The Popular Guide to Suffolk Churches

D.P. Mortlock: Former County Librarian of Norfolk was born at Wixoe, Suffolk – 100 yards from the county boundary so it was a close run thing! He spent most of his childhood at Mildenhall where he was a choirboy at St Mary's, one of the finest churches in the county. Grammar school was followed by service in the Indian Army. His library career began in 1947 with the old West Suffolk County. By this time 'church bagging' was a compulsive habit, continuing in the West Riding and Derbyshire before he came back to East Anglia in 1960. He started making notes on Norfolk churches at that time and in partnership with C.V. Roberts, produced the three-volume *Popular Guide to Norfolk Churches* between 1981 and 1985. In doing so, he completed the round of all the county's medieval churches and is looking forward to doing the same in Suffolk.

Front cover: Eye, St Peter and St Paul
Back cover: East Bergholt, St Mary: bell cage

Walk about Sion, and go round about her:
and tell the towers thereof,
Mark well her bulwarks, set up her houses:
that ye may tell them that come after.
Psalm XLVIII

D.P. Mortlock

The Popular Guide to Suffolk Churches

2: Central Suffolk

Foreword by the Duke of Grafton KG

With an encyclopaedic Glossary

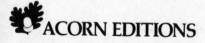

ACORN EDITIONS

For Barbara

Acorn Editions
P.O. Box 60
Cambridge
CB1 2NT

British Library Cataloguing in Publication Data
Mortlock, D.P.
  The popular guide to Suffolk churches.
  2: Central Suffolk
  1. Suffolk. Churches. Visitors guides
  I. Title
  914.26'404858
  ISBN 0-906554-13-6

Copyright © D.P. Mortlock 1990
First published 1990

Printed in Great Britain by
St Edmundsbury Press Limited, Bury St Edmunds, Suffolk

Contents

Foreword by the Duke of Grafton

As chairman of Trustees both of national and local bodies concerned with historic churches, I welcome this book and believe that it will prove to be an invaluable companion for all who visit Suffolk's churches. As more and more people discover the richness of our heritage, there is a need for guides that are authoritative but not boring, comprehensive yet pocketable, and this is what Mr Mortlock has provided.

It is not only in the grand churches of Lavenham and Long Melford that things of interest and beauty may be found. Virtually every village church has something to offer and this book will encourage its readers to go and see for themselves. When they do they will realise the tremendous efforts being made by hundreds of small parishes to maintain their churches, not only as places of worship, but as havens of rest and quiet refreshment for all who visit them. And having done so I hope that they too will lend their support.

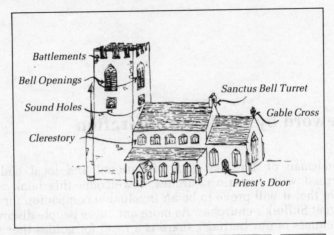

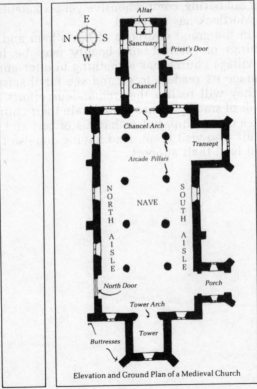

Elevation and Ground Plan of a Medieval Church

Introduction

The churches of Suffolk are among its abiding treasures, and to study them all in depth demands a lifetime. Nonetheless, a short visit to any one of them can be an adventure of discovery and delight, and this volume, the second of three, provides a concise guide in handy form to all those in the centre of the county. Because I am an enthusiast rather than an expert or a specialist, technical terms are avoided where possible but, when used, they are printed in **bold** and an explanation will be found in the encyclopaedic Glossary. There, entries will also be found for saints, famous persons, artists, architects and craftsmen, as well as historical notes for background information. The series covers all Anglican churches currently in use, and those cared for by the **Redundant Churches Fund** which are used for occasional services. Modern churches have their own fascination and surprises and do not deserve to be ignored, and I cannot recall a visit that did not provide something of interest.

The parish church is sometimes the only building in a village with any claim to architectural distinction, and is often an intriguing amalgam of alterations, additions, oddities and enigmas. More than that, it bears the impress of centuries of social, political and religious change, and has become the silent witness of its community. There is peace, a sense of continuity, and an invitation to take the long view. If it seems neglected, remember that this is nothing new. In 1562, *The Second Book of Homilies* talks of '... the sin and shame to see so many

churches so ruinous and so foully decayed in almost every corner ... Suffer them not to be defiled with rain and weather, with dung of doves, owls, choughs ... and other filthiness'. The Victorians in their turn inherited a legacy of neglect, and while many a restoration or rebuilding can be criticised, we owe them a debt that is not always acknowledged. In general, our churches are in better state than they have been for centuries, thanks to the energies and faith of local communities, the stirling work of the Suffolk Historic Churches Trust, and a growing national awareness of the scale of the problem.

For the casual visitor, access is sometimes difficult, but it was heartening to find that, of the 174 churches covered in this volume, 54% were open, 27% were locked but displayed a contact address (Burgh and Little Wenham are awarded gold stars for having a map as well), and only 18% were locked with no suggestion as to what to do about it. The remaining 1% had keys ingeniously hidden – convenient for those in the know but infuriating if you have spent half an hour or more scouring the village for help. History repeats itself even in this, for an 1846 guide to some Norfolk churches remarked:
It is very tiresome when one has travelled so far – in our case 12 miles – to see a church, to find that the parish clerk lives a mile off: and on reaching his cottage to hear that he has gone out and has taken the key in his pocket ...

If conditions demand that the church be locked, I would plead for a legible and up-to-date notice in the porch or on the outer door, giving an unambiguous address (Mrs Smith, The Street, is not always enough for strangers).

Visitors will find that binoculars are invaluable for picking out the often beautiful detail of roofs, wall paintings and stained glass.

I have read assiduously in preparing these guides – my debt to previous writers on the subject is massive. So many people have also helped me that to particularise seems invidious. However, I must record my grateful thanks to Birkin Haward, Roy Tricker, Peter Hollingham, Andrew Anderson, and the Suffolk Heraldry Society. The host of kind people that I met by chance along the way have treasure in store.

The Styles of Architecture

An instant check-list – but see 'Styles of Architecture' in the glossary (p. 1000) for detailed background.
All dates are approximate only.

Saxon – C7 to the Conquest (1066)

Norman – 1066 to about 1200

Transitional/Early English – 1200 to 1300

Decorated – 1300 to 1350

Perpendicular – 1350 to 1500

Tudor – 1500 to 1600

The Monarchs

William I, 1066-1087
William II, 1087-1100
Henry I, 1100-35
Stephen, 1135-54
Henry II, 1154-89
Richard I, 1189-99

John, 1199-1216
Henry III, 1216-72
Edward I, 1272-1307

Edward II, 1307-27
Edward III, 1327-77
Richard II, 1377-99

Henry IV, 1399-1413
Henry V, 1413-22
Henry VI, 1422-61
Edward IV, 1461-83
Richard II, 1483-5

Henry VII, 1485-1509
Henry VIII, 1509-47
Edward VI, 1547-53
Mary I, 1553-8
Elizabeth I, 1558-1603

Map references in brackets after church names refer to map on p. xii.
Glossary entries appear in **bold** type.

Central Suffolk

A B C D E F G

1

NORFOLK

Syleham
Wingfield
Stradbroke
Stuston   Hoxne   Denham   Wilby
Oakley
Thrandeston   Brome   Horham   Brundish
Burgate   Eye   Athelington   Worlingworth
Yaxley   Occold   Redlingfield   Tannington
Mellis   Thornham Parva   Bedingfield   Bedfield   Saxtead
Thornham Magna   Thorndon   Kenton   Monk Soham
Gislingham   Stoke Ash   Ashfield-Cum-Thorpe   Earl Soham   Kettleburgh
Wickham Skeith   Thwaite   Aspall   Brandeston   Easton
Wetheringsett   Debenham   Hoo   Letheringham
Cotton   Mendlesham   Winston   Cretingham   Monewden   Pettistree
Framsden   Charsfield   Dallinghoo
Gipping   Pettaugh   Helmingham   Bredfield
Little Stonham   Stonham Aspall   Otley   Clopton   Boulge
Old Newton   Crowfield   Gosbeck   Swilland   Burgh   Hasketon
Stowupland   Earl Stonham   Grundisburgh
Creeting St Peter   Ashbocking   Hemingstone   Henley   Culpho   Playford
Stowmarket   Creeting St Mary   Witnesham   Great Bealings
Needham Market   Badley   Coddenham   Claydon   Akenham   Little Bealings
Combs   Darmsden   Tuddenham   Kesgrave
Battisford   Baylham   Barham   Westerfield   Rushmere St Andrew
Little Finborough   Ringshall   Barking   Great Blakenham   Whitton
Hitcham   Willisham   Ipswich
Great Bricett   Little Blakenham   Flowton   Bramford
Offton   Nettlestead   Somersham   Sproughton
Naughton   Burstall
Bildeston   Elmsett   Washbrook
Whatfield   Hintlesham   Belstead
Nedging   Aldham   Copdock
Semer   Hadleigh   Chattisham   Little Wenham   Bentley
Milden   Lindsey   Kersey   Great Wenham   Capel St Mary
Little Waldingfield   Layham   Raydon   Holton St Mary
Great   Groton   Shelley   Brantham
Waldingfield   Edwardstone   Boxford   East Bergholt
Chilton   Polstead   Higham   Stratford St Mary
Newton   Assington   Stoke-by-Nayland
Great Cornard   Leavenheath   Nayland
Little Cornard   Wissington
Bures

ESSEX

1
2
3
4
5
6
7
8
9
10
11

Alphabetical Guide to Churches

Akenham, St Mary (E6): Just n. of the Ipswich suburb of Whitton a country lane meanders down into a little valley, and from it a rough farm track strikes off for half a mile until it reaches the church. Ipswich hovers on the skyline but the setting is genuinely rural, with just a house and a farm nearby; a charming spot. A stray landmine in 1940 badly damaged the church and it lay derelict for twenty years. Then, local enthusiasm backed by grants secured its repair but sadly it was declared redundant in 1976. However, the **Redundant Churches Fund** assumed responsibility two years later and it is now well maintained and still used for occasional services. As at a number of churches in this area, its C14 tower is placed on the s. side of the **nave** and serves also as a **porch**. Unbuttressed, it has one **set-off** below a bell stage that was shortened in the C18. Full-scale restoration of the church in 1854 included a rebuilding of the top of the tower and the battlements. The belfry has **cusped lancet** windows and one **jamb** of the entrance arch is bowed with age. On walking round, you will see that there are some substantial C18 and C19 table tombs of local gentry, and in the n. wall of the nave there is a **Norman** lancet confirming that the church has been here since the C11. Its miniature jamb shafts are an unusual embellishment for such a small window. There is a window with **Decorated tracery** on the n. side of the **chancel**, a **Perpendicular**

e. window, and two large late C13 lancets with a matching **priest's door** on the s. side. One of the window-sills here was deeply inscribed in the C15 or C16 with a name which could be 'Jo. Suckeym'. Nave and chancel have plastered walls, but in the C17 a short s. **aisle** was added, built in a dark red brick with **Tudor**-style windows, as a chapel for the Hawys family who were Lords of the Manor.

The interior is uncomplicated, with simple furniture and brick floors, but appealing nonetheless. Below a Perpendicular w. window the C15 **font** has an enterprising selection of tracery patterns in the bowl panels, including a **trefoil** with elaborate cusps and a block of nine **quatrefoils**; the shaft is decorated with miniature window designs. The nave **roof** is cross-braced with **king-posts**, and in front of the font there is a **ledger-stone** for Elizabeth Fynn who died in 1683 and her husband Robert who followed her three years later:

For nineteen yeares I liv'd a virgin life,
For seaventeen more beeing married liv'd a wife,
At thirty six pale death my life assail'd,
And as I liv'd I dy'd belov'd bewail'd.

Despite the profusion of apostrophes you will see that the mason was hard put to fit all the verse in. There is a small suite of pews with traceried ends and doors which have **linen-fold pan-**

els. They are C19 and may have been the work of George Drury, who was rector here. The heavily moulded pulpit stands on a shaft and dates from the late C18. Beyond a Tudor arch the chancel **weeps** slightly to the s., and although the ceiling is plastered the **castellated wall plate** of the medieval roof remains.

One would not expect such a small and humble church to be the setting for an important change in the law of the land, but in 1878 a Baptist couple in the parish sought to bury their unbaptised 2-year-old son in the churchyard, having no alternative. This was refused by the rector but permission was given for the grave to be sited n. of the church where still-born infants lay. When a Baptist minister attempted to hold a short service for the mourners just outside the gate of the churchyard he was peremptorily interrupted by the Revd Drury and an unseemly argument that came close to blows ensued. The corpse was eventually put to rest, but court proceedings followed and what became known as 'The Akenham Burial Case' was the prelude to the Burial Law Reform Act of 1880 which ensured that such a thing could not happen again. You may have seen the solitary stone n. of the church that was raised for little Joseph Ramsey, the unwitting cause of it all, and the full story is told in Ronald Fletcher's *In a Country Churchyard*.

Aldham, St Mary (C8): A lane leads only to the Hall and the church, which stands on a little knoll beyond the farm buildings, with a pond in the sunken meadow to the w. It is possible that the original church was **Saxon** and the base of the round tower may date from before the Conquest. The **quoins** at the s.w. corner of the **nave** are made up of flints and Roman bricks and this is generally taken as evidence of an early building. By the 1880s it was well-nigh ruinous and most of the tower was replaced, the s. nave wall was taken down completely, and all the windows

were restored or renewed. More work followed in the 1930s when the e. wall and its window were replaced. The tower is slim, with two small **lancets** set in brick surrounds to the w. and lancet bell openings. A number of brick **put-log holes** survived the rebuilding and there is a small lead spike above the plain parapet. The C14 n. doorway was unblocked in the 1880s and on that side there is 'Y' and **Decorated tracery** in the windows. A C19 'cottage' **vestry** with a chimney juts from the n. wall of the **chancel** and there is a s. **porch** which is probably of the same vintage. One s. chancel window has 'Y' tracery of about 1300 with rather nice medieval **headstops** and another has **Perpendicular** tracery.

Before going in, have a look at the fragment of **Norman** stone embedded in the s.w. corner of the nave, carved with an interlace design. It was probably part of a cross shaft and inside the church there is another section set in the e. **jamb** of the window nearest to the door. The interior is beautifully kept and redolent of wax polish. There are new doors to the C16 brick tower arch which was uncovered in 1933, and above hangs a large set of George II's **Royal Arms** – painted on board and very well restored recently. The complementary set of the present Queen's arms which hang over the n. door would look even better if they were framed. The **font** is square, with octagonal shafts at the corners of the bowl, four supporting columns, and a centre shaft. It looks neither Norman nor medieval and it would be interesting to know its date. The nave **roof** is a late C19 renewal of very high quality in pitch pine with **tie-beams** and **arch-braces**. The 1930s work included parquet flooring and the oak panelling which has a pierced trail along the top. Most of the benches were installed at that time and are beautifully made to match the few originals that had survived. You will find four at the w. end on the n. side which have token **poppyheads** (one with an original mask) and elbows roughly carved with roundels – a **Tudor rose**, a star, and a **St Andrew's** cross. There are also three medieval bench ends on the same side farther e. which have their poppyheads strangely offset and large oblong shields carved below, with a bear's head (?), a crown with spear, star and crescent, and a peculiar spike with forked ends. The lectern has a modern shaft and slope but the hexagonal base is C15 and very like the one at Kersey. The low screen and choir stalls in solid Perpendicular style came in with the nave benches, and the chancel arch was part of the 1880s restoration. However, the original C14 chancel and roof remains, with a tie-beam and **king-post** strutted four ways, with a runner e. to w. below the plastered ceiling. The **Stuart communion rails** have thin square shafts between the **balusters** and there is a C13 **piscina** in a deep recess with quarter-round shafts to the moulded arch. The modern e. window has large king and queen headstops, the jambs are panelled, and there are twin niches in Decorated style each side. The 1930s glass is by Walter Wilkinson and has large figures of the **Blessed Virgin** and Child, Elijah, and **St Paul** set in pale, intricate **tabernacles**. As you leave, note that faint traces of medieval painting survive on the inner jambs of the door.

Ashbocking, All Saints (D6): Well away from the village, the church stands by the Hall at the end of a lane off the road to Coddenham. The broad, slightly austere tower was probably built by Edmund Bockinge in the C16 and its red brick walls are patterned with lozenges of dark blue up to belfry level. The C14 **nave** windows have **mouchette** shapes in their **tracery**, and there are examples of late C13 **plate tracery** in the **chancel**. The e. window, with its three stepped **lights**, belongs to the same period but the wall was rebuilt in C16 (or later) red brick. A small window is rather curiously placed low in the nave s. wall and entry is by way of a lovely little **porch** in dark

red brick, again with diaper patterning. It has a crow-stepped gable and the stone demi-angel below, together with the side windows, probably dates from an 1872 restoration directed by **E.C. Hakewill**. The deeply moulded C14 inner doorway has worn **headstops** and there is a **stoup** to the r.

Seen from within, the nave walls have a decided lean and the **roof** is the plainest of **hammerbeams**, with rustic braces rising to **collars** and **king-posts** with four-way struts. The **font** shaft is modern but the bowl is an unusual **Norman** example shaped like a cauldron bulging out of a square frame. It had been encased in brick and plaster and was uncovered in 1842. The cover has a pinnacled corona at the base out of which a short **crocketted** spire rises to a **finial**. It is a handsome piece and is generally described as late C15, but parts at least are modern. The n. door is blocked and in front stands a large iron-bound C14 chest secured by four locks and a drawbar. There are some C15 bench ends at the back of the nave but the rest of the benches are C17, with heavy mouldings on the square tops and coarse triple **pilasters**. Theodore Beadle was the staunchly royalist vicar here before the Civil War and he had a set of **Royal Arms** painted on board, dated 1640, and inscribed 'God Save the King'. Restored in 1977, they still hang on the s. wall as a reminder that he 'spoke against the rebellion and Parliament' and ultimately died a prisoner in the Thames hulks for his obdurate loyalty. A little farther along is a splendid C14 tomb recess with no clue as to whose it was. The large **ogee** arch is very deeply moulded and the crockets are curiously varied so that they form strings of foliage and fruit on the l. side. The heavy **cusps** are carved, each with a terminal head, and the tall side pinnacles have two ranks of crocketted gables and shallow foliage in their front panels. The little window noticed outside lies within the arch and was obviously inserted later. A fine Elizabethan **brass** has been mounted on the opposite wall and displays the effigies of Edmund Bockinge, his wives Frances and Mary, and two daughters. Probably builder of the tower, he died in 1585 and wears typical armour of the period, while his wives have French bonnets and brocaded petticoats. The Latin of the second inscription is helpfully translated on a card below. C19 **deca-logue boards** hang at the e. end of the nave and, although there is now no screen, you will see that the chancel arch still has the slots in which a **tympanum** was secured. The **wall plate** of the roof beyond is medieval and there are late C17 **communion rails**, a tall set which have fluted columns at the centre and against the walls. In the floor by the **priest's door** is the brass inscription for Thomas Horseman who died in 1619, and it is an interesting example of an acrostic based on his name; a note nearby supplies a transla-tion of the verse. Within the **sanctuary** there is a tall and mis-shapen C14 **piscina** and the **altar** is a plain **Stuart** table which has been given a larger top. At the time of my visit it had a lovely lime-green frontal on which the text 'Gather my saints together unto me' was lettered in gold thread and leather appliqué.

Ashfield-cum-Thorpe, St Mary (E4): In 1810 it was recorded: 'the church has lain in ruins and has not been preached in these thirty years', and by 1839 there was not much more than a half of the square tower left. Although the churchyard continued in use, the peo-ple went to 'the chapel in Thorpe' for services. That may refer to St Peter's, of which the round tower remains. The present building dates from 1853 and is a simple but pleasing design in red brick with plum-coloured patterning designed by William Constable Woollard. It has a small wooden bellcote at the w. end of the **nave**, a tall s. porch, and a **vestry** on the n. side. Medieval convention was followed to the extent of having a **priest's door** on the s. side of the **chancel** and there are

crosses on the gables. The interior is light and airy and the short nave is lofty, with a deal **arch-brace** and **ham-mer-beam** roof above the brick floor. The small chamber organ has no case, giving it a rather avant-garde appearance, and the pulpit of 1939 incorporates three panels of typical **Jacobean** work. Were they perhaps salvaged from one of the earlier churches?

Aspall, St Mary of Grace (D4): There are over 150 churches in the county whose patron saint is the **Blessed Virgin** but this is the only one that particularises in this fashion. A narrow grove of holly and yew hugs the path right up to the tower, and on the n. side a path leads to cottages via an attractive **lych-gate** of 1869. The C15 tower has angle buttresses to the w. and **Perpendicular** bell openings, and the finely moulded door was blocked in the C19 with a **trefoil** window inserted in the head. The C17 n. **porch** of wood and red brick had nice barge boards added by the Victorians, and theirs is the large **vestry** and organ chamber n. of the short **chancel**. The 'Y' **tracery** of the windows and the plain **priest's door** on the s. side suggest an early C14 date for the chancel, but the **nave** was given tall late Perpendicular windows under deep **labels** with attractive little **headstops**. To the w. of the plain C14 s. door all that is left of a **scratch dial** on the buttress is the centre hole.

The tower arch within is devoid of ornament and two **hatchments** hang on the w. wall – for the Revd Temple Chevallier (1804, s. side) and Mary, his widow (1807). Most of the carving on the C15 **font** has been re-cut. It follows the common East Anglian pattern – profiled lions alternate with large **Tu-dor roses** and an angel bearing **Passion emblems** in the bowl panels, while four more lions squat round the shaft. Overhead is a plain C15 **arch-braced** and **tie-beam roof** with stone **corbels**, and the C19 nave benches are excel-lent. They have traceried ends with

TO SUFFOLK CHURCHES

Aspall, St Mary of Grace: C19 bench end

[Vol.1], where one of his forebears was bailiff to the Lord of the Manor. One of the s. nave windows has glass of the 1850s by **Powell & Sons** and is an example of their early work. The two oblong medallions portray Christ with children and the raising of Lazarus, the rest of the window being filled with **quarries** painted with the **sacred monogram**. The bold chancel arch has octagonal **responds** and **capitals** and you will find that sections of a C15 **screen** (and some copies) have been used in the fronts of the Victorian choir stalls. The tracery is compressed, with **castellated transoms** and flower terminals to the **cusps**. The **altar** is a small **Stuart** table with finely turned legs which has been raised on blocks, and it stands in front of a C19 **reredos** whose panels are painted with Creed, Lord's Prayer, and Commandments. There is a large, restored **piscina** under a trefoil arch, and the e. window contains three oval panels of stained glass by Powells of the Last Supper, Christ's baptism, and the Ascension set in **grisaille**.

poppyheads, and a variety of beasts and figures are carved on the elbows. On the s. side look especially for the rat at the w. end, a modern version of the **pelican** and her brood, a farmer binding a sheaf of corn, and, opposite him, the lovely little figure of a woman at her wash tub. High on the n. wall is a most attractive roundel of a naked, muscular young man sitting crouched with a dove on his knee, sculpted in deep bas relief. It commemorates Raulin Guild, who died young in 1966, and the epitaph is a single line from *As You Like It*: 'of all sorts enchantingly beloved'. Its gentleness seems to contrast strangely with the tablet opposite: 'Horatio Herbert Kitchener. A tribute of love and grief from countrymen overseas. Overseas Club, Kitchener Branch, Santa Barbara, California.' But that in its turn gives the lie to some aspects of *Oh What a Lovely War*. The World War I field marshal was not born here but his mother was, and in choosing the title 'Baron Kitchener of Khartoum and Aspall' he betrayed an affection for the place. There is another memorial to him at Lakenheath

Assington, St Edmund (B10): A splendid setting in parkland with enough of a rise to give the church prominence. It is in essence a late C14 to early C15 building but by 1827 the **chancel** was ruinous and had to be rebuilt. The C14 **priest's door** was retained but is now blocked and a **low side window** was left in place nearby. In the 1860s the vicar acted as his own architect and carried out a full-scale restoration, re-roofing the **nave** and adding a **vestry** to the n. The tower was rebuilt using the original materials and following the old design, although the **sound hole** to the w. is a Norfolk type and, like the door at the base of the stair turret, is unlikely to have figured in the original. The side windows of the tall C15 **porch** were blocked with brick but the inner doors are exceptionally good. The oak has faded to a silvery grey and one of the edges retains its band of vine carving in which birds peck at the grapes. The slim panels are ridged like **roofs**, with slender columns running up their centres to **capitals** on which perch lions, eagles, and angels, and there is dense **Perpendicular tracery** above them; the bottom rail is carved with shields within **quatrefoils** reminiscent of the screen at Great Cornard, and the doorway's **hood mould** has large bishop and queen **headstops**.

Lacking a **clerestory**, the church is a little dark inside and the nave **arcades** have capitals only within the arches, like those in St Gregory's, Sudbury [Vol.1]. The blocked original door to the tower stair is at the w. end of the s. **aisle** beyond the C19 **font**, and the pine benches have decorative lamp standards, each with a brass cup at the top to house the lamp and four prickets for candles. The Gurdons were C16 Lords of the Manor and resolute Puritans during the Civil War and Commonwealth. The first of their numerous monuments to catch the eye is a handsome **cartouche** on the n. wall for the Revd Nathaniel Gurdon, who died in 1695 secure in the family pardons granted by Charles II and James II. His **achievement of arms** at the top is backed by drapes which are caught up by cherub heads lower down, and there is a sharply carved winged skull at the base. In high contrast, a plain tablet below commemorates the life of William Warner who died at 80 in 1926, having been organist for fifty-five years. And he, like the organist at Bramford, was blind. Turning back to the s. door you will see the memorial of another clerical Gurdon – Philip, who died in 1817. It is an innocuous design by **John Bacon the Younger** but the prolix epitaph contains a peculiar phrase: 'whose gospel he had adorned and voluntarily proclaimed in this church for nearly 40 years with exemplary ability, fidelity and zeal'. Preachers seldom operate under duress, surely! A tablet to the e. of the s. aisle window is for John Gurdon who died in 1679. In his younger days he had been a Suffolk M.P. in the Short and Long Parliaments and a member of the Commonwealth Council of State in the early 1650s. Just beyond is the imposing monument for Brampton Gurdon, dated 1648. His portrait bust shows him wearing a spade beard and holding what might be a pomander. On either side are the demi-figures of his wives – Elizabeth wearing a ruff, and Meriell dressed in the Puritan fashion with a broad starched cape. The women's faces, particularly, are strong and full of character. All in alabaster, there are a dozen coloured shields arranged within the handsome **pediment** and frame, and veined marble columns separate the figures.

There is a small image niche with headstops to the hood mould by the aisle e. window and in the centre of the nave lies the church's only **brass**. The two 30in. figures are likely to be Robert and Letitia Taylboys (1506) and he wears **Tudor** armour with a large sword hung frontally, while she has a lavish **kennel head-dress** and a heavily ornamented tassel to her girdle. Taylboys was in the service of Thomas Rotherham, archbishop of York and chancellor of England, and his wife had been the widow of a Corbet whose family held the manor before the Gurdons. Parts of a C15 **screen** are built into the fronts of the choir stalls and more Gurdon monuments were replaced on the walls when the chancel was rebuilt. The largest is for Robert (1577) and John (1623) and their wives. The pairs of small figures kneel and face each other across prayer desks, and two children of each marriage are shown in the panels below. There are three shields and a skull at the top above flanking obelisks and a centre column. The e. window has 1860s glass by **Clayton & Bell** – an example from perhaps their best period. The ascended Christ is flanked by groups of angels above the disciples and the **Blessed Virgin**, and the general effect is cool, with dark reds and blues contrasting well with the steely grey of frames and **tabernacles**.

Athelington, St Peter (D3): Money was

bequeathed in the mid-C15 for the 'new tower' but it is unbuttressed and slim, which suggests that it dates from the C12 or C13 and was perhaps given a new upper storey later. Now, however, it is capped with a pyramid **roof** just above the bell openings – an alteration likely to date from the C19 when the stair turret was given a stone cap and exuberant **finial**. The w. window has **Decorated tracery** and there are plenty of **put-log holes** filled with brick. **Nave** and **chancel** lie under one C19 roof and on walking round you will see that the e. window has attractive **headstops** and intersecting 'Y' tracery of about 1300. Don't miss the interesting inscription cut in the sill: 'Dns Johns de Trun me fecit facere' (Master John de Trun had me made). The **porch** was built in 1873 and the village stocks have found a home here (as they have at Saxtead).

As with the w. door, the s. doorway was provided with new headstops when the porch was built, and one enters to find a neat, compact interior in which the separation of nave and chancel is marked only by the **rood beam**. This rests on substantial stone king and queen **corbels** which were moved to their present positions in 1873. The early C15 **font** stands in the base of the tower, its shallow bowl decorated with nicely varied tracery patterns. The C14 **scissors-braced** roof has wide **wall plates** which are **embattled** and decorated with **fleurons** in the chancel, and there you will find a **piscina** under a **trefoil** arch, with **dropped-sill sedilia** alongside. The **altar** is a small, almost square Stuart table. The choir stalls and pulpit date from the 1870s restoration, and although the rest of the benches were remade then, the ends next to the centre aisle are C15 in the main and are an interesting set. The scale is small and the sides are finely traceried in the style of **Perpendicular** windows, with each **poppyhead** flanked by little upright figures. Many of them can be identified by their symbols and on the s. side from w. to e. they are: **Saints Simon, Jude, Philip, James the Less (?),**

Athelington, St Peter: St Jude and St Simon

John, James the Great (?), Paul, Peter, Matthew (C19), **Bartholomew** (C19), **Andrew** (C19), **Thomas** (C19); on the n. side from w. to e. there are three female figures that might represent Chastity, Temperance, and Constancy or three saints whose identity is unknown, **Saints Margaret, Barbara** (C19), **Catherine** (C19), **Agnes** (C19), and the **Blessed Virgin** and Child (C19). In addition, there are bearded heads and a lion and an eagle on taller half-ends at the back of the church.

Badley, St Mary (C6): Newcomers are pouring into Suffolk, towns and villages spawn dormitories and factories, but there are still the secret places. Those who love them will notice the sign on the Stowmarket to Needham Market road which points to Badley church. A very rough track winds

Badley, St Mary: exterior

through fields for more than a mile and, topping a rise, there is the church set in a bowl of meadow land, with Badley Hall farm beyond it. The **Redundant Churches Fund** assumed responsibility in 1986 and within two years they had carried out a major restoration, making the building sound and watertight; a shining example, if one were needed, of the value of their work. The church is used for occasional services and is normally open at weekends; a key is kept at the farm.

The unbuttressed tower was probably built around 1300, but in the C15 a massive five-**light** w. window was inserted which takes up the whole width of the wall. The red brick belfry stage with its plain parapet is **Tudor**, and all has been meticulously restored. One interesting feature is that the **nave** walls are extended w. under tile caps to lap the tower, and the belfry stair fits neatly above on the n. side. On walking round, you will find brick buttresses to the n. and the remnant of a **rood stair** turret with a bricked-up top door. There has been a church here since the Norman Conquest and the blocked

lancet in the n. wall of the **chancel** dates from the early C13. All other windows are **Perpendicular** and it is strange that the e. window is rather small for the wall in contrast to the one in the tower. On the s. side a **dripstone** marks the site of a C14 window and just by it is a monument which would pass without much notice inside a church but which is unusually elaborate for an outside wall; a miniature sarcophagus and **cartouche** of arms are set within an architectural frame, and there is an urn with swags and flaming torches above the **pediment**. All trace of the epitaph has weathered away but it was for Henrietta Robins who died in 1728, and the original iron railings survive, having escaped the scrap metal drive in World War II that cleared most churchyards. The open wooden **porch** has a modern **roof** but the base and what remains of the barge boards are medieval, and it is guarded by a lift-gate that has to be teased out of its slots. Designed to deter farm stock, it looks as though it has always been there and I do not know another like it. The simple inner doorway is late C12, and the door itself may be as old – ridged boards in a heavy frame, with massive lock, original ironwork, and a grill window that was fitted with a shutter at one time.

One more step and you will see how important it is that this church should be preserved. In essence, nothing has been changed for two centuries; enthusiasms, doctrinaire theory, the obsession with domestic comfort, all have passed it by, and age has bestowed upon it an infinite charm. Below plastered ceilings, three cambered **tie-beams** support tall **king-posts** that have four-way struts under the ridge, and the **pamments** of the floor are interrupted haphazardly with **ledger-stones**. All the unstained oak has aged to a silvery grey, and the benches are an extraordinary mixture, made up from at least three sets. Some have full-size ends with **poppyheads** and the pair opposite the door have the remains of animals on the elbows. The mortice holes for a book slope show that they once belonged to a choir stall, and the singleton by the n. wall with its curious disc **finial** looks like a giant's cheese board. The boards at the e. end on that side are pierced with two **elevation squints**, and all the timbers are rough and sturdy, with the occasional hole where a knot or piece of rot was taken out. The plain **Stuart** pulpit is a tiny octagon that will not serve for anyone broader than 17in. unless they slide in sideways, but there is a commodious reading desk of the early C17 alongside whose door has a prettily carved top rail. The contemporary **box pews** beyond are crude but their makers could not altogether resist the beauty of the C14 **rood screen** that they or their fathers had taken out, and two sections of its **tracery** are fixed to the fronts. The base of the screen was left to serve as a division between one set of pews and another in the chancel, and there are traces of stencil flower decoration on its plum-coloured panels. Turned finials are the box pews' only ornament, and a few were added to the old screen in a jaunty attempt to draw it all together. Nearby is a plain C17 chest and there is another in the chancel, a little beauty which is unstained and has **linen-fold panels**.

The furniture is so beguiling that one moves about haphazardly to examine it, but there are other things to be seen. A simple C18 or early C19 **bier** hides behind the little chamber organ, and note that the step of the tower door is 7ft from the floor so that valuables could be kept up there with some security. A **stoup** is partly hidden by the wall panelling by the door, and the C13 **Purbeck marble font** has the usual pairs of blank arches in the sides of its deep, canted bowl. Its **ogee**-shaped panelled cover with acorn finial is probably C18. Beside it lies a C13 tomb slab with fragments of an inscription, and in the centre of the nave is a **brass** inscription for Edmund Brewster who died in 1633. Farther e. is Edmund Poley's, dated 1613 with three shields, set in a large **touchstone** slab. Part of the blocked doorway to the old rood stairs can be seen above the panelling on the n. wall. There is another brass inscription in the chancel floor for John and Dorothe Poley (1615):

Reade if thou canst & mourne not, his name & stocke being knowne, For they will tell what pitie twas, he was but borne & showne.

A ledger-stone on the n. side is unusual in having marble inserts – two inscriptions and a pair of shields for Peter Scrivener who died in 1604. On the wall above is the alabaster memorial for Edmund and Myrabel Poley (1548 and 1558) which was installed by one of their descendants in 1604. It has two inscription panels and a carved frame that once had six shields. These have been defaced but a larger one survives with traces of colour in a roundel at the top. On the s. side, the Edmund Poley who died in 1714 has a deeply cut ledger-stone, and on the wall is the tall and narrow memorial of 1707 for Henry Poley, in grey and white marble. The curved pediment carries a flaming urn and torches, and a delicately draped skull is poised over the epitaph. There are large C18 **decalogue boards** each side of the e. window, with an unusual addition above the altar: 'This do in Remembrance of me: Luke ye 22d ver.

ye 19:'. The church's only medieval glass is a shield of the de Badele family in a n. window, and **Dowsing** kept himself warm on a February day in 1643 by destroying thirty-four 'superstitious pictures'; a Mr Dove promised to take down the remaining twenty-eight and to level the chancel. It seems he did this because there is no change of level now, and the **sanctuary** step probably dates from 1830 when the iron **communion rails** were installed. Those apart, the only recognisable C19 touch is the 1860s glass in the e. window by Frederick Preedy, a good glazier who was often used by **William Butterfield**. This is a dense and quite attractive design, although there is scant animation in the figure work; narrow panels illustrate the Last Supper and Christ's encounters, after His Resurrection, with **St Thomas** and **St Mary Magdalene**. Dorothe Pooley died in 1625 and her grave in the n.e. corner of the sanctuary has a singular epitaph:

Staye Passinger, reade what this Marble tells,

Stones seldom speake but utter miracles . . .

Indeed they do, for in the lines that follow she, who was 'her Sexes Pride, her Ages wonder' is credited with no fewer than ten virtues.

This little church seduces the senses and sticks like a burr in the memory.

Barham, St Mary (D7): The church stands in a generous churchyard above the busy valley where industrial Claydon competes with the busy main road to distract the eye from the calm countryside beyond. The medieval building was heavily restored in the 1860s without detracting too much from its attraction and interest, but the large meeting room which has been added recently on the n. side does not blend happily with its senior partner. This is accentuated by the fact that the

Badley, St Mary: interior

tower is on the s. side so that the w. wall of the **nave** and the new work appear as a continuous facade when seen from the entrance. Beyond the annexe there is a blocked n. doorway, and although there are no **aisles**, a **clerestory** with brick windows was added in the early C16. The Middleton chapel juts out farther along, and beyond it there is an important and unusual window in the n. wall of the **vestry**. It came from Shrubland Old Hall, and the terracotta **mullions** and lintel were made from the same moulds that were used in Henley and Barking churches and are early examples of the **Renaissance** style. After the great house at Layer Marney in Essex had been finished in the 1520s, the specialist terracotta craftsmen probably dispersed to other projects, of which this may have been one. As a window it can hardly be called beautiful, despite its importance. The C19 **chancel** e. window fails on both counts. The position of the tower makes the nave seem short and very tall when seen from the s., and this accentuates the length of the chancel. Although extensively restored, the archway, narrow belfry slits with **ogee** tops, and 'Y' **tracery** of the bell openings date the tower as early C14, and it doubles as the main entrance.

Once inside, the size of the nave reasserts itself and light floods through the large w. window – a C19 replacement with flowing tracery. The **hammerbeam roof** is handsome, but everything above the hammers is modern work (and none the worse for that). Tall **king-posts** stand on collar beams that are no more than halfway up the slope of the roof, and demi-angels have been restored to the ends of the hammers. The **font** bowl is a huge octagon on a short stem, with a continuous blind tracery pattern on its sides. It is rather an anticlimax to lift the lid and find a recess the size of a washing-up bowl for the water. A Victorian oddity, but the shaft and base are C14. A new doorway leading to the meeting room has been made in the n.w. corner, and the old n. door com-

plete with drawbar survives, despite the fact that it has been walled up outside. The nave has an attractive brick floor in **herringbone** pattern, and leaving aside some original benches with **poppyheads** at the w. end, the main seating is C19. A good sequence of **hatchments** hangs on the n. wall; from e. to w. they were used for the funerals of Lady Harriot Fowle Middleton (1852); Sir William, her husband (1829); Sir William Fowle Fowle Middleton (1860); Anne, his widow (1867); and Sir George Nathaniel Broke-Middleton (1887). Most of the Victorian stained glass is low quality, but one s. clerestory window has an 1890s figure of Christ with a child – rich robes and **tabernacle work**, set in a yellowy-green vine trail, and possibly by **Clayton & Bell**.

Beyond a pair of arches on the n. side of the nave is the Middleton chapel, approached by four steps. This change of level provides a splendid setting for one of the Anglican Church's finest sculptures of this century. It is by Henry Moore and was commissioned in 1948 by Sir Jasper Ridley as a World War II memorial for Claydon. When that church became redundant, Moore himself supervised its removal. It was developed from the largest of the twelve models prepared for the sculptor's Madonna and Child at St Matthew's, Northampton, of which he said: 'The Divine and the human must co-exist in a sacred image without the one being wholly sacrificed to the other.' The sculpture has great presence and is relaxed but calmly dominant and vibrant, with the Christ child deeply protected within the **Blessed Virgin's** encircling arms. The e. half of the chapel has been cleared to honour it, although when I visited, a heavy oak lectern and a glass carboy had been thoughtlessly placed in the corner directly behind. The w. half of the chapel is enclosed with a **parclose**

Barham, St Mary: Henry Moore sculpture

screen, part C18 panelling and part beautifully dense **Perpendicular** tracery which, with the **cusped ogee** doorway, came from the C15 **rood screen**. This has created a compact chapel in which the Blessed Sacrament is reserved for the sick, and it is excellently furnished. On the wall is a large tablet for Sir William Middleton, his wife, and son, with three painted shields which echo the hatchments in the nave. There is a pretty **cartouche** on the e. wall – C17 in style but commemorating James and Jane St Vincent, who died in the 1930s. The stairs to the vanished **rood loft** go up from the s.e. corner. Sir William Fowle Middleton is commemorated in the window glass, which has lively heraldry and rich borders. There is an inscription, 'GR 1831', in the tracery lights and the window is probably the work of Yarington, a Norwich glazier.

The pulpit with its replacement top and base has been varnished to a dark brown, but the panels and some sections of cresting probably formed part of the rood loft. When he visited in January 1643, apart from destroying images, **Dowsing** 'digged down the steps' in his passion for degrading the status of chancels. It was to no avail in the long run, because the 1860s rebuilding restored them and, ironically, modern changes in corporate worship have called for a nave **altar** below the chancel arch. Beyond the organ in the n. wall there is a heavy C15 arch above a recessed tomb which lost its brass to Dowsing. It commemorates Richard Booth, or possibly his son who died in the reign of Edward IV. The arch, with its slight ogee shape, is **cusped** and sub-cusped, and one angel terminal survives. Heads of hound and boar decorate the **spandrels** and there are oak leaves in the moulding because Richard's crest was a boar's head and his wife was an Oke. Just in front is a **brass** of 1514 for Robert and Cecily Southwell that survived the Civil War. The 33in. figures are curiously attenuated, he in fur-lined gown and doublet, she with a deep **kennel head-**

dress. The border inscription has **quatrefoils** engraved with six shields at the corners and in the centre of the sides. A second brass lies on the s. side of the chancel, this time an inscription for Frances Southwell, 1607. There is a beautiful set of **communion rails** here, Italian work dated 1700, which I presume was part of the C19 reordering. The heavy bottom section is carved with **putti** pairing birds and dolphins, and the short **balusters** support little arches under a substantial top rail decorated with vine trails. The deep **sanctuary** is divided by a midway step, and the fussiness of the windows, with their spindly inner shafts and pierced tracery, is on a par with the outside. The early C14 **piscina** is humble by comparison. The large recess in the opposite wall was probably an **aumbry**, and it is rather overwhelmed by the monument next door. A massive **touchstone** chest supports the life-size alabaster figures, he on his back and she beyond and turned towards him, holding a tiny skull in her hand. There are pairs of columns each side of the backing arch, and a coloured **achievement** on top flanked by pairs of touchstone columns – all rather bald and ill-fitting, which is perhaps explained by the inscription:

> This monument is sent over from the Cittie of Limrick in Ireland by Sr Richard Southwell, second sonne of Jo Southwell of Barham Esq. and Margrett his wife as a pious remembrance of them to be left to their posteriti 1640.

An interesting exercise in the removers' art, no doubt, and Irish at that.

Barking, St Mary (C7): Approached by a long lane from the Needham Market road, the church stands on rising ground, with open views to the s. beyond a pair of stately cedars. The whole building is cement rendered except the e. wall and the tower, which was rebuilt in 1870 (presumably repeating the original design). It has

hexagonal buttresses which taper slightly in the centre stage and the w. door has **crocketted** pinnacles carved in the upper panels, with two vine trails below; the w. window has **Decorated tracery** and there are **Perpendicular** bell openings. Both **aisles** sport a splendid series of late C14 **gargoyles** (note those on the n. particularly), and a two-storeyed **sacristy** juts out squarely from the **chancel** n. wall. It has two small **cusped lancets** to the n. and what is probably C18 tracery in its e. window. Attractive cusped and intersected tracery of the early C14 fills the chancel e. window and below it is an odd little buttress placed centrally. The **clerestory** windows have dense Perpendicular tracery and those in the aisles are roughly the same date – except the one at the w. end of the s. aisle, which is early C14. The late C13 s. **porch** is set at a slight angle and the inner doorway has single attached columns with ring **capitals** and small **headstops** – the skull set at the top of the arch is a later insertion. Above it is a faded and damaged C17 text from Psalm 118; 'Open to me ye Gates of

Barking, St Mary: charcoal brazier

Righteousness, I will go into them and praise ye Lord', reminiscent of the one at Grundisburgh. The arch of a **stoup** survives here and the early C16 door is unusual in that the upper panels are carved with the **Blessed Virgin's** monogram enclosing the individual letters of her name. These caught **Dowsing's** eye when he came in 1644 but, perhaps because 'many superstitious pictures were down afore I came', he left them alone. They are very worn and one has been renewed – as have most of the lower panels.

Within, the **nave arcades** are similar in style but the s. is earlier, and above them is an impressive C14 **arch-braced tie-beam roof**. It has that delightful washed-out colour of unstained oak, and octagonal **king-posts** with four-way struts support a runner below the ridge. The e. section of this is patterned with colour and shows that there was a decorative **celure** above the **rood**. The n. aisle roof is surprisingly lavish with braces and principal timbers carved with leaf trails, traceried **spandrels** and centre **bosses**. There may be some connection between this richness and the window by the n. door. It is later than the others on that side and received very individual treatment. The **mullions** are formed from terracotta sections stamped with varying moulds, and down each side there is a running pattern of greyhounds. Sections of two unrelated patterns are inset in the **jambs** and the designs confirm that they are by the same craftsmen whose work can be found at Henley and Barham. Versed in the fashionable Italian style, the men probably came on from Layer Marney in Essex when Lord Marney's great house was finished about 1525.

The tall tower arch rests on inner-facing head **corbels**, and below the C15 **font** has fine and deeply cut **Evangelistic symbols** alternating with angels in the bowl panels; squat lions support the corners of the shaft and between them stand excellent little **woodwoses**. The charming late C15 cover is a compact design, with pinnacles and flying buttresses rising to a heavily crocketted **finial**. On either side stand iron braziers on delicate tripod stands. Like a pair of fat, black pumpkins with perforated lids, they were filled with charcoal and are a rare example of an early form of church heating. Another interesting reminder of the past is housed in a glass case at the w. end of the s. aisle – an early C19 serpent that once formed part of the church's orchestra. A C19 **bier** stands in front and over in the n. aisle there is a massive 9ft C14 chest, bound with iron and fitted with three locks. A large set of C18 **Commandment boards** in a **pedimented** frame hangs on the s. aisle wall, and moving e. you will find one of the church's best features in the form of matching C15 **parclose screens**, enclosing a Lady chapel in the s. aisle and the chapel of **St John** in the n. aisle. The tracery of the latter is well preserved, with beautifully delicate cusping in the entrance arch and pairs of **ogees** within each **light**. There is an attractive C14 **piscina** and **sedile** under cusped ogee arches in the r. hand corner of the chapel, and a doorway overhead led to the **rood loft**. Its position suggests that a walkway may have extended along the parclose screen. The Lady chapel screen retains no colour and the restored C13 piscina there is now low in the wall following changes in floor level. Overhead hangs a helm with a large sunburst and rose crest, and the e. window was blocked to accommodate the 1727 monument for John Crowley – a handsome, restrained design with a border of patterned marble to the tablet and a shaped back above to display the family arms and a cherub's head. Moving out into the nave, it is worth noticing that the parclose screens were carefully shaped at the bottom to fit the bases of the arcade **piers**. The pulpit is modern but a small late C16 or early C17 Flemish panel of the **Annunciation** has been incorporated on one face. Above it hangs the **hatchment** of Bertram, 4th Earl of Ashburnham, who lived at Barking Hall and died in 1878, a copy of which is to be found in

Ashburnham church in Sussex. On the opposite wall are **Royal Arms** in pale colour inscribed 'God save King Charles the second'; below them is the door to the rood stair (although the stairs themselves have been bricked up).

The rood screen retains the skeleton of the coving that ran below the loft and its design differs from most in the area in that the main divisions are split by mullions to form tall and narrow lights. There are remains of small figures acting as corbels for the coving ribs, and the lower panels retain some of their colouring. Eagles are carved in the spandrels of the centre arch, with others in the discs at the end of the cusps, but the best carving is to be found on the e. side where normally all is blank. Birds perch on the rim of the centre arch, there is a heart pierced by two daggers in a spandrel to the s., and two excellent dragons on the n. side. The valuables in the sacristy were very well protected in unusual fashion. C15 doors with fine tracery are fitted with two locks set vertically and covered with escutcheon plates, and behind them stands the original C14 door. This one illustrates the beginning of the dominance of carpenter over smith – crude hinges right across, massive lockplate, and very wide untrimmed boards. A range of pews in the chancel is enclosed by panelling that probably came from the rood loft, and there is fine small-scale carving in the spandrels; look particularly for the pair of fishes on the e. side, each with a smaller fish in its mouth – the carver's version of the predatory pike. The **sanctuary** has a large C14 piscina under a cusped ogee arch, with **dropped-sill sedilia** alongside, and the late C17 **communion rails** have an interesting variant of the twisted **baluster**, growing fatter as they go down.

Battisford, St Mary (C6): A minor road meanders towards nowhere in particular and the churchyard lies in a

pleasant spot by the lane leading to Battisford Hall. Limes shade the paths and the plain late C14 s. **porch** has a step made from a pair of **gargoyles** salvaged from the long-vanished tower. Within it, there are wonderfully gnarled planks for seats in front of a simple doorway of about 1300. Both **nave** and **chancel** date from this period, with most of the windows renewed and the walls partly plastered. To the n. of the nave is a C14 chapel whose **lancet** has little **headstops**. On the w. gable a substantial bellcote with tiled **roof** has taken the place of the tower. It is supported by an eccentric brick buttress shaped like a chimney, with no fewer than seven varying **set-offs**, as though the builder made it up as he went along (which he probably did).

Entering by the n. door, one finds a simple interior with **pamment** floors and stripped pitch pine pews. The w. range is likely to be C18 and above it is a raked **gallery** with a panelled and painted front. The blocked tower arch remains and the stubs of two timber joists suggest that there was an earlier gallery. It is worth climbing the stairs to view the **Royal Arms** – painted on board and placed on the w. **tie-beam**. They are for Queen Anne and have her individual motto 'Semper eadem' (Always the same), but the heraldry is not accurate. The gallery seats have panelled backs and gangway doors which, when closed, allow hinged flaps to fall and thus provide maximum accommodation – as at Thornham Parva. From here one has an excellent view of the C14 roof, with tie-beams chosen for their natural curve and **king-posts** with four-way struts. The thickly whitewashed **font** carries a range of varied window shapes in the bowl panels above a reeded shaft, and nearby there are two squares of roofing lead, clamped to the walls and embossed with simple designs together with the initials of early C18 and C19 churchwardens. The church acquired its organ in 1914 and it takes up the n. chapel which possibly served as the squire's pew in the previous century. In front, a **ledger-stone** retains one of its shields but the inscription has gone. The C18 pulpit in plain panelled oak opposite is a highly individual shape – five irregular sides set against the wall, to which the stem returns. There is an image stool resting on a demi-angel behind it, and a vestige of the **rood loft stair** can be detected above. A low door in the n. chancel wall leads to a **vestry** with a **Perpendicular** e. window, and in the **sanctuary** stands a plain, almost square C17 **Holy table**. Behind it are the **Commandments**, Creed and Lord's Prayer on slate panels. They were originally painted but were banished to the back of the organ some years ago; it was only in 1983 that they were salvaged, cleaned, and, with the lettering finely cut, replaced – not only restored but improved. The 1724 monuments to Edward Salter and John Lewis which flank the e. window are identical and attractive designs; standing **putti** blow gilded trumpets at the top of the obelisks and there are pretty, painted **cartouches** of arms, with side scrolls and cherub heads below. Walter Rust's tablet is interesting because it tells us that at his death in 1685 he established a charity which specified that on a particular day each year (his birthday?) bread should be given to poor people in the church porch – one of the many ways in which the porch figured in parish life.

Baylham, St Peter (D7): The church stands on a hill within a spacious churchyard and there are pleasant views to the s. The architect Frederick Barnes carried out a full-scale restoration here in 1870 when he rebuilt the **chancel** and added **transepts** to it – 'Domus Dei, porta caeli 1870' (This is the House of God, this is the gate of heaven) is cut above the s. doorway. The C14 tower has **Decorated tracery** in the w. window but the blocked n. doorway betrays the true age of the church. It has a square **Norman** lintel

and the **tympanum** above it is incised with a pattern of lozenges. The C19 work on that side included a tall chimney in the corner between **nave** and transept which was given peculiar **trefoil** smoke holes at the top in a forlorn attempt to afford it some Gothic character. There is nice flowing Decorated tracery in a s. nave window and entry is via the 1870s **porch** and s. door.

The C15 **font** is a familiar East Anglian design, with four lions that have lost their heads round the shaft and defaced angels beneath the bowl. Six of the bowl panels are carved with two lions and four **Tudor roses**, but the other two are of more than usual interest. When **Dowsing** came here, probably in August 1644, he noted that 'there was the Trinity in a triangle on the Font, and a cross', and although he doubtless ordered their defacement, the shields held by the angels in the n. and s. panels of the bowl can still be identified as a **Trinity emblem** (s.) and the **instruments of the Passion**. The nave roof retains its original **tie-beams** but Barnes inserted additional **kingposts** and panelled out the ceiling in chestnut. A new chancel arch was part of the reconstruction and the partial door shape just w. of the transept was probably the entrance to the old **rood loft stairs**. Parts of the medieval **screen** were found when the pews were replaced and they were incorporated in the **vestry** screen under the tower and in the front panels of the reading desk. The C17 monument of John and Elizabeth Acton was reinstated on the n. wall of the chancel and their little alabaster figures kneel and face each other over a prayer desk, with a gruesome skeleton reared behind them; there is an **achievement of arms** above the cornice, three sons and two daughters kneel in compartments below, and a **pelican** is carved in a roundel at the bottom – there are traces of colour here and there. The **communion rails** by Hart & Co. are the ingenious tubular variety in brass, with telescopic centre sections, and the

e. window has the risen Christ flanked by two of the **three Marys** and two apostles in attractive glass by **Clayton & Bell**, with their individual red typically dominant.

Bedfield, St Nicholas (E3): The church is to be found at the end of a lane off the village street to the e. and when I visited in 1988 the restoration of the C14 tower was nearing completion. It has a panelled **base course** and the **Perpendicular** w. doorway has **fleurons** in the mouldings. There are three canopied niches around the w. window and **flushwork** decorates the buttresses and battlements. On walking round, you will find evidence of **Norman** origins in the form of an early C12 n. doorway with zigzag bobbin decoration in the arch, and there is an abrupt change in the make-up of the **chancel** wall on that side where Norman coursed flints give way to random placing. There, a single C14 **lancet** contrasts with the variety of Perpendicular windows in the **nave**. The stonework of the e. window and the **priest's door** are reminders that J.K. Colling supervised the big restoration of the chancel in 1870. The C14 **porch** is simple but most attractive, with a niche over the wide outer arch and a **king-post roof**. The side lancets in their deep splays have been blocked and the homely brick floor is worn and undulating.

Within, the tall tower arch is blocked by a combination of C19 screen and painted hardboard but just below is an interesting range of C17 benches. Their ends are cut from 2in. plank and curve up to scrolls decorated with simple gouge cuts at the rear. The deep bowl of the C14 **font** is decorated with window **tracery** and three shields, and stands on a plain shaft, but its C17 cover is much more unusual. Over 6ft tall, its body is panelled, with columns at the angles, and the curved strapwork brackets on top are carved with masks where they meet the centre shaft and **finial**. Its individuality lies in the way

it is prepared for use. The three w. sections are lifted away in one piece, and three of the e. panels are hinged at the top so that they can be folded inwards and secured by a hook. This allows people standing on that side to watch the priest as he christens the baby. A chest with typical **Jacobean** decoration stands by the n. door and the later C17 pulpit has plain panels and carved scroll supports to the canted book ledge. Overhead is a single-framed and braced rafter roof, and the stairs to the old **rood loft** are set in the s. window embrasure. Judging by the size of the top opening one would have crawled rather than walked onto the loft. There are image niches on both sides of the chancel arch and the base of the C15 **screen** has narrow painted panels. At least some of the subjects were Old Testament prophets for two survive on the s. side – Joel and Baruch – and there is a fragment of the donors' inscription below: 'Robert and his wife Alice'. It may be that this section was masked by a former pulpit and so escaped the fate of the rest. The chancel roof was part of Colling's restoration, together with the Caen stone **reredos** bearing painted Creed, Commandments and Lord's Prayer panels. Floor levels were altered and the plain C14 **piscina** is now very low in the wall. The **altar** is a simple C17 table. Returning down the nave you will walk over Thomas Dunston's **ledger-stone** of 1657. It is decorated with a skull and that popular comment: 'Hodie mihi cras tibi' (My turn today, yours tomorrow).

Bedingfield, St Mary (D3): The church stands in a bosky churchyard by the village crossroads, and walking up the path you will see that the stumps of crosses crown the gables of **nave** and **chancel**. They are a reminder that **Dowsing** paid a visit in April 1643, when he gave orders for them to be taken down, having broken 'fourteen superstitious pictures, one of God the Father, and two doves, and another of

St Catherine and her wheel'. The late C13 or early C14 tower is unbuttressed to belfry level where there are small **trefoil lancets**, with no window above the small, plain w. doorway. The bell openings have the remains of **Decorated tracery** and, at that level, there are shallow angle buttresses with three **set-offs**. Some of the windows in nave and chancel are square headed with Decorated tracery, there is an earlier lancet on the n. side of the chancel, and a late **Perpendicular** design, with deep **label** and stepped **embattled transoms**, in the s. wall of the nave. The e. window is C19, and so is the tracery of the round window w. of the **porch**. One wonders whether it was **Saxon** originally, possibly uncovered during restoration work. A good deal of that was done in the C19 and a **vestry** was built onto the n. wall of the nave in 1834. The C15 porch is intriguing because, above the heavily moulded **tie-beams** and **wall plates**, the ridge is supported lengthwise by slim **arch-braces**. They have the remains of very delicate pierced tracery in the **spandrels**, and the uprights are slotted to take transverse braces which have largely gone. It is the latter that makes one suspect that either the original **roof** was a different shape or the frame came from elsewhere (it is distinctly darker than the rest). The inner doorway is finely moulded and the niche high on the r. has most unusual mouldings for its size – five shallow ranks back to a trefoil arch.

Within, the nave lies under a well-proportioned **double hammerbeam** roof which has very little ornamentation. Arch-braces rise to collars under the ridge and there were angels or shields attached to the ends of the hammers but they have all gone. Painted Victorian **Royal Arms** are framed above the tower arch, and below stands a massive chest over 7ft long, completely sheathed and banded in iron. C14 or early C15, it is very like the one at Horham, but is divided in two, with separate lids. A visitor in 1887 found parish papers in one half

and coal in the other, and apparently thought nothing of it! The plain C15 octagonal bowl of the **font** is decorated with simple tracery shapes and it stands on an earlier shaft. The nave benches are an interesting mixture. The ends against the wall are the remains of a C15 set with varied **poppyheads** and the shattered remains of a whole range of figures and beasts, while the remainder date from 1612 and are typically **Jacobean** in style. They have pairs of scrolls with rosette centres below a **finial**, with more scrolls on the elbows. Unlike the earlier craftsmen, the C17 joiners were content to carve only the side facing the aisle, but the backs of two ends on the s. side bear 'R.1612L.' and 'G.1612P.' (churchwardens, no doubt), and one at the w. end simply has the date. On the other side at the w. end, one back has 'B.Bond' carved in relief. The front range are C19 along with the pulpit. There is now no **screen** but remains of the stairs that led to the **rood loft** survive in the n. wall. The centre **light** of the Perpendicular s. nave window has glass by **William Morris & Co.**, but it dates from 1929 when the firm was limply reiterating all that had gone before. The design is probably by Dearle and has the **Blessed Virgin** kneeling with a book before her which has fallen open at the words of the **Annunciation. Gabriel** holds St Mary's lily emblem, and there is a clump of foliage which has the faint echo of **pre-Raphaelite** richness. The large and brash figures of **St James the Great, St Stephen** (?), and **St John** in the chancel e. window have much more character. Its maker is unknown but the glass probably dates from the 1850s, and the Bedingfield arms at the top may link it with the **hatchment** that hangs on the chancel s. wall; it was used at the funeral of John James Bedingfield in 1853. The early C17 **altar** is an oak table with austere lines but of a most interesting design. The legs are turned and four slimmer versions are set along the single central stretcher.

Belstead, St Mary (E8): Like those of a number of churches in the Ipswich area, Belstead's tower is on the s. side of the **nave** and doubles as a **porch**. It is small scale and unbuttressed, and at some time the battlements were renewed in brick. The bell openings probably had **tracery** originally, and in the C19 a cross was outlined in flint above the little belfry **lancet**. On walking round, you will find that the large **Perpendicular** w. window has been renewed and there is a blocked n. door. A chapel was added on that side in the C16, with three-**light** windows and a doorway in brick (the latter and one of the windows have since been blocked). The **chancel roof** continues down over a n.e. **vestry** whose window has 'Y' tracery of about 1300, but the main e. window is Perpendicular. A window on the s. side of the nave has attractive **Decorated** tracery, and before going inside there are **scratch dials** to be found on the s.w. and s.e. **quoins** of the tower. The entrance arch is small but robust and the inner doorway is set within an earlier, larger arch.

C19 **decalogue** boards stand at the w. end and the n. doorway now houses a restored charity board. The C15 **font** is in fine condition and in one of the bowl panels an angel holds a shield carved with three fishes, one of Christianity's oldest symbols. In the other panels there are **Tudor roses**, a **Trinity** shield, the arms of Bury abbey, and those of the Norwich diocese–of which Suffolk once formed a part; demi-angels spread their wings under the bowl and fine upstanding lions support the shaft. The range of benches with square-topped ends and heavy mouldings on the s. side w. of the entrance date from the C16, and a set of George III **Royal Arms** painted on canvas hangs above the door. The tall tablet on the s. wall is for Sir Robert Harland, an admiral who died in 1784. By way of epitaph his widow composed an extraordinary thirty-line résumé of his not very distinguished career. Farther along, the sill of the window was crudely lowered to form **sedilia** and to give

access to the **rood loft stairs** that rise in the wall. The tall bottom doorway still retains its hinge hooks and the upper exit is partially framed with thin tiles which may have been filched from an earlier building. The **piscina** below served a nave **altar** nearby but the three worn heads around the arch do not belong to it. The nice **Jacobean** pulpit has an abundance of shallow carving, with a typical range of blind-arched panels; the base and steps are modern. Over by the reading desk lies the church's only **brass** and it is a good one. It commemorates John Goldingham, who died in 1518, and his wives Jane and Thomasine. He was Lord of Belstead Parva Manor and is shown wearing Tudor armour with his sword eccentrically slung. The women wear **kennel head-dresses** and have massive rosaries, together with missals hung from their girdles. The inscription is missing but there are three shields which were originally inlaid with colour, displaying the arms of Goldingham and his wives' families. The n. chapel was built for the use of the Blosse family and is separated from the nave by a three-bay **arcade**, with one bay taken up by the organ. Just inside is a huge **ledger-stone** for Tobias Blosse, rector here for forty years until he died in 1693. His **achievement** is deeply cut and displays three **griffins** with curly tails. Over the blocked door beyond is a tablet for an earlier Tobias who died in 1630, carved by John Stone, son of the better-known **Nicholas Stone**. Not installed until 1656, it is a lozenge of marble which is carved as though it hung from a beribboned ring, and the epitaph is meticulously arranged. At the same time, Stone also carved the more elaborate tablet in the n.e. corner for Elizabeth Blosse, Tobias's daughter-in-law, who died in 1653. It is a slightly domed oval tablet set within an oblong frame, with an achievement and bunched drapes at the top, and little figures of her three sons and four daughters kneeling at the bottom. Note how the epitaph was phrased to add lustre to her in-laws' family by dwelling on the services rendered to royalty by her Darcy forebears. Partially hidden by the organ is the large tablet for Elizabeth Hunt, wife of Tobias's grandson, who died in 1727. It has chaste scrolls each side but a riotous **cartouche** was placed on top. The chapel's w. window was filled in to make space for the largest of the family monuments. Thomas Blosse died in 1722 and is commemorated there by a mottled grey marble composition which has skulls at the top on either side of a seated **putto**, while standing putti flank the large tablet, one piping his eye while resting his foot on another skull.

The C14 **scissors-braced** roof in the nave has been restored and there is no chancel arch now, the division being marked only by a change in roof level and flushed boarding. However, the base of the **rood screen** remains below and the painted panels are interesting. The work dates from the end of the C15 and the figures are set against a continuous landscape panorama, with lakes, hills, and castles. Although badly defaced, the colours are still bright and the paintings display a strong Flemish influence. Starting from the l., the first two panels are blank, then we have good figures of **St Osyth** and **St Ursula**, and a poor **St Margaret** followed by another female saint who is probably **St Mary Magdalene**. The next two are blank and then there are two bishops, the first of whom might be **St Thomas of Canterbury**. Then comes **St Laurence**, followed by **St Stephen** and **St Edmund** robed in red trimmed with ermine and holding a spear-like arrow. The last figure is **St Sebastian** in hunting green, with fashionable epaulettes on his doublet and a feather in his hat. The chancel lies under a plastered ceiling and there is a text over the **priest's door** which may be the survivor of a sequence like the examples at Witnesham and Hemingstone. The doorway to the vestry is C14 and the door itself is contemporary, with lapped boards and strap hinges as at Capel St Mary. Within the vestry there is a section of a C17 pew fixed to the wall, with turned uprights and a line of hat pegs. There is no piscina now in the **sanctuary** and the modern oak **reredos** frames a C19 painting of Christ blessing the bread and wine of the Eucharist. The simple **Holy table** in front of it has '1621' carved on the inside of the top frame but, like many others, it has had extensions screwed on to the top to make it a fashionable size.

Bentley, St Mary (E9): The church stands about a mile n. of the village by the lane that leads to Bentley Park. A row of limes fronts the churchyard but only one of the three large cedars survived the great gale of 1987. The sturdy **Perpendicular** tower has a simple **base course**, buttresses angled to the w., and the **flushwork** in the battlements has been partially filled with brick. The barn-like n. **aisle** under a double pitched **roof** was an addition of 1858 when **R.M. Phipson** carried out a major restoration. The organ chamber/**vestry** to the e. is almost as lofty, with a circular window in the gable. The **chancel** was rebuilt in the 1880s and given a new e. window with flowing **tracery**, but there is a **Norman lancet** in the n. wall which marks its true age. The lancets on the s. side are late C13, with the exception of the largest, which is C19 (the old **priest's door** disappeared in the course of the rebuilding). The low s. porch has Victorian king and bishop **headstops** to the outer arch, and there is a modern statue in the niche above. Passing a fine upstanding pair of boot scrapers, one is confronted by a full-scale replica of a Norman doorway which, save perhaps for painted decoration, is what the original might well have looked like. The only real evidence left is a section of **chevron moulding** which rests on a windowsill.

The church once had a C13 **font** of **Purbeck marble**, and its square base with the outline of shafts remains almost flush with the floor. The present font has lions round the shaft and dates from the early C16, but it looks as though it was re-cut by the restorers. The e. panel of the bowl is carved with the **Blessed Virgin** and Child within an aureole, and is flanked by angels bearing Tollemache shields. Others hold shields bearing initials and the cross of **St George**, and the rest of the panels are carved with a **Tudor rose**, a pomegranate, and a curious interlaced strap. The **decalogue boards** on the aisle w. wall are brightly lettered in the High Victorian style, and a dark set of George III **Royal Arms** hangs above the arch at the e. end. Below, a C13 font bowl stands in the corner, but curiously enough it does not match the old base. Nearby is a single C15 bench with **poppyheads**, a lively horse carved on one elbow, and what is possibly a **cockatrice** on the other. The glass of 1900 in the s.w. **nave** window is probably by **Powells** and has the figures of Martha and Mary, with two vignettes below. In the other window the **three Marys** gather at the tomb, with the emphasis on the Magdalene with her long golden tresses; this is the work of **Heaton, Butler & Bayne**. The nave roof is a simple C15 **hammerbeam** construction, with collar beams and **king-posts**, and the **rood beam** is still in place. The chancel has a panelled wagon roof which was installed at a lower level during the rebuilding. **Henry Ringham** carried out the woodwork for Phipson's restoration, but although the choir stalls are very much in his style, they date from the 1880s, long after his death. The e. window is filled with the scene of the disciples after the Ascension, with an angel host hovering above them and Jerusalem in the distance. It contrasts nicely with the other windows although it too is by Heaton, Butler & Bayne. The whole of the e. wall below is clad with mosaic panels and, unlike most modern versions, the **piscina** in a window ledge was provided with a drain.

Bildeston, St Mary Magdalene (B8): This was an important village in the

great days of the wool trade but, even before that, the church had been sited half a mile away on the hill to the w. Standing in a well-wooded churchyard, its tallness is emphasised by the lack of a tower, although there was one until 1975 when the s.e. corner collapsed onto the **nave** and much of the rest had to be pulled down. Now it is capped level with the nave **roof**, and between the remains of angle buttresses there is a finely moulded **Perpendicular** w. doorway, with triple niches under **cusped** and **crocketted ogees** above it. The C14 **aisles** stop short just one bay from the e. end and their e. windows have **reticulated tracery**. There is more **Decorated** tracery in the n.w. window but the others are Perpendicular – very tall and **transomed**. The C15 **clerestory** continues over the **chancel**, with thin red bricks in the window arches and **gargoyles** in the parapet. On the n. side there is a C14 doorway and a projecting slab that marks the site of the **rood loft stairs**. A small **vestry** is tucked in the n.e. angle and the chancel e. window displays interesting Decorated tracery – an irregular **cinquefoil** shape above five tall ogee-headed **lights**. The s. **sanctuary** window matches it and a **priest's door** is set in the corner by the s. aisle. The tall **porch** is very similar to Hitcham's and has an **ashlar** parapet, in the centre of which a feathery angel holds a shield. Facade and buttresses are all panelled **flushwork** and there are three particularly good niches; tall, with vaulting and the remains of angels below the stools, their crocketted canopies are formed by pairs of little ogee arches. The lower buttress faces are carved with recessed panels in ashlar and the arch has roses in the **spandrels** and lion masks with more roses in the mouldings. The inner doorway is equally impressive, with its double rank of deep mouldings set with shields and crowns rising to an angel at the apex; there are large lion stops to the **hood mould** and the original doors have a broad band of vines round the edge and tracery cut in the solid (rather than applied) in the tops of the panels. The upper room was once used as a treasury and you will see that iron rods still run through the timbers of its floor.

The interior is immaculate and bears witness to the tremendous efforts of the parish in the years of repair and restoration that followed the tower's collapse. One of those deeply involved is commemorated in a new s. aisle w. **lancet** which has glass by Pippa Heskett (whose work can also be seen at Withersfield [Vol.1]);the subject is **St Mary Magdalene** kneeling with her companion below an angel and it was completed in 1981. A small early C14 doorway to the tower is blocked and high above the main arch there is a **quatrefoil sanctus-bell window** looking rather lost in the expanse of wall. Having no step, the C15 **font** seems squat, and there are battered carvings of extra-large **Evangelistic symbols** in the bowl panels alternating with angels bearing shields. On these you will find a **Trinity emblem** (e.), a chalice and wafer for the mass (n.), and possibly the three crowns of Ely (w.). Only fragments of the **woodwoses** and lions that supported the shaft remain. The large door to the porch upper room is no longer accessible but it once opened onto a gallery and stairway above the entrance. The body of the church is tall and open, with beautiful **arcades** that sweep through to the e. end uninterrupted by a chancel arch. Their quatrefoil **piers** support finely moulded arches which have angels at the top, and the **capitals** are carved either with demi-angels or oak leaves. In the roof, cambered **tie-beams** alternate with **hammerbeams** whose ends carry newly painted angels in the chancel. The stone **corbels** are carved with foliage, shields, and some more angels with strawberry-pink hands and faces. There were a number of restorations in the C19 and the benches, pulpit, and choir stalls date from then.

In 1977 the parishes of Bildeston and Wattisham were united, and in 1980 the s. aisle chapel was re-dedicated to **St Nicholas**, patron saint of the redun-

dant church. Some of its fittings found a home here and its chancel **screen** is now the **reredos**. With a new cresting, the buttresses have crocketted pinnacles with little mask stops and, below Decorated tracery, the panels have totally repainted figures of four male and four female saints. One can identify **St John** (far l.), **St Paul** (3rd from l.), possibly **St Ursula** (4th from r.), **St Agnes** (3rd from r.), possibly **St Helen** (2nd from r.), and **St Barbara** (far r.). Nearby, the square **label** of the **piscina** encloses a pair of crocketted canopies and on the wall overhead there is an 1837 **cartouche** by Gaffin of London for Richard and Percy Wilson. The plain tablet with crossed palms to the w. is by the same firm for the same family. Above it, a stark but interesting tablet commemorates Capt. Edward Rotheram, who was with Lord Howe on the 'glorious 1st of June' and commanded the *Royal Sovereign*, which led the battle line at Trafalgar. The window here is a good 1890s example of the characteristic style of **Kempe & Co. Censing** angels flank the Virgin and Child in the upper panels, with the **Annunciation** beneath. The bottom panels portray the **Visitation, Zachariah** in the Temple, and the angel in peacock robes appearing to shepherds who obviously had a talent for music. All very sumptuous. Farther w., is a tablet carved as an open book – 'This durable volume is inscribed to the memory of John Parker . . . 1831'- by J.H. Elmes, a little-known London mason. Across the n. aisle, a slab set against the wall at the e. end carries the **brass** of Alice Wade. Her 22in. figure is dressed in a voluminous gown, parted to display a brocaded petticoat, and she wears a fashionable Elizabethan hat. The inscription dated 1599 is for her and her husband William but his effigy has gone, although little groups of sons and daughters survive at the bottom.

Because there was no chancel arch, the **rood screen** stretched from wall to wall and faint traces of the entrance can be seen at high level. **Cautley** reminds us that it survived the Puritans only to be torn out in the C18. The stalls in the chancel are largely Victorian but incorporate C15 **poppyheads**, and behind them are stalls which came from the now vanished chapel of St Leonard in the village. They all have **misericords** in a fairly shaky state and those that could be examined have been mutilated. They were mostly human faces but there are the remains of a **pelican** on the n. side. The late C17 **communion rails** have clusters of four **balusters** to mark the entrance to the sanctuary and beyond them to the r. is a heavy C19 **piscina** and **sedilia**. William Wailes had worked with **Pugin** in the 1840s and his Newcastle firm of Wailes & Strang produced a great deal of richly coloured glass in the C19. The e. window is characteristic and the large **cinquefoil** contains a scene from St Luke's Gospel, while the two long quatrefoils illustrate episodes from the Acts of the Apostles. For those with keen eyes (or binoculars) the text references are lettered in the borders. The main lights are filled with patterned **quarries** crossed with diagonal text labels, and at the bottom is a beautifully painted crest of a cock. This is unlikely to be Wailes's work and is the device of Admiral James Cockburn, C. in C. naval forces in India. He died in Calcutta in 1872 and the window is his memorial.

Boulge, St Michael and All Angels (F5): Boulge Hall was pulled down in 1956 and the parish is a mere handful of scattered cottages and farms. There are two routes across the park, but the one from the Bredfield/Debach road is ungated and winds through the fields until it comes to a leafy tunnel of trees that leads to the churchyard. In the C13 an older building was replaced, and a modest brick tower was added in the early C16, but the character of the present church was largely determined by the Victorians. An 1858 restoration by W.G. & E. Habershon rebuilt the e. end and added a s. **aisle**, and nine years later a s. **transept** was added, the **chancel** was rebuilt, and the walls were re-faced by Habershon & Pite. Finally, in 1895, a new **vestry**/organ chamber was built on the s. side. Coming in from the s.e. corner of the churchyard one is faced with the two large flint-faced gables – the vestry with a circular window over the door, and the transept. The latter has its own door and (rather confusingly) is placed where one would expect a s. **porch** to be. The **knapped** flintwork is exceptionally good, particularly round the s. window. The C14 n. doorway was untouched by the restorations and there is one 'Y' **tracery** window of about 1300 on that side. The large C19 mausoleum of the Fitzgerald family stands s.w. of the tower. It has a hipped, stone-slated **roof** and is half submerged, with steps down to its C13-style doorway. Guarded by heavy iron railings, it is crumbling gradually to ruin, and is in no way remarkable but for the fact that the one member of the family with a claim to fame is not buried within but has his own simple grave slab alongside. Edward Fitzgerald lived most of his life in this part of Suffolk, a gentle scholar who numbered Thackeray and Tennyson among his friends. His work would have been forgotten by the world at large had he not issued a little anonymous pamphlet in 1859 entitled: *The Rubáiyát of Omar Khayyám*. Few other single poems of its class have been so widely known and loved, a singular tribute to the genius of its translator. He died in 1883 and ten years later a rose was planted at the head of his grave – no ordinary rose, however, for artist William Simpson had been to Omar Khayyám's tomb at Nishapur; the seeds he took from the roses blooming there were cultivated at Kew and one of the bushes was planted here. Six more roses came from Iran in 1972 to mark the 2500th anniversary of the Persian empire.

The interior is rather dark but once the lights are switched on it is remarkably attractive. The massive **font** that stands in the tower is one of a group of only eight in England and is made of black marble quarried at Tournai in Belgium. Dating from 1150-70, the best-known ones are in Winchester and Lincoln cathedrals, but there is another in the redundant church of St Peter, Ipswich. The sides are normally sculpted with scriptural or legendary subjects but unfortunately this one has had all its decoration carefully chiselled away, save for a few fragments beneath the corners. Nearby hangs a C19 **decalogue board** set in an oak frame, and round the corner on the w. wall is an elegant tablet of 1792 for William Whitby. Excellently lettered within a narrow beige border, it has a small urn **finial** between scrolls above and a shield of arms with palm fronds below. The glass in the nearby **lancet** celebrated Queen Victoria's Diamond Jubilee and has a profile portrait held aloft by a pair of youthful angels above the **Royal Arms**. A set of George IV arms painted on canvas hangs above the n. door. Farther along on that side, stained glass which may be by **Clayton & Bell** commemorates a Suffolk Regiment lieutenant and his comrades who fell near Colesberg in the Boer War; the regimental badge is in the tracery above the figures of **St Michael** and **Gabriel**. The transept is two bays wide, and e. of it, beyond a half-arch, is a family pew which has its own arch to the nave resting on large leafy **capitals**. Stiff Victorian Gothic memorials to the Fitzgeralds abound, and the glass by Arthur J. Dick in the transept window dates from 1906. The centre Crucifixion is reminiscent of the one by **Kempe** at Burgh and is flanked by figures of **St Edmund** and **St Felix**. The tracery has Christ the King, an **Annunciation** and Christ's baptism, and all is very lush. The glass of 1940 in the window farther along is not particularly distinguished – figures of Justice and Charity alongside Christ as the Light of the World – but look for the sweet little vignettes slipped in under the main figures: a view of the church, a wagon being loaded, and a cow. The artist is unknown but he may also have de-

signed the glass in the n. chancel window which commemorates Lieut. Cdr Robert White and the ship's company of H.M.S. *Duchess*, sunk in action in 1939. There is a figure of **St Faith** and one of **St Nicholas** carrying a model of the ship. Strangely, and apparently as an afterthought, someone has added crudely painted anchors to the front of his chasuble. There is a blocked C13 window on the n. side of the **sanctuary**, and a few C14 tiles have been re-set within its splay. They probably formed part of the floor (like those at Icklingham, All Saints [Vol.I]), and one bears an heraldic shield. The **altar** is a simple **Stuart** table which stands in front of a white marble **reredos** of 1913 whose design is taken from the C5 sarcophagus of Valentinian III, the Western emperor at Ravenna. A lamb, with two doves perching on a cross behind it, stands in a shallow portico with twisted columns and matching arches each side.

Boxford, St Mary (C9): This was one of Suffolk's prosperous wool villages, with a population of over 400 in the early C16, and the houses cluster attractively round its splendid church. The tower is C14 and grotesques crouch on the lowest **weatherings** of the w. buttresses (like those at Great Waldingfield). Note that the **dripstones** of the weatherings are continued up into the corners to finish with more grotesques. The C16 w. doors are panelled, with a carved border, and the **transomed Perpendicular** window overhead is flanked by remnants of niches and a **flushwork arcade**. There is a stair turret on the s. side to belfry level bearing a C19(?) slate sundial, and the tower is crowned by a pretty little wooden octagon with a ring of wooden spirelets and flying buttresses round the leaded spike on top. The main entrance was originally on the n. side where the bulk of the village lay and there one finds the county's finest example of a C14 wooden **porch**. It is tall, with an entrance arch formed from two moulded planks flanked by niches,

Boxford, St Mary

and there are pairs of large windows each side with **Decorated tracery** cut from 2ft wide planks laid crosswise. Within, triple-shafted columns with ring **capitals** support the skeletal ribs of a **groined** ceiling which would have been panelled out originally. Overall, it illustrates perfectly the way in which C14 carpenters copied the patterns and designs of the masons before evolving their own disciplines. The arch of the inner doorway rests on angel **headstops** with two ranks of eroded **paterae** in the mouldings and the doors have a band of **quatrefoils** at the edge. Circling the church, you will find a **vestry** rather like a little doll's house with a tall chimney tucked into the angle by the **chancel**, and an e. window with panel tracery above five **ogee**-headed **lights**. Just below the e. window of the s.e. chapel there is an unusual headstone of 1821 which has a cast-iron plaque of two maidens and an urn clamped to the top which bids fair to outlast the stone itself. There is a

priest's door on this side and the main entrance is now through the splendid C15 s. porch. Money was bequeathed for it between 1441 and 1480 and there were burials there in 1465 – always a spot favoured by the medieval wealthy. Unfortunately the soft stone has perished badly but it is one of the most lavish in Suffolk, particularly in its minor details. The **jambs** of the four-light side windows, for instance, are enriched with miniature stooled and vaulted niches and the buttresses are intricately panelled. The porch has a double **base course** of shields in quatrefoils and the side parapets are panelled and pierced. The frontage is terribly worn and only parts of the **Annunciation** scene in the **spandrels** survive – the archangel on the l. bears a scroll and the **Blessed Virgin's** lily emblem can be seen on the r. Above, there are seven niches in a line, all groined, with a vine trail underneath. The entrance doors have some tracery and a quatrefoiled rim, and note how the step has been worn away by countless people making use of the l. hand door only.

The body of the church was rebuilt in the C15 and the arcades rest on quatrefoil **piers** with bold **hood moulds** to the arches. The size of the chancel and its side chapels makes the **nave** seem short for its height, and the heavy cambered **tie-beams** of the **roof** have **wall posts** resting on small head **corbels**. The w. **gallery** with its moulded front beam is set just below the spring of the tower arch and was probably installed in the early C16. Below it there is an C18 charity board and a section of roof lead embossed with the names of churchwardens, carpenter, and plumber in 1805. The **font** stands by a pillar opposite the s. door and although the bowl is modern its C15 shaft is panelled in the form of **mullioned** windows. What makes it special is the C17 octagonal cover, which is built like a cupboard, with two hinged doors and a graceful ogee cap. The faded green of the inside is painted with red and cream scrolls which are lettered with texts from **St John's** Gospel: 'How can a man be borne which is old?', 'Except a man be borne of water and of the spirit, he cannot enter the Kingdom', and 'If I wash the not thou hast no part with me'. The new step has been finely cut with a text from the Beatitudes: 'Blessed are the pure in heart . . .'. The iron-bound chest in the n. **aisle** is probably late C14 but, unlike the majority of medieval examples, it is made of softwood rather than oak or chestnut. The C18 pulpit has a typically restrained marquetry design with the **sacred monogram** in one panel, and the fact that capitals from **Corinthian pilasters** are strangely attached underneath suggests that its parts may have come from a **reredos**. The shaped stair rail is beautifully done, with pairs of **balusters** like old-fashioned sticks of barley sugar.

The chancel arch is tall and wide and there is no longer a **screen**. However, the upper door to the old **rood loft** is prominent on the n. side, and there is a second opening towards the n. aisle which means that it probably connected with another loft over a **parclose screen**. Above the chancel arch is a fine painting of two **censing** angels which was uncovered in 1955. They have pale blue wings and between them is a tiny Christ in Majesty. To the l. on the **clerestory** wall is another fragment and it must have formed part of a large scheme designed to complement the rood below, painted soon after the C15 clerestory was built. A shield dated 1685 on the e. tie-beam indicates that the roof was altered slightly then, partially obscuring the angels. Before the **Reformation** there were **guilds** of **St John, St Peter, St Christopher**, and the **Trinity**, and the two chancel chapels may have been associated with them. The arcade to the s. matches the nave but the lozenge shape of the pier on the n. side indicates a slightly later date. The e. wall of the s. chapel has two niches, one above the other, on either side of the window, groined and stooled but with their canopies shorn

away. Those on the l. retain a great deal of their original colour and the shadowy marks within show the size of the images that once filled them. By the window on that side is a painting of **St Edmund** clutching one of the arrows of his martyrdom. There are sections of **linen-fold panelling** behind the late C17 **Holy table** and, to the r., a **piscina** lies below a mutilated ogee arch. A plain tablet on the s. wall of the chapel carries the singular epitaph of Elizabeth Hyam: ' . . . for the fourth time widow; who by a fall that brought on a mortification was at last hastened to her end on the 4th May 1748 in her 113th year'. An earlier and equally engaging memorial is the tiny **brass** in the n.e. corner of the chapel. It is for David Birde, the rector's son, who died a few months old in 1606. The tiny engraving shows him in a cradle with rockers and turned corner posts. A larger brass at the w. end of the chancel is for John Brond, who died four years later, and the inscription is less than specific: '. . . having in his life time two wives & left behind him by either of his wives divers children'. There could be a lot felt but left unsaid behind that! The n.e. chapel is now taken up by the organ and vestry but it is worth exploring if possible because there are some more brasses – for William Birde, 'sometyme Pastor of this churche' (1599), Robert Bird, another of the rector's sons (1612), and a plate within a strapwork border for William Doggett with his wife Avis. He died in 1610 and was 'Marchant adve(n)terer, citizen and mercer of London and free of the East India Company'. There were never effigies but four shields carry the arms of the City of London (top l.), the Mercers' Company (top r.), the Merchant Adventurers (bottom l. with faulty heraldry), and the East India Company (bottom r. and also inaccurate). The shields were originally inlaid with colour and some of the lead infilling survives. The C18 **communion rails** in the chancel have elegantly turned balusters and the e. window is filled with striking 1970s

glass by Rosemary Rutherford. It is a Transfiguration scene in which tremendously elongated figures of Christ flanked by Moses and Elijah tower above the crouching figures of the disciples. The red and yellow flame-like centre splinters outwards into cooler colours, and the lead lines radiate and encircle the centre. More of this artist's work can be found at Hinderclay [Vol.1].

Bramford, St Mary (E7): If you approach, as I did, across the wide expanse of churchyard on the s. side, the church seems large but unremarkable. The C14 tower has attractive **Decorated tracery** in the bell openings, **quatrefoil** belfry windows, and a wide and shallow niche beneath the w. window. There is a triple **base course** in flint chequerwork, and the **dripstones** on the buttresses continue into the corners, with grotesques on the lower **weatherings** reminiscent of those at Boxford; a slim C18 spire rises behind the battlements. It is not until one sees the n. side that the richness of the C15 rebuilding can be appreciated. A continuous parapet carved with a frieze of shields and **Tudor** flowers links the **aisle** with the tall **porch**, and above it there are pinnacles crowned with figures. Look particularly for the figure of **St Edmund** with his arrow on the n.w. corner of the porch, and a cowled ape carrying a flask which is seated cross-legged on the pinnacle to the e. of the porch (satirising the doctors). There are more figures above the richly traceried battlements of the **clerestory**, and the aisle buttresses each have niches at high level. The substantial 1890s **vestry** projecting from the **chancel** was designed by Cheston & Perkin and matches the C15 work very well. The facade of the porch is in **knapped** flint and the central canopied niche contains a statue of the **Blessed Virgin** and Child which was given in 1908 (unlike many

modern replacements, it is just the right size). As with the w. window of the n. aisle, the C14 e. window of the porch was re-used at the rebuilding and so was the inner doorway, although this entailed offsetting the porch to the l.

Within, the very tall tower arch has leaf **stops** to the **hood mould** and for some reason it does not align with the nave. This is emphasised by the differing widths of the blind **ogee** arches on either side. There seems little doubt that the tower was completed before the **nave** was rebuilt because the w. bays of the **arcades** are halved where they meet its substantial e. buttresses. By the organ there is a huge glacial boulder below the base of the tower buttress and, like those at Shelley and other churches nearby, it may have been a pagan cult object which was cleansed and converted to the service of the new religion. Large stone **corbels** high up in the tower show that there was vaulting originally (or at least a substantial floor) and two of them are remarkably like those below the chancel arch at nearby Hintlesham. One is a handsome man with curly hair, one a devil, and the last is a mask with arms that pull the mouth wide open. There are C19 **decalogue boards** on the walls below and the C15 **font** has been moved within the tower. The panels are carved alternately with shields and angels bearing books or crowns, and the flat underside carries **paterae** above a traceried stem. The carcase of the elaborate early C16 cover is hinged so that it can be opened out, and the base of each panel carries triple pedestals below shallow canopies. The domed top is **crocketted** with a **finial** and the carved detail throughout is an interesting mixture of Gothic and **Renaissance** motifs. It is supported by a thick, rather crude, post at the back – I wonder whether this was always so. The nave arcades have octagonal **piers** and the hood mould of the arch by the organ has a stop carved as a dragon biting its tail; the dove in a vine farther along is C19 but there is a

Bramford, St Mary: stone screen

nice little medieval dog opposite. It is likely that there were extensive wall paintings in the C14 but only a fragment remains on the s.e. buttress of the tower. **Dowsing** records that he broke down 841 'superstitious pictures' in 1643 and he may have been responsible for the mutilation of the angels which form the **hammerbeams** of the C15 nave **roof**. Some have only lost their heads but others have been replaced with roughly shaped blocks. The **arch-braced** aisle roofs have large **bosses** and in the s. aisle canopied **wall posts** carried figures, two of which are still recognisable. There are two most attractive oval bronze tablets for Rear-Admiral Sir Lambson Loraine (1950) and Sir Percy Loraine (1961) at the w. end. The arcade pier nearest the s. door has a very interesting incised inscription: 'Remember ye pore the scripture doth record what to them is geven is lent unto the Lord 1591'. There would have been an alms box below; the present one is C19. At the e. end of the s. aisle there is a plain C14 **piscina** and

the tall recess in the e. wall may have been the entrance to the **rood loft** stair. The suite of choir stalls nearby was designed by W.D. Caröe for the chancel in 1904 and was obviously so uncomfortable that extra backboards in pine were added. The attractive late C16 **Holy table** is now used as a nave **altar** and, to the w. of it, Thomas Sicklemore's **ledger-stone** is dated 1619. The plain Elizabethan pulpit has two ranks of **linen-fold panelling**. Across on the wall of the n. aisle is a memorial for Eliza Mee, who died in 1912 aged 87. She had been blind since birth but led the choir when it sang in the old w. **gallery** and played the church's first organ for thirty-five years. Another memorial for a blind organist can be found at Assington.

Bramford's chancel **screen** is one of the rare examples in stone. Although the cresting and the pierced quatrefoils in the **spandrels** are C19, the rest has been unchanged since the late C13 or early C14. It has three equal arches and there are triple shafts with ring **capitals** against the outer **jambs**; more shafts face e. and w. on either side of the entrance but the centre arch is unmoulded. The chancel arch overhead was designed by **Ewan Christian** as part of the 1864 restoration, but the roof beyond is a C15 single hammerbeam and again there are defaced angels. The C13 chancel is the earliest part of the building and the window embrasure on the s. side has a moulded arch and jamb shafts. The **sedilia** are divided by octagonal detached shafts and their plain arches match the piscina alongside. Attractively carpeted, the chancel is now used as a chapel for small congregations, and the **reredos** is another of Caröe's designs, reminiscent of his magnum opus at Elveden [Vol.1]. In oak, gilded and enriched with red, there are chunky canopies below four standing angels on pinnacles; painted shields with **Passion emblems** are set on the side panels and there is a beautifully carved crucifix in the centre. The five-**light Perpendicular** e. window is filled with 1905 glass by **Kempe**. The Blessed Virgin and Christ are flanked by **Saints Edmund, Laurence, Giles**, and **Etheldreda**, with musical angels below.

Brandeston, All Saints (E4): The church stands by the entrance to Brandeston Hall (now a school) and the path to the n. door is bordered snugly by rounded hedges of clipped yew. The C14 tower has a simple **flushwork base course** and the w. door has shields and crowns in the mouldings. There are shields carved with a **Trinity** emblem and the three crowns of East Anglia (or Ely) in the **spandrels**, the **headstops** are crowned and the **label** is decorated with **paterae**. The tall, late **Perpendicular** w. window is flanked by niches with **crocketted ogee** arches, and another above it is made more elaborate by having a canopy, and a mask below the image stool (just like the arrangement at nearby Earl Soham). The bell openings have **Decorated tracery** and there is more

flushwork in the stepped battlements. The walls of the **nave** and **chancel** are startlingly white, and on the s. side there is one **scratch dial** on a nave buttress with two more on the s.e. buttress of the chancel, one of which has traces of numerals. The chancel dates from the end of the C12, with a group of three **lancets** within a single arch on the s. side, but it had become ruinous by the early C17. In the 1860s **R.M. Phipson** directed a heavy restoration in which new **roofs** were provided, the s. porch was demolished, and a new one was provided for the n. door.

The interior is neat with a rather cool feel. A **sanctus-bell window** is tucked under the ridge above the tower arch and to the l. of the organ is a decorative and unusually interesting peal board of 1749–50. Its scrolly outline has six pendent bells and it records a peal in seven methods, two of which were composed by the local band who thought it worthwhile to list the course ends and calls on each side. The C13 **Purbeck marble font** has a deep, canted bowl with the usual pairs of shallow arches in the panels, and the s. door still has its original drawbar in place. A reminder that it was once the main entrance is the **stoup** recess to the l. There are two **brass** inscriptions set in the floor e. of the font, for Jane and Elizabeth Stebbing (1616 and 1621). The Perpendicular nave windows all have places for images and there are over a dozen C15 bench ends. Some of the tracery has been skimmed off and they bear heavy **poppyheads** flanked by remnants of beasts and one or two figures – one seated with an open book (3rd from back n. side), and a man astride a beast (3rd from back against the s. wall). A **piscina** in the wall farther along shows that there was an **altar** nearby in the C14. The **rood stairs** go up from a window embrasure on the n. side and the rebuilt pulpit nearby made use of C17 blind arches and the strapwork panels above them. Behind it there is an oddly placed door shape and another section of it can be seen beyond the chancel arch. It lies partly within the wall and may have some connection with the low blank arch in the chancel n. wall. At a guess there was a chapel or **sacristy** on that side. The little enclosed stall in front has two painted shields and a monogram with the date 1868, but 'A.D. 1745' is painted inside. Another C18 piece that has been re-used is the panel in the reading desk on the s. side. It bears the painted shield of the Revett family and a quote from Psalm 26: 'Domine dilexi decorum domus tuee, locum habitationis gloriae tuee' (Lord, I have loved the beauty of thy house, the place where thy glory dwelleth). The **communion rails** also have a quotation; it is lettered in gilt on the top rail and this time is from Psalm 28: 'Exaudi meam Vocem supplicem quate, Sublatis ad tuum sacrum Penetrale Manibus, Imploro' (Hear the voice of my humble petitions, when I cry unto thee: when I hold up my hands towards the mercy-seat of thy holy temple); it ends, 'Impensis Jos. Revett Gen: A.D. 1711'. It may have been added when what were three-sided rails were altered to stretch across the chancel. They are high-quality work and the **balusters** are turned in two stages, with barley sugar twist at the top and conventional sections below. Two more C15 benches stand in the **sanctuary** and one has a man holding something astride a beast. On the wall above is the 1671 monument for John Revett. **Corinthian** columns flank a **touchstone** tablet lettered in a wilful mixture of italic and capitals which has a laurel-wreathed skull at the foot and a cherub's head at the top; a well-carved coloured **achievement** in the **pediment** is supported by **putti** holding reversed torches. No piscina survives for the **high altar** but there is an admirable panel in the s. sanctuary window of the head and shoulders of a bearded man which has the look of the 1890s. The window farther w. contains some very interesting early C16 glass. There is a **Blessed Virgin** enthroned at the top, and below are the figures of a monk robed in blue (l.) and a kneeling abbot

(r.). They were placed here by John de Bury who was vicar 1501-11 and the abbot may commemorate his former superior William de Coddenham, abbot of Bury. Some of the **quarries** deserve inspection too. **St Edmund's** crown and arrows occur below the monk, and below the abbot is the crown and rose with 'H.8' for Henry VIII. Just beneath is perhaps the most interesting of all, the pomegranate badge of his first wife Catherine of Aragon with the Latin text which translates: 'Whom God hath joined let no man put asunder.' Historic irony is nearly always accidental. The edges of the window are filled with examples of the beautifully delicate leaf and spray designs which have so often been destroyed. There is the chilling memory of a vicar of this quiet parish who was harried to his death for supposed witchcraft. John Lowes was priest here for close on fifty years and, it must be admitted, was often at loggerheads with his flock. Then in 1646 he was accused by Matthew Hopkins, witchfinder general, of being in league with the devil and was cruelly deprived of sleep for nights on end, while his tormentors 'ran him backwards and forwards about the room, until he was out of breath; then they rested him a little, and then ran him again'. He underwent the ordeal by swimming at Framlingham and was seen to be guilty by not sinking, and finally the poor man confessed and was hanged with seventeen others, having read his own burial service.

Brantham, St Michael and All Angels (E9): St Michael's has a particularly nice 1890s **lych-gate** in the **Arts and Crafts** style, designed by Edward Schroder Prior, a founder-member and sometime master of the Art Workers' Guild. Its retaining walls curve to the roadside outside the gates, and the shingle roof has gently rounded hoods n. and s. The eaves and braces are carved with a bine and leaf pattern which is echoed on the 'S'-shaped bars of the sides; an evocative period piece. The church was more or less rebuilt by **Edward Hakewill** in 1869 but the indications are that it dates from the C14. The tower has a small **Decorated** w. window, strong **string courses**, and buttresses to belfry level. Above that, the work is largely new, including the **flushwork** roundels in the parapet and the **gargoyles**. There is a **vestry** on the s. side covered by an extension of the **nave roof**, and an odd little porch-cum-mini-vestry is tucked into the angle between nave and **chancel**. There are glimpses of the Stour estuary from this side of the churchyard, and on walking round you will see that the chancel was wholly rebuilt. Hakewill added a n. **aisle** under a continuation of the nave roof, and the steep roof of his n. **porch** drops to within 5ft of the ground.

The glass in the tower window has a look of the 1920s but I have not been able to identify the glazier. It sets **St John the Baptist** and three other figures against an attractive landscape background and is very pleasing. The good early C15 **font** came from the redundant church of St Martin at Palace, Norwich, in 1977; its bowl has a **castellated** rim with **quatrefoil** roundels in the panels, and there is delicate Decorated **tracery** between the shafts of the stem. Overhead, a small and dark set of George III **Royal Arms** hangs above the tower arch. The single-braced nave roof, with its **tie-beams** and tall **king-posts**, dates from the rebuilding and so does the n. **arcade**, but there is Decorated tracery in the s. windows. Some C15 glass has survived there too – figures of an archbishop and a civilian, three initials, and some miscellaneous fragments. The C14 **angle piscina** nearby has no drain now but it would have served a nave **altar**, and the **trefoil**-headed niche by the n. aisle altar may have been removed from another piscina on that side of the nave. The oak pulpit is a striking piece of work in Arts and Crafts style. On it, a Tree of Life is carved to form a lattice across three panels with an overlaying scroll: 'From death unto life'. It was

given in 1900 by a parishioner whose wife had a penchant for pokerwork, and she added her initials and the date inside. Her husband also gave the ancient bishop's chair in the **sanctuary**, but her addition of 'Rest in the Lord' on the back was tactfully removed after her death. The chancel is offset to the n. but this may merely be one of the side-effects of the rebuilding. Its C19 arch rests on stub columns above **corbels** carved with the church's patron saint on the n. and **St Gabriel** on the s. Although rebuilt, the chancel retains another C14 angle piscina, and the e. window is filled with glass which looks like the work of **Lavers & Barraud** – Christ the King flanked by four angels below pretty patterns in the tracery. John Constable only painted three altar pieces, one each for Nayland and Manningtree, and one for Brantham on the theme of 'Suffer little children to come unto me'. Many have come especially to see it but it is, alas, no longer here. Security has dictated that it has to be housed in the Ipswich museum, a depressing reflection upon our largely godless generation.

Bredfield, St Andrew (F5): There are fine, mature lime trees along the frontage and this compact little church stands well in its churchyard. The shortness of **nave** and **chancel** is accentuated by their height, and the smoothly uniform finish is largely the result of a full-scale restoration by **R.M. Phipson** in 1875. He repaired the nave and renewed its tall **Perpendicular** windows, gave the chancel a new roof, and added a **vestry** on the s. side. There is a pretty little e. window, and the **priest's door** to the n. has been blocked like the s. door in the nave. The **base course** of the early C15 tower is decorated with crowned 'Ms' for the **Blessed Virgin** and unusual **flushwork** roundels, each enclosing a pair of **mouchettes** and a **quatrefoil**. The narrow w. doorway has roses in the **spandrels**, there is more flushwork on the buttresses, and the battlements in stepped brick have corner pillars which project to give the top of the tower a more than usual emphasis. The tall and shallow n. **porch** was restored by Phipson but its steep C15 **roof** is intact, a miniature **hammerbeam** with carved spandrels that is quite remarkable. The only other example that I remember seeing in a porch is at Great Bealings.

Within, one finds a full-scale version above the nave that is exceptional on a number of counts. The **wall plate** is pierced with **tracery** and so is the deep cornice above it, this time in two bands. There were once angels or shields on the ends of the hammers and at the base of the **wall posts**, and two bays at the e. end (rather than the usual one) provided a **celure** for the **rood**. Faint traces of the painted decoration remain on the hammers and in chevron form on the rafters, and the sides of the upper ribs have crowned 'Ms', the **sacred monogram**, and distinctive foliage patterns. The **font** is C19 and the benches are modern. There is a **stoup** by the s. door which means that it was the principal entrance when the nave was built. At the w. end, metal **Commandment boards** are framed on the wall, and the church has been presented with a fine array of hassocks embroidered with English and Australian flowers worked by ladies of the village and of Australia. A **brass** of 1611 has been preserved in the s. doorway and commemorates Leonard and Elizabeth Farrington; their 14in. figures show him wearing a cloak and his wife a fashionable hat, and there are groups of six sons and two daughters below. Two Arthur Jenneys have **hatchments** here, over the n. door for the one who died in 1729, and on the s. wall for Arthur of Rendlesham who died in 1742. The **Stuart** pulpit has three ranges of panels and pierced brackets below the book ledge; for a long time its **tester** hung on the wall in Bredfield House but it came back to the church eventually and now serves as a table top in the **sanctuary**. On the s. wall there is a bronze tablet for Joseph

and Emily White which is an interesting period piece of **Art Nouveau** design dating from the early 1900s – swirling, languorous female angels in a vague seascape. Moving into the chancel, the window on the n. side has attractive glass of 1860 by an unidentified firm; panels illustrating four of the **Seven Works of Mercy** are set in a bright blue latticed with dark red. On the s. wall a plain tablet by Stephenson of Woodbridge commemorates George Crabbe, rector here from 1835 to 1856. He was the poet's son and biographer, and a great friend of Edward Fitzgerald, who lived at nearby Boulge. Dale of Wickham Market provided the tablet for the Revd John Dufton on the n. wall and also for his brother William on the e. wall; the latter was a Birmingham surgeon who died in 1859 having founded the Institution for the Relief of Deafness in that city. From an earlier age is the severe **touchstone** tablet and flanking columns on the other side of the **altar**. It commemorates Robert Marryot who died in 1675 and his coloured **achievement** is displayed at the top with another shield at the base. Turning back, one can just make out the tiny **sanctus-bell window** in the wall of the tower just below the roof ridge, but it is so placed that only the altar can be seen from there – a convincing proof of its original purpose.

Brome, St Mary (B3): There is a clamorous rookery e. of the church and peacocks from the farm next door emerge as startling flashes of colour among the sombre shrubberies. The church was enthusiastically rebuilt between 1857 and 1863 to the designs of Thomas Jeckell, a wayward and idiosyncratic architect with practices in Norwich and London. A n. **transept** was added in 1865, the **aisle** was extended westward, doing away with the n. **porch**, and the upper stage of the **Norman** round tower was remodelled in 1875. Jeckell toyed with every style in the book but the s. porch (now a vestry) was altered very little.

Within, there is a heavy three-bay **arcade** in Norman style and matching n. transept. The **font** has been raised on steps within the tower to form a baptistery and its familiar East Anglian style has **Evangelistic symbols** in the bowl panels, together with angels bearing shields carved with **instruments of the Passion** and a **Trinity** emblem; there are demi-angels below the bowl and four snooty lions support the base. The wide **Early English**-style **chancel** arch has stiff-leaf **capitals** and opens up a vista to the **high altar** uninterrupted by a **screen**. The stone pulpit has figures of the apostles within open arches and is designed 'en suite' with a reading desk which now (surprisingly) shows signs of decay. The sculptor was James Williams of Ipswich and the **reredos** is his also. This unusual and interesting piece was shown at the 1881 London Exhibition and the panels are carved in deep relief – the visit of the Magi, Christ in Gethsemane, the Resurrection, and Our Lord with doubting **St Thomas**. In the central Crucifixion scene, the two thieves are tied writhing to their crosses, in sharp contrast to the calm figure nailed between them. Williams also supplied the **piscina, sedilia**, and heavy **communion rails** to match. Lady Caroline Kerrison painted much of the glass in the body of the church but the windows in the chancel contain very good work of the 1860s by **Heaton, Butler & Bayne**. The vivid panels of the e. window portray **St George** and **St Michael**, while the damned in hell cringe below the urgent hand of the avenging angel on the r., in contrast to the company of the blessed being gathered on the other side. The s. **sanctuary** window has figures of the **Blessed Virgin**, Christ, and **St John the Baptist**, while the s. chancel window contains panels illustrating Christ's baptism, His presentation in the Temple, the visit of the Magi, the miracle at Cana, and the Last Supper. There are brilliant blues and reds and the patterns are lively. Brome Hall was the ancestral home of the Cornwallis family. Charles, 1st Marquis, was patron of the living but is better remembered for his enforced surrender at Yorktown in the American War of Independence and his governor generalship of India. There is an interesting selection of family memorials in the n.e. chapel, and the tomb under the arch just n. of the sanctuary is that of Sir John Cornwallis and his wife (although he was actually buried at Berkhamstead). The stone is painted buff, picked out with gilt and colour; there are eight painted shields on the chest and a large relief **achievement of arms** against the wall at the foot of the effigies, where two nicely individual hounds lie. The wife wears a **kennel head-dress** and has a large golden locket on a long chain. Sir John is in full armour and holds the white staff which was the symbol of his office as steward in the household of the young prince who was to become Edward VI. He was knighted for bravery at Morlaix in Brittany and died in 1544. In the n.e. corner the tomb of his eldest son, Thomas, is closely modelled on his own. He too is in full armour, while his wife wears a Paris cap and scarlet gown; a large stag lies at their feet. Sir Thomas was one of the knights who put down Kett's rebellion in 1549 and he was sheriff of Norfolk and Suffolk in 1553. He was a fervent Catholic supporter of Queen Mary and comptroller of her household until her death in 1558. As treasurer of Calais he was widely accused of its loss to the French and his epitaph sums up:

> in special grace and trust of his Mistress who untimely losing her life retired him self home to this towne wher he spent the rest of his own privately and loyally all the rayne of Queen Elizabeth her sister and died heer the second yeer of King James the 26 of December 1604 in the 86 yeer of his age.

On the wall above, a large marble **cartouche** carries the worn gilt epitaph of Elizabeth, Lady Cornwallis, who died in 1680. Over it, two **putti** draw aside drapes from an oval frame containing a bas relief bust which, with its décolleté shift and pert mouth, has a hint of the voluptuous. In the s.e. corner of the chapel is a large and distinguished mural tablet for Frederick, 1st Lord Cornwallis, who died in 1661, just after Charles II's restoration. Part of the epitaph translates:

> for his unshaken loyalty to the King and having suffered proscription and exile by his enemies has entered into the celestial fatherland and in the bosom of a church restored has fallen peacefully asleep.

The last memorial to note is on the n. wall by the organ where a small painted and gilt figure kneels within a coffered arch, with six shields displayed around. It commemorates Henry Cornwallis, Sir Thomas's brother, who lived in Norfolk and was buried here in 1598.

Brundish, St Laurence (E2): The church stands in a spacious churchyard by a quiet lane at the e. end of this straggling village. The unbuttressed **Norman** tower was heightened during a C14 rebuilding but the bell opening on the e. side was retained and there are outlines of **lancets** to w., s., and n. farther down. The w. doorway and the rest of the bell openings are later. There are tall **Perpendicular** windows in the **nave**, their **hood moulds** linked by a **string course**, and the date of the **chancel** restoration is cast on one of the drainpipe hoppers. When you walk round, you will find a low granite stone almost hidden by the yew to the n.w. of the tower. It marks the grave of Reginald Livesey, who died in 1932, having earlier in his life explored the interior of Queensland and studied birds in the Pacific. The s. **porch** was added after the nave had been rebuilt and could only be fitted on by overlapping half of one of the windows. Its facade is decorated with **flushwork** and there is a niche over the outer arch which has

large roses in the **spandrels** and little **fleurons** on the **label**. The entrance door is medieval and the shaft of a **stoup** remains to the r.

Once inside you will see that when the window was partly blocked by the porch, the C15 builders did not bother to remove the glazing bars but merely filled the spaces between them with plaster. The outline of the old Norman w. arch shows up plainly in the tower wall, and above it is a very attractive set of George III **Royal Arms** dated 1765 in a cut-out frame complete with dummy candlesticks. The church is well blessed with **biers** – there are three in the base of the tower, one of which is child-sized like the one at Mendlesham. The plain C14 **font** rests on a low drum shaft and by it stands a single stall complete with **misericord** that must have come from a chancel set somewhere. The two panels by the n. door are all that remain of the C15 **rood screen**. The nave has a homely brick floor, C18 plastered ceiling, and a low range of C15 benches with **poppyheads** and later backs. A suite of C18 plain **box pews** was installed at the e. end and most of them merely encase the old benches (as at Gislingham). The low arch in the n. wall probably marks the grave of the founder but it now shelters an interesting 28in. **brass**, that of Sire Edmound de Burnedissh. It is the earliest of the four brasses in the county illustrating priests in vestments and dates from about 1360. In the nave floor another brass commemorates John Colby who died in 1540. The engraving of his armour is heavily cross-hatched and shaded but the figure of his wife Alice and the inscription have gone; there are groups of four sons and nine daughters and three shields. The very coarse pulpit has C15 **tracery** in the body panels but the back panel and **tester** are **Jacobean**. The statue niche in the window embrasure to the l. shows traces of original colouring and there are the remains of its twin on the s. side. The chancel arch is wide, with small **headstops**, and marks show where the old rood screen was fixed. The **angle piscina** in the **sanctuary** is most attractive, with a **cusped** and **crocketted ogee** arch flanked by pinnacles. There are **dropped-sill sedilia** to the r. and to the l. two small and oddly proportioned recesses. In the n.e. corner is the brass for Sir John Colby who died in 1559. There are three shields and a verse inscription but when I visited the effigy was missing. The brass in the s.e. corner shows Thomas Glemham as a kneeling youth of about 1570 and has a verse inscription and five shields. There are sections of C15 glass in the tracery of the e. window, including a very good head and shoulders of a bearded king and a devil/monster.

Bures, St Mary (B11): A handsome, chunky church in a spacious setting. The lower section of the tower is late C13 with tall, thin **lancets** to the w. and s., and there is an exterior tomb recess on the n. side below a **finialed** gable. Most of the tower was built by Sir Richard Waldegrave in the late C14 or early C15 and there are two chambers with small lancets below the bell openings with their **Decorated tracery**; a stair lies within the n.w. buttress and rises almost to the top. The late C15 or early C16 s. **porch** is very stately in red brick and the wide outer arch incorporates two earlier stone head **corbels**. There is an niche overhead above sloping steps in the brickwork reminiscent of Little Waldingfield's n. porch. The **dripstone** of the C14 inner doorway has large **headstops** and the one on the r. is a knight wearing the chainmail 'camail' to protect his head and shoulders. The **stoup** below is most unusual in that the ledge of the bowl is supported by two figures, one of which is a bishop raising his hand in blessing. The C15 doors have the remains of tracery and a border trail of vines and birds. At the e. end of the s. **aisle** is the bulky **chantry chapel** built in brick by Sir William Waldegrave in 1514, with generous windows and some **flushwork** on the e. face. The centre

buttress cunningly incorporates a **priest's door** with **fleurons** in the moulding and the table tomb nearby has a barely legible inscription on the top in which the name 'Constable' can still be recognised – apparently the last resting place of the famous landscape painter's grandfather. The window of the **vestry** on the n. side of the **chancel** has an angel with a curly trumpet as one of the headstops while his partner bears a **Trinity** emblem shield. The C14 n. porch is lovely, its timbers grooved and worn like driftwood. The **cusped** barge boards are pierced with **mouchette** roundels matching those below, and the moulded entrance arch is cut from two massive planks. Sympathetically restored in 1873, there are varying Decorated forms in the tracery of the side panels.

It seems that the wide **nave** and aisles were built in one continuous operation and the C14 **arcades**, with their octagonal **piers**, are low and wide. The original nave **roof** was replaced when the **Perpendicular clerestory** was added and altered again in the C19. The brutal flat ceiling probably dates from an 1860s restoration by **Ewan Christian** and now houses modern recessed lighting, but below it on the walls are large corbels which once supported **wall posts**. There are bland angels with shields and the three interesting heads and a grotesque in the corners no doubt survive from the original roof. A vaulted ceiling was planned for the ground floor of the tower and again there are two excellent grotesques at the base of the rib stubs – one snarling and the other sticking its tongue out. The **font** stands at the w. end of the s. aisle and its traceried stem has battered **Evangelistic symbols** at the corners. The bowl is likely to be a replacement of the 1540s and has very deeply cut angels bearing shields in the panels. These are now coloured, and clockwise from the e. they are: England, De Vere, Fitzralph, Mortimer, Cornard, Waldegrave, De Bures, and Mortimer of Clare. On a tomb chest in a n. aisle window

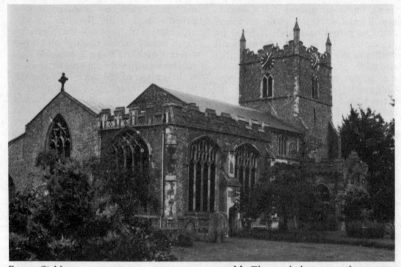

Bures, St Mary

embrasure is the superb effigy carved in sweet chestnut of a knight dating from around 1330 (the only other wooden example from this period in Suffolk is at Heveningham). It probably commemorates Sir Richard de Cornard, and his head rests on a pillow borne up by a pair of angels, while his crossed, spurred feet rest on a lion which has a cloth draped and tied around its neck. I wonder why. The shields of effigies like this were usually pegged on and most have vanished but this one is complete. Both pulpit and low chancel screen are C19 but on the e. of the chancel arch (s. side just below the **capital**) is a most interesting survival. **Rood lofts** occasionally carried an **altar** and there must have been one here because the **piscina** that was used for washing the chalice is built into the **respond** of the arch and its fluted underside can be seen from below.

The late C14 n.e. vestry was altered, probably in the C16, and the doorway from the chancel has fleurons and masks in the moulding, with smiling faces on the headstops of the **hood** **mould**. The arch between the vestry and the **sanctuary** is blocked by a massive table tomb and indents show that the top once carried a large **brass**. Its placing and the nature of the brass make it virtually certain that this is the tomb of Sir Richard Waldegrave, builder of much of the church, who died in 1410, and his wife Joan. It is strange that the style of the chest is C16 rather than C15 but it is possible that it was rebuilt when the vestry was altered. Above it, angels with shields jut out and under them there is a figure with a floriated cross on one side, and a chained dog on the other. Originally, the tomb had an elaborate wooden canopy and, like many in this position, it was used as an **Easter sepulchre**. The mid–C19 glass in the e. window is of poor quality and very eroded while the contemporary **reredos** is flanked by equally vapid panels of the **Annunciation**. The Waldegrave chantry on the s. side of the chancel was also known as the Jesus chapel and although its founder's tomb has disappeared, the one below the s.e. window is likely to be that of his son Sir George Waldegrave who died in 1528. The chest has lozenges with shields deeply

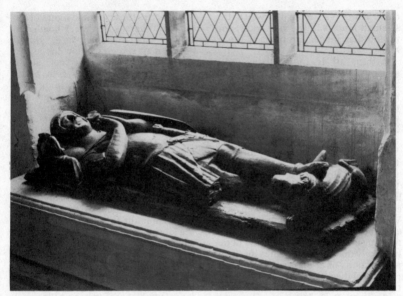

Bures, St Mary: C14 wooden effigy

set within them and **spandrels** carved with leaves. What was the back now lies canted at an angle on the top and shows the marks of missing brasses. **Dowsing** perhaps removed them in 1643 when he 'brake down above 600 superstitious pictures'. The chapel e. window now contains a large modern Christ in Majesty within a glory, trumpeting angels each side, and three panels of script at the bottom commemorating the chantry's founder – all set in plain glass and attractive. Another William Waldegrave, who died in 1613, and his wife Elizabeth have a large free-standing tomb in the chapel. The chest is plain except for grooved **pilasters** and the upper section has pairs of **Corinthian** columns flanking coloured **achievements**, with **pediments** and balls at the corners above. Strangely, the inscription tablet is on the back and the only effigies are those of the twelve children – little kneeling figures in alabaster.

Bures, St Stephen's chapel (B11): The road to Assington climbs Cuckoo Hill out of Bures and at the top a track leads through a farmyard and open fields to a lovely hill-top site where stands the chapel. There is a firm tradition that **St Edmund** was crowned king here on Christmas Day 855, and it is certain that Stephen Langton, archbishop of Canterbury, consecrated a private chapel here on the Feast of Stephen in 1218. This is the building we see and, although it is not a parish church, at least one service is held a year so it comes within the scope of this guide. At some time it fell into disuse and over the years it was divided into cottages and then used as a barn, with a brick and timber extension added to the w. end. Its walls were breached so that wagons could be driven in and it was not until the 1930s that restoration was put in hand leading to a re-dedication in 1940. The whole building lies under thatch, with a two-storeyed porch on the n. side and the brick and weatherboard section to the w., but the plain oblong of the original chapel is clear. There is a simple doorway to the s., small **lancets** in the side walls, and three taller lancets grouped at the e. end.

Within, all is immaculate under single-framed **roofs** and the w. wall has been rebuilt. Some of the 'mock masonry' wall painting and the original **consecration crosses** have been uncovered, and the panelled shaft of a C15 **font** stands at the w. end. In a niche beyond is the fine wooden figure of a bishop which is Continental work, but the real surprise is to find three magnificent tombs. At the **Reformation**, Earls Colne priory in Essex fell into disuse and was later sold by the earl of Oxford. It contained many De Vere monuments and when the estate changed hands in the 1930s the remaining effigies were transferred here. It is likely that the three tombs incorporate sections of at least seven, but the identity of the effigies seems certain. In the n.w. corner lies the figure of Robert De Vere, 5th Earl of Oxford and master chamberlain of England, who died in 1296. His sword is slung from a broad belt, his crossed feet rest on a ridge-backed hog, and the angels that support his pillow are very like those on the wooden effigy at Bures. The chest he lies on is later and has deep niches with **cusped** and **crocketted ogee** arches and shields hung in the **spandrels**; within, they are delicately **groined** and panelled and, between them, smaller shallow niches contain little figures in typically early C14 poses which are beautiful despite their mutilation. The other two tombs carved in alabaster stand in the centre of the chapel and the westernmost is that of Richard De Vere, 11th Earl of Oxford, who died in 1412, and Countess Alice. His head rests on a hog-crested helm, there is a lion at his feet, and his wife's horned head-dress lies on a pillow supported by angels; at her feet two engaging little dogs with bell collars tug at her skirts in play. The side panels of the chest have standing angels holding shields, with the arms of England at the e. end and **St George's** cross to the w. The last

tomb carries the armoured figure of the 8th Earl, Thomas De Vere, who died in 1371 – mail-sheathed face, gloved hands, mail showing below his jupon, and a lion beneath his feet, all in remarkable condition. The sides of the chest are carved with nodding ogee arches over niches in which pairs of diminutive cloaked figures stand. The last monument to look for is in fact the oldest – a fragmentary C12 coffin lid in the s.w. corner carved with the stumpy feet and legs of an effigy. It probably lay on the tomb of Alberic De Vere, first great chamberlain and father of the 1st Earl, who died in 1141. There is a brass on the n. wall commemorating Isabel Badcock whose dedication was largely responsible for the restoration, and in the lancet alongside is a small figure of a bishop with an arrow emblem in C17 Flemish glass. Across the nave another Flemish panel portrays **St Mary Magdalene**. The **sanctuary** n. lancet displays the Scourging of Christ and on the s. side there is a Flemish or German roundel of Christ being taken from the Cross, with a kneeling C15 figure below. Most if not all of this glass came from the priory house at Earls Colne. In the e. lancets there are small figures of **St Edmund, St Stephen, St Laurence, Edward the Confessor**, and two bishops, framed by dense patterning in which a beautiful deep blue predominates (maker unknown). The **altar** and stone balustrade **communion rails** are modern but there is a heavy **piscina** with a square drain under a **trefoil** arch, and an **aumbry** with a modern door in the n. wall.

Burgate, St Mary (B3): The C14 tower has an unusual window arrangement, with **quatrefoil** belfry windows and **Decorated** bell openings which have three quatrefoil openings above them on all sides. The tall s. **porch** has blocked side windows, with a plain niche over the inner door and a shallow recess to the r. which housed the **stoup**. **R.M. Phipson** carried out a heavy-handed restoration of the **nave**

in the 1860s, giving it a new **roof**, and there is now no **chancel** arch; the division is marked only by an embellished **arch-brace** in the roof with **wall posts** resting on slightly fungoid **corbels**. Phipson continued with the chancel in 1872, raising the walls to take a new roof, inserting a new e. window and replacing **tracery** in the side windows. His bench designs for the nave are attractive, with chunky and varied **poppyheads**. C18 Creed and Lord's Prayer boards flank the tower arch and a little chapel dedicated to **St Edmund** was formed earlier this century by screening the area at the side of the organ. The **font** is a common East Anglian design but the **Evangelistic symbols** have been hacked from the bowl panels, leaving only a shield held by an angel to the w. Fat lions squat round the stem and the top step carries an inscription which says that it was given by Sir William Burgate and his wife (whose tomb you will see in the chancel), which dates it around 1400. There is a modern screen across the wide nave just e. of the entrance and a set of **Royal Arms** hangs on the n. wall. They are **Stuart** but were refurbished for George II in 1735. Farther along, the **rood stairs** remain in the wall and the **piscina** of a vanished nave **altar** dedicated to the Trinity survives on the s. side. A headless figure labelled **St Augustine** can be found among the fragments of medieval glass in the top of a nave n. window. The square Stuart pulpit has shallow relief panels below the ledge and, beneath them, pairs of blind arches are duplicated on each side. Traces of paint inside suggest that it was made out of sections from an old **screen**. The arched recess in the chancel n. wall is in the right place for an **Easter sepulchre** but if it was it is unusually large and it is more likely to have been the entrance to a chapel. It now frames a wooden altar which has standing candlesticks and other ornaments made from shell cases and shells themselves by convalescent soldiers in Belgium in 1917. A central glass case contains the communion set used by a

chaplain in France during World War I. The turned **balusters** of the choir stall fronts look as though they were part of a C17 set of **communion rails**, and on the s. side by the **priest's door** stands a large early C15 chest whose front and sides are tinged with colour. One can just distinguish the figure of a knight on horseback and so it was probably a jousting scene or a portrait of **St George**. The only C19 stained glass is in a s. chancel window and is likely to be the work of **Lavers, Barraud & Westlake**. The main panels portray three of Christ's miracles of restoring life, with a **Trinity** emblem at the top and three angels with scrolls below. The large **piscina** in the **sanctuary** has had all its cresting and **cusping** chopped away, but the shields in the **spandrels** link it with Sir William Burgate, Lord of the Manor. That brings us to his tomb, the church's most interesting feature, standing proudly in the centre of the chancel. The tomb chest has close-set niches all round, with **crocketted ogee** arches and blank stone shields hung in alternate spaces, plus two Sacred Hearts at the e. end. The bevel of the **Purbeck marble** slab carries an exceptionally good inscription with a leaf design between each word. It translates: 'William de Burgate Knight of Burgate who died on the vigil of St James the Apostle 1409 and Alianora his wife daughter of Sir Thomas Vyzdelou who died ...'. Thus one assumes that the wife installed the tomb but that her date of death was never added. The **brass** on top is possibly the best in the county for the period. The two figures lie within a double canopy which is all but intact, although four shields and Sir William's helm have gone. His armour is a fine example of the age and he wears a heavily ornamented sword belt. There is a sprightly lion beneath his feet and Lady Alianora's dog has a collar of bells. Her figure and that of Lady Margaret Drury at Rougham [Vol.1] are so similar that the two brasses are likely to have come from the same workshop.

Burgh, St Botolph (F5): This most attractive little church stands on a tump above the Otley/Grundisburgh road, and like Clopton (which is just a couple of fields away) it has a tower which also serves as a s. **porch**. There was a time when it had a joint dedication of **St Botolph** and **St Andrew**, but originally it was for St Botoph alone, and it has been suggested that the rather shadowy saint was actually buried here before being transferred to Bury St Edmunds. There is a neat parish room of 1835 by the gate and the path rises steeply to the church. The C14 unbuttressed tower has recently been restored, there are **quatrefoil** windows and a single **string course** below the **Decorated** bell openings, and deep, **flushwork** battlements. There are **Perpendicular** windows in the **nave**, the n. door is blocked, and the raised mortar round all the flints in the walls gives the building a distinctive texture which must date from a C19 or early C20 restoration. There is one Decorated window on the s. side of the **chancel**, and the **dripstone** of the C14 **priest's door** has C19 **stops** carved with wheat and vines. A large iron bootscraper was provided for those who used to walk through the mud to church and they would then have to squeeze round the ringers, for the six bells are rung from the ground floor. Nowadays the sallies are cheerfully wasp-coloured rather than the conventional red, white, and blue. The inner door carries a closing ring set on a massive boss 10in. in diameter. It dates from the C13 and on the ring one can just discern the outlines of twin lizards, those ancient emblems of good fortune.

The interior is dark but distinctly nice. By the door is the C15 **font** and it has an interesting range of carvings in the bowl panels, despite the fact that the heads were drastically re-cut in the C19. There are the **Evangelistic symbols**, an angel holding a crown (n.), a totally feathered angel (e.), and an **Annunciation** (w. and s.) in which the

Blessed Virgin has been given rather masculine features. Burgh has a range of late **Kempe** glass and the 1906 w. window is not his best – figures of **St George, St Paul**, and **St Stephen**. The n. doorway frames a lovely painting by Anna Zinkeisen which illustrates all the birds of the Bible and is a memorial to her husband, who died in 1967. Bands of swallows swirl down from the dove of the Holy Spirit to meet swans flying upwards, and the others perch and strut within a dream landscape; there is even a realistic **pelican** and her brood in the bottom corner. The C19 **arch-braced roofs** are enlivened by demi-angels, and there is some interesting early C19 glass in the nave windows – Crucifixion and Resurrection scenes of 1817 possibly by Cox & Son on the n. side and, in the s. window, two roundels set in bright geometric patterns. The pulpit is **Jacobean** in style, with coarse carving, but there is an inscription at the base, 'John Vance 1708', so it was presumably about 100 years behind the fashion. A simple **piscina** on the s. side shows that there was once an **altar** nearby, and although there is now no **screen**, you will see that the **imposts** of the C14 chancel arch were cut back to take one in the C15. Like the nave benches, the choir stalls are C19, and the Kempe glass of 1879 in the s.w. window is much better – a Nativity with the Holy Family bathed in light on one side and the shepherds in sombre colours against a darkling landscape on the other. A tablet by Robert Brown on the n. wall commemorates three sons of the rectory, one of whom was only 23 when he died in 1827 as adjutant of a regiment of Bombay Native Infantry. Brown also provided a tablet for the parents in 1850 on which drapes partially mask the **pediment**. A large arch n. of the **sanctuary** opens into the **vestry**, and on the s. side there is a particularly good C14 chest which has recently been restored. It is completely sheathed in iron and has three hasps, a securing bar, and a lock. Above it is more Kempe glass, this time of 1902, an

Burgh, St Botolph: C13 closing ring

Annunciation in typical style. It was installed 'for mercies vouchsafed in an hour of great personal danger' – an instance where pious reticence merely triggers off an unholy desire to know what happened in the fullest possible detail. Kempe's e. window is a year later and has an elongated Crucifixion in the centre **light** which is faintly bizarre – spurts of blood from oversize nails, and a fringed carpet hung behind against a background of blue oak leaves and sprays; St Andrew to the l. and St Botolph cradling a church to the r. There is a piscina under a **cinquefoil** arch, and the oak altar and **reredos** of 1876 were carved by Gambier Parry. This is an interesting design because the pierced tracery of the front is backed by fabric embroidered with grapes and ears of corn, and the three reredos panels have grapes, sheaves, and the dove of the Holy Spirit in raised embroidery on cream-patterned damask. A very attractive period piece.

Burstall, St Mary (D8): The C14 unbuttressed tower has one **set-off** below the **lancet** bell openings and the **quatrefoil** belfry windows have **dripstones**; there is a blocked lancet below the w. window. The tall and wide n. **aisle** dates from the early C14 and its windows contain a variety of beautiful **Decorated tracery**. There are small **mouchettes** and quatrefoils, and a most unusual arrangement of **trefoils** within a curved triangle in the n.e. window. Round the corner you will find that the aisle e. window displays a variation of the four-petalled flower above the three **lights**. A **string course** links the dripstones on the n. facade and another runs below. A brick **rood stair** turret rises in the corner between aisle and **chancel** and the lancet alongside was probably used as a **low side window**. The chancel e. window has

Burstall, St Mary: C14 parclose screen

intersected 'Y' tracery of about 1300
and on the s. side there is a **priest's door**
which has been brutally used to admit
a large and ugly stove flue. The walls
on this side are plastered and the C15
wooden **porch** stands on a brick base.
The form of the outer arch suggests
that it was originally constructed in the
C14 but the **cusped** and carved barge
boards are C15, and the centre upright
had a niche which is still just
recognisable by its **crocketted finial**.
The open sides have cusped arches
with carved **spandrels**. The inner
doorway is deeply moulded, with king
and queen **headstops**, and the **jambs**
are a mass of graffiti. There is a C15
name cut on the e. side (it recurs in a
chancel n. window embrasure) and the
date 1599 can be found opposite.

On entering, one is immediately
struck by the beauty of the early C14 n.
arcade. The fine mouldings sweep up
into the steep arches and the **hood
moulds** meet in fine, large headstops.
There are **capitals** within the arches
only, and they are adorned with two
ranks of **paterae**. Some of these are
intricately pierced and undercut and a
number incorporate tiny masks. As
with the outside, the hood moulds of
the aisle windows are linked by a string
course; notice how this even lifts over
the finials of the niches that flank the e.
window. All the interior arches are
moulded, and although the builder of
the aisle has not been identified, he
must have been a wealthy man who
was content with nothing but the best.
The **parclose screen** is of the same
period and the chapel it encloses on
two sides may have been a **chantry**
originally. The screen has a base of
plain, lapped boards, with the entrance
offset to the l. It has turned shafts
rather than **mullions** and a fine variety
of small Decorated motifs is carved on
both sides of the tracery. The blocked
door to the rood stair is in the corner,
and the floor level of the chapel is two
steps above the aisle (this change of

level may date from the period when it
was used as a family pew). The **ledger-
stone** of William Cage is covered but a
transcript of the inscription is provided, by which you can tell that he
married his father's wife's daughter.
Think about it! The aisle contains some
C16 rugged benches with rough fleur
de lys **poppyheads** and they were
copied on those of the C19 that complete the suite. There is now a fine new
organ set against the tower arch and
above it you will see the outline of a
quatrefoil **sanctus-bell window**. The
church was extensively restored by
Frederick Barnes in the 1870s, and
Thomas Stopher of Ipswich carved
demi-angels bearing emblems and instruments for the **hammerbeams** in the
nave roof. It has a pierced **wall plate**
and is very dark, and was probably
stained at the same time. The **font** is
not the usual East Anglian type.
Instead, there are buttresses at the
angles of the plain bowl which rests on
a drum shaft and four octagonal pillars.
The World War I memorial window in
the nave is by **Heaton, Butler & Bayne**,
and rather than the usual **St George**,
the two panels illustrate texts from the
Old Testament: Joshua 5: 13 – 15
(Joshua and the captain of the Lord's
host), and 1 Samuel 26: 9 ('who can
stretch forth his hand against the
Lord's anointed, and be guiltless?).
The base of the C15 **rood screen** is
still in place, its narrow panels placed
between heavy mullions. **Cautley**
apparently recommended putting the
desk lectern on the top of the n. side
(convenient but untypically naughty),
and he may well have designed the
very handsome pulpit, with its pierced
Perpendicular tracery, which was
placed at the s. end of the screen in
1945. There is a single framed, **scissors-
braced** C14 roof in the chancel, effectively outlined against a blue
background. The C14 **piscina** has a
trefoil arch and there are ogee shapes
cut in the embrasure of the **dropped-
sill sedilia** alongside. Below, a glacial
boulder or sarsen heaves up like a
foreign body through the **encaustic**

tiles, and was probably a pagan cult object before it was pressed into service for the new religion. It is one of a number in this area which were used in the same way. The **communion rails** and **reredos** are modern and the 1913 e. window has attractive glass which is probably by Heaton, Butler & Bayne: the **Blessed Virgin** and Child in the centre, with an **Annunciation** on the l. and St Mary with **St John** by the cross on the r.

Capel St Mary, St Mary (E9): The church stands prominently above the village street and has a robust C15 tower with a broad, three-**light Perpendicular** w. window. There are two strong **drip courses** and the surface texture is an interesting mixture which includes bands of narrow red bricks and tiles. In the **base course**, flint has replaced most of what were **ashlar** panels decorated with very finely cut blind **arcades**; it has a very worn angel with a shield in the centre on the s. side and there is a writhing figure on the s.w. buttress. There is now a plain cement parapet and until 1818 the tower carried a spire. On walking round, you will see large Perpendicular windows on the n. side of the **nave** with **embattled transoms**, and they illustrate how the **ogee** shape came back into fashion. Opposite the n. door stands the gravestone of William Manning, 'Police Constable in this county' who died in the 1870s. The stone was 'erected as a token of respect by the members of the Suffolk Constabulary' and must be one of the earliest memorials to a local bobby in the county. At the e. end of the nave there is the shape of a round-headed door in the wall and, together with some **herringbone work** nearby, it suggests that the building is **Norman** in origin. The **chancel**, however, was built or rebuilt in the early C14 and its n. windows have two worn grotesques and two good female **headstops**. The e. end had to be given brick buttresses at some stage and the insertion of the tall,

four-light Perpendicular window may have weakened the wall. The **Decorated** windows on the s. side of the chancel each have a curved triangle above two lights and the most unusual **tracery** has **cusps** that are forked. The most easterly headstop is a very good example of the pagan **green man** symbol which masons persisted in using all through the Middle Ages, and there is a lively grinning head at the other end of the sequence. One of the female headstops of the **priest's door** is partly covered by a later buttress but the **dripstone** is nicely carved with a trail of flowers. All the s. **aisle** windows are Perpendicular except the one w. of the C15 **porch**. A modern **Blessed Virgin** and Child occupies the niche above the entrance, and there are **quatrefoil** roundels in the arch **spandrels** with widely spaced **paterae** in the mouldings. Pale oak **arch-braces** and **wall plates** remain of the original **roof** and the inner doorway has pilgrim crosses scratched in the **jambs**. The door itself, with its lapped boards and long strap hinges, can be no later than C14.

The interior is bright and beautifully kept, and despite its sturdiness the four-bay arcade between· nave and aisle leans outward. The nave roof is a compact design with diminutive **hammerbeams** and there are collar beams and **king-posts** under the ridge. At the w. end, the organ masks the tower arch and a C19 **font** stands in the s.w. corner. The tablet on the aisle wall is for William Press who died in 1809 and has drapes bunched at the top corners and over a centred **achievement**. Its interest lies in the signature at the bottom: 'Coade & Sealy', the firm founded by that remarkable business woman Mrs Eleanor Coade. She popularised the use of artificial stone (Coade stone) as a cheap and effective alternative to marble, and only employed the best designers. Having said that, one has to admit that the results are always mud-coloured. Although the epitaph concludes: 'His remains are deposited in this churchyard', the

Capel registers apparently contain no record of the burial – which is a mite odd. The s. aisle is designated as the chapel of **St Edmund** and the 1920s e. window glass by Frederick Eden has the Virgin and Child flanked by figures of that saint and **St Felix**; in the tracery you will see the shields of Capel, the province of Canterbury, and the dioceses of Ely, Norwich, and St Edmundsbury & Ipswich. A centre panel of the window to the s. contains a figure of the risen Christ by the Canterbury firm of Maile & Son, placed there in the 1970s. The design is naturalistic, with attractive use of colour and very clever leading. Although much restored, the aisle roof is medieval and there are original shields to be seen: the Debenham family arms above the window e. of the door, the Loudham arms opposite, Bishop Nykke's (of Norwich) above the s. door, and Ely's opposite. A fine, large statue of the Blessed Virgin in natural wood stands by the entrance to the chancel, and on the n. side the C18 pulpit is in oak on a wine-glass stem, with a **sacred monogram** within a sunburst on one of the panels; the **tester** has been injudiciously restored. A C19 arch-braced beam spans the chancel arch, and the figures of the **rood** group on it were carved by the renowned Lang family of Oberammergau in Bavaria. Beyond it, the chancel roof was renewed in the C19 but is, for East Anglia, a rare example of the 'cradle' type. Deep coving rises each side to a longitudinal beam above which the roof is arched in a gentle curve to the ridge, with closely spaced moulded ribs overall. Some time between 1880 and 1920 large but dumpy angels playing harps, pipes, and cymbals, their feet enveloped in medieval-style clouds, were placed on the e.- w. beams. They do not suit the roof and are quite out of scale. The painted C19 **high altar reredos** came from a Belgian church and has sharply gabled arches with gold diapered backgrounds and a centre canopy over the crucifix. In 1918 the upper half of the e. window

was filled with stained glass and displays the figures of the Archangels **Uriel, Michael, Gabriel,** and **Raphael** in steely colour, with dark red behind the heads and blue below the feet.

Charsfield, St Peter (F5): The handsome C16 brick tower, patterned overall with diamonds of darker hue, is more than usually interesting because its builder made use of parts of its C15 predecessor. The panelled **base course** was retained and on the s. side there is a **St Edmund** emblem and 'MR' for the **Blessed Virgin**. To the r. of the w. door, part of an inscription survives and to the l. there is a panel carved with the chalice and wafer symbol of the Eucharist which has the Virgin's initial at each corner. The doorway and w. window were also saved and so were the stepped **flushwork** battlements with **gargoyles** below them. On the n. side of the **nave** the plain doorway has brick **jambs** and nearby, a small **Norman lancet** shows that the building has been here since the early C12. Judging by the form of its windows, the **chancel** was added or rebuilt in the C13. At some time the s. wall of the nave was heavily repaired in brick and part of another Norman lancet is still embedded there. The brick **porch** is the same age as the tower and it too has an older base course with symbols in **ashlar** and flushwork. The polygonal corner buttresses rise to little domes that have clumsy brick **crockets**, and there is a niche below the crow-stepped gable. There was leaf carving at one time in the arch **spandrels**, and the **paterae** in the mouldings include the badge of the Wingfields, showing that they contributed to the building. The outer door is medieval and just inside stands a very interesting bell. It is badly damaged now but the inscription recalls a fierce C18 controversy: 'Sic Sacheverellus ore melos immortali olli ecclesiae defensori hanc dicat Gulielmus Leman de Chersfield Eques 1710' (Since Sacheverell's eloquence is so musical, so this [bell] is dedicated to him, the immortal defender of the church, by Sir William Leman of Charsfield 1710). Henry Sacheverell was a High Church divine and pamphleteer who was a rabid opponent of the Whig government and of all dissenters. On 5 November 1709 he preached a sermon in St Paul's before the lord mayor in which he warned in violent language of the perils of Whig toleration for nonconformists, and openly attacked Burnet, the bishop of Salisbury. The sermon was declared a seditious libel by the House of Commons and he was impeached. But 40,000 copies were sold and all London was on his side. At his trial in March 1710 he was found guilty but was only suspended from preaching for three years and became a popular hero. The case brought down the government and when the Tories came in, Queen Anne rewarded Sacheverell with the Crown living of St Andrew's, Holborn. A contemporary sourly labelled him 'a man of much noise but little sincerity', so a bell is perhaps appropriate, but he obviously found favour here with the family who had provided London with at least one lord mayor.

Inside the tower, the little organ with decorative pipework is neatly placed on the old ringers' **gallery**, and the beam below dated 1585 came from the old rectory. The C15 **font** is the familiar East Anglian pattern, with fragments of lions and **woodwoses** around the shaft and **Evangelistic symbols** in four of the bowl panels. Three of the remainder have angels with scrolls but the n.w. panel contains a seated figure holding a cruciform church. Apart from the head it is well preserved and probably represents **St Botolph**. The **hammerbeam** and **arch-braced** nave roof has been in-filled with plaster, and there are demi-figures holding shields below the **wall posts**. Four little shields hang on the walls and are painted with the arms of gentlemen associated with the parish, including Sir John Leman, a C17 lord mayor of London. Half of the base of the **screen** remains below the chancel arch, and the stairs that led to

the **rood loft** are in the n. wall. The modern choir stalls are the work of a Framlingham craftsman, with good **poppyheads** in the local tradition and a very nice variety of subjects on the elbows – squirrel, owl, **pelican**, muzzled dog, and a small boy being punished in the stocks. The modern **communion rails** copy a good C17 pattern and the C19 stone **reredos** is painted with Creed, Lord's Prayer, and Commandments. There must have been a **piscina** once but there is no trace now. On the n. wall a marble tablet of 1730 reads:

> Here also mingled with his Parents' Dust
> Sleeps till ye Resurrection of the Just
> Of William Leman Esq. their beloved son . . .

Odd how the 'Esq.' creeps in. His parents' little **touchstone** tablet of 1690 is to the r., signed with his monogram. You will have seen a **hatchment** on the nave wall for Henrietta Orgill who died in 1843, and in the chancel is her husband's; he was the Revd Naunton Thomas Orgill and died in 1837. It is an interesting example because, having assumed the name and arms of Leman by licence in 1808, the rector had two crests and the one on the l. is a pun on the name – a pelican perches in a lemon tree.

Chattisham, St Margaret and All Saints (D8): There are countless medieval churches dedicated to All Saints, and many whose patronal saint is **St Margaret**, but this is the only one in England that honours them jointly. Tiny belfry **lancets** probably date the tower as C13 and it seems squat now because it lost the upper stage prior to a restoration in 1770. It was repaired with brick at that time, battlements were added, and, more recently, a **Decorated**-style w. window has been inserted. On the n. side of the **nave** there is a plain C14 door and a window of the same period, while farther along there is a blocked **low side window** and a blocked **Tudor**

priest's door in the chancel. The e. window is modern and there is a small vestry on the s. side. All the walls are plastered and the C19 timber porch stands on a flint and brick base.

The simple interior has been lime-washed recently and is very comely, with brick floors and walls that incline gently outwards. There is a plain tower arch and in front of it stands a neat little late C18 chamber organ with a fine mahogany case, given to the church recently as a thank-offering. The font is C19, and there are pine tie-beams below plastered ceilings. The C18 restoration also involved removing the chancel arch, and only rough shapes in the walls betray its position. The rood screen was destroyed at the same time but the blocked door leading to the loft stairway remains in the n. wall. An attractive modern figure of St Margaret stands in the low side window embrasure in the chancel, sculpted by Derek Jarman from driftwood found in the River Orwell. The saint was a shepherdess and is here portrayed cradling a lamb rather than overcoming the legendary dragon that is her usual symbol. There are two heavy C17 stone frames for tablets on the chancel walls carved with crude swags and skulls, but instead of being engraved the inscriptions were painted and have all but vanished. The communion rails are C19 and in the sanctuary there is a very simple C14 angle piscina (minus its drain) with dropped-sill sedilia alongside. In the floor on the n. side is the 1592 brass for John and Mary Revers and their family, but only the inscription and the plate engraved with the little figures of the three sons and seven daughters are still in place. The 12in. indents for their parents' effigies are clear and you will find Mary's figure in its wide-brimmed hat fixed to the chancel s. wall. There are two more brass inscriptions in the floor of the nave: John Bennett (1608) and Daniel Meadowe (1651, with a Latin verse). As you go, have a look at the medieval octagonal poorbox set on a pedestal by the door.

Chilton, St Mary (A10): This little church lies in the middle of fields beyond an industrial estate on the n.e. edge of Sudbury and is now in the care of the Redundant Churches Fund. Access is by footpaths and it is advisable to make enquiries about the key before a visit. The building is largely C15 but the heavily buttressed tower is C16 brick, with a solid stair turret to the s. The battlements are probably C19 but the Decorated bell openings may have been saved from an earlier tower and re-used. C16 too is the n.e. Crane chantry chapel and its w. window was blocked to make space for a monument inside. The n. door of the nave is blocked and there are two oddly proportioned windows on that side – the one to the w. of about 1500. The large late C15 windows on the s. side are very like those in Long Melford's s. aisle [Vol.1]. The s. porch is modern and entry now is normally via the chantry chapel. This has a fine late C15 roof with heavily moulded timbers and there are some excellent monuments. The earliest is a table tomb below and to the r. of the e. window and is for George Crane who died in 1491. Despite the loss of the hands, his alabaster figure is well preserved and shows traces of colour, with the feet resting on a unicorn. There was a brass inscription on the bevel originally and the quatrefoils in the side panels contain blank shields. Within the arch that links the chapel with the chancel stands a second tomb chest on which lie the alabaster effigies of Robert Crane, who died in 1500, and his wife Anne. He wears full armour, long hair lapping his helm, and again the feet rest on a unicorn. His wife was evidently of gentle birth because she wears the Collar of SS and the lappet of her head-dress retains traces of the coloured pattern. Like the first tomb, this one had a brass inscription on the bevel of the top but the shields of Crane, Ogard, and Lovell on the sides are set within lozenges and have been recoloured. Portraits of Robert, the founder of the chantry, and his wife can be found in the glass at Long Melford. On the w. wall is the last and best of the Crane monuments, for Sir Robert, M.P. for Sudbury in the Long Parliament, and his two wives. Of alabaster, it was sculpted in 1626 by **Gerard Christmas** and the three stubby figures kneel within niches separated by columns of polished **touchstone** with **Corinthian capitals**. Sir Robert faces front and his first wife, Dorothy (who was a Norfolk Hobart from Blickling), is on the l., with Susan, her successor, on the r. They are in profile, the faces aquiline and forceful, and Dorothy has more than a passing resemblance to Queen Elizabeth I. There are three shields of arms at the top and strangely placed behind Sir Robert's head is a pencilled inscription: 'S.Brown and A.Porter restored the chancel end of this church in the month of September 1860 assisted by J.Partridge' – a little credit note from the past that is a reminder that there was a major re-ordering at that time when the position of the s. nave windows was changed, the s. wall rebuilt, the roof replaced, and **box pews** removed – all under the direction of George Grimwood of Sudbury.Two good C15 figures have survived in the **tracery** of the chapel e. window – **St Appollonia** on the l. and **St Michael** beating down a blue dragon on the r.

The door to the nave has rudimentary **linen-fold panelling** and the **jambs** retain a portion of the decoration which was applied to all the walls in 1875 (there is another fragment by the s. door). In the tower there is an C18 **Commandment board** framed on the n. wall, with a section of its counterpart standing close by, and another C19 set leaning against the w. wall. The C15 **font** has quatrefoils in the bowl panels, a traceried stem, and **paterae** carved on the foot. The base of the late C15 **screen** still stands in the chancel arch and the rail is carved with two heads and two dragons biting their tails. There is a similarity with Great Cornard's screen

and they may have been carved by the same man. Yet another pair of Commandment boards hang on the e. wall and, below them, a C19 or early C20 **reredos** of mosaic panels with fleur de lys and centre text set in marble. The churchyard is pleasant to stroll in, and e. of the chancel lies Thomas Creaton who, after '36 years as Steward to the elder John Addison Esq. of Chilton Hall in this Parish', died in 1835. Status is status after all, even at one remove.

Claydon, St Peter (D6): The church stands above the village, overlooking the Gipping valley, and it is now in the care of the **Redundant Churches Fund**. In their report for 1987 the fund had this to say:

> Within sight of new housing and burgeoning prosperity the diocese left this historic church to rot for eleven years while attempts to find an alternative use came to nothing. It is one of the most conspicuous cases of neglect that we have encountered.

When I visited in 1988, the church was still in the hands of the builders, with all the windows boarded up, and so this description is necessarily provisional. Even so, much had already been done to overcome the sorry sequence of neglect and vandalism, including an entire re-tiling.

The C15 tower has **flushwork** on the angle buttresses to the w. and the upper stages have been re-faced in a much lighter colour than the base; the stepped battlements are rendered. It is highly likely that the original church was **Saxon**, judging by the **long and short work** at the w. corners of the **nave**. The C15 n. **porch**, with its crow-stepped gable, was never pretentious and when I was there it was roofless with the doorway bricked up; restoration, however, was imminent. The church's strongest feature is the massive pair of **transepts** whose continuous **roof** ridge runs across above the level of the nave. They were part of an ambitious scheme of restoration in **Decorated** style which was initiated by the rector, George Drury, in the early 1850s. It so happens that he was the same man who caused the rumpus over a nonconformist burial at nearby Akenham, and he had a reputation for savaging medieval buildings. Here, however, his ideas are interesting and, as we shall see, his own artistic skills were involved. His architect was **R.M. Phipson**, whose suspect methods are confirmed here by the poor construction of the transept walls. The rearrangement n. of the **chancel** is confused, with a small bell turret attached to the e. face of the transept and a **vestry** at right angles to the chancel. On the s. side there is a large organ chamber, and the naive **ball flower** decoration of the **priest's door** and the **headstops** of Victoria and Prince Albert's death mask are likely to be some of Drury's work. His grave in High Victorian style lies under the yew tree not far away.

Entry is via a plain C14 s. doorway, and inside you will see that it was set within a tall, narrow **Norman** arch. The tower arch was reconstituted in plain style by Drury in 1849, and when the present restoration is complete the w. window will again display glass that was designed and painted by him then. Hopefully, the early C15 **font** will also return from storage. Its bowl panels are carved with **crocketted trefoil** arches in which crowns and angels holding shields alternate; there are large heads below the bowl and the shaft is panelled. The scale of the transepts makes the nave with its simple **arch-braced roof** seem short. There is a single C17 or early C18 text painted within a leaf border on the n. wall which is probably the survivor from a sequence like the one at Witnesham. The glass of 1912 in the s. nave window is by Albert Moore, more of whose work can be found at Dallinghoo and Little Bealings. The spacious centre crossing has a **groined** timber ceiling with a large painted lozenge at the centre. There are further examples of Moore's glass, this time of the 1890s, in

the n. and s. transept windows, and in the w. window on the n. side you will find a good example of the early work of **Lavers, Barraud & Westlake** which dates from 1867. The panelled barrel roofs of the transepts have **bosses** which were carved by **Henry Ringham**. He also contracted with Drury in 1851 for the benches, reading desk, and wooden pulpit, but the diaper patterns on the pew ends are not his style at all and were probably dictated by the rector. The standing figures that he carved as **finials** have, alas, gone. Drury carved the gross **corbels** smothered with foliage that support the triple stub shafts of the transept arches. He is also credited with the stone pulpit – an interesting and inventive design. It stands on a low plinth and there are three large panels (the front one curved) pierced with intricate and spiky **tracery**; the two projecting niches contained figures until relatively recently.

The chancel reconstruction included a new arch-braced roof and Drury applied painted decoration to the timbers which is not the run-of-the-mill stencil work so often used at that time. His corbels are worth noting too – serpent, ram, owl, and **green man**. The **sanctuary's** e. wall was faced with blind **arcading**, and the **piscina** set at an angle in the corner is matched by a **credence** recess on the n. side. Drury's best glass is to be seen in the 1852 e. window. He designed and painted pointed ovals and smaller roundels for the three **lights** (including Crucifixion, Resurrection and the **Evangelistic symbols**) and filled the rest of the space with small squares rather than **quarries**, all within leafy borders. This important work by a gifted amateur came at a time when the C19 revival in stained glass was gathering momentum, and despite the recent vandalism it will be both repaired and restored. A landmine blew in the s. sanctuary window in World War II and the figure of **St Peter** was replaced in the 1950s. The s.e. organ chamber (with no organ now) has a faded section of painted pattern on the e. wall which probably backed an **altar** originally, and the stained glass cockerel in the high roundel window may be re-set medieval work from elsewhere. There is a fireplace in the corner and the flap in the priest's door obviously had a specific purpose, so was this designed as a C19 priest's cell? Drury had High Church sympathies and Father Ignatius (of Llanthony fame), together with his four monks, enjoyed the rector's hospitality in 1862 before moving on to Norwich and founding a short-lived Anglican order. The strange little vestry is puzzling too, divided into unequal and inconvenient parts by a stub wall. Plans must have been changed without coming to a coherent conclusion. The **wall plates** of the roof were salvaged from a medieval predecessor. Claydon's war memorial was a fine **Blessed Virgin** and Child group sculpted by Henry Moore. When the church became redundant it was moved to Barham. The man who secured its commission was Sir Jasper Nicholas Ridley, whose grave lies by the n. porch – a good stone, with a bas relief of a bull in a roundel.

Clopton, St Mary (F5): The village is scattered, with the church well down the Grundisburgh road within hailing distance of Burgh's St Botolph. Like a number of others in the area, the C15 tower stands to the s. of the **nave** and doubles as a **porch**. It is plain and very solid, its doorway dwarfed by the expanse of blank wall above. Just to the r. and a little higher up there is a **consecration cross** which has probably been moved from its original position. Mock **gargoyles** without spouts were sometimes used for decoration, and there is one carved as a pig's head on the s. face here, with the genuine article e. and w. On walking round, you will see **Perpendicular** windows in the nave with varying **tracery**, but one on the n. side at the e. end has 'Y' tracery of about 1300, and the coursed flints in the wall close by suggest that the fabric

is at least a hundred years older than that. Only a faint outline shows where the n. door once was. The **chancel** was replaced in the early C19 and then entirely rebuilt as part of a major restoration in the 1880s. It has a very strange lean-to organ chamber and **vestry** on the n. side, built of wood and entirely sheathed in roofing felt, a 'temporary' solution that seems to have become permanent. Within the porch/tower, the late C13 inner doorway has two exceptionally wide chamfer mouldings rather like a window splay, and on the l. hand **jamb** there is a fine example of medieval graffiti. It is a merchant's mark of a cross and flag above a heart and is precisely dated '8th April 1570'. Just below is a C14 'M.S.', and someone later cut a large 'T.C.' on the opposite jamb.

The interior is light and airy and the nave has a good **hammerbeam, arch-braced roof**. There are **king-posts** on the collar beams and, when it was restored in the 1880s, excellent demi-angels with shields were placed on the hammers, those at e. and w. having gilded wings. The lower **spandrels** are carved with some variety; there is a shield of arms at the w. end n. side, a crowned 'M' for the dedication w. of the entrance and, just to the e., a distinctly indelicate figure. The plain early C15 **font** has small shields within pointed **quatrefoils** in the bowl panels and there are quatrefoils below the step; the shaft has been renewed. The United States flag which hangs at the w. end once flew over the local air base, and below it is a panel commemorating forty-five men of the 8th Air Force who died on missions from Clopton. The small, plain **piscina** in the s. wall shows that there was an **altar** nearby, and the boldly lettered mid-C18 tablet for John and Ann Jeaffreson has a coloured **achievement** above it. The 1880s chancel arch comes down to stub jamb shafts which rest on large carved **corbels**. These are more enterprising than the usual forms of the period and portray the Good Shepherd on one side and the Good Samaritan on the other. **Balusters** from a C17 set of **communion rails** have been used to form a low screen at the chancel entrance. The austere **reredos** and altar in oak date from 1950, and the e. window has interesting glass by **Ward & Hughes** of 1887. The three main **lights** illustrate the sacrifice of Isaac, with attractive colour and sensitive modelling.

Coddenham, St Mary (D6): An attractive village in a valley, and the church stands well in a spacious churchyard. Its layout is unconventional, with a C14 tower at the w. end of the n. **aisle** rather than the **nave**, and a quite eccentric n. **porch** which is sharply angled to the e. It is too marked a variation to have been an error in setting out and seems to have been aligned for convenience with the path from the street. The tower is rather bald in its upper stages below **flushwork** battlements but this is more than balanced by the richness of the nave **clerestory**. It is deep, with a profusion of flushwork below the **ashlar** battlements, and at the e. end on the n. side an inscription for the C15 donors reads: 'Orate pro animae Johannis Frenche et Margarete' (Pray for the souls of John and Margaret French). Look also for the **sacred monogram**, an 'M' for the dedication, and a **Trinity** roundel which makes use of the ancient Christian fish symbol. A **sanctus-bell turret** stands on the gable with a niche below it, and the line of a previous **chancel roof** shows in the wall. The chancel was partially rebuilt about 1840 with another restoration following in 1893, and there is a C19 **vestry** on the s. side, but it does retain evidence of the church's early years. There is a **Norman lancet** on the n. side and a change in wall texture shows where the chancel was extended in the C14. A brick **rood turret** nestles in the corner by the n. aisle and its insertion partially masked a **Perpendicular** window. The C14 s. aisle has very nice flowing **tracery** in its e. window and

just round the corner is a large tablet for Matthias Candler who died in 1663, having been minister of the Gospel for thirty-three years, 'solid in Divinity, Laborious in ministry, Heavenly in society, a mirrour of sound piety'. The outer arch of the porch has the remains of a Trinity shield and sacred monogram in the **spandrels**, with a decayed inscription above them, and rather fine little lion **stops**.

Passing a **stoup** by the entrance, one finds within that the tower arch to the r. has been blocked and an C18 door inserted. The interior is spacious, with robust C14 **arcades** below a lovely and exceptionally shallow **double hammerbeam** roof. It is unstained, with **king-posts** on the collars under the ridge, and the hammers are adorned with demi-angels (many renewed); the **wall posts** have mutilated figures within canopied niches and they are all decorated with rosettes or stars on the underside. This is all late C15 or early C16 work and the aisle roofs are the same age and quality, their **wall plates** and main timbers nicely carved and studded with **bosses**. A number of **hatchments** are displayed and they belonged to: Dorothy Bacon (1758, n. aisle e.); Nicholas, her widower (1767, s. aisle e.); Revd John Longe (1834, n. aisle w.); Anna Maria Bacon (1783, n. nave); Revd Nicholas, her widower (1796, s. aisle w.); and an unidentified member of the Bacon family (1740s, s. nave). The stairs that led to the rood loft are entered from the n. aisle, and the painting of Christ being shown to the multitude, which hangs opposite, is probably an C18 Dutch work. There is a C14 chest sheathed in iron close by and also a crude late C17 or C18 **bier** which now serves as a table for the children. At the w. end of the s. aisle is a well-carved C19 version of a C15 **font**, and in the corner is the mechanism of an early iron-framed clock housed in a four-post wooden frame stamped 'I.W.' The aisle chapel has a large, handsome C14 **piscina** with leafy **crockets, finial**, and shallow carving in the spandrels of the

trefoil arch. The **altar** here is a most
attractive **Stuart** table whose heavy
stretcher has four slender turned shafts
set upon it and a deep, canted top
frame. On the ledge behind stands a
small C15 alabaster panel that no doubt
formed part of a **reredos**. Coloured and
gilt with a lettered scroll, it has Christ
crucified crowded round with figures;
an angel holds a chalice below His feet.
The chapel's late C17 **communion rails**
are good quality, with barley sugar
balusters in clusters of four each side
of the entrance and they, together with
the range under the chancel arch,
originally formed a three-sided set for
the **high altar**. Between the chapel and
the nave is a low screen which has an
interesting series of little carvings in
low relief in the upper panels; they
illustrate the **Annunciation**, the visits
of the shepherds and wise men, the
Flight into Egypt, and Christ's circumcision, baptism, and temptation. The
nave seating is in modern pitch pine
and the pulpit has a new stone base,
although its blind-arched panels are
Jacobean.

There is no longer a **screen** and
although **Cautley** commented on its
remains I could not locate them. After
reading the account of Bishop
Redman's visitation in 1597, one is not
surprised that the chancel needed so
much attention in the C19:

> The chauncell is in great decay in
> the rooffe, pavement and glasse
> wyndows, in so much that beggars
> creep into the chauncell through
> the wyndows and lye in the
> church abusing the same to the
> great anoyance of the parishioners.

Now all is neat and seemly. The
modern stalls incorporate a medieval
pair with **misericords** on the s. side. On
the n. wall is the memorial for Philip
Bacon, a naval captain who helped see
off the Dutch at Sole Bay and died in
the North Foreland engagement of
1666. Flanked by fluted columns, the
immense epitaph is replete with nauti-
cal detail. Farther along is a beautifully
proportioned tablet with a large urn on
the classical pediment and books piled

at the corners. It commemorates the
Revd Baltazar Gardemau, a French-
man who died in 1739, having fled from
persecution and married Lady Catherine Bacon. Her family have a **ledger-
stone** nearby inscribed 'Crypta
Baconorum' with no fewer than fourteen subsidiary shields of arms. The
simple C14 **angle piscina** stands next to
dropped-sill sedilia and there is rich
and attractive glass by Percy Bacon, an
artist not often found in East Anglia
although there are windows by him at
Tuddenham (St Martin) and Haverhill
[Vol.1]; it dates from 1894 and Bethlehem scenes fill the three **lights**, with an
Annunciation in the top tracery.

Combs, St Mary (C6): A grand church
that still manages to preserve its sense
of isolation and tranquillity, despite
the suburbs of Stowmarket that have
crept up from the n. A longish lane
through open fields leads to the
churchyard on rising ground, and note
that the C14 tower is hard up against
the w. boundary – which explains why
there are large archways n. and s.
Although blocked now, they once
allowed processions to circle the
church and still remain within consecrated ground. The tower has a
flushwork base course, the arms of
Ufford, earls of Suffolk, above each
entrance, and the bell openings have
Perpendicular tracery. There is 'Y'
tracery of about 1300 in the s. **aisle** w.
window, and the large **Tudor** brick
porch, with its polygonal buttresses,
has had the crow-step gables recently
capped and the replacement arch
bricked up. The s. aisle was remodelled
in the late C15 and the elongated
windows have stepped **transoms**. The
early C14 **chancel** is unusual in a
number of ways; look first at its w.
windows. They have **ogee** arches, and a
low transom forms a pair of **low side
windows** in both of them. The frames
were rebated to take external shutters
and one hinge survives in each. Beyond the blocked **priest's door** there is
a large circular window with four-leaf

tracery which is placed high enough to give light above the **sedilia** within. Deep, angled buttresses flank the e. window with its intersected 'Y' tracery, and a low **string course** links them. There is another priest's door on the n. side (now a **vestry**), and the **rood stair turret** shows in the angle between chancel and aisle.The Perpendicular windows on this side have no transoms and those in the C15 **clerestory** are linked by a continuous string course. The tall C14 wooden n. porch has been heavily overlaid with modern plaster but the entrance **jambs** remain, and although the door has lost its surround, the thin closing ring still serves. The early C14 inner doorway has single shafts and a finely moulded arch rests on oak leaf **capitals**, with large **headstops** – male to the l., a queen to the r.

This is a lovely church inside – all light and height. Note that the tower buttresses obtrude to merge with the w. bays of the **arcades**, whose tall octagonal **piers** have wide capitals. There is a narrow **sanctus-bell window** and below it is the original w. door, with slots for a drawbar. The base of the tower has been enclosed to form a vestry and boiler room and, hidden behind the pipework, the **stoup** is still in place; this unusual position indicates that the principal entrance was here. The C15 **nave roof** was **archbraced** to begin with, but some weakness developed which called for new **tie-beams**, **king-posts** and arch-braces. Both aisles have arch-braced roofs with crested **wall plates** and there are heavy **bosses** at the base of the braces in the s. aisle. The deep, canted bowl of the late C14 **font** is carved with nubbly roses, squares, and shields, and the stem has miniature replicas of complete **Decorated** windows. Three bells stand in the n.w. corner and provide a rare opportunity to study bell founders' marks and inscriptions. The largest was cast by Richard Brayser (father or son) in Norwich during the C15 and their shield charged with three bells is easily identified. The inscription has

excellent decorated capitals and the text is unusual: 'Nos prece Baptiste salvent tua vulnera Christe' (May thy wounds, O Christ, save us, by the Baptist's prayers). The other two bells are dated 1619 and 1662 and were cast by Miles Graye and John Darbie of Ipswich. The fine C15 benches in the nave have very varied **poppyheads** on the panelled ends and a nice selection of animals on the elbows – lions, dogs, a **griffin**, a **pelican**, a chained and muzzled bear, and an engaging hare looking typically startled. A very good C19 carver made the front three ranges (**Henry Ringham**?) and there is clever replacement on some of the others (the men 4th from the e. in the aisles, for example). There is a large, plain **piscina** in the s. aisle chapel and the surrounding **parclose screen** has been extensively restored, having lost the applied mouldings and **crockets** to the tracery (another section is against the organ). The **Stuart** pulpit has the familiar style of panelling but the design is individual – instead of single blank arches, two in each panel come down to a centre fret pendant, and the book ledge is carried on outsize scroll brackets.

The loft and upper range of the **rood screen** has been destroyed but the base remains; the tracery of its broad panels is formed by pairs of flattened **ogee** arches, above which there are small triple **quatrefoils**. The chancel lies under a C19 cross-braced wagon roof, with double wall plates adorned with demi-angels and **paterae**. Some of the stall ends are C15, and again there is dexterous Victorian restoration – examine the two heads at the e. end of the n. range. The large **piscina** and sedilia suite was largely replaced with undecorated and clumsy sections but the crockets and **cusps** are original and the vaulting comes down at the back to three diminutive leaf **corbels**. The tall niches that flank the e. window were similarly treated but you will see that one leaf capital on the n. side still shows original colour. On the wall below is the **brass** of Katherine, wife of the Revd Thomas Sotherbie, who died in 1624 – a shield of arms and parallel Latin and English verses in elegant italic:

> Fare well deare wife, since thou art now
> Absent from mortalls sight . . . .

The two plain tablets that face each other across the chancel are not inspiring but it is interesting that they match, although separated by thirty years and cut by different masons, the first of whom was local.

Combs is noted for its fine late C15 glass, given by Sir Christopher Willoughby who was Lord of the Manor. The Stowmarket gun cotton explosion of 1871 blew in many of the windows and most of the remaining glass has been collected in the s. aisle. (binoculars are invaluable here). In the window w. of the parclose screen are panels from a life of **St Margaret**: top centre, she receives God's blessing while tending her sheep and Olybrius, the governor, in rich red robe and steeple hat, sits on his charger while an attendant points her out; in the panel below two men at arms push her forward in front of the governor, with the green and blue devil she refused to worship overhead; in the top l. panel she is chained by her neck to a prison gateway; bottom l., she stands over a cauldron of boiling oil and the warder has a vicious looking prong; the top r. panel is a composite, with the saint being swallowed by the dragon on the l. and emerging to birch it on the r. The bottom r. panel has a baptism scene with bishop, saintly mother and child, and godparents. The s. window of the chapel contains two scenes from a **Seven Works of Mercy** sequence – food for the hungry to the l. and drink for the thirsty to the r. – both with angels hovering. The upper tracery of this, the e. window, and another farther w. contains labelled figures which must originally have formed a genealogy of Christ. The names of Abraham, Isaac, Jacob, and others are easily recognised, as are Old Testament kings like Josias. The many fragments in the e. window

are worth studying and there is in the centre the remains of a Christ in Majesty, the hand raised in blessing.

Copdock, St Peter (E8): The suburbs of Ipswich and the busy A12 are not far away, but the churchyard within its surrounding trees is a peaceful spot. Except for minor alterations the whole building is **Perpendicular** in style, and a panelled **base course** extends round the tower and along the **nave** and n. **transept** walls. There are **flushwork** panels in the angled buttresses of the tower, with more above the w. door, and the w. window has a **crocketted dripstone** with **finial** and angel **headstops**. There are brick battlements, and the jaunty weathervane is a cut-out of King David playing his harp; it was made in the 1850s by a Mr Trent, a friend of the rector. It is worth walking round to examine the n. door, which dates from the early C15. Its panels are keeled and the **tracery** at the top is overlaid rather than carved in the solid and incorporates little **mouchette** roundels. Beyond the tall, three-**light** windows of the nave there is a blocked door in the w. wall of the transept, and a large n.e. **vestry** was added in 1901. The **chancel** is almost as tall as the nave and its walls are faced with close-set flint pebbles whose shapes are emphasised by raised pointing. Don't miss a tombstone that stands s.w. of the **priest's door**. It commemorates John Marven, a celebrated bellringer who died aged only 34 in 1789. He was one of the early composers of change ringing methods and the head of the stone is carved with an oval relief of a woman holding a book and leaning against a bell. This is particularly interesting because the design was copied from one of Bartolozzi's engravings for the *Oxford Youths*. The s. **porch** is tall to match the rest of the building but relatively shallow, and had a stepped brick gable added in the C17. A large stone sundial was placed above the entrance in 1935 bearing the legend: 'The greater light to rule the

Day', and its C17 predecessor is lodged on the windowsill within. The outer arch has hung shields in the **spandrels**, with shields and crowns in the moulding, and the **stoup** by the inner door still has the whole of its bowl intact.

A deep **gallery** installed in 1901 spans the w. end of the nave and five small C16 panels have been placed on the front. The two outer ones are carved with leaf patterns, the centre is a shield of arms, a lady plays a harp on the fourth, but the best one is carved with the little figure of Edward VI on horseback. When **Dowsing** came here in January 1643 the windows must have been full of stained glass because he records having broken down 150 'superstitious pictures'. He also says that he defaced a cross on the **font** but it looks as though the bowl was comprehensively re-cut in the C19 anyway. The panels have kneeling angels holding open books (with texts), two pomegranates, a **Tudor rose**, and an interlace design – all in deep relief; the shaft is Victorian. So too is the handsome cover, a design that is an elaboration of the fine late C15 model at Barking. The nave **roof** was replaced in 1901 in celebration of Queen Victoria's long reign, but the C15 transept roof remains, low pitched and heavily moulded, with leaf and flower **bosses**. The transept was originally a **chantry chapel** associated with Copdock Hall, and the priest who served its **altar** will have made use of the long **squint** that cuts through the wall at an angle to emerge in the chancel aligned with the **high altar**. The tall transept arch has hung shields in the moulding, three of which have traces of painted arms, and the **jambs** of the chancel arch were cut short in the C19 to rest on new stone **corbels**. A **brass** shield below the one on the n. side displays the arms of Goldingham impaling those of the Hacon family. The organ chamber dates from 1901 and there is a large tablet carved with a floriated cross above the vestry door. It commemorates Arnald de Grey, the rector who died in 1889 and was responsible for

much of the restoration. A C19 stone **reredos** in **Decorated** style stretches the full width of the e. wall, with a central Last Supper tableau sculpted in relief. It is strange that the **sanctuary** floor was later raised to such an extent that the carving is now almost at floor level and completely hidden by the altar. Somebody obviously didn't like it. The large, plain **piscina** is also well down the wall. The e. window has a crowded scene spread across three lights of Christ carrying the cross. Despite the theatrical poses it is curiously lifeless, and the paint is deteriorating here and there.

Cotton, St Andrew (B4): This large and handsome church stands within a spacious shady churchyard and tends, perhaps, to receive less attention than it deserves. The tower shares with Wetheringsett the strange distinction of having a tall C15 open arch in its w. face, and the ground floor serves as the draughtiest ringing chamber that I have ever experienced. Unlike Wetheringsett's, the inner wall contains a three-**light** window and it has been suggested that this was why the outer arch was left open. The **tracery** is certainly attractive and unusual, with a large **ogee** bisected by an inverted curve. Ponderous buttresses stop short at the second stage and others which are much lighter continue diagonally to the bell chamber. A group of three niches is placed above the arch, with singles n. and s., while the bell openings have **Decorated** tracery and there are **gargoyles** below the shallow battlements. The odd shape best described as a triangle with curved sides crops up in the C14 s. **aisle** windows and there is excellent **reticulated** tracery in the aisle e. window. A **string course** on the s. wall of the C14 **chancel** links the **dripstones** of the windows and another beneath them lifts to form a dripstone with a fat **finial** for the **priest's door**. At the chancel corners, gabled pinnacles decorated with **crockets** and finials have pretty little niches facing e., each with small **corbel** heads below their ogee arches. Between them is a great e. window with a singular tracery pattern over the five tall lights. Two large ogees enclose a pair of curved triangles each, plus a **quatrefoil**. This leaves a large oval at the top and two side slivers, all containing weak subsidiary divisions, and it is these that sabotage the design so that it is more interesting than beautiful. There was once a **vestry** or **sacristy** on the n. side which disturbed the window/buttress pattern, and the Decorated tracery in the aisle contains variants of that seen on the s. side. The C14 **nave** received a new **roof** in the late C15 and the **clerestory** was built with it. Nine windows each side, their arches emphasised with red brick, are linked by a string course, and there are **flushwork** panels between them plus a large patch at the w. end of the s. side.

Entry is through a mid-C14 s. **porch** whose windows match the aisles. The front is decorated with flushwork, including crowned 'MR's for the **Blessed Virgin** in the **spandrels** of the outer arch with its leafy **capitals**. Some of the strange mixture of patterns in the parapet would seem to be C19. The tall inner doorway is one of the finest surviving C14 examples and a remarkable amount of its colouring remains. The capitals of the triple shafts are densely carved with oak leaves and acorns, and you will discover the face and hands of a tiny **green man** among the foliage on one of them to the r. of the doorway. The **hood mould** rested on large corbels and the shape of the remains on the l. suggests that it may have been a lizard – a symbol of good fortune that was often chosen for doorways. The outer moulding of the arch is carved with roses and foliage coloured in green and yellow against red, and the centre band features bunches of blue grapes. Follow it down to the r. hand base and you will come across a little pagan Pan with goat feet, matched by a less distinct human figure on the other side. The doors themselves are C14 with tracery at the top, and there are remains of a

stoup to the r.

Within, the C14 **arcades** lean alarmingly outwards under the pressure of roof and clerestory, particularly to the n., and there are attractive, undulating brick floors throughout. The w. end of the s. aisle is used as a vestry but within it a stair leads to the tower, and its iron-clad door shows that parish valuables were once protected there. The C15 **font** lacks the figures that once stood at the corners of the shaft, its panels have been re-cut with strange little monks, and the bowl is modern. Nearby stands the table that served as the **high altar** in the C17. Light from the clerestory emphasises the beauty of the pale oak roof – a rich double **hammerbeam** design whose e. bay was panelled to form a **celure** above the **rood** that stood or hung below. There are demi-angels fronting the ends of the upper hammers and pendants on the range below. Huge flat flower **bosses** abound, some divided by the principal timbers. Four ranges of cresting run lengthways and along the hammerbeams, pierced tracery is set behind the posts, and **king-posts** rise to the ridge above **embattled** collar beams. Similar in many ways to nearby Bacton [Vol.1], this is one of Suffolk's loveliest roofs. While studying it, use binoculars if you can to look at the C15 angels in the n. clerestory windows – ten are tonsured like monks and six are crowned, some have pink wings, some have blue. A pair of bench ends at the back of the church are intricately carved and one on the n. side has a most unusual representation of a door, complete with closing ring and strap hinges. The main range is completely plain, its thick ends warped to a gentle curve, and the pews with doors at the e. end probably date from the 1903 restoration. A low tomb recess lies in the n. aisle wall below an arch which has just a hint of the ogee shape.

The early C17 pulpit is not, for a change, darkened by stain, and it is remarkable that in this case the familiar blind arches in the panels have no **pilasters** – nor had they ever. There is attractive scrollery below the canted book ledge, and the curved rail of the modern stairs carries an extraordinarily vicious **griffin** which, as a handhold, is acquiring a fine patina as successive parsons climb to preach. The **chancel** arch capitals were roughly chopped back and morticed to house the **rood screen** and the stairs which led to the loft above it are tucked behind on the e. side rather than the more usual w. At least part of the reading desk dates from the C17 and the **Stuart communion rails** are a good set with close-set **balusters**. A small recess high in the n. **sanctuary** wall indicates that the vanished sacristy (or it might have been an **anchorite's cell**) had an upper chamber. Opposite are the beautiful remains of the C14 **piscina** and **sedilia** suite. The design placed two of the sedilia seats within the window embrasure, and although these have lost their canopies, their companion to the w. is complete. Like the piscina at the other end, its ogee arch is multi-**cusped**, the crockets are very crinkly, and the tall finial is flanked by pinnacles.

Creeting St Mary, St Mary (C6): At one time there were four Creeting parishes but St Olave's church had disappeared by the C17 and in 1801 All Saints, whose churchyard adjoined this one, was demolished and St Mary's a n. **transept** was added to St Mary's a year later to accommodate the joint congregation. The spire and top of the tower had by this time collapsed and been replaced by a pyramid **roof**, but in 1885 this in turn was followed by the present bell stage and battlements. About the same time the transept was enlarged into an **aisle** and the C13 **chancel** was largely rebuilt. The w. window of the tower is tall and thin with **Decorated tracery**, and an oblong stone above it is carved with the arms of Ufford, earls of Suffolk. The whole facade of the C15 s. **porch** is covered with **flushwork** and a modern **Blessed Virgin** and Child occupies the niche over the entrance. The

dripstone rests on worn **headstops** and beyond the half-gates there is a **stoup** which has **paterae** on the bevel of its recess. The inner **Norman** doorway reveals the true age of the church. Thoroughly restored, the arch has a roll moulding and an outer band of semi-circles, and rests on scalloped **capitals** and single shafts.

The C15 **font** stands in the base of the tower and the **Evangelistic symbols** in the bowl panels alternate with angels holding shields – a **Trinity emblem** to the w. and a well-cut arms of St **Edmund** to the e.; four lions guard the shaft and above them is a prominent range of defaced angels. The **crocketted ogee** cover was restored and supplemented by a deep skirt in 1907. Nearby are **Commandment boards** and a memorial for Rear-Admiral Samuel Uvedale, who died in 1808 after a distinguished career in which he commanded the *Ajax* at the battle of Cape St Vincent. The roofs, **arcade**, and furnishings are modern, including a **screen** of 1902, but the **altar** is an excellent **Jacobean** table. Its substantial turned legs are carved and the very odd metal cylinder used for storing documents that was fastened underneath at one time now rests on the floor. St Mary's has a fine array of **Kempe & Co.** glass dating from the late C19 and early C20 which illustrates the consistency of their style and the variations introduced by Tower. The e. window includes figures of St **Alban** and **St Olave**, the s. chancel windows have **St Laurence, St Stephen, St Cecilia**, and **St Agnes**, while in the nave there is an especially rich King David group dating from 1903. In the n. aisle are two Kempe & Tower designs – an **Annunciation** and a **St George** and **St Edmund**, and in the lower borders of both you will find the firm's emblem of a tower within a wheatsheaf (the wheatsheaf alone figures in the chancel windows). In complete contrast in the n.w. aisle window there is an arresting 1950s Nativity by Brian Thomas in which the Holy Family is grouped with shepherds and their dog while **putti** float overhead. The colouring is vivid and the rough outlines of the naturalistic figures have the texture of a charcoal drawing.

Creeting St Peter, St Peter (C6): Approached by a long gravelled lane from the s., this little church nestles in a grove of trees above the busy A45 which now cuts between it and the village. There was a time in the C18 when it lay derelict and roofless but now, despite all difficulties, it is well cared for and the C14 **porch** with its original **roof** has recently been restored. There are flint **consecration crosses** on the **nave** buttresses and a faint **scratch dial** can be found on one of them. The small doorway of the C14 tower has plain chamfers and there is no w. window, although the bell openings have **Decorated tracery** like one of the nave n. windows. The round arch of the little n. door shows that the building was **Norman** originally. The e. window and one s. window have 'Y' tracery of about 1300 and the narrow **priest's door** is the same age. The small **ogee**-headed windows each side of the **chancel** are slightly later and were probably **low side windows**.

There is a neat interior, and under the C19 **gallery** there is a C15 **font** in beautiful condition which does not seem to be the result of re-cutting. It is so like Earl Stonham's that they may well have been carved by the same mason. In the bowl panels there is a pomegranate and crown of thorns (s.e.), a lattice with fleur de lys terminals (n.e.), and a fat **Tudor rose** (s.w.). Angels with shields fill the rest, others link wings underneath, and four proud lions slightly turn their heads against the shaft. The solid C19 pews have **poppyheads** and doors, and hassocks embroidered with saints' emblems make a colourful display on the ledges. Beyond the plastered-over n. door there is a most interesting **St Christopher** painting. It is faded and one of the roof braces obliterated the saint's face, but his arm and staff are clear and so is

the Christ child on his l. shoulder. Behind the figures an elongated scroll carried the message: 'Christopheri sancti speciem quicumque tuetur illa nempe die nullo languore gravetur' (Whoever looks at the picture of St Christopher shall assuredly on that day be burdened with no weariness). The red background has a pale blue border on which a red and white ribbon is folded and, farther down, the head and shoulders of a mermaid holding mirror and comb were probably in the legendary river to be crossed. Instead of the more usual eight, the C15 pulpit has seven sides of which two make up the door, and each panel has a pair of **crocketted** and **finialed** ogee arches with tracery behind them. All the bevels carry **paterae** and the underside is coved, but of the original shaft only the **capital** remains. By it stands a repaired early C17 table and in the s. wall opposite, the recess is likely to have been the entrance to the **rood loft stair**. The chancel roof is C19, as are the stalls, but they have rather nice standing figures against the walls. The **communion rails** are composed of a series of wrought iron upright scrolls, both unusual and decorative – Victorian or C20? There is a plain **piscina** and the e. window glass dates from the formative period of the 1840s before the large firms became established. It was designed by Mr Rawnsley, the curate, and made by an Ipswich glazier. There is a central figure of the patron saint and the rest of the window is taken up with lozenge and scroll patterns in blue, red, and yellow against cross-hatched backgrounds. George Paske of the Hon. East India Company died on his way home in 1822 and was buried on St Helena, but the memorial for him and his wives on the chancel wall is quintessential High Victorian Gothic of 1874.

A cast-iron lamppost twisted like traditional barley sugar stands by the porch and the peaceful churchyard invites a stroll in search of epitaphs like Henry Ellis's, twenty yards s. of the priest's door: 'O how uncertain are the days of man ...'.

Cretingham, St Peter (E4): It is probably pure coincidence, but both Cretingham and neighbouring Earl Soham were originally dedicated to **St Andrew**, although in Cretingham's case the change of allegiance was delayed until the beginning of this century and the reason for it is unknown. The present building probably dates from the early C14 but there have been gradual, piecemeal alterations over the years, and the tower has a **Decorated** w. window and slightly later bell openings. The w. door has been bricked up and there are large **flushwork quatrefoils** in the stepped battlements. A **Perpendicular** window in the n. wall of the **nave** has to make do with wooden glazing bars and there has been a good deal of patching up in brick. The e. window has intersected 'Y' **tracery** and there is a **lancet**, more 'Y' tracery and a small **priest's door** on the s. side of the **chancel**, all of around 1300. The modest **rood stair turret** to the w. has a sloping stone slab **roof** and little slit window, and one of the late Perpendicular nave windows on that side has recently been renewed. There are three small niches around the entrance of the C14 **porch**, and one of its timbers is secured by a massive peg on the outside of the wall. At some stage the roof was renewed at a higher level and the side windows were blocked.

The interior is charming, largely because nobody in the C19 was minded to wield a new broom and sweep away all that was old-fashioned. The n. wall leans lazily outwards (which explains the brick buttress outside) and there is a good **hammerbeam** and **arch-braced** roof with **collars** tight under the ridge. Its **spandrels** are pierced with tracery, and so is the **wall plate**, which has carved spandrels running e.-w. below it. It is worth using binoculars to study the **St George** and dragon in the 3rd bay from the e. on the n. side. There is an 'A.T.' monogram in the corner behind the dragon and the saint's long sword and large hand project from the r. The head of a man and a recumbent figure can be found in the 3rd bay from the w. on the s. side. Half a dozen C15 benches with rustic tracery and the remains of **poppyheads** stand at the w. end on either side of the chunky **font** of the same period. Plain shields and **Tudor roses** in **cusped** squares decorate its bowl panels, with angel heads below, smiling lions round the shaft, and quite a lot of the original red and green paint survives. A little organ stands by the blocked n. door, and by its side there is one high-backed late C16 pew with turned **finials**. The rest of the seating is in the form of plain C18 **box pews** painted black, and above them on the n. wall there is a set of C18 or early C19 **decalogue boards**. Opposite hang the **Royal Arms** of Charles II, dulled by age but well painted on board. Two boys' heads peep out from below the Garter roundel and **Cautley** thought that it was the work of the same artist who painted the set in St Margaret's, Ipswich. It has been discovered that the Commandments are lettered on the back, suggesting that the arms were originally for Charles I, reversed during the Commonwealth, and revised at the **Restoration**. The pulpit is a handsome **Stuart three-decker** that lost its clerk's pew when the box pews were installed. The blind-arched panels are more delicate than usual and there are pierced brackets to the steeply canted book ledge; the hexagonal **tester** is adorned with acorn pendants. Moving into the chancel, note the curious recess below the window on the s. side – possibly the remains of a **low side window**. Two more C15 benches stand farther e. and the **altar** is a small, simple C17 table, enclosed on three sides by **communion rails**. This was a late C17 fashion but these may have come in a little later and they are painted to match the C18 box pews. A tiny parish chest no more than 2ft by 14in stands by the altar and the top is lettered: 'This box is for the towne evedence A.C:C.H. 1660' (i.e., the parish's official documents). On the n. wall the C16 monument to Lionel Louth retains much of its original colour. There are two shields and an **achievement** with strapwork at the top, and he kneels within a coffered arch (minus half his legs) with a helm in front. His daughter Margaret married Richard Cornwallis (brother of Sir Thomas, whose memorial can be found at Brome) and her memorial of 1603 on the s. wall of the **sanctuary** has a **touchstone** tablet within a broad surround decorated with six small coloured shields; her arms are in a coloured roundel at the top. Her son John is commemorated on the e. wall with a touchstone tablet set in an architectural alabaster frame, achievement on top and shield below. He died in 1615 and because his second wife was related to the Wolseys, the arms of the cardinal feature in miniature on the l. The roundel painted with the head of the **Blessed Virgin** in the e. window is likely to be C19 work, and at the top there is a small but well-painted achievement of the Chenery family arms.

Crowfield, All Saints (D5): Like nearby Gosbeck and Ashbocking, Crowfield's church is well away from its village that lines the old Roman road. Beautifully placed, it is masked from the s. and e. by trees and there is a substantial moat close by. The owners of the house that stood within it probably sited the church for their convenience. For most of its history it has been a daughter chapel of Coddenham and it was only in the 1920s that it was advanced to the status of a parish church. There was a restoration here in 1862 under **E.C. Hakewill** that went so far as to rebuild the C14 **nave** from the foundations, retaining the ground plan and re-using much of the material. It is unlikely that there was ever a tower but a bellcote was sited towards the centre of the nave **roof**. In the C18 this became an attractive cupola but Hakewill replaced it with a banal little

Crowfield, All Saints: chancel

turret, and he added a **vestry** outside the n. door. A new **lancet** and **cinquefoil** roundel were inserted in the w. wall and stone blocks carved with an animal and a grotesque head were found new homes level with the gable ends. Quite the most interesting thing about Crowfield is the C15 **chancel**. Timber-framed like a cottage, there is nothing like it in either Norfolk or Suffolk and, with its wooden **mullioned** windows and **priest's door** on the s. side, it is very pleasing. So too is the contemporary s. **porch** which has been unobtrusively glazed. Its roof is braced by cambered **tie-beams**, crested like the **wall plates**, and the **spandrels** are carved with a lively selection – an angel with a crown, a **green man**, two birds pecking grapes, and a defaced mask.

The re-used C14 doorway was given new **headstops** and just inside there is a **stoup** in a new niche. The nave **hammerbeam** and **arch-braced roof** is late C15 in essence and, like Ufford chancel, the arch-braces are interrupted by a short post partway up. The **collars** under the ridge are **castellated** and all the timbers are unstained except the C19 additions. These take the form of standing angels placed in front of the hammers and smaller ones added at the bottom of the **wall posts** and halfway up the braces. There is a good shield of Victorian **Royal Arms** in the top w. window and the 1860s **font** is quite attractive, although it is cramped up right in the s.w. corner. Hakewill's instinct for sympathetic design faltered when it came to the nave windows and he inserted pairs of internal arches with bald **trefoil** tops which were surely unnecessary. The tablet on the n. wall is a grateful tenantry's tribute to Sir William Middleton of Shrubland Park and has a profile portrait at the top. He was buried at Barham and the restoration here was funded by his widow in his memory. C19 woodcarvers were often very talented

and the benches here are the work of James Wormald and William Polly. Each **poppyhead** is different and they took a generous selection of tree foliage, fruit, and corn for their subjects. They also carved the two groups of standing and kneeling angels which flank the entrance to the chancel (more of Polly's work at Rushmere St Andrew). There is now no medieval **screen** but you will see that the arch overhead is nicked in three places where the **tympanum** once fitted. Beyond it the roof has cambered tie-beams with plain and heavy braces below them and C19 work above. Above wainscot panelling the wall timbers are exposed, and on the e. wall there is an excellent set of **decalogue boards** painted and gilt in true High Victorian style. The light-weight C18 **communion rails** have turning in two sections and the **altar** is a robust **Stuart** table with a carved top rail. **Brasses** were very much out of fashion in the C18 but there is an inscription of 1775 for William Middleton on the s. wall of the **sanctuary**, and two attractive mid-C19 examples opposite mark the return of this style of memorial. The church's only **hatchment** is in the chancel and was used at the funeral of Sir William Fowle Fowle Middleton in 1860; its twin is to be found at Barham. All the stained glass is by **Ward & Hughes** and the e. window has shaped panels of the Resurrection, and the raising of the widow's son and of Jairus's daughter; the rest of the space is filled with bright geometric shapes and foliage and is quite attractive at a distance.

Culpho, St Botolph (F6): There has never been more than a handful of houses scattered across this little parish, but a church has stood here since the Conquest and it may indeed have been one of those founded by St Botolph himself in the C7. The core of the walls is no doubt older, but most of what we see dates from about 1300, with characteristic 'Y' **tracery** in the

windows, although the **lancets** in the **chancel** are probably a little earlier. The n. door has been blocked and there is a generous **priest's door** with small, worn **headstops** on the s. side of the chancel. As with a number of churches in this area, the unbuttressed tower with its tall entrance arch stands to the s. of the **nave**, its ground floor acting as a **porch**; the upper stage has been removed and it is capped with a tiled pyramid **roof**. There is a **scratch dial** to be found on its s.e. corner and the inner C14 doorway is finely moulded, with the unusual accompaniment of a square **label**. This is partially obscured by the outer arch, which indicates that the tower was added a little later. The builders provided a **stoup** to the r. although you will find that there was one already set in the wall just inside.

The interior is bright and neat but it was not always so. In 1602 it was described as 'exceeding ruinous' and it must have been about that time that the e. wall of the nave was rebuilt in brick and a new chancel arch inserted. There was a full-scale restoration in the 1880s and in 1976 the church was entirely re-roofed with attractive small red tiles, the tower restored and the interior re-plastered, leaving exposed flints in the window splays. The late C15 **font** has **quatrefoils** in the bowl panels with flowers and leaves at their centres, there are large **fleurons** underneath, and the medieval staple used to secure the cover survives on the rim. The C17 framework of the present cover was found in the stable loft at Playford vicarage in 1935 and was newly panelled for use here. Floors are brick, and the pattern on the n. side shows where **box pews** once stood. Overhead, the nave roof is **arch-braced** and plastered out, with two heavy **tie-beams** set well below the top of the walls. C18 **decalogue** texts painted on canvas hang on the walls, and over the n. door there is a banner with decorative swags of dried flowers. The small pulpit, with its acorn-cum-pineapple **finials**, dates from 1959, and the 1970s work uncovered a late C14

Dallinghoo, St Mary: Tudor Royal Arms

piscina in the s. wall, indicating that there was at least one nave **altar**, even in a church as small as this. A plaque on the n. wall records that Robert Thornhagh Gurdon, 1st Baron Cranworth, 'rebuilt and furnished the chancel' in 1883, but the altar that was provided has been relegated to the back of the church and the C17 communion table reinstated. The piscina in the **sanctuary** matches the one in the nave and has small-scale **dropped-sill sedilia** alongside. The plain rectangular recess in the n. wall was no doubt an **aumbry**, and although the roof is Victorian, parts of the **wall plate** are original.

Dallinghoo, St Mary (F5): At first sight, the church seems to have been built the wrong way round with a tower at the e. end, but on walking round you will see that it was a central tower originally and that the **chancel** has been demolished. The **herringbone** patterns in the flints of the tower walls suggest that it dates from the C12, although there is C15 **flushwork** on the e. buttresses and later brick battle-

ments. The C19 window was perhaps inserted in the e. arch when the chancel was removed. A very large brick **vestry** was added on the n. side (early C19?) and served for a time as the village school. The w. window has attractive C14 flowing **tracery** and the little Victorian **transept** on the s. side of the **nave** is actually an organ chamber. The **porch** has all the signs of C19 rebuilding, but the **spandrels** of the C15 outer arch have shields with **Trinity** and **Passion emblems**, there are **fleurons** in the mouldings, and the **stops** are lions like those often seen in font panels. The inner doorway has **headstops** and the spandrels are filled with flushwork, just as they are at Charsfield.

C19 **decalogue boards** hang on the w. wall and there are **Royal Arms** of George III above the n. door. The font is C19. The nave is fairly wide and is spanned by a shallow **arch-braced roof** which has collars and short **king-posts** under the ridge. Strange little cut-out emblems were added to the bottom of the **wall posts** in the late C17, and between them there are carved lateral braces. The e. bay of the roof was once a **celure** for the **rood** below, and faint traces of decoration remain on the n.

Dallinghoo, St Mary: C17 Holy Table

side. The shields in the corners repeat those on the porch but they may be modern. The mid-C17 pulpit is particularly good and rises from a short stem of bunched scrolls. The body has flattened **acanthus** scrolls at the angles, with blind-arched panels between, and the range above is carved with a fish scale and fleur de lys pattern. The **tester** cornice is decorated with a vine trail and turned pendants, and there are sharp gables above each face. The backboard has a double blind arch at the top, and at the bottom a very interesting panel was incorporated from elsewhere which is carved with miniature **Tudor** arms flanked by a rose and the pomegranate of Catherine of Aragon. The large reading desk in front has been formed by using sections of late C16/early C17 woodwork, including what looks like part of an Elizabethan court cupboard. The base of the tower now serves as a chancel and the C18 **communion rails** have fine

twisted **balusters** and fluted gate-posts. There is a C14 **piscina** within a **trefoil** arch but this must have been moved to its present position from the old chancel. C17 panelling has been brought from elsewhere to form a **reredos**, and in front of it stands a most attractive C17 **Holy table** with a solid bottom shelf, short bulbous legs, and a deep carved top rail. The 1880s e. window glass is by Albert Moore, an artist who had been a designer for **Powell & Sons** twenty years before. The subjects are identified by Gospel texts, the colouring is pleasing, but the figures are poor. There is another of his windows at Little Bealings. Before leaving you may like to examine the figure of Hope with her anchor that stands in the n.e. churchyard. It is a typically bland piece by that prolific statuary Matthew Wharton Johnson, whose work is scattered all over England, and it must date from the 1840s. The vault in front contains the remains of Rector Ellis Walford's family and was once enclosed by railings and a gate.

Darmsden, St Andrew (D6): A sign on the road between Needham Market and Baylham points to Darmsden, and a pretty lane climbs out of the valley to the tiny hamlet; its church which lies beyond is nearly a mile from the main road. This is a quiet and peaceful spot, with spacious views across the Gipping to the Creetings and Shrubland Park, and the tiny building is an object lesson in the virtues of tenacity and faith. The diocese closed it in 1973 and declared it redundant in 1979, but parishioners and friends bought the church and formed the St Andrew's Trust which maintains it and ensures that there is a service at least once a month. The poem by one of them on the door may not be great verse but it deserves its place:

> . . . Now this little church is up for sale,
> Some folks say 'Well it's getting old'
> But others say 'Yes so it might be But we'll fight like mad to keep it free.
> It's too beautiful to close for ever, When so many friends get together,
> Once a month on a Sunday afternoon,
> To say a prayer and sing a hymn, And thank the Lord for everything . . .

There was a small medieval building on the same site, but by the C19 it was in poor shape and was entirely replaced in 1880. Designed by Herbert J. Green of Norwich, the successor is an excellent example of the small Victorian church, and unlike his other church at Willisham, it is distinguished by its quality. Everything is small in scale, with a continuous **roof** over **nave** and **chancel**, and the bell was re-hung in the bellcote on the w. gable in 1983. The flint pebble walls have stone facings, and the general style is **Decorated**. Above the w. door there is a handsome rose window enclosing four **quatrefoils** and there is a diminutive s. **porch**.

Within, everything has an extraordinary compactness. A heavy drum **font** stands on one side at the w. end, and the neat benches are not only made of oak but they have **poppyheads** excellently carved with sprays of vine, pomegranate, hops, roses, and thistles. This is work by Cornish & Gaymer's men and overhead the roof, again in oak, has **arch-braces** which project to curious stubs which are at right angles to the **purlins**. There is no chancel arch, but three steps mark off the **sanctuary**, flanked by open-work pulpit and reading desk. The Cornish & Gaymer oak **reredos** has pierced and **crocketted** gables in keeping with the chosen style, and below them the figure of Christ as the Good Shepherd stands flanked by **St Paul** and **St Andrew**, all well carved in deep relief within **cusped** panels. Carved sprays of corn and vine, and painted texts of the Creed and Lord's Prayer complete the range but above, on each side of the e. window, the early C19 **decalogue boards** from the old building were replaced in their traditional position. So too, was the **piscina**, and part of its stonework looks original. All is meticulously kept, a credit to Darmsden and an example to many, in more ways than one.

Debenham, St Mary Magdalene (D4): The main village street rises to a hump with the church on the crest, its graveyard sloping gently s. towards a little open plain. The bluff and solid tower has distinctive **long and short quoins** which are normally a sure sign of **Saxon** work, but you will find that the simple **imposts** of the arch within appear to be **Norman** and it may well date from the Conquest period when the two traditions overlapped. There are small **lancets** at ground and first-floor level but the stage above is C14, with **Decorated tracery** in the bell openings. The tower was some 20ft higher until 1667 when it was struck by lightning and had to have the top removed – which accounts for its squat appearance in relation to the **nave**; tie-bars secured by 'S' plates were used to strengthen it. A large two-storeyed **Galilee porch** was added to the w. in the C14, the upper room being a Lady chapel that was probably used by one of the two village **guilds**. Its facade is very worn, with niches in the side buttresses and another one over the entrance, and the **roof** has its own **gargoyle**. The spacious churchyard allows a clear view of the impressive **Perpendicular** nave and s. **aisle**; the three-**light clerestory** windows have stepped **transoms** as do the tall windows of the aisle whose buttresses are decorated with **flushwork** panels – all, that is, except two in the centre which, with a section of the wall, were replaced in red brick. The C13 **chancel** windows on the s. side have **plate tracery** which has been partially filled in, and the **priest's door** has single shafts below a renewed arch. The bold triple-lancet e. window is C19 work but round the corner on the n. side one of the three tall lancets is original. All the nave windows look as though they were renewed in the C19 and the finely moulded n. door has large **Tudor roses** in the **spandrels**.

Entry is normally via the Galilee porch and tower, and you will see that one of the **imposts** of the inner arch is crudely decorated with diagonal lines on the chamfer. Above it there is a tiny slit **sanctus-bell window** in the wall. The early C15 nave **arcades** are beautifully proportioned, with **quatrefoil** piers whose **capitals** are decorated with angels, **acanthus** leaves, or vine trails, each within bands of narrow mouldings enriched with tiny **paterae**. The pattern is repeated on the chancel arch but all the angels have been defaced unfortunately. Overhead, the **roof** has alternate **tie-beams** and **hammerbeams**, all **embattled**, and tenons projecting from the hammers indicate that there were originally angels on them. Some of the small stone **corbels** below the **wall posts** have been renewed. The nave floor is

Debenham, St Mary Magdalene: galilee porch

patterned with a **herringbone** of local red and yellow bricks and there are small diamond rosette tiles at the intersections. Part of the restoration work in 1871, the floor was a product of Debenham's only C19 industry and is remarkably attractive. The benches date from the same time. By the s. door stands the memorial to the Revd John Simson, who died in 1697. His handsome half-length marble effigy stands within an arched niche with one hand raised, the other on his breast. His face is full and fat, his hair falls to his shoulders, and one astonished **putto** sits on an adjoining ledge, his twin having fallen off. With a flaming urn on top, the surround displays a selection of Latin tags, and the black marble top of the table tomb below carries a long English epitaph which is worth reading as an illustration of the contemporary attitude to funeral monuments. In case the deceased's scholarship should be in doubt the base carries a line of Greek below another epitaph in Latin. Nearby stands a C14 chest with scrolled straps, and the C15 **font** is over by the n. door. It is very worn, and defaced shields alternate with **Evangelistic symbols** in the bowl panels. The candle-snuffer cover is C19. A wooden chiming drum from a clock mechanism stands by the nearest arcade pillar, together with a decayed section of C17 **communion rails**. There are fragments of medieval glass gathered together in one of the n. aisle windows, and although the **piscina** at the e. end is a jumble of bits and pieces, there is a fine bishop's head of about 1300 at the top and shields in the spandrels. Across on the s. aisle wall is an oval tablet for the Revd John Davie who died aged 36 in 1813. His father was master of Sidney Sussex and vice-chancellor of Cambridge University, but the ambiguous wording could have you thinking the son held those posts, but for his age. A restored piscina at the e. end of the s.

aisle shows that there was an **altar** here, and an C18 Lord's Prayer board stands on the windowsill. To the l., a generous doorway leads to the **rood stair**, and moving back into the nave you will see that although the top exit is blocked, the heavy, embattled rood beam still spans the chancel arch.

The arch itself is interesting because the C15 builders re-used it by inserting extra sections of shaft and new capitals above the old caps, thus raising the whole thing to marry with their nave. Before leaving the nave, have a look at the **Stuart** pulpit. It stands on a modern stone base, but the panels are well carved with typical blind arches and strapwork. Behind it on the wall is a plain tablet by Robert Tovell whose work is not uncommon in the county. It commemorates Robert Green, a young lieutenant of marines who fell at the battle of Trafalgar while serving in the *Royal Sovereign*, and his brother Samuel of the Madras Native Infantry who succumbed in 1818. The second phase of restoration in 1883 dealt with the chancel but the floor levels remained unchanged and there is a step down from the nave. The 1909 glass in the centre s. window has figures of the **Blessed Virgin** and **St Columba**. The **Annunciation** panel has Our Lady dressed in red and green rather than blue, for a change, and the message comes via a ray of light instead of the usual figure of **Gabriel**. St Columba bears a dove on his shoulder, and both colour and composition are pleasing; the maker is unknown. Farther along is the large tomb of Sir Charles Framlingham, who died in 1595. He lies in full armour alongside his wife, who wears a huge ruff and bulky skirt whose voluminous folds only show at the end round her feet. There is **Renaissance** detail on the chest, with remains of two figures within shallow niches. Large shields with innumerable quarterings decorate the ends and there is a full **achievement** within an architectural frame on the wall above – no trace of colour anywhere. On the wall overhead hang two **hatchments**,

that of Lady Mary Gawdy (1691), daughter of the Earl of Desmond, to the r., and Sir Charles Gawdy's to the l. This has attractive heraldry within a **cartouche** and, having been used at his funeral in 1650, it is one of the earliest in the county. On the wall by the priest's door is Sir Charles's coffin plate. These are seldom seen, and this one is memorable for the lengthy epitaph. He was 'blessed in the happie choice of a most vertuous wife', and he 'lived and died a zealous prooffessor of the reformed religion settled and established in the reigne of Qu' Elizabeth by Act of Parliament'. He had 'an undaunted loyalty to his Sovereigne Charles the First which he frequently manifested by espousing his cause and quarrell to ye uttermost hazard of his life and Fortune'. The restored C13 piscina in the **sanctuary** lies under a steep gable and **trefoil** arch. Debenham's bells are some of the mellowest in the county and they have always been popular with ringers. It is a ground-floor ring of eight. As you leave have a look at the peal boards in the tower. An early long length of 10,080 changes of Bob Major was rung in 1767, and in 1892 there was a record peal of 16,088 Oxford Treble Bob which was rung in 10hrs 32mins. and thoroughly deserved the stone tablet.

Denham, St John the Baptist (C2): The church is set apart from the hamlet a short way down a narrow lane in pleasant, open countryside. There is now no trace of a tower and the w. wall is of red brick plastered over, with a small **Perpendicular** window set within it. The little n. door has no **porch** and at some time heavy brick buttresses were added on that side. Further to the e. there was once a chapel and the large arch that linked it with the **nave** remains in the wall, filled with red brick. A small **vestry** was added to the n. side of the late C13 **chancel**, possibly at the time of a major restoration in 1873, and the e. window in **Tudor** form is of the same period. The square-headed side windows have **ogee** shapes in the **tracery**, and the **priest's door** has a continuous deep roll moulding and simple **dripstone**. Two more heavy red brick buttresses were added close together where the chancel joins the nave on the s. side, and they stand on the foundations of the **rood loft** stair turret; between them you will see part of the little upper doorway that gave access to the rood. Judging by the shape of the outer arch, the tall brick **porch** dates from the C17, and that may be a clue to the age of the other brickwork. There is a **scratch dial** on the e. **jamb** of the inner doorway dating from a time when there was no porch, and a C13 closing ring has survived on the door itself.

The **roof** of the nave has continuous **arch-braces** which rise to stub posts under the ridge, and below the w. window is a most interesting inscription. The Latin text translates: 'William de Kirksby, Prior of Norwich placed me here. On whose soul may God have mercy Amen.' He was prior from 1280 to 1290 and the parish was one of the Benedictines' benefices. The small, oblong slab of stone was originally outside in the e. wall; its new position will ensure that the inscription remains legible. There is a C15 angel in yellow stain holding a scroll in the tracery of the window above, together with a few simply patterned **quarries**. The bowl of the octagonal **font** carries an inscription recording its restoration in 1876, and across the nave you will find that the n. doorway still has its drawbar in a deep slot. Nearby stands a bell cast by John Darbie of Ipswich in 1614, and that implies that the tower was still standing in the early C17. The arch with its triple shafts that led to the C13 n. chapel shows up boldly, and just beyond, under a low arch, lies a lovely late C13 stone effigy of a lady. She was probably a member of the Bedingfield family and her tomb may have been in the chapel originally. The figure is only 4ft 4in. long, and she wears a typical head-dress of the period graced by a chaplet decorated with little roses and

shields; her hands clasp a heart to her breast, and her feet rest on a mutilated but still recognisable lion. Two small angels each support her head with a wing; see how the naked foot of the nearer one is exposed as he kneels. There is no sign of the rood stair inside the church and the medieval **screen** itself has gone. Over the chancel arch hangs a framed set of Charles I **Royal Arms**. Well painted on board, with lively mantling, it is rated the best of the five in the county from that period.

The choir stalls in the chancel are C19, but they made use of C14 bench ends with **poppyheads**, and against the wall on both sides there are three stalls with **misericords**. They have leaf supporters and plain pendant centres, and 'T.B.' inscribed his initials on one of them on the s. side in 1719. A **ledgerstone** under the **altar** shows the outline of a **brass** which commemorated Edward Bedingfield, who died in 1574. There is a rubbing displayed in the vestry which shows his 25in. figure clad in a long gown trimmed with fur above a clear inscription. It was engraved on the back of an older Flemish brass which was made for Jacobus Weghechede, a religious of the abbey of Bergues St Winock. The extraordinary thing is that another section of this brass was put to similar use in 1580 for a tomb in the church at Yealhampton, Devon. That displays the heads of the **Blessed Virgin, St James**, and Weghechede. One can only assume that the original was taken from its tomb and used in a London workshop to provide the two memorials in Devon and Suffolk. The brass is not displayed but may be seen by arrangement.

Earl Soham, St Mary (E4): Set attractively on slightly rising ground, the church presents its w. face to the village street and the tower is one of those whose proportions seem instinctively good, with four subtly proportioned **set-offs** and **flushwork** decoration in the **base course**,

Earl Soham, St Mary

---

buttresses, and battlements. The w. doorway has **fleurons** in the mouldings, **Tudor roses** in the **spandrels**, a niche each side of the w. window, and another above it. The latter is distinguished by a more elaborate canopy which has a little head pendant and there is a demi-angel below the image stool. Farther up a flushwork shield carries a **St Andrew's** cross, a reminder that the church was originally dedicated to that saint. The tower was built in the 1470s and its real distinction lies in the fact that it is one of the very few that are signed both by donor and builder, with inscriptions on the w. buttresses about 12ft up. One would need a ladder and some patience to decipher them but they read: (n.w.) 'Campanilis eius thomus edouard fuit autor huius christopher simus optimus auxiliator' (Thomas Edward built this tower with Christopher his best helper); (s.w.) 'Ranulphus Colnitt bona maxima contulit isti ecclesiae sacrae cui prosit gratia christia' (Ranulph Colnett conferred the greatest gifts upon this sacred church; may the grace of Christ advantage this). The **nave** is cement-rendered and the 'Y' **tracery** windows with their worn **headstops** on the s. side of the **chancel** point to a date around 1300. Canon Abbay was rector from 1880 to 1928 and was responsible for much restoration work – the e. window has a **corbel** head which is a portrait of him, the other being Sir Aukland Colvin, the patron. There is a **priest's door** to the s. and the s.e. nave buttress has one complete **scratch dial** and traces of two more. The low C15 s. **porch** has late **Perpendicular** side windows and the tall medieval figure holding a staff on the gable may have been a statue of St Andrew. Below it is a worn rampant lion and a modern inscription: 'Christ who died upon the rood, grant us grace, our end be good'. Just inside, the stone block on the floor may have been the shaft of a **preaching cross**, and you will see shields bearing **emblems of the Trinity** and **instruments of the Passion** set against foliage in the spandrels of the inner doorway.

Within, there is a modern **screen** with massive turned uprights and false **gallery** front in the tower arch, and beyond it is a good C17 **Holy table**. The C15 **font** is a familiar local design, with squat lions seated round the shaft, angel heads below the bowl, and angels bearing shields in the panels – all effectively defaced. A Robert Kinge was apparently the donor but the inscription round the base is no longer legible. The C17 cover is in excellent condition, with solid scrolls reaching up to a turned **finial**. The nave was rebuilt in the C15 and given a handsome double **hammerbeam roof**, with carved spandrels and cambered collar beams carrying **king-posts** under the ridge. The **wall posts** come down to niches under **ogee** canopies, and although the carved figures remain they have nearly all lost their heads. The C15 benches below were saved from demolition by Canon Abbay and were restored by Archdeacon Darling's group of woodworkers at Eyke. They caught the spirit of the originals so well that it is quite difficult to tell old from new in some cases. The ends are 3in. thick and have window tracery deeply carved in the solid; the large, squat **poppyheads** are flanked by animals and figures. Look particularly for the C15 figures on the 5th bench from the e., s. side – a man with a log on his shoulder and a woman setting up a sheaf of corn, and there is a good standing figure with a basket 4th from the e. on the n. side. For comparison, examples of the modern work are the two heads 6th from the w., n. side and the elephant against the s. wall. Nearby hangs a fine set of Charles II **Royal Arms** painted on canvas, and Gaffin provided a characteristic early C19 tablet for members of the Hinde family on the n. wall – deep sarcophagus with urn and drooping willow branches on top. The pulpit is a pleasing **Jacobean** piece, tall, with blind arched panels and strapwork under the canted book ledge, and a hexagonal **tester** above the backboard. There is a little **piscina** in a recess close by marking the site of a nave **altar** and, although there is no drain, the cavity in the opposite wall was probably another. The chancel arch would seem to date from the time when the nave was rebuilt, and the concave faces of the **responds** are matched by the **capitals**. There is now no screen and just beyond on the r. is a window in memory of Canon Abbay with beautiful glass by **Margaret E. Aldrich Rope**, one of her last commissions. In glowing colours, **St Edmund** stands against a background of oak tree and flowers, while **St Felix** has a church on a cliff behind him. The **communion rails** have turned **balusters** below a heavy top rail and are probably late C17, and the tall C14 piscina has a hint of the ogee shape in the arch and remnants of **crocket** and **cusp** decoration. The excellent Jacobean chest in the n.w. corner has typical decoration like the pulpit but is longer than usual, with four rather than three front panels. The pallid 1880s glass in the e. window is not memorable but turning back one has a good view of the w. window – a much better design which may have been provided by **Burlison & Grylls**; the Bethlehem angels and shepherds fill the centre of the three **lights**, and two of Christ's miracles flank a little vignette of Noah's ark below.

Earl Stonham, St Mary (C5): This is a cruciform church with **transepts** but there is no firm evidence to show whether or not it ever had a central tower, and a single **lancet** in the **chancel** n. wall is an indication that it was begun no later than the C13. Close by, a brick **rood stair** with blocked window is set in the corner. The n. transept was rebuilt and much work was done on the e. end generally in an 1870s restoration by Cory & Ferguson of Carlisle. There are no **aisles** and the **nave** was widened in the C14; then

about 1460 it was given a lavish **clerestory** entirely panelled in **flushwork** so that the new **roof** should be well lit. The C15 tower replaced one that had stood at the s.w. corner of the church and the old w. window of the nave, with its **reticulated tracery**, was re-used. Below it are doors with their original tracery, the archway has **paterae** and crowns in the mouldings, and there is a flushwork **base course**. Nicely graduated buttresses rise to the bell stage where one of the large **Perpendicular** bell openings is offset to leave room for the stair turret. They have a line of **quatrefoils** under them and there are stepped flushwork battlements with more quatrefoils ranged below them. The C14 s. **porch** has remnants of barge boards above a wide **trefoil** niche and the windows are set within large blank arches.

Passing the remains of a **stoup**, one enters a lofty interior dominated by the magnificent chestnut roof. Its **hammerbeams** are carved as angels (now minus their heads) bearing shields, some of which still have recognisable **Passion emblems** – the hammer and pincers are on the s. side above the door and there is a chalice and wafer representing the mass at the w. end on the n. side. The hammerbeams alternate with false hammerbeams whose posts continue down to form richly carved octagonal pendants which match those below the collar beams and **king-posts**. Heavy **wall posts** with shields at their bases carry canopied figures, and the **wall plates** with demi-angels are widened by two more ranges of decoration. All **arch-braces** are richly carved – largely with leaf forms, but look for the fox with a goose in his mouth and a large duck on the s. side above the door. On the tower wall a 1680s tablet for Thomas Goodall says that he was a true member of the Church of England, approving its discipline and practising its doctrine, and adds that his father-in-law was 'exemplary for piety towards God and loyalty to his martyred sovereign Charles I'. No doubt

Earl Stonham, St Mary

the widow had the wording of it! The C15 **font** has good carvings in the bowl panels: w., a seeded pomegranate within a crown of thorns, and an angel with a **Trinity emblem**; s., a pierced Sacred Heart within a wreath of leaves; n., a seeded rose; e., a lattice of ribbons with fleur de lys terminals. These are so like those at Creeting St Peter that both fonts must have been carved by the same mason. Most of the benches at the w. end are original and the worn inscription on the front elbow n. side reads: 'Orate pro [anima] Necolai Houk' (Pray for the soul of Nicholas Hook). In front of the n. door is a most interesting chest of the late C13. Ironwork does not play an important part (as in the C14 Icklingham chest [Vol.1]) and the roundels of chip carving are strongly reminiscent of **Norman** stonework. The nave benches with varied **poppyheads** were made by local joiner James Gibbons in 1874 and carved by Robert Godbold of Harleston.

The early C14 arches to the transepts have **paterae** in the mouldings, and above the chancel arch there is a **Doom** painting which is still recognisable. (As with the roof, binoculars are helpful for appreciation of the detail). A small window was inserted just to the r. to give extra light for both Doom and rood. On the s. transept wall there is a large fragment of a **St George** painting and in the n. transept hang sketches of two more frescoes that have been destroyed. The pulpit of the 1680s is a good example of the period and on a shelf behind stand three unique **hour-glasses**. They contained differing amounts of sand to record a quarter, half, and three-quarters of an hour. The iron holder to the r. held a standard hour-glass. The first range of choir stalls is Victorian and carries **Evangelistic symbols** but the others are medieval, with wide book slopes, and there are figures of a bagpiper, a man with an axe, and a **pelican in her piety** on the n., with remains of a **woodwose** and a dragon on the s. Two of the poppyheads are carved with triple faces like the one at Hawkedon [Vol.1] and three of the stall fronts were adapted at an early stage to take tracery which probably came from the **rood screen**. The roof was remodelled in the 1870s restoration to match the nave roof, as were those in the transepts. In the **sanctuary** there is a C14 **piscina** under a **crocketted** gable, but note that the double drain slab was part of a C13 model. The **dropped-sill sedilia** alongside are divided by a stone arm rest carved with a hound (now minus his head). Across in the n. wall a plain oblong recess served either as an **Easter sepulchre** or an **aumbry** and the cross at the back of it was found in the floor of the s. transept. Henry Hughes of **Ward & Hughes** designed the e. window in 1874 – insipid figures of the risen Christ flanked by a Nativity and the **three Marys** at the tomb. The early C17 **altar**, with its turned and carved legs, was probably a domestic table originally and has been cut down and extended for its present role.

East Bergholt, St Mary (E9): Constable country attracts a host of visitors and many of them come to visit this beautiful and interesting church in the village where the artist was born. One of the pleasures of a tour of the churchyard is to identify the vantage points for his various paintings and sketches – from the s.w. in 1796, the n. arch of the tower 1806, from the n.e. 1818, and his first exhibited work in oils of the **porch**, possibly in 1810. The 1818 pencil sketch includes his parents' tomb which lies in the far n.e. corner of the churchyard – a broad, low slab resting on a wide plinth. The church's unique bell cage stood to the e. of the **chancel** until the late C17 when it was moved to its present position. It dates from the C16 and was probably a compromise solution when plans for completing the tower were abandoned. It sits attractively under a tiled pyramid roof, and the bells in their heavy frame can be seen through the lattice of the timbered walls. It is the only ring in the world that is handled by ringers standing on the frame and controlling the bells with wooden stays rather than ropes.

Turning to the church itself, we have a fine building that is both impressive and picturesque. There was an earlier tower, but tradition has it that Cardinal Wolsey financed its replacement as a sop to local opinion when he acquired nearby Dodnash priory. It was begun

about 1525 but Wolsey's death in 1530 brought things to a standstill. Judging by the polygonal buttresses, **ashlar base course**, and broad side arches, it was to have been a massive and lavish design with echoes of Dedham. Stubs of vaulting show within and, having been built up to the limit of consecrated ground and beyond, the arches to n. and s. would still have allowed processions to circle the church. The **aisles** date from the C16, with tall **transomed** windows on the s. side; note how the flint work varies there, with the later and better work at the w. end. Delicately canopied niches are set in the buttresses and a profusion of tiny shields in the battlements. Above them, the **clerestory** forms virtually a wall of glass. There is a sharp drop in height to the aisle chapel, and that too has canopied niches in the buttresses. The mid-C14 chancel has later windows, plastered walls, and a **flushwork** base course. The n. aisle and chapel are largely in brick and there is a substantial **rood stair** turret at the corner of the aisle. Polygonal in plan, it has two **set-offs**, and the star (the heraldic 'mullet') of the De Vere earls of Oxford is incorporated in a little window. They were Lords of the Manor and this particular 'star-on-star' badge was used by John, the 14th Earl, 1513-26. The n. aisle windows are simpler, with four plain **lights** under **Tudor** arches, but the n. doorway is quite elaborate, with initials and merchant's mark in the **spandrels** and a band of shallow niches set in the arch. Above the shell of the tower base, which is all open to the sky, the **nave** w. wall is all brick, and the windows were not inserted until 1905. Above them on the gable, the clock made by Nathaniel Hedge of Colchester in 1764 is crowned with an attractive cupola. The inscription on the w. door is a copy made in 1886 of the medieval original. The initials represent a Latin text which translates: 'For Holy Church John Fine, Francis Yual and others made [this gift] in honour of Jesus and Mary'. The tall C15 s. porch has plain plastered walls, although the buttresses retain their niches and flushwork; a handsome sundial is centred below the gable. A stair turret leading to the upper room is set in the angle between porch and aisle and rises well above the **roof** line.

Within, the early C16 nave **arcades** are tall, with elegant **quatrefoil piers** and deep hollow mouldings. The aisle roofs are largely original but the nave roof dates from 1854. A major restoration in 1870 cleared out all the **box pews** but luckily the attractive pale brick floors were not replaced by tiles. Solid oak screens enclose choir **vestries** at the w. end of both aisles. The **font** of 1862 is a cumbrous affair with a variety of symbols in the bowl panels. The nave w. window contains fine **Arts and Crafts** glass by Hugh Arnold. He was one of **Christopher Whall's** pupils and was killed in 1915 after only a few years' work. Dating from 1906, there are lovely figures of the Four Virtues in the lower lights, with Patience holding an hour-glass. They are set in clear glass with simple borders, and above are displayed the shields of the province of Canterbury, Norwich and St Edmundsbury & Ipswich dioceses, and Emmanuel College, Cambridge. The n. aisle windows are filled with **Lavers & Barraud** glass commemorating members of the Hughes family – Sir Richard (1862), Sir Edward (1880), and Sir Alfred (1890). Scenes and individual figures are largely drawn from the New Testament and are very attractive. Under the centre window is the remnant of Anna Parker's tomb of 1656, a shield flanked by crests of camel and muzzled bear. To the l. is an anonymous epitaph cut in stone which probably dates from the C16 or early C17:

> What ere thou art here reader see
> In this pale glass what thou shalt be,
> Despised wormes and putrid slime,
> Then dust forgot & lost in time.
> Birth, beuty, welth may gild thy east,

> But ye black grave shadowes thy west.
> Ther earthly glorys shorte liv'd light,
> Sets in a long & unknown night.
> Here till the sun of glory rise,
> My dearest darke and dusty lyes,
> But clothed with his morning raye,
> Ther polish't with dust shall shine for aye.
> Reader first pay to this bedewed stone
> The tribute of thy tear & then be gone.

At the e. end of the aisle stands a large late C14 chest with a curved, worm-eaten top; the centre hasp and broad backplate were clearly designed to resist forcing. Nearby, John Mattinson's epitaph tells us that he was 'eleven years the beloved schoolmaster of this Town and then unfortunately shott' in 1723. In the corner is the door leading to the **rood stair** turret and its position shows that the medieval loft and **screens** stretched right across the church.

Over in the s. aisle there is a C19 architect's drawing of a projected tower completion design and many will be glad that nothing came of it (although Long Melford shows how successful such projects can be). A little farther along is a most interesting drawing by John Constable of the chancel as it was before the Victorian's version of the wind of change. As at Whitby in Yorkshire, the arch was spanned by a substantial **gallery** resting on classical pillars. The 1877 glass in the centre window is the artist's memorial by the Cambridge firm of his namesake. **St Luke** sketches the **Blessed Virgin** in the centre and the Ascension spans the three lights at the top, but it is ironic that the window is the worst in the church when it should have been the best. There are C19 painted boards with the Creed and Lord's Prayer above the arch into the aisle chapel, and the modern screen below, with its coved canopy, is excellent. The chapel was at one time walled off and used as a vestry, but it was restored to use in the mid-C19 and the roof dates from 1866. The **communion rails** incorporate sections of medieval screen work that were discovered in 1905 and some of the old choir stalls were installed as benches. The compact e. window has good glass of 1900 by Lavers & Westlake – six of the **Seven Works of Mercy** in well-painted panels, with angels in the **tracery**. The glass in the side windows of 1873 and 1892 is by the same firm but not of the same quality. There is a tall image niche to the l. of the **altar**, and a **consecration cross** roundel can be seen on the n. wall by the rails.

Moving back into the nave, have a look at the **brass** in the floor at the e. end. It is the only one that remains and is most attractive; it commemorates Robert Alfounder. He was once a churchwarden here, dying in 1639, and the 23in. figure has him sporting a Van Dyck beard and wearing a cloak, high boots, and spurs. With shield and inscription, it is the only example of its period in the county, and I wonder whether it was laid after **Dowsing** came breaking things in 1641. There is no mention in his journal but it is said that he ripped up 80lb of brasses and destroyed the parish registers. The piers of the chancel arch are mid-C14 but the arch was renewed when the nave was rebuilt, and on either side there are ledges that lent support to the rood loft. The heavy octagonal pulpit was both carved and given by a Mr Rimmer in the 1870s, while the chancel screen with its pretty fan-vaulted coving was designed by Sir T.G. Jackson in 1920 and made by Farmer & Brindley. At one time the n.e. chapel was the preserve of the Lords of the Manor but it now houses the organ, and just beyond it, in the n. wall, is an interesting example of an **Easter sepulchre**. Restored in 1920, the red and black C15 painting at the back has the hazy outline of the resurrected Christ set within luxurious foliage (possibly of lily and pine, alluding to the prophecy in the Book of Joel). The grandfather of John Constable's intended was

the Revd Durand Rhudde, the rector, and for a while he was strongly opposed to the marriage. After Maria's death and burial at Hampstead, Constable commissioned the sculptor Alfred Stothard to cut the plain tablet on the wall above the Easter sepulchre to commemorate her and her grandparents. Next to it is a **touchstone** tablet in an alabaster frame for an earlier rector, William Jones, who died in 1636. A charming little library of books is carved on the top and painted as though they were bound in scarlet calf and vellum with gilt edges. Opposite on the s. wall is the monument to Edward Lamb, a Lord of the Manor who endowed the local school and died in 1617. It is in alabaster, with traces of colour, and two finely carved figures draw curtains aside from the niche where his little effigy kneels in flowing robes. A quirky acrostic is arranged on the brackets at the bottom (Elizabeth Bull's monument at Sproughton is similar and, as she was a relative, one mason may have carved both). The communion rails are good specimens of the brass telescopic variety that combined utility with ingenuity in the eyes of the mid-Victorians. Prior to his screen, Sir T.G. Jackson had designed the oak choir stalls and **reredos** in 1904, and the latter has a relief of the supper at Emmaus flanked by the **Annunciation** figures below a curved top and angel **finials**. The **piscina** has a thick stone **credence shelf** and there are **dropped-sill sedilia** alongside. East Bergholt has the best range of Lavers, Barraud & Westlake glass in the county, and the n. **sanctuary** window has an Annunciation paired with a **Visitation** of 1892, while on the s. side there is a full-length scene of Christ meeting the fishermen on the shore. There is a considerable contrast between the creamy tones of these designs and the much sharper colours of the e. window (the firm's first commission here in 1867), where the subjects of the five main panels are: the Nativity, Christ's baptism, the Crucifixion, the **three Marys**, and doubting **St Thomas**.

Easton, All Saints (F4): The great house was demolished in 1923 and there are new developments within the park, but the 1830s crinkle crankle wall is largely intact and is said to be the longest in the world. A section of it lines the w. boundary of the churchyard and joins the tower, while on the n. side the **porch** was enclosed to afford a private entrance for the earls of Rochford – a nice example of noble exclusiveness. The lower stages of the unbuttressed tower are C13, but an octagonal belfry with stepped battlements decorated with **flushwork** was added some two hundred years later. The body of the church must have been built in the late C13 but a variety of **Decorated** and **Perpendicular** windows were inserted later, and a C19 **vestry** was added to the s. wall of the **chancel**. A **scratch dial** can be found low down on a **nave** buttress, and there

Easton, All Saints: C17 Wingfield pew

is a small niche above the decayed outer arch of the porch.

Seen from outside, there is a variation in the **roof** lines of nave and chancel, but the timber framework within is uninterrupted and there are heavy **tie-beams** with **king-posts** cross-braced to the rafters – all of which looks C19. There is a small **sanctus-bell window** in the tower and the C14 octagonal **font** has a bowl whose sides angle outwards slightly to a horizontal centre line. The heraldry of the **Hanoverian Royal Arms** over the n. door dates them before 1801 and, although uncoloured, they are a particularly fine set, beautifully carved and pierced in deep relief. The range of low **box pews** in stained pine was installed in 1816, and on the n. wall is the memorial for William, 5th (and last) Earl of Rochford, who, when he died in 1830, was the last of the House of Nassau that came over with William of Orange. The tall tablet has a bas relief of a praying woman kneeling by an urn, with a shield in scrolls at the top and an epitaph panel below. The Rochfords

gave way to the dukes of Hamilton, and the window opposite is a memorial for the 11th Duke, a stylised Nativity across three **lights** of 1863. The window to the w. of the pulpit contains more interesting glass and at the very top there is a C14 figure of a crowned woman in a blue and brown robe; her face is now very dark. Identification is debatable but she may represent **St Helen**. Below it are remains of C15 canopies and two delightful 1960s roundels of flower shapes with sun, moon, and other symbols. Across the nave a window has more C15 canopy work and below, the glass of 1964 by Michael Farrar Bell takes the form of two **Annunciation** panels in a modern version of C14 style. The **rood loft stairs** in the window embrasure show where the chancel arch stood, and the plain, panelled pulpit forms part of the suite of pews that extends a little to the e. of it to include a reader's desk. On the n. wall Dame Mary Wingfield's handsome memorial of 1675 is a large **touchstone** tablet flanked by matching Ionic columns with looped garlands at the base, and beyond, within a blocked window, is the Hon. George Savage Nassau's monument of 1823. This is a coarser version of the kneeling woman and is signed by William Pistell, so one wonders whether he provided both pieces. It is the only example of his work identified in the county. There are three **brasses** under the carpet in front of the **sanctuary** and the one on the n. side is particularly fine. It is the 3ft effigy of Radcliff Wingfeld (that is how she spelt it) who died in 1601. First wife of Sir Thomas Wingfield, her Christian name was her mother's maiden name, and she wears a farthingale drawn back to display a brocaded petticoat, with a pendent jewel below her French bonnet. On the s. side is a smooth 26in. figure in armour of the 1420s. It probably commemorates Sir Thomas Charles whose family were Lords of the Manor before the Wingfields. Alongside is the excellent brass for John Wingfeld who died in 1584, a classic example of Elizabethan

armour, with peascod breastplate, elaborate buckles, and lots of shading. The family was established in Suffolk before the Conquest and the twenty quarterings of the shield include the arms of many ancient lines. The sturdy **communion rails** are late C17 and two more sections screwed to the e. wall indicate that they were once three-sided. The late C13 **piscina** and **sedilia** have shafts with ring bases and **capitals** but are partially masked by the family pew which occupies the corner of the sanctuary. It is one of a pair installed by Sir Henry Wingfield about 1650, and though their placing on either side of the **altar** is distinctly eccentric, they are rather attractive. They have no ceilings and the low cornices, carved with wreaths and the Wingfield badge, are supported by turned shafts, with strapwork below the book ledge; the end panels are moulded and each door has a blind-arched panel. The stone **reredos** is C19 and grouped on the chancel walls are **hatchments** which form one of the best collections in the county. In date order they are for: Dame Susan Wingfield (1652 e. wall, l.); Dr Ralph Cotton (1705 e. wall, r.); Hon. Henry Nassau [?] (1741 s. wall top l.); Hon. George Richard Savage Nassau [?] (1823 s. wall bottom); Anne Nassau (1771 s. wall top r.); William, 5th Earl of Rochford (1830 nave n. wall); Alexander, 10th Duke of Hamilton (1852 n. wall top); Susan, Duchess of Hamilton (1859 n. wall bottom r.); William, 11th Duke of Hamilton (1863 n. wall bottom l.).

Edwardstone, St Mary (B9): A rough drive leads from the gatehouse into the park and from the church there are views over rolling fields with a farmhouse nearby. Edwardstone was one of Suffolk's thriving wool villages and the handsome church, well restored both in the C19 and recently, is meticulously maintained. The C15 tower, with its flint panelled **base course**, has a renewed w. window and bell openings, and there are generous **Perpendicular**

windows in the 1460s n. **aisle**. The C14 n. door was re-used and the solid n.e. **vestry** under its own gabled **roof** is as least as old as the **chancel** of about 1300. There is a C19 e. window in Perpendicular style but those on the s. side are early C14. Two new windows have been inserted in the s. wall of the **nave** and the low brick s. **porch** is largely C19, although an old cambered **tie-beam** survives below its plastered ceiling.

The interior is lovely , with a graceful C15 n. **arcade** and a single-framed **roof** above the nave. **King-posts** rise from the tie-beams, one of which is heavily warped, and the roof timbers are decorated with gilded shafts – part of the scheme devised by **G.F. Bodley** in the 1870s. He placed **sacred monograms** within sunbursts as **bosses** along the centre line of the n. aisle and designed the very attractive organ case in the chapel at the e. end. In plum and gilt, it has pierced **tracery** wings and cresting, and decorative stars link it with the roof theme. The instrument itself was rebuilt at the same time around a 'Father Smith' organ of 1670 which came from the Sheldonian in Oxford. The octagonal C14 **font** stands on a new base and has a C17 panelled **ogee** cover. Beyond it on the n. wall there are **Commandment**, Creed, and Lord's Prayer boards in triptych form matching the benefactions board over the s. door; both are likely to be Bodley designs. The **censing** angel painted high in the n.w. corner of the aisle seems to be C18 – period and placement are both unusual. The pews with their stepped square ends could be taken as typical of Bodley but in this case, as it happens, he merely repeated the form of the old seats to be found under the tower and at the w. end. The **linen-fold panelling** at the back of the nave range is a copy taken from a C16 screen that fronted the aisle chapel. Nave and aisle are lit by extremely handsome wrought iron candelabra and the **Stuart** pulpit belongs to the same family as those at nearby Milden and Little Waldingfield. On a tall turned stem, it has similar scrolls and acorn pendants below the body, blind-arched panels, and heavy scroll brackets under the canted book ledge. Unlike the others, however, this one retains its backboard and **tester**. The **rood stairs** are just behind it, and across the nave stands a double-sided lectern on a triangular shaft with lion feet. Good Victorian craftsmanship of the 1870s. An 1860s tablet with draped standards by Gaffin on the s. wall commemorates Major Richard Magenis of the 7th Fusiliers who saw action at Copenhagen and retired here, having lost an arm at Albuera in the Peninsular War. There are two early C19 tablets by **John Bacon the Younger** in the n. aisle – one commonplace for William Shepherd, and the other with a little more style for Thomas Dawson; it has an urn with knotted drapes against a grey obelisk. Farther along is the C19 **brass** of Armar Lowry-Corry, 3rd Earl Belmore, and his family and just inside the n. chapel is a largely lettered tablet for Joseph Brand, 'a pious, prudent, charitable person' who died in 1674. Below is a brass with the family arms and John Brand's epitaph. He died in 1642, 'a freind and lover of pious & godly ministers' (in other words, a thoroughgoing Puritan). The Brands were wealthy clothiers and C17 Lords of the Manor and at the e. end of the aisle is an excellent brass of about 1620 for Benjamin and Elizabeth. They are both in ruffs and gowns and she wears the fashionable calash hood; a dozen children kneel in neatly descending order and the inscription is memorable:

> To ye precious memory of Benjamin Brand of Edwardstone Hall, Esq., and Elizabeth his wife, whom when Providence, after 35 yeares of conjunction, divided, Death, after 12 dayes divorcment, reunited; who leaveing their rare examples to 6 sonnes and 6 daughters, (All nursed with her unborrowed milk), blest with poormen's prayers, embaulmed with numerous teares, Lye here reposed.

Bodley replaced the chancel roof in 1880 and it is gilded and painted overall in striking fashion, with sacred monograms at the panel intersections and heavy **wall plates** pierced with **quatrefoils**. The vicar, George Augustus Dawson, died in 1848 and Robert De Carle of Bury provided an austere tablet on the **sanctuary** n. wall which is effectively enlivened by a coloured shield of arms at the top. The elaborate **reredos** of 1910 in dark oak and muted gold is by C.G. Hare, Bodley's successor, and faithfully continues his style; pierced canopies range along the top and in the centre niche **St Mary Magdalene** kneels at the foot of the cross with the **Blessed Virgin** and **St John** each side while **Annunciation** figures take up the flanking niches. The C14 **piscina** lies under a **trefoil** arch and was probably canopied originally. The church has some interesting modern glass in varying styles. The e. window is a fine example of **Burlison & Grylls** in C15 idiom – a Crucifixion in the tracery, the Blessed Virgin and Child and **St Edmund** in the centre **light** flanked by two bishops, **St Anne**, and **St Margaret**. By the pulpit, an 1870s window contains six scenes with identifying labels in C15 style, and to the w. a 1920s Lowry-Corry memorial window has a large figure of Melchizedek in company with a very unusual pair – Abbot Samson of Bury St Edmunds and **St Edith**. In both cases the glass is probably by Burlison & Grylls.

Elmsett, St Peter (D8): The church lies n. of the village proper with only a farm for company, and its buttressed C13 tower has **lancet** windows and bell openings of varying sizes. 'Y' **tracery** of 1300 and **Perpendicular** windows are to be seen on the n. side of the **nave** as well as a blocked **Norman** lancet, and a large C17 or C18 brick buttress supports the n.e. corner of the **chancel**. The flowing **Decorated** tracery of the e. window has been renewed but is likely to have repeated the original, and in

the s. wall, the windows and **priest's door** are C14 too. A **scratch dial** can be found on the bottom r. hand corner of the s.w. chancel window and a date is cut on its sill – 1625? Another blocked Norman lancet in the s. nave wall confirms the building's age and a two-**light** C14 window has **mouchettes** and a **quatrefoil** in the tracery. The C14 **porch** was well restored in the 1970s and still has its outer wooden arch and barge boards. There is a triangular **stoup** by the inner doorway and the door itself retains its closing ring and broad bands of C14 iron work decorated with curious little pieces like tenterhooks along the edges.

Within, there are **pamment** floors and the plain w. **gallery** houses the organ. Below on the n. wall hangs a late C17 painted version of the Table of Kindred and Affinity, which was first published by Archbishop Parker in 1563 and later printed in the Book of Common Prayer. It is but right and proper that unlawful unions between close relatives should be avoided, but many of the curious conjunctions must have stemmed from a lively imagination. Examples like this one are rare and the sign-writer had a job to fit the last four of the thirty categories in at the bottom. An interesting photograph on the opposite wall shows the church decked for a Harvest Festival in the days when there were high **box pews**, and their discarded panelling now lines the nave. There is a small table placed centrally whose lovely top is a thick slice taken from an elm which blew down in 1879, and beyond it is a square Norman **font** of **Purbeck marble**. It has long been plastered over but one of the familiar blank arches shows on one corner. The plain and time-worn pyramid cover is C17 and a chest of the same period stands nearby with inlaid lozenges in the front panels. On the wall above hangs a large, handsome **Royal Arms** of Anne – subsequently dated 1758 for George II.

Dowsing paid a visit in August 1644 but found that a deputy had done his work for him and he had to be content

Elmsett, St Peter: Table of Kindred and Affinity

with rending the parson's hood and surplice – the only mention of vestments in that sorry catalogue of vandalism that is his journal. St Mary-at-Quay, Ipswich, is now redundant but its fine early C17 pulpit has found a home here. The small upper panels contain **Renaissance** motifs while below there are perspective arches in which centre pendants are applied. The bottom range consists of subdivided moulded panels between turned columns at the angles. Beyond it, a niche with a multi-**cusped** arch has a single hinge left in the rebate and so must once have had a door. The chancel arch is rather rudimentary and at high level each side there are strange masonry ledges that may have supported a **rood loft**. The **hatchment** on the chancel s. wall bears the arms of Skinner/Jones but is not precisely identifiable and opposite there is a fine monument for Edward Sherland, who died in 1609. Its design is conventional and his effigy in black gown kneels before a prayer desk within a square alabaster recess; there are painted ribbons on the frame pinned by hourglass, scythe, pick, shovel, and Bible, with a coloured **achievement of arms** between obelisks on top. The epitaph, however, is thoughtful: '. . . a painted sepulchre is but a rotten trustless treasure, and a faire gate built to oblivion . . .'. Farther along, the Revd William Talbot's 1812 memorial is a plain sarcophagus above a tablet large enough to give elbow room for an extract from his will, including the plea: '. . . I earnestly beg the parishioners of Elmset will read the inscription every time they go into the church . . .'. The **altar** is enclosed by substantial and handsome three-sided **communion rails** that were made about 1670, and there are **Commandment boards** on the e. wall. Beside the C14 **angle piscina** there are **dropped-sill sedilia** which have a little **trefoil** arch at the w. end.

A C16 rector of Elmsett achieved immortality at one remove, for his son was John Bois, one of the translators of the Authorised Version of the Bible. Thomas Fuller said: 'Whilst St Chrysostom lives, Mr Bois shall not die.' One wonders what a more recent rector felt about the stone monolith that stands defiantly across the road from the church gate: '1934. To commemorate the Tithe seizure at Elmsett Hall of furniture including baby's bed and blankets, herd of dairy cows, eight corn stacks and seed stacks valued at £1200 for tithe valued at £385.'

Eye, St Peter and St Paul (C3): Eye is one of Suffolk's ancient boroughs and the splendid and beautifully kept church is set attractively just to the e. of the old castle mound. The mighty tower rises to just over 100ft and has much in common with Redenhall,

Eye, St Peter and St Paul

the **aisle** windows have miniature **embattled transoms** in the **Perpendicular tracery**. There is no n. porch and on that side the battlements are boldly chequered above prominent **gargoyles**. The aisles lap the **chancel** as far as the **sanctuary** and there is a n.e. **vestry** with an upper room. The e. window was probably renewed as part of the restoration carried out by J.K. Colling in 1868 and the buttresses with their careful flushwork were re-worked then or a little later. The n. **clerestory** wall is plain but on the s. side there are flushwork panels between the windows. The s.e. chapel follows the line of the s. aisle but the brick battlements are lower and have terracotta tiles inserted in them deco-rated with crowned boars and lions. The **priest's door** lies snugly below a miniature flying buttress and there is another blocked doorway at the e. end of the aisle. The late C15 **porch** has suffered over the years and the dressed flints within the narrow ashlar panels on the e. side were replaced with brick at some stage. The s. face is entirely of stone and the octagonal corner buttresses are blind panelled in two stages. The base course was once decorated with monograms and the De La Pole shield crops up again, along with the **Tudor** portcullis badge and the **Blessed Virgin's** monogram. Access to the porch is now from within and one enters the church through the w. door.

The ground floor of the tower has a **fan vault** set around a circular trap door and the **gallery** above is a smaller version of the one at Mildenhall [Vol.1]. There are **hatchments** for Mary D'Eye (1749), John Sayer (1761), and Rear-Admiral Sir Charles Cunningham (1834), together with two Tudor helmets on the s. wall, and an excellent set of George III **Royal Arms** are displayed opposite. Before explor-ing the body of the church, have a look at the s. porch. Built into its w. wall is a dole table of brick with a stone top which was given by Henry Cutler in 1601. This is the place where debts,

which is a few miles away over the Norfolk border – the octagonal buttresses and a w. face completely covered with a fine web of **flushwork** in elongated panels. Begun in the 1450s, it was completed when the bells were hung in 1488, and it is interesting to see how the shape of the window arches varied significantly during those thirty years. There is a **base course** of shields set in multi-**foils** and the niches flanking the door have had their canopies chipped away. The bell openings are pairs of windows linked by a **label** and the deep parapet below the stepped battlements is panelled in **ashlar**; on the s. side an angel holds the shield of John De La Pole, Duke of Suffolk, whose badge occurs on Redenhall tower and probably ex-plains why the two have so much in common. In contrast to the w. face, the rest of the tower is severely plain up to the bell stage. The majority of the church was rebuilt in the late C15 and tithes, and church dues were traditionally paid and where bread and other charities were distributed to the poor. There is some sage advice inscribed on the tablet above:

> Seale not to soone lest thou repent to late,
>
> Yet helpe thy frende, but hinder not thy state.
>
> If ought thou lende or borrow, truly pay,
>
> Ne give, ne take advantage, though thou may,
>
> Let conscience be thy guide, so helpe thy frend,
>
> With loving peace and concord make thy end.

Corner shafts remain of the original **groined** ceiling and the C15 rebuilding thought well enough of the C13 inner doorway to use it again – rightly, for it is a fine piece. The flanking columns have stiff-leaf **capitals**, and there is a line of **dogtooth** decoration within the deeply cut mouldings of the arch. The C19 **font** has a 1930s cover designed by **Sir Ninian Comper**, who played a decisive role in beautifying the church. Turned pillars support the octagonal base of a skeletal tabernacle and it is prettily painted and gilt. The n. door is blocked by the tomb of Nicholas Cutler (1568) and his wife Elionora (1549), which was originally in the sanctuary. The **Purbeck marble** chest has small **cusped** lozenges that once contained brass shields, and there were more above the shallow, panelled recess. There are flanking columns and collared **griffins** on the pinnacles, while the pale **St Christopher** of 1921 in the window above is another Comper design. Farther along in the n. aisle wall is an additional reminder of the earlier building in the form of a shallow mid-C14 tomb recess. Its tall **ogee** arch is **crocketted**, the deep cusps are carved with shallow leaf patterns, and two of the head terminals survive. The crockets of the flanking pinnacles sport tiny heads at their bases and the arch provides a lovely setting for an outstanding figure of the Blessed Virgin and Child. Carved in natural wood

Eye, St Peter and St Paul: C15 screen panels

by Lough Pendred in the 1960s, the widely flowing and swirling cloak of Our Lady shows up boldly against a dark green background. The C14 **nave arcades** have octagonal **piers** and there are minor variations in the capitals, with the **hood moulds** on the s. side coming down to small **headstops**. The C16 **roof** is **arch-braced** and the deep **wall posts** rest on wooden **corbels** carved as heads. The w. end of the nave angles in towards the tower and there the wall posts are longer. The **roof** was extensively restored in 1868 and the small recumbent figures at the base of the braces appear to be largely C19. There are generous flower **bosses**, a canted cornice decorated with demi-angels and **paterae**, and at the e. end is a **celure**. Its panels are painted with the **sacred monogram** in red within a green wreath sprouting flowers. This is modern work but the original may well have been similar.

Below stands the church's master-piece, the 1480s **screen** that had its loft and **rood** figures replaced by Comper in 1925. The base has deep, cusped, and crocketted ogee arches above the painted panels and there are curly leaves carved and pierced in the **spandrels**. At the base is a line of crisply carved roundels containing triple **trefoils**, and note how each one is accompanied by a little panel to take up the space between the buttresses (a similar adjustment on a larger scale is the slim panel at the l. hand side of the screen which was inserted to take up the full width of the arch). The **mullions** are painted with red and green scrollery on a white ground, and there are traces of **gesso** which can also be found on the leaf trail along the top rail. The arch of the centre doorway is a particularly good example of intricate elaboration and sensitive design, with a triple range of cusping (the doors themselves have gone, together with the tracery in the main **lights**). To the r. of the entrance, one of the arches carries the inscription: 'Pray for John Gold' – a reference to the probable donor. The underside of the loft is **groined** and decorated with stars and flowers on a blue ground, and the front arches come down to tiny demi-angels. There is a **pelican in her piety** at the base of the rood cross and dragons reach out below the feet of the Virgin and **St John**, while seraphs attend on either side. The lower panels have a full range of painted figures which are by no means great art, but they have not been so badly defaced as others elsewhere and they were meticulously restored (not repainted) by Miss Pauline Plummer in the 1960s. The selection of subjects is of more than usual interest; from l. to r. they are: **Saints Paul** (or a king?), **Helen** with the true cross, **Edmund**, **Ursula** with the virgins under her cloak, Henry VI (d. 1471 but never canonised), **Dorothy**, **Barbara**, **Agnes**, **Edward the Confessor** holding the legendary ring, **John**, **Catherine** with large sword and tiny wheel in the bottom corner, **William of**

Norwich, **Lucy** smiling sweetly while carrying her bloody eyes on a book, **Thomas of Canterbury** (Blaize has been suggested but there is no sign of his wool comb), and **Cecilia**.

The C19 chamber organ in the s. aisle was restored and given by the local Bach choir in 1978, and the window to the e. of it has glass of 1876 by **Heaton, Butler & Bayne**. In the s.e. chapel there is the 1569 tomb of William Honyng which matches the Cutler monument in the n. aisle, and the e. window contains 1890s glass by H.A. Hymes on the 'Suffer little children to come unto me' theme. The side chapels are separated from the chancel by two-bay C14 arcades with **quatrefoil** pillars on tall bases and the organ is enclosed on the n. side by a handsome modern limed oak screen. The C15 clerestory continues over the chancel and the braces and **wall plates** of the roof are gaily painted. The C14 doorway to the **vestry** has been restored and the door itself is in lovely pale oak, still with its original lockplate. On the n. wall is a tablet by Harvey of Diss for the Revd Thomas Wythe who died in 1835, having been vicar here for fifty years. John Brown was a naval surgeon who died in 1732 and his memorial is on the s. wall – a shapely tablet in a dark frame below a curly cornice. At the base is a lively bas relief tableau of the Good Samaritan whose horse grazes quietly as he tends the injured man, while the two other travellers 'pass by on the other side'. After the experience of the opulence of his rood, Comper's e. window glass seems pale and vapid, with conventional figures of Christ, St John, **St Peter**, and St Paul. It does, however, include the kneeling figure of a vicar, John Polycarp Oakey (1927), in front of **St Polycarp** – seldom seen in ancient or modern glass.

Flowton, St Mary (E7): Except for minor alterations, repairs, and renewals, this small, attractive church has changed but little since it was built in the late C13 or early C14. The unbuttressed tower was originally a good deal higher but in the mid-C18 it was in danger of collapse and the bell chamber was removed; in its place we have a brick parapet and tiled pyramid **roof** complete with a little dormer door, and the **quatrefoils** that were once the belfry windows are now just below the top. It is strange to find the ground-floor entrance in the s. wall. There is a tall w. window with 'Y' **tracery** flanked by deep niches under multi-**cusped** arches. There is a small n. door and 'Y' tracery windows on the n. side of the **nave**, and a brick **vestry** rather like a little cottage complete with a chimney and sash window was added to the n. side of the **chancel** in the C18 or early C19. The e. window is small in scale but has lovely **Decorated** tracery, with three **reticulations** enclosing four quatrefoils each. On the s. side of the nave a very large slab-shaped **rood stair** turret was added in the early **Tudor** period and the large window with brick panel tracery alongside dates from about the same time. **Scratch dials** can be found on both of the nave buttresses. The low s. **porch** stands on a renewed brick base but the timbers of its frame are medieval and the outer archway is moulded.

The interior is homely, with brick floors and original **tie-beams** and **king-posts** below plaster ceilings in nave and chancel, and there is another tie-beam placed very eccentrically just in front of the e. window. A plain **gallery** is set slightly forward in the tower arch and the bowl panels of the C13 **font** are decorated with pairs of shallow blind arches typical of the period. The C17 cover has a centre **baluster** supported by gawky scroll brackets. A fragment of C14 wall decoration was uncovered on the s. side of the nave in 1973 – a scroll pattern in dark red, and farther along there is the outline of the large door that led to the rood stair. Both **screen** and loft have gone but notches below the **capitals** of the chancel arch show where they were fitted. The boxy pulpit is squeezed right into the corner and is a **Cautley** design made by Ernest

Barnes, with pierced quatrefoils under the rim. A section of C17 carving forms part of the front of the priest's stall, and there are sturdy oak **communion rails**; beyond is a C14 **lancet piscina** which still has its original wooden **credence shelf**. Before leaving the chancel, note the roof **corbel** on the n. wall carved as a devil's head with enormous ears, and back in the nave there is an interesting **ledger-stone**:

> waiting for ye Second Coming Wm. Boggis Gent. deere to his contrey by whoes free choyce he was called to be captayne of their voluntaries raysed for their defence. Pious towards God meeke & just towards men & being about 40 yeeres of age departed this life March 18 1643.

In such a fashion the Civil War touched even this little community and they thought it worthy of record.

Framsden, St Mary (E5): A lane from the village street crosses a stream and a picturesque **lych-gate** of 1899 gives access to the churchyard. The C15 tower was chosen as a model for the one to be built at Helmingham and it has four **set-offs** with linking **string courses**. There is a panelled **base course** and niches flank the w. doorway, which has **fleurons** in the mouldings and shields in the **spandrels** carved with **Passion emblems** and the arrows and crown of **St Edmund**. On walking round, one finds that the n. side of the **nave** has two tall and thin late **Perpendicular** windows in brick, with three more at **clerestory** level. The **chancel** is C14 although the e. window is again Perpendicular, and there is a **scratch dial** on the s.e. buttress. The s. **aisle** too is C14 and its e. window has three stepped and **cusped lancets**, with 'Y' **tracery** of about 1300 in the side windows. Above the **roof** the clerestory range is in **Tudor** brick. The s. **porch** has a good **flushwork** facade with three niches and the condensed dragon in the r. hand spandrel is matched by a figure

with a club like those at Cratfield and
Badingham. Overhead, the stepped
battlements continue along the w. wall
of the aisle. The inner doorway is early
C14 and the door itself is contemporary, with a closing ring combined with
one of the strap hinges.

The double **hammerbeam roof** to the
nave is much less heavy in appearance
than most and has long top hammers,
with **king-posts** on the collars and
carved spandrels. The C15 **font** is the
familiar local pattern, with battered
lions round the shaft, and mutilated
angels bearing books and shields alternate with lions in the bowl panels. The
aisle roof is apparently dated 1620 and
1676 but despite a careful look I could
not confirm this. According to **Cautley**,
it also has the name of William
Stebbing somewhere; his memorial
tablet is on the s. wall. Farther along
there is an early C14 **piscina** within a
trefoil arch resting on half-round **jamb
shafts**. C19 benches and pulpit are in
the nave and the **rood loft stairs** rise in
the n. wall although the upper doorway
has been blocked. The chancel roof and
panelled **reredos** are Victorian but, by
way of contrast, an ancient carving has
survived in the n.w. window surround.
It is a little **Saxon** figure about 8in. long
and lies on its side at the r. hand spring
of the arch. It has a triangular face, one
arm is akimbo, and it wears a full-
length tunic. Is this perhaps a remnant
of Framsden's first church or is it a
pagan cult figure? In the **sanctuary**
there is a C14 angle piscina with a
cusped ogee arch and curly **stop** to the
hood mould. The **altar** is a very nice
table of 1628 in excellent condition
which has turned columns at an angle
outside each leg and pairs of **balusters**
back and front; the shapely skirt is
pierced and the bottom stretchers are
covered by boards to form a shelf. The
stalls on the n. side of the sanctuary
have **misericords** with some mutilated
but interesting carvings. A man holds a
cruciform church with a spire, there is
a crouching lion and another beast,
both with very strange supporters, and
possibly the bottom half of an

Annunciation. Two good bench ends
form part of the choir stalls and they
have varied tracery on one side with
two quite different patterns on the
other. The Revd Loder Allen and his
wife Lydia have both a **ledger-stone**
and a marble tablet. He died in 1811,
she in 1814, and of him we learn that
'Loder had Talents for a wider Sphere',
and of his wife 'Her features stampt
with Virtue's ripen'd hue, Thus
polishing her charms with Age'. No
doubt the author knew what he meant
even if we don't. The executors of
Edmund and Margaret Barker cannot
have been too pleased with the mason
who cut the lettering on their stone by
the **priest's door**. He managed to foul
up both death dates.

Gipping, chapel of St Nicholas (B5): A
lane with broad verges leads to a pink-
washed Tudor farmhouse on one side
and this lovely little building on the
other. Open fields lie all around and
the hamlet itself is only a scattered
handful of houses. Gipping has never
had a parish church and, although the
abbey of St Osyth provided a chapel
here in the C14, this is the private
chapel built in the 1470s by Sir James
Tyrell, Lord of the Manor. His
friendship with Edmund De La Pole,
Earl of Suffolk, brought a charge of
high treason and cost him his head in
1502. Until 1850 the family mansion
stood a little way to the e. but only a
few farm buildings and a large pond are
left to mark the spot. Tombstones have
not been cleared from the churchyard
for, not being a parish church, there
never were any (although it has been
noted that Thomas Tyrell was buried
here in 1585). It became a free chapel
administered by trustees to cater for
the local people in the C18 and so it
remains today. After crossing the
footbridge from the lane, it is worth a
stroll to the s. boundary to view the
chapel as a whole and to appreciate its
remarkable beauty. Tall for its length,
there is chequered **flushwork** below
the broad eaves, and **transomed**

Gipping, Chapel of St Nicholas

windows fill most of the wall space. There are variations in the **tracery** between **nave** and **chancel** but the **ogee** shape figures in both. Doorways are centred on both sides of the nave and form a cleverly integrated design with the windows above them (a feature encountered again at Elmswell [Vol.1] and Woodbridge [Vol.3]). On either side, blank arches filled with dressed flints align with two-**light** windows overhead, and the narrow space between the pairs of lights is filled with a band of dainty flushwork flanked at the top by **mouchette** roundels. Contained beneath a **dripstone** which matches the other windows, the unit merges with the whole facade. Nave and chancel buttresses are worked with small flushwork panels which have **crocketted finials** delicately cut in the **ashlar** above each. The badge of the Tyrell family is a triangular interlace of bow shapes called the 'Tyrell knot' (a **rebus** on 'tirailleur', which is French for bowman). To be seen all over the building, it is matched by two interlaced hearts because Sir James married Anne, daughter of Sir John Arundell, and it was her family's badge. More puzzling is the inscription 'AMLA' carved on diagonal labels on the buttresses. Some have said that it stands for 'Ave Maria laetare alleluia' (Hail Mary, rejoice! alleluia'), but another possibility is that it is some form of Anne's name – possibly Anne Morley Lanherne Arundell. Sir James's mother was a Darcy and their shield of three rosettes is to be found on a chancel s. buttress, while the shaped shields on the e. buttresses carry the arms of Tyrell (s.e.) and Arundell (n.e.). There are tiny **sacred monograms**, crowned 'AMRs' for the **Blessed Virgin**, and 'T' for Tyrell on the n.e. buttress, and round the corner is the **vestry** which, judging by its junction with the chancel, was slightly later than the rest of the building. It originally had two windows and may well have been designed as quarters for a chaplain; it has a fireplace. The chimney shaft is elaborately disguised as a blind bay

window, with transomed lights filled
with flushwork, and above the set-
back upper section the Tyrell arms
have their two panther supporters – a
rare instance of a commoner being
granted this distinction. Five shields in
the upper panels are carved with
various combinations of family arms
and from e. to w. they are:
Clopton/Darcy,   Tyrell/Darcy,
Tyrell/Arundell, Arundell/Morley,
and Tyrell/Morley. Round the corner,
a little doorway with the now familiar
badge in the **spandrels** has 'Pray for Sir
Jamys Tirell. Dame Anne his wyf'
carved in the moulding, and the
wording shows that it was done in their
lifetime. Unlike many churches, the n.
side equals the s. in richness, but then
one comes to the tower. In brick but
faced with stucco and given commonplace windows, it was probably added
in the late C16 or C17 and mars the
perfection of the chapel itself.

The charming interior is full of light
and beautifully maintained. Looking
up at the almost flat C15 ceiling, with
its panels of heavily moulded timbers
and folded leaf motif on the **wall plate**,
you will realise that the present **roof**
was placed above it and the e. wall
heightened in consequence. There was
a major restoration in 1938 and the
seating and woodwork were refurbished in 1970. The oak benches at the
w. end have been stripped of paint and
those on the s. side are quite plain. The
range opposite came in the early C19
from the Tyrell chapel in Stowmarket
church and once again the family
badge appears; there is a tiny face
worked on the corner of a moulding on
the back bench and three of the others
have broad book slopes. This fact,
taken with the tracery at the front,
suggests that they were once part of a
set of stalls. Note the interesting little
pattern incised on part of the leading
edge. A **hatchment** for Edmund Tyrell
who died in 1799 hangs in the blank
tower arch and the C15 drum **font** has
large **paterae** above the octagonal stem.
The C18 panelled pews and matching
pulpit in deal are painted pale cream,

with the tops left bare – a convention
continued in the churches of New
England. The flattened chancel arch
has token **castellated capitals** and although there is now no **screen**, the
stairs to the **rood loft** remain in the s.
wall. Had the Victorians carried out a
re-ordering here, the interesting painting on the e. wall would surely not
have survived. Carefully restored by
Maurice Keevil in 1971, it displays
olive-brown classical columns draped
with gold-fringed scarlet curtains
which spread over the top of the
window, their tassels hanging the
length of the splays. The **balusters** of
the **communion rails** are like those
seen in countless C18 country house
staircases and there is a small plain
piscina. All the windows probably
contained stained glass originally but
the chapel suffered badly during the
Civil War and Commonwealth. The
remnants   were   restored   and
rearranged in the e. window in 1938. It
has been suggested that the style of
painting indicates work by late C15
Westminster glaziers for there are **Renaissance** motifs and the modelling
and shading are much more subtle
than usual. At the bottom, Tyrell
names and family arms appear again,
with their crest in the l. hand light – a
splendid yellow peacock's tail issuing
from a boar's mouth. The centre panel
now has five **Passion emblems** on little
shields held by angels' hands, and to
the l. is a figure of the Blessed Virgin in
exquisitely delicate colouring. Her
hands are crossed against her breast
and tears course down her cheeks. On
the other side **St John**, wearing a
matching robe, weeps with her. No
doubt they were separated by a Crucifixion panel that was destroyed in the
C17. Above in the centre is the figure of
an archbishop in red cope and embroidered   gloves   (**St   Thomas   of
Canterbury**?), to the l., a bishop (**St
Nicholas**, or more probably, an abbot of
St Osyth's?), to the r., a king (**St Edward
the Confessor**?). Everything else is
fragmentary except some fine golden
canopies. When leaving this charming

Gipping, Chapel of St Nicholas: C15 Blessed Virgin

place, note the pilgrim cross incised on the e. **jamb** of the door.

Gislingham, St Mary (B4): This is a generously proportioned church for a small village – over 120ft from end to end, and the distinctive red brick tower with diminishing polygonal buttresses was a relatively late addition, being built by Robert Petto of Bramford in 1639. There is a heavy stair turret to the s. with a faded sundial, and a stone in the n. wall records that John Darbie gave £100 towards the rebuilding. He may have been the Ipswich bell founder who cast two of the bells in 1671. The early C14 **chancel** has a fine e. window with **reticulated tracery** beneath a later arch, and there is a **priest's door** in the s. wall. The **nave** was lengthened westward in the late

C15 and the original tower was replaced by another which collapsed in 1598. So things remained until the advent of the new tower forty years later. The late C15 n. **porch** is handsome and the inscription across the front translates: 'Pray for the souls of Robert Chapman and Rose his wife who built this porch to the honour of God.' There are large flat lion supporters to the outer arch, an angel holds a shield at the apex, and suspended shields are carved within the moulding and on the inner surface. The shields in the **spandrels** carry the arms of **St Edmund** and East Anglia, and there is a panelled parapet with central canopied niche. The **roof** was renewed in 1661 (see the churchwardens' initials over the inner door) and the principal timbers have attractive gouge-cut decoration.

There are no **aisles** and the nave is over 20ft wide, spanned by a lovely double **hammerbeam** roof. The struts resting on the lower hammers are tall and there is plenty of space between the collars and the ridge. The wooden pulleys which remain on the 6th and 9th collar beams were probably used to raise and lower lights, and another to the r. of the chancel arch was possibly used for the **Lenten veil**. The new tower was offset to the n. and a murky set of George III **Royal Arms** on a shaped board hangs above the arch. Below it is a gimcrack boarded **gallery**. The C15 **font** stands in the centre of the nave and there are remnants of an inscription on the top step which showed that it, like the porch, was a gift of the Chapman family. Four fat lions guard the base and the bowl panels are carved with the **Evangelistic symbols** alternating with angels holding shields – w., a **Trinity** emblem; n., arms of St Edmund; s., chalice and wafer symbolising the sacrament of the mass; e., what I think is the pot and lily emblem of the **Blessed Virgin**. To the w. of the s. door are the remains of **consecration crosses** which mark the beginning of the C15 extension. The w. range of medieval benches has small

poppyheads, and backs with turned **finials** were added in the C17. There are early C19 plain deal **box pews** of low quality and in poor condition e. of the font, but on the n. side they are built round a fine C18 **three-decker pulpit**. It is severe in style and grained to represent oak; the deep and compact **tester** has small painted flower discs in its panels, there is a seat in the pulpit, and a large **hour-glass stand** is attached to the reading pew. Its position well down the nave is typical of the arrangement to be found in a **Prayer book church**. To the r. are traces of Elizabethan texts and long ranges of C18 hat pegs are to be found farther w. on both sides of the nave. The box pews conceal more medieval seating and the front bench end on the s. side has a very worn seated figure on the elbow. The nave n.e. window contains a considerable amount of C15 glass. The figure of **St Catherine** minus her face can be recognised top l., there is a fine eagle roundel, and below it are the shields of the Toppesfield, Chirche, and Clouting families. They are surrounded by lovely tendrils of the blue columbine, and white flowers which **Cautley** identified as meadow saffron. These are some of the earliest flower paintings in the county.

Like the tower, the chancel is offset to the n. and there is a large square opening to the l. of the arch. Beyond is an **arch-braced** roof and the **corbels** carry figures bearing texts, books, and (possibly) musical instruments. The one over the priest's door looks like a small organ, with a lute to the w. There is a well-turned set of sturdy C17 **communion rails** and the top of the rather nice Elizabethan melon-legged table was grained to match the pulpit. The **reredos** and **decalogue** panels painted on zinc are C19 and there is an elaborate pair of 1890s Gothic niches for memorial tablets – one on each wall by the rails. The Victorian restoration apparently did away with the **piscina**. Anthony Bedingfield, who died in 1652, has a large monument on the chancel n. wall. The heavy kneeling figure, in black robes, clutches white gloves and is set in a round-headed niche with grey **Corinthian** columns each side; a **cartouche** of arms sits within the broken **pediment** and the Greek and Latin epitaph is cut in a square **touchstone** tablet below. Mary Darby's memorial on the opposite wall is much more restrained and attractive. The alabaster oval records that she died in 1646 and gave money 'for teaching poore children to reade Englishe by their exsample'.

When leaving via the tower, have a look at the record of a long-length peal rung in 1822 – 10,080 changes of Grandsire in 6hrs 35mins. Its real interest lies in the fact that round the edge the tools of each ringer's trade are shown. The treble ringer was a sexton (spade and coffin), the 2nd and 5th were blacksmiths, the 3rd was a bricklayer, the 4th has, I believe, a turf-cutter's spade, and the tenor ringer was probably a carpenter. In 1987 the huge **Perpendicular** nave windows had recently been re-leaded but the whole interior was in a distressing condition of filth and decay. There was no sign of the panels of the old **rood screen** or the font cover and it was difficult to do justice to an intrinsically fine building. I hope that progress towards complete restoration has not been long delayed.

Gosbeck, St Mary (D6): Like neighbouring Ashbocking and Crowfield, the church is well away from its parent village and the ancient moats to the n.e. suggest that the original settlement was in that direction. It is a tiny building almost overwhelmed by the late C14 tower that stands on the s. side and serves as a **porch**. Above the outer arch a pretty little niche has shields in the **spandrels** of its **cusped ogee** arch, and there is **Decorated tracery** in the bell openings below the **flushwork** battlements. On walking round, one finds three graves to the w. with curious humpbacked brick bodies between head and foot stones, and there is a C14 w. window in the **nave**. The body of the church, however, is a good deal older, for the plain n. doorway and the **lancet** beyond it are **Norman** or even late **Saxon**. The earlier dating is made more likely by the **long and short work** that survives in the n.e. and s.e. corners of the nave. The **vestry** and **chancel** were rebuilt in 1848 and the e. window appears to date from another restoration in 1883.

The entrance door is made of ancient lapped boards, and just inside to the l. the small iron-clad door leading to the tower is a reminder that church and parish valuables were often stored there in the Middle Ages. The **font** is C19 and a memorial screen of 1900 divides the nave behind the pitch pine benches. Overhead is a restored **hammerbeam roof** with collars and **king-posts** under the ridge and large flowers applied to the hammers. The pulpit was reconstructed on a new stone base but the blind-arched panels at least are **Jacobean**. The chancel arch was apparently removed during one of the restorations but a section of the old **rood screen** was saved and the five panels now hang on the n. wall. They have rather an unusual pattern of tracery, with lozenges at the bottom enclosing small shields, and there are dull but extensive remains of gilt and colour. C19 metal **decalogue** panels flank a somewhat later **reredos** which has well-painted figures within panels enriched with **gesso** backgrounds; there is a Crucifixion in the centre with the raising of Jairus's daughter on the l. and the raising of Lazarus on the r. The 1890s glass displays panels of Christ in the Garden of Gethsemane, the Resurrection, and Ascension above scenes of Bethlehem, the presentation in the Temple, and Christ's baptism. Terribly solemn but well drawn and not unpleasing, it is by **Heaton, Butler & Bayne**.

Great Bealings, St Mary (F6): A row of stately limes comes up across the meadow from the bridge to line the n. side of the churchyard. They once bordered a path leading to the Hall which lay behind the high brick wall e. of the church and they help to make this a most attractive setting. There are over 150 churches in the county under the patronage of the **Blessed Virgin**, and Great Bealings is one of the few that can be precisely linked to one of her Feast Days – a will of 1523 refers to the full dedication as 'the Nativity of Our Blessed Lady'. Although there is known to have been a church here just after the Conquest, the earliest dateable work is C13, and on walking round you will see that the w. window has **reticulated tracery** of about 1330. A number of C15 bequests mention the tower, whose **flushwork** buttresses rise to stepped battlements, and there is an **ogee**-headed niche in the n. face. The nave walls are of flint pebbles but a full-scale restoration in the 1840s and 1850s rebuilt the s. side, renewed many of the windows, and faced the **chancel** with very dense dressed flint. There is a **priest's door** to the n. and, on that side of the nave, a C19 **lancet** and a late **Perpendicular** window with stepped **transoms**. Red brick was a fashionable material in the early C16 and about 1505 Thomas Seckford used it for a new n. **porch**. The inscription over the entrance is nearly all worn away now but it asked us to pray for his soul and that of his wife Margaret. There is a canopied niche above it and the flanking polygonal buttresses are crowned with stone angels. The porch **roof** is a delightful miniature **hammerbeam** very like the one at Bredfield, and it shelters a fine pair of carved doors in good condition – another of Seckford's gifts, in all probability. Their narrow, keeled panels have ogee tracery and three small figures stand within niches on the uprights, the one on the r. bearing a heavy rosary. As you close the door, see how the backs of the panels were finished with an adze.

The rather dark interior lies under single-framed and braced rafter roofs with a section of panelling below the **wall plates**. It is just possible that some of the tracery in the bottom panels of

Great Bealings, St Mary: Henry Ringham carving

the tower screen is C15, and beyond it the w. window is filled with glass by Henry Hughes of **Ward & Hughes**. This dates from 1879 and a sentimental Good Shepherd is surrounded by illustrations of four of the **Seven Works of Mercy**, an example of what mass production did for the firm. The **font** of **Purbeck marble** is another example of mass production, this time from the C13, with its typical canted bowl whose panels are decorated with pairs of shallow arches. Edward Moor, the mid-C19 rector who restored the church so effectively, was able to secure the services of **Henry Ringham**, who did wonders with the remains of the C15 benches. Using the same techniques as he did at Tuddenham, St Martin, he spliced in new bottoms to the bench ends where necessary, and matched **poppyheads**, grotesques, and emblems to such good effect that it takes a keen eye to tell old from new. Look particularly for the medieval figure holding the Christian symbol of two fishes by the s. wall opposite the organ, three **pelicans** nearby, and two cocks for **St Peter**. Ringham essayed four versions of the pelican farther e. and provided both lectern and reading desk. The pulpit, however, is a C17 piece with coarse blind-arched panels and smaller foliage panels below the rim. It stands on a modern base and the octagonal **tester** has acorn pendants. The three shields in the tracery of the n. window were inserted in the 1840s and display the arms of Meadows, Henniker-Major, and Seckford. The glass in the s.e. nave window is an **Annunciation** of 1874 by **Lavers, Barraud & Westlake**, and the lower two-thirds of the window is blocked by a memorial inserted in 1583 for Thomas and Margaret Seckford by their son, who was the founder of Woodbridge School. It has a large painted **achievement** set within a classical frame beneath a **portico**, and the Latin inscription on the lintel is helpfully translated below. In the chancel, Ringham excelled himself with a brilliant series of **finials** on the choir stalls. They were designed by Major Edward Moor, author of *Suffolk Words and Phrases* and father of the rector, and display the crests of successive Lords of the Manor, churchwardens, and rector. On the n. side from the e., the front rank are for Moor (rector 1844-86), Morrison (James Morrison, M.P. for Ipswich 1832-5, a self-made man whose motto in business was 'small profits and quick returns'), Major (Sir John, Lord of the Manor 1770-1781); the back rank are Webb (Henry, Lord of the Manor 1692-1710), Meadows (Daniel, churchwarden), Cage (Seckford, Lord of Seckford Hall Manor 1673-1713). On the s. side from the e., the front rank are for Bridges (Lords of the Manor 1770-81), Clench (Lords of the Manor 1585-1680), Henniker (Lords of the Manor from 1781 and later patrons of the living); the back rank are Heard (Thomas, churchwarden), Seckford (Lords of the Manor of Seckford Hall 1185-1673), Wood (Thomas, bishop of Lichfield and Coventry, Lord of the Manor 1680-92). The C19 glass in the chancel is of varying quality. The e. window of 1874 is by Lavers, Barraud & Westlake and flanks the Crucifixion with the Gethsemane vigil and the **three Marys** at the tomb; the panels are set as though on pedestals within canopied niches. The windows on the n. side and s. of the **sanctuary** are poor designs, but the s.w. window contains pleasing work by Mayer & Co., a Munich-based firm which was active in this country in the latter half of the C19. It portrays the young Christ in the Temple, and there is a vivid contrast between the brightness of the child and the rich, dark robes of the elders. The

heavy stone **reredos** takes the form of two traceried windows flanking a central **cusped** arch, with sharply **crocketted** gables and pinnacles. It was designed by the architect William Bassett Smith in 1882 as a memorial to William Page Wood, 1st Baron Hatherley, who was Gladstone's first lord chancellor. To the r. is a C14 **angle piscina** with **dropped-sill sedilia** alongside, and on the wall above is an impressive monument for John Clenche, who died in 1628, and his wife Joan, who followed him a year later. Their alabaster busts face boldly forward, with closed prayer books placed before them, and quite a lot of the original colour survives. Four kneeling figures of their sons line the panel below, with skulls by two of them to show that they predeceased their parents; a coloured achievement and two shields on top, and a small **touchstone** tablet at the bottom, complete the piece.

Great Blakenham, St Mary (D7): A small but very interesting church, beautifully kept. Although the w. window and bell openings have **Decorated tracery**, the tower was probably **Norman** in its lower stages and the **nave** has a bricked-up Norman n. doorway, a simple s. doorway, and contemporary **lancets**. The **chancel** dates from the late C12 and there is a small round window well above the three small, widely spaced lancets in the e. wall. An early **scratch dial** with deep holes instead of lines can be found on a s.e. **quoin**, there is another above it, a third on the s.e. corner of the **nave**, and yet another on the r. hand side of the nave lancet. A **vestry** and an organ chamber were added to the sides of the chancel in the C19 and the **roof** neatly extends to cover both. In doing so, the **priest's door** and one lancet were left undisturbed in the old s. wall. The C15 wooden **porch** with its original **archbraced roof** has open sides and the mortices in the **mullions** show where panels of tracery once fitted. A singular survival is the shadowy remnant of a figure of the **Blessed Virgin** carved in wood beneath a **crocketted** canopy above the outer arch.

The shaft of the early C15 **font** is unusually elaborate, with panelling both between and on the buttresses, and four of the bowl panels display intricate tracery. The others are carved with **Passion emblems**: the Sacred Heart within a crown of thorns (e.); the scourging pillar with a crowing cock, ropes, and sword (n.); nails and spear (w.); cross, rod, and branch of hyssop (s.). Within the tower is the table tomb of Richard Swift, a merchant who died in 1645. Kneeling **putti** flank the tablet and there is a notable epitaph:

Reader knowe, this narrow earth
Incloseth one, whose name and worth
Can live, when marble falls to dust,
Honoured abroad for wise, and just,
Alike the Russe, and Sweden, theis
Report his prudence with their peace,
Deare when at home, to his faith given
Steadfast as earth, devout to heaven.
Wise merchant he (some stormes endur'd)
In the best porte his soule secur'd
For feare, thou shouldst forgett his name
'Tis the first epitaph of fame.

The open-framed and braced roofs of both nave and chancel are likely to be C13 and combine with the chancel lancets in their generous splays to form a vista which is deeply impressive in its simplicity. Although there are rough projecting **jambs** there is, oddly, no chancel arch, but stairs for the **rood loft** remain in the s. wall. The **Stuart** pulpit nearby is pleasantly rustic, with shallow carved blind arches and embellished lozenges in the panels, and the **tester** has acorn pendants to its skirt. There are well-carved **poppyheads** on the C19 pews and choir

stalls, and the **communion rails** make very decorative use of tracery which probably formed part of the medieval **rood screen** – pairs of roundels over **cusped ogee** arches. Within the **sanctuary**, the round-arched **piscina** is, like the rest of the chancel, late C12.

A tombstone e. of the chancel outside caught my eye. John Haward died aged 47 in 1870, having served in the 1st Suffolk Rifle Volunteers, one of the many local units that were raised for home defence in the 1860s and eventually formed the Territorial Army. His stone carries the badge of the National Rifle Association inscribed 'Wimbledon 1864' and it was at that rifle meeting that his moment of glory came. He had earned a place in the county team almost by chance but in the first stage of the Queen's Prize he swept the board against stiff opposition to take the silver medal which was, according to the association's report, 'deservedly awarded to ... an excellent shot' – a distinction that was not forgotten in his village.

Great Bricett, St Mary and St Laurence (C7): A church with a rare dedication – one of only three medieval examples in England – and the building has a most interesting history. It began as a priory of Augustinian canons founded in 1110 and later became a cell of Saint-Léonard near Limoges. All priories controlled from abroad were suppressed in the early C15 and this one became the parish church. Although it now has a straightforward **nave** and **chancel** under one **roof**, it was originally more elaborate and clues can be found on the outside. Excavation has shown that there were **transepts**, each with an e. **apse**, and the chancel was probably apsidal too. In the late C13 lateral chapels were added to the chancel and their arches remain embedded in the walls. A manor house was subsequently built directly on to the n.w. corner and covers much of the priory complex. There is a useful plan of the church displayed within which

Great Bricett, St Mary and St Laurence: scratch dial

explains the layout and identifies the various building stages. The bellcote is a 1907 replacement and below it a small blocked **lancet** shows in the w. wall. The s. frontage displays a bewildering variety of windows, including a blocked lancet by the **porch** and several examples of 'Y' **tracery** of about 1300 – the date of the **priest's door**. To the e. of the porch is a fragment of the original **Norman** s. door and above it is a **scratch dial** cut on a large circular stone; which is likely to be the earliest in the county. It has four deeply incised lines, one of which is marked with a cross. The very decorative e. window was inserted in 1868 but its tracery almost certainly repeats the pattern of the C14 original. The 1850s wooden porch has an attractive tile and pebble patterned floor and leads to an interesting Norman doorway of about 1160 that was formerly elsewhere. The arch is carved with **billet** and zigzag

mouldings and the keystone has a **trefoil** pendant. The **jambs** are also decorated and an inscription runs down the whole of the l. hand side. In it 'Leonardus' can be plainly seen. There is a smaller section below the r. hand **capital**.

The interior is broad and spacious under a single roof in which **arch-braced tie-beams** support **king-posts**, and the lack of a chancel arch accentuates its length. A tall blocked Norman arch at the w. end shows that there was once a tower, and in front of it a modern screen carries large **Commandment boards** lettered in a favourite late Victorian style of Gothic with coloured initials. The square late C12 **font** is carved with interlaced arches e. and w. and trefoil **arcades** n. and s., and there is a good deal of inventive difference between them. Beyond it, a low C16 brick doorway leads to what is now a private garden. Although it does not show from inside, there was a C13 n. doorway farther along. The C15 **rood loft stair** remains in the n. wall and to the w. is a blocked Norman lancet. Just to the l. of this are two small head **corbels** which I think may have been re-sited. A s. nave window contains four unusually good C14 panels of the **Evangelists**. They came from the tracery of the e. window and are now placed so that they can be examined easily; it is a pity that they had to be surrounded by inferior patterned glass in the C19. Each winged figure is shown with pen poised, and has a name label, with his symbol cleverly introduced at the top. The tall lancet farther along contains the figures of the two patron saints in a nice uncomplicated design of 1975 by the Maile Studios of Canterbury. On the n. wall John Bright's memorial of 1680 is an attractive composition in alabaster and **touchstone** – leafy side scrolls, urns, and an **achievement of arms** on top, swags and cherubs with a shield below. The pulpit has one traceried panel, with **quatrefoils** and shields in the rest and, like the reading desk, is, I think, largely Victorian. The C14

*Great Bricett, St Mary and St Laurence:
C14 Evangelists*

piscina set in a blocked chapel arch
now has no drain and its **crocketted
ogee** arch rises to a **finial**. By it stands
a compact C17 table and there is a nice
early **Stuart** chest with blind arches in
the front panels standing in the n.e.
corner.

Great Cornard, St Andrew (A10):
Alongside the road to Bures, the early
C14 tower carries a graceful shingled
spire like those to be found in Essex on
the other side of the Stour. There are
very worn niches unusually placed
within the angle of the buttresses on
either side of the renewed w. window;
they have steep gables and there are

remnants of masks below the stools.
The bell openings are roundels and a
polygonal brick turret was added to the
n. side in the C16. The s. **porch** matches
it and was probably built at the same
time. In the mid-C19 the body of the
church was faced with flint and the s.
aisle of 1887 joins up with the porch. By
1908 extensive repairs were necessary
and the **nave roof** was replaced. On
walking round, you will find that the n.
aisle windows have **headstops** with
exceptionally large ears, and under the
e. wall there are C18 headstones
carved with cherub heads.

Through the small, plain C14
doorway, one comes into a neat interior
where the organ is placed on a **gallery**
within the tower. The **piers** of the C14
n. **arcade** have semi-circular shafts
with **capitals** towards the arch openings – a scaled-down version of those in
Sudbury, St Gregory's [Vol.1], and the
Victorian architect sensibly designed
his s. arcade to match. The aisle roofs
are almost flat and most of the timbers
on the n. side are medieval. The stem of
the **font** is C19 but the late C15 bowl
has shields within **quatrefoils** on four
sides – e., the cross of **St George**, s., the
arms of Ogard (?), w., an unidentified
shield, and n., the arms of Crane (?).
The two-**light** window at the e. end of
the n. aisle has glass by Jones & Willis of
1927; the figure of **St Andrew** and a
version of Holman Hunt's *The Light of
the World* are conventional enough but
competently done. The parable of the
sower in the s. aisle e. window is in
another class altogether and quite exceptional, although I cannot name the
artist or give a precise date. In the small
upper panels the tares are sown by a
devil with glinting eye and cast at
length into the flames, while below are
the larger figures of Christ as the sower
of good seed and the fair harvesters –
sound draughtsmanship and subtle
colour. The pulpit is C19 but the base of
the C15 **screen** remains, with **paterae**
and masks cut on the top rail. These
and the shields at the bottom are very
like those at Chilton and may well have
been carved by the same man. The base

Great Cornard, St Andrew: parable of the sower

Manchester for his temerity.

Great Waldingfield, St Laurence (B9):
A handsome church which was largely
rebuilt in the late C14 by John
Appleton, whose family were Lords of
the Manor of Little Waldingfield. An
inscription asking for prayers for his
soul is distributed along the battlements on the s. side of the **nave roof**. A
stair turret rises above the parapet of
the tower on the s. side and a lion
crouches on the lowest **weathering** of
the s.w. buttress, with a matching
griffin to the n.w. **Groined** niches with
their canopies shorn away flank the w.
window and a modern figure of **St
Laurence** stands in one of them. The
C15 w. doors are **traceried** and shields
of the Boteler and Carbonell families
are set in the **spandrels** of the doorway.
Its mouldings are carved with large
paterae and you will find that one of
them is a **green man** and another an
eagle. By the early C19 the church was
in poor state and work in the 1820s
included a new n. **porch**. Walking
along that side you will see the
buttressed turret of the stair that led to
the **rood loft**, which must have
stretched right across the church. In
1866 the **chancel** was entirely rebuilt
by **William Butterfield** and the walls
are faced with flint in which broken
lines of tiles are set edgewise; the e.
window repeats the outline if not the
design of the original which was found
embedded in the wall. Like the tower
and **aisles**, the tall s. porch has a flint
chequer **base course** and it once had an
upper room whose stair turret rises
well above the aisle roof. There are
fleurons in the mouldings of the outer
and inner arches and the C19 doors
have an attractive figure carved at top
centre. This was part of an extensive
1870s restoration under the direction
of **J.H. Hakewill**; he replaced all the
roofs and the window tracery and
opened up the arch to the tower.

Just inside the entrance to the l. is the
tiny door to the porch stair; even in an

now supports a light wrought iron
screen and, in the **chancel** beyond, the
choir stalls incorporate C15 bench ends
with **poppyheads**. Overhead there is a
C16 roof which is almost flat but the e.
end was apparently altered in the C19
and there are shallow niches on either
side of five stepped **lancets**. Below is a
modern oak **reredos** with small shields
bearing **Passion emblems**, and under
the s. **sanctuary** window set in the wall
is a worn tomb which has lateral
moulded bands and three raised
shields carved with arms that have not
been identified. **Dowsing** called here in
February 1643 when he ripped up a
couple of **brass** inscriptions and
ordered a cross to be taken off the
steeple. The interesting thing is that
John Pain, the churchwarden, refused
to pay the fee for this legalised vandalism and was haled before the Earl of

Great Waldingfield, St Laurence: C17 altar rails

age of small men it must have been a tight squeeze for the average and impossible for the generously built. The **font** is interesting because although there are **quatrefoils** containing shields and paterae carved on all but one of the panels, the w. face has a small section of triangular patterning. This is undoubtedly **Norman** and shows that the bowl was re-cut in the C15. The graceful tabernacle cover commemorates a brother and sister who died in World War I. In the tower beyond is a nicely lettered Table of Fees which reveals that it paid to live in the village if you wanted to be buried there in 1882, and opposite, the updated version of 1948 is an unusually late example. The 1877 w. window glass is by Alexander Gibbs, whose workshop supplied some excellent designs to a number of Suffolk churches. Here, there are three panels of the Resurrection (with wide-awake soldiers, for a change) and musical angels in the tracery – strong reds and blues dominating. The tall nave **arcades** have quatrefoil **piers** and below the **clerestory** a **string course** is decorated with paterae and some very nice little heads with an interesting line in period hats. The pews below are from 1877 but they make use of C15 bench ends and there is a **pelican in her piety** on the n. side 4th from the w. Above the tower arch is a small gilt and coloured set of George III **Royal Arms** carved in relief, and in the n. aisle w. window, 1880s glass by **Lavers & Westlake** – Christ flanked by angels and blessing the peoples of all nations. There is more of their glass in the window by the organ – Christ expounding in the Temple as a child, with figures in the tracery of **Zachariah, St Elizabeth, St Joseph**, the **Blessed Virgin, St Simeon** (in a mitre, which seems a little odd for a Jewish priest), and **St Anne**. The central n. window of Christ's miracles is by Westlake and one **light** of the centre s. aisle window by him shows the sacrifice of Isaac within a canopied niche, with Old Testament figures in the tracery. There is a small **piscina** in the s. aisle chapel and the e. window there contains a jumble of medieval fragments in which very little of consequence can be distinguished.

There is no trace of the C15 **rood screen** that stretched from wall to wall (except the entry door to the n.), but when St Michael's, Cornhill, was being restored by **Scott** in the C19 he discarded the **altar rails**, and by some happy chance they were bought by the rector and placed within the chancel arch. They are a lovely set dating from the 1670s and **Pevsner** believed them to be the work of William Cleere. With centre gates, there are **acanthus** carved **balusters** which continue up in spiral form to a heavy top rail bearing an acanthus mould on both sides. Scrolls with swags of fruit support the gate-posts and two matching ranges of balusters are worked into the fronts of the choir stalls. Butterfield's chancel is not one of his most endearing works. The walls have a rather bald pattern of tiles and the **sanctuary** is lined with panels of marble fragments collected by two maiden ladies in an excess of zeal from the temples of Rome and Egypt (with a portion of Mount Sinai for good measure). The e. window glass of 1869 by Gibbs provides an interesting contrast with his later work at the w. end. There is no clear glass and the colours are bright and jolly. Not so the figures of the shepherds and the wise men, although their camel attempts a small smile.

Great Wenham, St John (D9): A fine cedar stands to the w. but does not mask the fine proportions of the C15 tower. The angle buttresses stop short at belfry level and they have simple **flushwork** to match the **base course**. There is a small **Perpendicular** w. window with a tiny niche above it just like the one at Little Wenham, and the bell openings have their lower sections roughly filled with flint. The rest of the building dates from about 1300 and has been rather harshly faced overall with plaster. On walking round, you will see that there is a small windowless shed in place of a n. **porch** and on that side of the **nave** the **rood stair** projects as a

shallow slab capped with red bricks. There is a **low side window** and a pair of **lancets** in the n. wall of the **chancel**, and its e. window comprises three stepped lancets with **trefoil** heads. From the s. it seems as though a miniature porch has been added to the chancel to match the one at the s. door, but it is actually a little **vestry** which was built in the mid-C19. Above its door the tablet in memory of Spencer Fell, a rector who died in 1676, was originally on the chancel wall. The porch is Victorian but shelters a **stoup** by the plain C14 doorway on whose **jambs** are carved plenty of C17 graffiti.

The organ is placed in the tower and fills the arch entirely, flanked by raised C19 **choir stalls** with **linen-fold panelled** fronts. Rather oddly, an arch almost at floor level and five steps give access to an excavated cubby hole beneath the organ. The C19 **font** is cumbrous and by it lies a short section saved from the old **roof** which was replaced in 1867. Its pine successor is panelled out in wagon style, with **kingposts** on **tie-beams**. A large, pale but lively set of **Royal Arms** of George II painted on board hangs over the unused n. door, and to the r. there is a 3ft by 2ft 6in. recess under a **Tudor** arch. This is possibly a late example of an **aumbry** in which oil and other necessaries for baptism were kept conveniently close to the font, but it could also have been designed to house a small memorial **brass** which has since disappeared. However, if so, **Dowsing** saw nothing of it when he came here in February 1643, for his journal reports that there was 'nothing to reform'. The raked metal rack with pegs that runs the whole length of the nave n. wall has been called an C18 wig rack, although I would not have thought that a parish of this size could raise as many wigs as that, even in its heyday. Perhaps hats were taken into account. The pews are Victorian and it may be that the 1860s restoration removed the chancel arch. There is now only a break in the masonry to mark the division, although a door shape in the n. wall shows where the stairs led to the old **rood loft**. Above it, a helm with a large horse crest, a short sword, and a **cartouche** of arms are mounted on a board. They were probably carried at the C17 funeral of a member of the East family. The generous pulpit matches the pews and has rather a nice bookrest with deeply cut oak leaves and acorns on the underside. The range of pews continues up to the **sanctuary** steps where the **communion rails** are in Victorian Gothic style, with turned **balusters** like **Early English** shafts. The memorial to John and Susan Bailey on the s. wall of the chancel dates from 1813 and is by a minor sculptor, Robert Ashton the Younger. It is a small sarcophagus resting on lion paw feet, with lifting rings carved at each side, all set against a black background. The floor levels in the chancel have been changed and some C15 tiles have been relaid in the sanctuary. There are two patterns, each using four tiles, and the smaller design has crowned **sacred monograms** in roundels about a centre **quatrefoil** (many of the tiles are good C19 copies). The small, plain C14 **piscina** has a groove in the arch where a wooden **credence shelf** once fitted and there are **dropped-sill sedilia** alongside. The panels of the C19 wooden **reredos** are painted with the Commandments, Lord's Prayer, and Creed.

Groton, St Bartholomew (B9): The churchyard is extensive and Groton Hall with its farm buildings lies along the s. boundary. The church is largely C15 but the tower has a w. window of about 1300 and below the stepped battlements the bell openings have lost their **tracery**. There are fine **gargoyles** everywhere and those on the **nave** are well above the **clerestory** windows with their **cusped** 'Y' tracery. The **chancel** parapet is plain and although the s. windows are **Perpendicular**, the e. window has attractive C14 **reticulated** tracery. On the n. side is a brick lean-to **vestry** and, in the nave, a small blocked door. On walking round, one

comes across the first indication that this church has a very special place in the hearts of Americans and the history of the United States. A table tomb in the corner between the s. **aisle** and the chancel has a modern inscription which identifies it as the grave of Adam and Anne Winthrop, the parents of John Winthrop, first governor of Massachusetts and founder of the city of Boston. A man of exceptional qualities, he was, like his father before Him, Lord of the Manor here in 1618 but, at odds with Church and government, he led the Puritan exodus to New England in 1630.

Entry is by the s. **porch** and just inside there is a **stoup** with a very strange recess within it. Although blocked now, it was angled to emerge in the porch like a **squint** but the siting is difficult to understand. Below it stands a C14 chest with the curved top eaten away between the heavy iron bands. Under the tower two sheets of roofing lead are framed on the wall. Dated 1698, one bears the names of the churchwardens and the other: 'This done by me William Chenery Plummer'. Bells are not normally easily accessible and it is nice to find that trouble has been taken here to display casts of the interesting marks of two C15 London founders, Chamberlain and Keteyll. The **piers** of the tall four-bay **arcades** are a little gawky, with **capitals** only on the shafts within the arches, and overhead the pale **arch-braced** nave roof has churchwardens' initials cut at both ends and is dated 1665 (e.), 1671 (w.). Floors are **pamment** and brick, the walls are a cheerful pink, and in the heads of the aisle windows there is some mainly C18 heraldic glass which is now very worn in places. In the s. aisle (w. to e.) the shields are for: Adam Winthrop 1560, John Winthrop 1605, Winthrop/Clopton 1615, Winthrop/Tyndal 1618 (marking the second and third of John's four marriages); n. aisle (w. to e.), Anne Sears (a Winthrop girl), John Savile Halifax of Edwardstone, and John Weller Poley of Boxted. A niche in the n. aisle contains a 1950s **Blessed Virgin** and Child and the e. window (which now opens into the organ chamber) is fitted with a decorative modern iron grille which incorporates the shields of Winthrop and the state of Massachusetts. Groton was one of the cluster of prosperous Suffolk wool villages and it is notable that when Henry Dawson died in 1677 his **ledger-stone** in the centre pavement still described him as a 'Groton clothier' although the great days were long gone. There is 1870s glass by the **O'Connors** in the s. aisle e. window – a post-Resurrection Christ and **St Thomas**, with the influence of photography showing clearly in the treatment of the faces. The upper opening leading to the old **rood loft** can be seen on the n. side of the chancel arch, and although the pulpit below is Victorian, the panels and stem appear to be C15.

In the chancel the e. window is dominant, with its glass of 1875 by Cox & Sons; there are angels with scrolls in the tracery and the four main **lights** illustrate the text, 'I command thee this day to love the Lord thy God' (Deuteronomy), and **St Paul's** charge to the elders at Ephesus. It was given by John Winthrop's American descendants and in 1878 Robert Winthrop of Boston restored to the church the **brass** inscription which once lay on the tomb of his ancestor Adam Winthrop, who was the grandfather of the Puritan leader and died in 1562. It is now placed on the chancel s. wall near the **priest's door**. The **sanctuary** s. window contains 1880s glass by John Cameron (undistinguished figures of Faith and Charity). The light and golden figures of angels in the s. chancel window are much more attractive, although I have not been able to identify the maker. They are retrospective memorials for Mary and Thomasina, John Winthrop's first two wives. Before leaving, have a look at the stone in the s.e. corner of the churchyard which is claimed as the oldest (outside, that is) in Suffolk. The edge inscription identifies it as the grave of 'Lewes Kedbye whoe had to wyfe Jane Kedbye' and it is dated 1598.

It once formed the top of a table tomb and there was a graven effigy and epitaph. Faint traces of the latter can still be seen and it read:

Christ is to me as life on earth
And deathe to me is gaine,
Because I trust through him alone
Salvation to obtain.

Grundisburgh, St Mary (F6): There was obviously a fashion in this part of Suffolk for putting the tower on the s. side of the **nave** and using its ground floor as the main **porch**. In Grundisburgh's case the medieval original was replaced in the C18, and one can have some sympathy with **Edward Hakewill's** comment: 'We know not whether to mourn over the fall or the restoration.' Had it been built a century earlier or later it would probably have sat more easily with the rest of the building. As it is, the outline is severe, with clasping buttresses, round-headed arches to doors and windows, and a plain parapet. The plain red brick is relieved by patterns of darker hue on the e. and w. faces, and there is an inscription above the entrance: 'This steeple was built The bells set in order And Fixt at the charge of Robert Thinge Gent. lately deceased 1731-1732.' The clock has the traditional 'Tempus fugit' (Time flies) on its face, and I like the inscription on the C18 sundial which uses the Suffolk form of the present tense: 'Life pass like a shadow.' One feels bound to echo it with: 'That that do!' The C14 s. **aisle** has **Decorated** windows with peaked arches, and there are startled **gargoyles** below the parapet. The position of the tower makes the sway-backed leaded nave **roof** seem low when seen from the s., and below it is a C15 **clerestory** whose windows are set within a band of lovely **flushwork**. From w. to e. one can recognise **St Edmund's** emblem, the Tudenham arms, a 'T' (Sir Thomas Tudenham?), the lily emblem of the **Blessed Virgin**, crowned letters that make up 'Ave Maria' (Hail Mary), an 'A' (Alice Tudenham?), and finally the

Grundisburgh, St Mary: double hammerbeam roof

---

sacred monogram. At the e. end of the aisle is the chapel built by Thomas Wale in 1527. He was a London salt merchant who had property locally and lived near the church. He had no coat of arms but made up for it by decorating the chapel with the shields of the city of London and the Salters' Company (three salt cellars), and his own angular merchant's mark. The inscription is very worn in places now but reads, 'Orate p. aiabus Thome Wale et Alicie uxor eius xvcxxvii' (Pray for the souls of Thomas Wale and his wife Alice 1527), and is decorated with the rose and pomegranate of Henry VIII and Catherine of Aragon. The buttress below widens at the base to form a snug little porch for the **priest's door**, and a C19 Virgin and Child occupies the canopied niche. Wale's merchant's mark appears again above the doorway and there is a **scratch dial** on the plinth of the buttress to the l. After all that, the n. side is very humble, plain and plastered, with no aisle, and an ugly chimney rears up against the blocked n. door. Hakewill's full-scale restoration of 1872 included replacement e. and w. windows and he died before the work was completed. Grundisburgh's light ring of ten bells is well known in Suffolk and beyond, and a bell wheel serves as a wall decoration in the porch. To the r. of the C14 inner doorway is an C18 text from Leviticus which was placed there specifically to make a point: 'Ye shall keep my Sabbaths and reverence my Sanctuary. I am the Lord.' It is reminiscent of those at Hemingstone and Witnesham and may be the survivor of a sequence.

In contrast to the porch, the nave is full of light, and overhead is one of the finest roofs in the county. It is a double **hammerbeam** design, with **king-posts** on the collar beams and pendent bosses below the upper hammer posts. There is a deep, richly carved cornice and the roof is all aflutter with angels – over fifty of them perch on hammers, **wall posts**, and even on the collar beams below the ridge. They nearly all have new heads and wings which date from a restoration of 1888. The nice **pamments** of the nave floor have been replaced at the w. end by sickly yellow tiles, and the C15 **font** stands in the centre raised on steps provided by Hakewill. It is a familiar East Anglian pattern although the lions in the bowl panels are more squat than usual. Those that support the shaft sit on human heads in the same strange way as those at Helmingham and Ipswich, St Mary le Tower, but these have lost their features and only the **kennel head-dresses** identify the two women. Nearby, the colourful Garter banner from St George's chapel, Windsor, serves as a memorial for Bertram Francis, Baron Cranworth, who died in 1964. On the n. wall is a C15 **St Christopher** painting which was uncovered in 1956 and restored in 1961. The huge figure in red and blue robe carries the Christ child on his shoulder and leans on a rough staff which sprouts leaves. There are buildings in the background on both sides, and the hermit fisherman stands bottom r. Fishes and eels abound and there is even a tiny mermaid to the l. of the saint's r. leg. Also on the n. wall is a good memorial in oak for Robert Brampton Gurdon, who served in the Long Range Desert Group. It is a measure of the toughness of that legendary unit that he was 38 when he was killed in 1942. Farther along, a large door led to the **rood loft** stairs, blocked now after the 4th step, and a faded C13 painting above has the remains of four figures and part of a decorative frieze. The subject is said to be Christ's appearance before the high priest.

The bulky open-work stone pulpit of 1881 stands here, and within the late C13 **chancel** arch is a lovely mid-C14 **rood screen**. The deep tracery has a **crocketted ogee** arch applied to each bay, the uprights carry pinnacled buttresses, and many of the mouldings are deeply undercut. Although most of the **cusping** has been broken from the entrance arch, there is a **green man** lurking in the l. hand **spandrel**. The low base has stencil decoration on a plum-coloured ground, and the whole screen was restored by Maurice Keevil in 1967. The plain C14 **arcade** of three bays between nave and aisle has octagonal **piers**, and the aisle roof had its angels and **bosses** replaced in the 1870s. On the w. wall, a tablet by Brown of Russell Street has a wreath and sword on the **pediment** and commemorates Lieut. Henry Freeland of the Royal Marines, who died on the *Royal George* off Sweden in 1854. The aisle is separated from Thomas Wale's chapel by a C15 **parclose screen** which must have belonged to an earlier chapel. It has been skilfully repaired and was restored at the same time as the rood screen. It has sharp ogee shapes in the **tracery**, and there are fleur de lys and roses stencilled on the uprights. The base panels have a pattern of sacred monograms on an olive-green ground, and there are fainter 'MRs' which indicate that the chapel was dedicated to the Virgin. It is largely taken up now by the organ, but there is a **piscina** under an ogee arch that belonged, like the screen, to the earlier chapel. The stone roof **corbels** again display Wale's merchant's mark and the arms of the city and his company. Three **brass** inscriptions have been taken from their slabs and mounted on the e. wall here. Two are for Anne Manocke (1610) of 'Stooke Nayland' and her son-in-law Thomas Sullyard (1612). Both families clung to the Catholic faith and suffered loss and persecution on that account. The third of 1501 begins: 'In heven God giveth everlastyng lyffe to the soulle of John Awall & Margery hys wyfe', and probably relates to the parents of Thomas, who rebuilt the chapel.

Between chapel and chancel there is a two-bay arcade with a **quatrefoil** pier and flattened arches, and although the chancel roof was lowered it still retains

the medieval braced **tie-beams**. The now familiar Wale mark and Salters' arms crop up again on the s. corbels, and below is a range of choir stalls designed by Hakewill. He made good use of four C15 bench ends which have heavy **poppyheads** and a nice selection of tracery; the **Evangelistic symbols** are additions. The Blois family were Lords of the Manor for 200 years and there is a good range of their **ledger-stones** in the chancel, including one of 1631 and another of 1652 that was unfortunately masked by the C19 **sanctuary** step at one end. A fragment of C14 wall painting has been uncovered on the s. wall; it has a vigorous drawing of **St Margaret's** head in black line and the yellow wing of her attendant dragon. Three Blois memorials of consequence are on the n. wall. That for Martha (1645) has an oval inscription tablet set in drapes, below which man and wife face each other across a prayer desk backed by four sons and three daughters; all within an oblong frame, with an **achievement** at the top. William (1658) has a grey alabaster and **touchstone** tablet with shallow carving and five shields of arms. In a typical progression, Sir Charles's monument of 1738 is a great deal larger. It has side **pilasters** adorned with cherub heads and swags, there is a coloured **cartouche** below, and a **putto** with a golden trumpet has his own miniature portal flanked by urns on the top. In the sanctuary there is a large piscina with a fine specimen of **dogtooth decoration** on the rim of the arch and part of an outer matching band. This confirms that the chancel was built in the late C13. The e. window glass of 1887 is by Wyndham Hughes – a slightly unusual Ascension scene, with angels in pastel shades floating on either side of Christ, above the disciples clad in sombre robes.

Hadleigh, St Mary (C8): This grand church reflects the town's importance as a thriving centre of the medieval wool trade and the e. end rears majestically beyond a short cul-de-sac which leads from the High Street. Beyond, the churchyard is as spacious as a park and the ochre-coloured C15 Guildhall stands on the s. boundary. To the w. is the glorious red brick gatehouse which survives from the Deanery built in 1495. The base of the tower may well be as early as the late C12 or early C13, but there is 'Y' **tracery** of about 1300 in the belfry windows and the bell openings have intersected tracery of the same period. In addition, there are small circular sexfoil (see **foils**) openings each side of them just below the parapet. A stair turret on the s. side has a very individual selection of windows – a pair and a trio of minute **lancets**. Suffolk has few spires and none older than this one. It is probably early C14 and its 70ft frame is sheathed in lead laid in attractive **herringbone** pattern. The clock bell which hangs below a little gable on the e. face was cast about 1280 and is almost certainly the oldest in the county. A major reconstruction in the C15 added a tall **clerestory** with widely separated pairs of windows which extends over the **chancel**, and the line of the **aisles** is continued by chapels at the e. end – all adding to an impression of tremendous length. The wide n. aisle has **Perpendicular** windows but the door is C14 with remnants of **headstops** and there is a massive two-storeyed **vestry** at the e. end which probably provided living accommodation for a priest. It is interesting that it was built at an acute angle to the chancel chapel to keep it within the bounds of the churchyard. The **priest's door** on the s. side cuts into the corner of the window above it and there used to be another entrance to the church (complete with two-storeyed porch) by the side of the 5th window from the e. end – conveniently placed for processions from the Guildhall opposite (there were at least five medieval **guilds**). The early C15 s. **porch** is wide and tall, with pairs of windows each side but with surprisingly little decoration. There are three plain niches over the entrance and

within, the stumps of vaulting remain to show that there was an upper room originally. The inner doors are panelled, with a **quatrefoil** border, and the wrought iron fittings repay some study – note particularly that the strap hinges pass underneath the mouldings.

The church within is very wide and open, with sharply raked aisle **roofs** and a coved and boarded ceiling in the **nave** above encased **tie-beams** which have shaped iron brackets resting on **corbels**. This was all part of an 1870s restoration that changed the character of the interior significantly. The C15 **arcades** are tall and slim and the chancel arch is very wide. The mouldings of the C14 tower arch fade into the **imposts** and there is a nice oak screen below installed in 1946 which has a rich, pierced cresting. On the w. wall there are some **hatchments**: top l. for Sir Henry Bunbury, 2nd Bt (1748), top r. for David Wilkins, a rector who died in 1745, bottom l. for the Very Revd Edward Hay-Drummond (1829), bottom r. for Mary Tanner, the wife of a rector, who died in 1779. The late C14 **font** was re-cut in the C19 but is a fine specimen; the bowl panels have pairs of shallow niches set with tiny **paterae** under **cusped** and **crocketted ogee** arches with almost flat **groining**. The stem has larger versions with gabled buttresses and there are **Tudor roses** set at the base. The cover was made by Charles Sidney Spooner, a member of the **Arts and Crafts Movement**; it is a tall tabernacle with two ranks of shafts carved with overlapping feather motifs and has a range of small painted shields halfway up – anti-clockwise from the s.: the arms of the diocese; Hadleigh; 'MR' for the dedication; (unidentified); the dioceses of Norwich, Lichfield, and Ely; and the province of Canterbury. The cover was dedicated by the archbishop of Canterbury in 1925 and commemorates John Overall, who was baptised here in 1559. Professor of Divinity, dean of St Paul's, bishop of Coventry and Lichfield, and finally bishop of Norwich, he drafted much of the catechism that is to be found in the

Book of Common Prayer, including that memorable definition of 'Sacrament': 'an outward and visible sign of an inward and spiritual grace'. A fine specimen of a ringers' gotch or ale jug is displayed in a glass case nearby, with a crudely lettered inscription:

> If ye love me due not lend me,
> Use me often keep me clenly,
> Fill me full or not at all,
> And that with strong and not with small.

The long benches in the nave were made in 1869 and children collected wild flowers so that the carvers could use them as models for the carvings in the quatrefoils on the elbows. The 1871 pulpit was designed by Farmer & Brindley – it has a typically Victorian stone and marble base but an oak body nicely carved by John Spurgeon of Stowmarket. The lectern is an interesting essay in C19 Gothic style and was designed by **Hardman**.

The church has a variety of chests and the one by the s. door has a domed lid that is formed from a half tree trunk. Joseph Beaumont died in 1681 and his memorial is an attractive little marble **cartouche** by the n. door, with fat, trumpeting cherubs holding a heart above it. Two brass measures belonging to the town are displayed in a case in the n. aisle and there are two more wagon chests there. At the e. end on the wall is a **brass** for Richard and Elizabeth Glanfield (1637). Like a number of others in the church, it has been moved from its original position; it shows the couple hand in hand, he in a furred robe and she wearing a stylish wide-brimmed hat. There is now no **rood screen** but openings on either side of the chancel arch show that its loft probably continued across the aisles. Two matching C15 **parclose screens** remain. They are tall, with wide divisions, and the delicate tracery is unlike most of the period. It is cut and carved as double units out of thin board and inserted between the uprights. In the s. aisle wall is a C14 tomb recess which was left undisturbed at the rebuilding a

century later. The wide ogee arch has remains of crockets and a nubbly **finial**, and the heavy cusps are carved and partially pierced. Nearby, the World War I memorial is another piece of work by Charles Spooner – finely lettered on a painted panel, with Christ crucified at the top and an oak panel below inset with little painted flowers. The n. chancel chapel houses an organ with a fine early C18 oak case which came from Donyland Hall in Essex; there are pairs of chubby cherub heads under the corner pipe clusters and an attractive pierced **acanthus** frieze between them matches the hoods and surrounds to the pipes above. In the floor to the w. is a brass inscription and **achievement** for William and Dorothy Foorthe (1599), and on the wall by the vestry door is another for Anne Still, the wife of a bishop of Bath and Wells, who died in 1593; the figure is worn and there is part of a curved edge inscription and a Latin epitaph. Above this brass is a memorial for Sarah Johnson who died in 1793. The obelisk above the tablet has two mourning **putti**, one reclining and one standing by an urn; it is by Charles Regnart, a competent mason whose work is found all over England, with other Suffolk examples at Mendlesham and Higham, St Mary. The large oak chest by the organ is initialled 'W.S.' below a fascinating little ball padlock. The e. window of the n. chapel contains a number of heraldic panels and roundels set in closely patterned glass. At the top from l. to r.: the shield of **St George**, the badge of Queen Elizabeth I, the arms of Tudor England, and those of England quartered with France. Lower down is a selection of arms borne by various archbishops of Canterbury – Sancroft (bottom l.), Howley (centre middle), Juxon (centre bottom), and Wareham (bottom r.)

The two-bay arcades which separate the chancel and its chapels rest on quatrefoil **piers** and at the junction of the **hood moulds** there are headstops carved as angels on the n. and devils on the s. (one would expect it to be the other way round). Unlike the nave, the chancel roof was undisturbed by restorers and is richly panelled, with **bosses** along the centre line. The mighty Perpendicular e. window is filled with glass by **Ward & Hughes** from their worst period, and to the l. is a C15 tomb set within the wall with an opening above it through to the chapel beyond. The three shields in quatrefoils along the front were once inlaid and there are indents for brasses on the walls above the slab. Whose it was is not known but it was obviously designed for use as an **Easter sepulchre**. The **piscina** and **sedilia** on the s. side of the **sanctuary** are C19 but three medieval **squints** remain in the wall behind them, giving a view of the **high altar** from the s. chapel. The e. window of the chapel is something which attracts the eye the moment one enters the church. It is filled with glass of 1857 by George Hedgeland, best known for the great w. window of Norwich cathedral. On the theme of 'Suffer little children to come unto me' it is an uncomplicated design across the three **lights** in the fashion of a large painting; the colours are clear and vivid and the artist used a great deal of textured shading both in features and drapery. The small C14 piscina to the r. is now used as a tabernacle for the Blessed Sacrament and has been fitted with a door on which is carved a gilded **Agnus Dei**. On the n. wall of the chapel sanctuary is Thomas Alabaster's brass – a kneeling figure crudely engraved within a niche. He died in 1592 'having lived in this towne a clothier about 50 yeeres'. On the s. wall John Alabaster's brass of 1637 shows him in ruff and gown within a **Renaissance** arch. Another brass to the l. of the altar and the window to the r. both commemorate the most famous of Hadleigh's rectors – Rowland Taylor, installed by Cranmer in 1544. A diligent preacher of the new doctrine, he was arrested within six days of Queen Mary's accession and, obstinate in his refusal to recant, was sent back to Hadleigh to be burnt, meeting his end with fortitude

on Aldham Common. Below his brass there are two oblong tablets commemorating Dean Francis Carter (1927) and his wife Sibella (1940); the beautiful inscriptions in red and black Roman and italic lettering were cut by Eric Gill, that modern master of typography. A bench end opposite is carved with an animal holding a human head in its mouth, and it is often identified as the wolf guarding the head of **St Edmund**. However, the creature wears a parody of priestly vestments and its back feet are cloven and so it is more likely to be a medieval carver's sardonic comment on the clergy.The windows on the s. side are again by Ward & Hughes and it is interesting to see the distinct difference in style of the three to the w. They were designed by Thomas Curtis around the turn of the century and look more like **Kempe's** work – steely grey and pale yellow, with muted colours for the robes of the **pre-Raphaelite** figures.

Hasketon, St Andrew (F6): It is generally agreed that the round tower is **Norman**, and there are tall, thin **lancets** at belfry level. However, it was remodelled around 1300 when a w. window was inserted and a leggy octagonal bell stage added, making it the tallest round tower in Suffolk after Mutford [Vol.3]. Perched on the brick parapet is a pretty little weathervane in the form of a ship, a replica of one on the training ship *Britannia* and presented in 1946. Despite a C14 doorway and lancet, and a **Perpendicular** window, the **herringbone** flintwork in the n. wall of the **nave** confirms that it is Norman. On walking round, you will find that the e. wall of the **chancel** was rebuilt, a **vestry** added, and the **porch** renewed in 1850. Nevertheless, there is an unusual two-**light** Perpendicular window in the chancel s. wall, very tall and thin under a **label** shaped like a **kennel head-dress** with small **headstops**. An attractive **Decorated** window on that side of the nave has

mouchettes and a **quatrefoil** in the **tracery**, and to the w. of it there are three sections of a small lancet embedded in the wall. It is likely that this is a **Saxon** window that was re-used by the Normans, and when it was uncovered in the C19 there were fragments of wood and bark in the holes drilled on the bevel. Apparently the early builders inserted sticks as part of a wattle framework for the inner splay, but if this is the explanation for the holes the stones must have been reversed in the wall. One of the porch windows has a 1960s picture of a monk playing the organ, and the early C14 inner doorway is deeply moulded with no **capitals**.

The tower arch within is taken up by the organ, but note the doorway above it, a common feature in round towers of this period which lends substance to the theory that they served as places of refuge. The **font** is in such good condition that I suspect it was plastered over in the C17 to protect it against the Puritan despoilers. In the bowl panels fat **Tudor roses** alternate with angels holding shields whose heraldry is still crisp and legible. It was probably given in the 1450s by Sir Robert Brewes, one of a family who were lords of four Suffolk manors, two in Lincolnshire, and one in Norfolk. Their arms are on the w. side and those of other families linked with them by marriage are carved on the other shields: Ufford (e.), and Shardelow and Stapylton (n. and s.). The shaft has been replaced but the base shows that there were four lions around the original. There are three **embattled tie-beams** under the wagon **roof** of the nave, and the C19 window in the s. wall contains attractive and unusual glass of 1858. The maker is unknown and it has a thick border of holly and ivy around the lights and the tracery; there are two **cartouches** of arms (one with a 'hawk on hand' crest) set within plain **quarries**, and the overall effect is Christmassy. The blocked doorway of the **rood loft** stair is in the n. wall, and by it is a very decorative memorial in alabaster and **touchstone** for William Godwin, who

died in 1663, and two of his sons, who were Smyrna merchants. A large roundel contains a coloured **achievement** on top, there are four other shields, and a cherub head is set at the bottom within a coarse garland of fruit. The C13 chancel arch with its minimal **imposts** is almost as wide as the nave, and by it stands a modern, heavy oak pulpit on a stone base. There is no **screen**. On the n. chancel wall, a tablet commemorates two young Wait brothers who were killed in 1916 – Percy, a midshipman at Jutland, and Charles, a lieutenant in the KOYLIs, who fell on the Somme. The **reredos** in C14 mode was given in their memory. On the s. wall a shaped tablet in an alabaster frame has a cherub head above, a skull and bones below, for William Farrer who died in 1635 aged 15:

> Here lies his kindred's hope, his Parents' joy,
> A man in manners though in years a boy.
> If on his yeares you looke, hee dyd but younge,
> If on his vertues, then hee lived long.

The C19 window nearby has 1860s glass by **Lavers, Barraud & Westlake**; two crowded little scenes·of Christ's betrayal and the Via Dolorosa. The tall, thin window noticed outside is equally attractive within and has **jamb shafts** with moulded capitals. The Brewes arms can be seen again, this time in C15 glass, with the deep red lion's shield set on a blue ground, and there are contemporary fragments in the heads of the lights and in the borders.

Helmingham, St Mary (E5): A spacious, pleasant setting, and there are glimpses of the great house across the lake to the w. The tower is attractive, with four **set-offs**, deep stepped battlements with pinnacles and **flushwork** that embodies 'MR' for the dedication and the Tollemache family arms (a family signature that will be very familiar by the time you leave). The w. doorway is flanked by niches while the flushwork above it displays a **sacred monogram** and a crowned 'M'. The **base course** on the s. side has a bold inscription: 'Scandit ad ethera Virgo puerpera virgula Jesse' (The Virgin Mother, branch of Jesse's stem, ascends to heaven). Of particular interest is the date 1543 which can be seen on the s.w. corner of the battlements and, more than that, the fact that this is one of the very few towers whose building contract still survives. In 1487 Thomas Aldrych of Lopham in Norfolk agreed with four parishioners to build a 60ft steeple to the same design as the ones at Framsden and 'Bramston' (Brampton?). Ten years were allowed and work was only to be done between June and September to guard against frost damage. The parish was to provide all materials and plant and no bells were to be hung until four years after completion. There was a proviso for making the tower higher and this must have been done in the early years of the C16 by Lionel Tollemache, with completion in 1543. On walking round, you will find a substantial addition to the n. side of the **chancel** which covers the dank steps leading down to the Tollemache vault. The e. window has flowing **tracery**; in passing note the **scratch dial** on the s.e. buttress. There are renewed **Decorated** windows and a **priest's door** on the s. side, and the **nave** sports a curious dormer window with wooden **mullions** whose purpose will be seen within. The s. **porch** has rudimentary flushwork with a small niche above the arch whose **stops** are a little out of the ordinary, being small pendent shields. The C13 inner doorway has squared-off **capitals** and deep, ribbed mouldings, while the door itself dates from the C16 and has deep tracery cut in the solid, with two ranks of **mouchette** roundels.

First impressions inside are of a multitude of Tollemache memorials counterbalanced by a succession of bold C19 texts writ large over arches and on walls. The nave **roof** is either late C16 or early C17 and its slim **arch-braces** are interrupted by squared pen-

dants below the collar **spandrels**, with plastered ceiling between the main timbers. The deep **wall plate** is pierced and carved with kneeling angels holding scrolls, their wings widespread. The C15 **font** has been carefully restored and is the familiar East Anglian design, with lions and angels in the bowl panels, compact angels beneath each corner, and lions round the shaft. The latter, however, have an odd distinction because they sit on male and female human heads like the ones at Grundisburgh and Ipswich, St Mary le Tower. This little local example of symbolism must have had a particular significance and I wonder what it was. Lionel Tollemache's **ledger-stone** of 1610 has been clamped to the s.wall at the w. end and the epitaph begins:

Wise Teare turn hither here's a stone

Would not be left to weep alone . . . Much grander is the monument to Maria, Countess of Dysart, on the opposite wall. Sculpted by **Nollekens** in 1804, it is a large bas relief of a woman musing with a book on her lap, while a **putto** weeps and caresses a lamb on the other side of an urn. The figures are sharply silhouetted, beautifully modelled in high relief, and the piece illustrates how sentiment was creeping into the work of fashionable sculptors at this time. Beyond the n. door is another and quite different piece by Nollekens for Lionel Robert Tollemache, an 18-year-old ensign in the 1st Foot Guards who 'died nobly fighting for his king and country' at the siege of Valenciennes in 1793. A pile of ordnance and flags is set against a grey arch shape and there is a bas relief bust in an oval at the top. It was set up in 1810 and the epitaph records the deaths of his father (killed in a New York duel) and two uncles (lost at sea). It understandably concludes: 'So many instance of disaster are rarely to be met with in the same family!' Flanking the s. door are two unexceptional tablets by Bedford for two early Victorian members of the family, and farther

---

along on the n. wall is the large monument commemorating the Lionel who died in 1640. The armoured effigy lies stiffly on its side, carved in alabaster and gilt, with a painted face above a wide ruff; the backing is a double arch coffered in alabaster with **touchstone Corinthian** columns and his shields above.

Across the nave towers a multiple memorial of 1615 for four more Lionels (a confusing family fixation), starting with the one who built the tower and finishing with his great-grandson who died in 1605. They each kneel in profile within coffered arches, the senior in his judge's robes and the others in black and gilt armour. There is **Renaissance** detail on the massive frame and two vaguely pagan figures flank the upper arch; a large **achievement** within a roundel stands at the top, and a rhyming epitaph is painted below each figure. The whole thing was transferred from Bentley and its size demanded alterations to the roof, which explains the dormer window. Some have thought that the window was originally inserted to light the **rood** but it is too far w. for that. The seating and the pulpit are C19. The chancel arch was renewed, possibly during a restoration, in the 1840s. There is no **screen** now and on the n. wall of the chancel Lieut. Gen. Thomas Tollemache has his memorial, having served in Ireland at the taking of Athlone and died in the attack on Brest harbour in 1694. The monument probably came rather later and has a large bust backed by martial trophies above a potted biography of an epitaph. To the e. is a very impressive but unsigned monument for yet another Lionel – Baron Huntingtower and Earl of Dysart, who died in 1727. The life-size muscular figure reclines in Roman costume but incongruously holds his coronet, and his mourning Countess is seated to the r. The epitaph dilates at length upon his lineage and

attainments. On the opposite wall John, 1st Baron, has a bust by Thomas Mayes in a square recess flanked by touchstone columns. He died in 1890 and his memorial is a noble patrician head instinct with Victorian rectitude. To the r. one jumps back in time with a small touchstone tablet within a painted and gilt border; there is a roundel of arms with supporters topped by a little hour-glass. It commemorates Dame Catherine who died in 1620. Very decorative. Pleasing in quite a different fashion is the little kneeling figure within an alabaster niche on the n. side of the **sanctuary**. For Minnie, Lady Tollemache, it dates from 1918 and is signed with a monogram that I could not decipher.

Hemingstone, St Gregory (D6): Caught in the loop of a minor road that leads nowhere in particular, this charming little church is well away from its village. Fields drop away to the n. into a miniature valley, and four venerable sycamores line the grassy path up to the n. **porch**. The unbuttressed late C14 tower has a single **string course** which lifts to form a **label** for the canopied niche on the w. face, and the **Perpendicular** window below is relatively large. There are shallow battlements and a 'G' for the dedication can be seen in the **flushwork** to the w. The first sign that this building has been here a very long time is the **long and short work** at the s.w. corner of the **nave**. A good example which reaches to the eaves, it must be **Saxon** of the C11 or earlier. Nave and **chancel** lie under one **roof**, with the s. door blocked up long ago and C18 glazing inserted in the head. The windows range from the 'Y' **tracery** of about 1300 to Perpendicular, and there is a **Tudor priest's door** on the s. side. The porch is the same age or a little later, and darker bricks pattern the walls; a niche and two small recesses are set above the outer arch. At first glance, there is duplicate porch tacked on to the nave n. wall – some 4 yds square, with the outline of a door and high window under the gable, a chimney, a side door, and a largish window. But more about that later.

Entry is by way of a simple doorway of about 1300, still with its first door, and straight ahead is a superb C14 **font**. The Victorian tiled floor laps the step, robbing it of height, but the deep bowl panels are beautifully carved with **crocketted** gables, and there is tracery within them and in the **spandrels**; worn little heads jut out below the slim corner buttresses, and the rim is **castellated**. The base of the cover is modern – very well made to match and carry the crocketted top of the C15 original. The opening into the tower is tall and thin, and an arch of Tudor shape on stub **jambs** was inserted later. For those interested in heraldry and family history, there are three **hatchments** in the tower: n. wall, for Richard Bartholomew Martin (1865), with a nice monkey and mirror crest; on the floor, for William Martin (1842); s. wall, for one of his three daughters(1842-70). In the n.w. corner of the nave a plain deal cover lifts away to reveal the C14 door to the tower stair. It is completely sheathed in iron and has two locks, a sure indication that the upper room was used as a safe for church and village valuables. Except for the **embattled wall plate**, all the roof timbers are hidden by a plastered ceiling, but the **rood beam** remains to mark the entrance to the chancel. The pine benches and pulpit are Victorian, and the remnants of an interesting set of painted texts in small, shaped panels on the walls can be dated by the one over the entrance. It shows that the church was repaired by a churchwarden in 1773, and the rest of the set are virtually identical to those at nearby Witnesham. They were chosen and placed to make specific points, so that the one over the s. door reads: 'This is none other than the House of God, this is the Gate of Heaven' (Genesis 28: 17), and others emphasised the significance of font, pulpit, and **altar**. The small bronze

plaque of 1907 for Col. Sir Richard Martin on the s. wall of the nave is worth looking at; signed by E.A.C. Harris and E. Godwin, it has a miniature roundel portrait at the top. On the n. side is William Cantrell's tomb of 1585, a compact and fairly modest effort, with three shields on the chest, and a shell shape with flanking spikes above the back. There are dainty marble columns each side, and three more shields (coloured this time) above an epitaph:

Man here thou mayste yntombed see,
A man of honest fame
Come home to earthe, who in his life bare
Willm Cantrels name ...

The mason rectified one mistake but missed another. See if you can spot it. All that remains of the C16 **rood screen** is a section of the base on the s. side, and that was varnished a dark brown at some time, but the piece of C14 glazing in the tracery 'eye'of the window on the n. side of the chancel is rare because it is virtually intact. The muted yellow border encloses pale green **quarries** decorated with delicate leaf sprays in black. The battered C14 **piscina** in the **sanctuary** has remnants of **cusping** like decayed teeth, and above is a tablet for Robert and Amelia Colvile by Humphrey Hopper, a sculptor whose genius seemed to fail him when prestigious commissions like Gen. Hay's pile of marble in St Paul's came his way. In smaller things he was always competent, and here we have a tablet of 1825 on which curtains are drawn aside between pillars to reveal the inscription, with a small coloured **achievement of arms** on top. As far as I know, his only other Suffolk work is at Worlington [Vol.1]. Set in round-headed recesses on the opposite wall is a pair of matching sarcophagi by James Smith, another fashionable sculptor (for whom Mrs Siddons sat) but whose reputation is dogged by his largest work – the Nelson memorial in London's Guildhall, which nearly beggared him in 1810. He died in his

40s and these monuments to members of the Brand family were done in his last decade.

Now for the mysterious little annexe on the n. side of the nave. It now serves as a **vestry** and is reached by a little connecting passage from the chancel, which was added later. Within you will find a set of **William and Mary Royal Arms** in the last stages of decay, and Sarah Martin's hatchment of 1841. But the fascinating thing about the building is that it was apparently added by Ralph Cantrell, a Roman Catholic who would not transfer his allegiance to the Protestant faith but who wished to avoid the penalties involved. It has always been known as 'Ralph's Hole'. By using its outer door he could attend in comfort, listen to the service, and watch it through the **squint** in the wall opposite the pulpit, but salve his conscience by not actually entering the church. Tradition does not say how he avoided taking the sacrament, but then the village had a certain reputation for waywardness with the authorities. In 1597 the entire parish was cited because 'their children, servantes and apprentyzes [had not] com to church to be catechised for a year past'. Under the rules of 1559 they should have been there every Sunday, and the backsliding coupled with Ralph's example adds point to the wall texts of two centuries on.

Henley, St Peter (E6): Meticulously maintained and surrounded by a manicured churchyard, St Peter's is obviously appreciated by its parishioners. It has that sharp look so often associated with full-scale Victorian restoration, and indeed there were major upheavals in 1846, 1895, and 1904, but the building is welcoming and there is much of interest. The tower has angle buttresses to the w. decorated with good **flushwork**, and a panel above the w. door contains the inscription: 'Orate pro anymab: thome Sekeford et margarete uxor eius' (Pray for the soul of Thomas Seckford and Margaret his

Henley, St Peter: terracotta window

wife). He was a clothier who died in 1505 and doubtless provided most of the money for the new tower; his shield of arms and shears merchant's mark feature on the panel. The little shields in the doorway **spandrels** are interesting because they combine, in two variations, the keys of **St Peter** with the sword of **St Paul**. Was the dedication shared at one time? A circuit of the building entails a detour round a large extension to the n., the village school of 1838, rebuilt in 1904 to serve as a **vestry** and Sunday School. It is as big as the average cottage of the period, with hipped gables and a generous w. window, and it has its own diminutive **porch**. It fits happily with the church and is still useful. The C15 **nave** windows have been renewed but on the s. side there is one that deserves closer attention. Square-headed, with terracotta lintel and **mullions**, it dates from the early 1520s and is likely to have been taken from Shrubland Old Hall. There are large curly dolphin heads with urns at the top, masks on the mullions, and three shields with beasts between below – all in what was then the new Italian **Renaissance** style. The same moulds can be found in windows at Barking and Barham, and the workmen who used them probably came up into Suffolk after they had finished decorating the great house at Layer Marney. A stone mask is set in the wall to the l. and it may be a companion to the purely ornamental **gargoyle** that keeps company with others more active below the tower battlements. The e. window is modern but the **chancel** as a whole dates from the late C13 to early C14, with **lancets** to the n. and **Decorated** windows to the s. The **rood stair** turret shows as a slight projection between nave and chancel on the s. side, and there are two **scratch dials** – one on the s.w. corner of the nave and another on the s.e. corner of the porch.

The inner doorway could be labelled **Transitional** because its **Norman chevron** and **billet** decorations are used in a pointed arch, but there is an incomplete C12 **capital** on the l. and the **jambs** seem to have been remade, so it may be a case of Norman components re-assembled. There are remains of a **stoup** to the r., and the C14 door of lapped boards has strap hinges right across. Just beyond, a showcase contains a copy of the Bible printed by John Baskett in 1716 which has become known as the 'Vinegar Bible' by reason of a single misprint. Beyond it is an 1840s **font**, and there are three **hatchments** to be seen: over the s. door to the e., for Henrietta Sleorgin (1808), who used her parents' arms because her husband was but a cornet in the Horse Guards; to the r. of it, for Mary Medows (1809), who had no family arms of her own and made do with her husband's; and on the n. wall for Harriet Ibbetson (1843), the donor of the schoolroom. Incidentally, the connecting doorway below is the origi-

nal n. entrance and is only 27in. wide. To the r. is a well-lettered **touchstone** tablet in a marble frame patterned with drapes and sprays; an elegant little **cartouche** perches on top, and it commemorates Elizabeth Vere who died in 1717, one of the De Veres who were in the parish for over 200 years. The nave lies under a plaster ceiling and there are substantial C19 benches with **poppyheads**. The **gallery**, with its 'Gothick' tracery balustrade, was reduced to its present width in 1846 and in more recent times the ringing chamber beyond has been glazed in. Although heavily lime-washed, the details of the terracotta s. window mouldings show up clearly from within, and farther along there are the tall and thin doorways of the rood stair. The **rood beam**, with its plain cross, is modern pine and goes with the wagon **roof** of the chancel. The C13 **piscina** beyond **dropped-sill sedilia** in the **sanctuary** is interesting because the bowl previously belonged to a Norman pillar piscina. Some have suggested that it came from the stoup in the porch, but I do not think so. A small **aumbry** in the opposite wall has holes drilled in the surround that would have taken a wooden frame for a door or an iron grille. By it stands a very ornate C19 lectern in oak, with a turned and carved pedestal and double book shelf. It is rather a chaotic mixture of styles, but is remarkable for one thing. The two slopes, with their broad, carved borders of **acanthus** leaves, are cut from a single block; I could find no trace of a join at the ridge, which is itself carved.

Higham, St Mary (D10): The setting is most attractive; the church stands by the Hall and the water meadows of the Stour reach up to the edges of the churchyard. The tower is likely to have been built in the C13 but above the small w. doorway a short and broad window has **Decorated tracery** with pairs of **mouchettes** above flattened **ogees**. The bell openings are

Perpendicular and there is a slab turret on the s. side up to the belfry. Recently restored, the s. wall of the **nave** is spotted with lumps of **septaria** and, like the **priest's door** farther along, the doorway has been blocked up. All the Perpendicular windows on that side have been renewed and so has the **chancel** e. window. If its intersected 'Y' tracery is a copy of the original it means that nave and chancel were probably built soon after the tower. A narrow n. **aisle** was added in the early C15 and entry now is through a C19 wooden **porch** and a small but substantial n. doorway.

For a little church, the four-bay **arcade** between nave and aisle is remarkably elaborate and decorative. The lobes of the **quatrefoil piers** are ogee-shaped and their **capitals** are carved alternately with vines and **paterae**. The **hood moulds** come down to **headstops** decorated with leaves on the n. but on the nave side there are four excellent heads, including two women wearing the net head-dress known as a crespine. The **roofs** are C19 but the stone **corbels** in the aisle appear to be original and the nave roof incorporates medieval **arch-braces** which rest on wooden slabs that are worth studying. There is a man with his tongue out in the s.e. corner, an angel with a shield, and in the s.w corner a cowled figure with a book grins knowingly. The simple C14 **font** has quatrefoils in the bowl panels above a traceried stem and there is another bowl on the floor nearby. Small blank shields are carved on four of its faces and it was originally set against a wall or pillar; although sometimes described as a font, it is almost certainly a large **stoup** and may have formed part of the vanished s. porch. The 1811 memorial for Robert and Marian Hoy on the n. wall is by Charles Regnart, a prolific monumental mason, some of whose work was good enough to exhibit at the Royal Academy. Here, however, he is not at his best. It is a bas relief in which an awkwardly posed woman clasps an urn which she seems

to have caught just in time, and the folds of flimsy drapery serve only to confuse the anatomy. In contrast to the stiff Victorian Gothic tablets over the n. and s. doors, there is a sweet little design on the s. wall for Helen Dawson, who died young in 1863 – an obelisk over a chaplet of flowers in relief which frames the epitaph. The glass in the window to the r. is a World War I memorial, with conventional regimental crests and a figure of **St George**, but it is interesting that the designer chose to pair the patron saint with Richard Coeur de Lion. In a window farther along there are two **pre-Raphaelite** figures of Faith and Charity, with peaches-and-cream complexions and deeply coloured brocade dresses; a good turn-of-the-century period piece by **Powell & Sons**. Just below, a **piscina** under a **cusped** ogee arch shows that there was a nave **altar** nearby.

The chancel roof was reconstructed in the 1880s restoration but retained the old arch-braces and **castellated wall plates**. There must have been a masonry arch between nave and chancel previously but the replacement is wood and comes down to large canopied oak figures of **St Peter** and **St Paul** resting on stone corbels. The choir stalls probably date from the same time and have **Evangelistic symbols** on the elbows and two curiously flat lions at the front. The 1820s memorial in artificial Coade stone on the n. wall is not very attractive but it is interesting that its design is the same as a tablet in Layham church which was cut by E.J. Physick much later; this one may have been done by his father. The **sanctuary** is tiled and so is the **reredos** on either side of the alabaster centre panels. Some of the colours are fairly startling but the design includes nicely lettered **decalogue**, Lord's Prayer and Creed. There is a plain **touchstone** tablet in the corner for Alice Dokenfielde who died in 1622, and below it is a C16 piscina with small paterae in the moulding, a wooden **credence shelf**, and an interesting drain shaped like a **Tudor rose**.

The chancel floor was probably tiled in the C14 and some examples have been found which are now embedded in the s. windowsill; two are heraldic shields and were once glazed.

Hintlesham, St Nicholas (D8): The church stands back from the village street in a pleasant setting, and the tower has a late **Perpendicular** window above a plain w. door. There are three recently restored **clerestory** windows on the s. side, but the n. **aisle** was re-roofed at a steeper angle at some time, thus covering the upper windows on that side. The n. door is blocked and farther to the e. there is a C13 window composed of three **lancets**. There are more tall lancets in the **chancel** and a large modern brick and flint n.e. **vestry**. A small **priest's door** is set in the wall on the other side, and the windows on the s. frontage have **Decorated tracery** with **mouchette** patterns like those at Washbrook; all that is, except the one nearest the porch, which has intersected 'Y' tracery of about 1300. The s. **porch** was restored to celebrate the coronation of King George V and the inner doorway has very deep continuous mouldings.

The character of the interior is established by the simplicity and solidity of the C13 **nave arcades**. The chamfered arches rest on well-moulded **capitals** and the **piers** are circular and octagonal alternately. But it is interesting that they are not paired and one shape faces the other across the nave. The blocked clerestory windows are outlined above them on the n. side and there is a C19 **tie-beam** and **king-post roof**. The **font** and the benches are Victorian too and the organ stands on a square C19 w. **gallery** which carries two **hatchments**: for Frances Burrell, who died in 1846 (l.), and Capt. Heneage Lloyd of the Coldstream Guards, who died in 1776. Fragments of a medieval wall painting survive above the n. arcade, and although nothing is left that can be recognised, its position opposite the door suggests that it was a **St Christo-**

pher. The glass in the s. aisle windows was made and engraved at Ipswich School and there are skilfully lettered names on the clear **quarries**, recording baptisms, marriages, and deaths in a way that is both imaginative and attractive. There is a **piscina** in a square recess by the **altar** farther along, and a tall niche in the e. wall contains a large 1930s statue of the church's patron saint. Judging by the timbers, the n. aisle roof was restructured in the C15 or C16, and below the three-**light** window there is a C13 piscina within a bold **trefoil** arch. As a **retable**, the altar there has a modern, fresh-coloured painting of fisherman hauling their nets, thoughtfully combining an allusion to the disciples as fishers of men and **St Nicholas's** role as the patron saint of seamen. There is no chancel arch now but a cross is set on a modern, braced beam which rests on two huge stone **corbels**. They may have been elsewhere originally, but if not they are surprisingly pagan for this position. One is a devil pulling his mouth open and the other is a **green man**, although the leaves that issue from his mouth are rudimentary. The stair to the vanished **rood loft** is within the chancel on the s. side and is a late construction in **Tudor** brick. The chancel roof is apparently a C19 reconstruction and has curious pierced braces under a plastered ceiling. On the n. wall, a **touchstone** tablet for Charles Vesey (1657) is set within a lozenge like a hatchment and is engraved with his arms and crest. Farther along, there is an unusual and attractive memorial for Capt. John Timperley who died in 1629. It is a 6ft touchstone slab engraved with his effigy in half-armour, and he wears his hair long over a lace collar. The architectural frame contains martial trophies and his **achievement**, with all the lines emphasised by white mastic filling. The verse below has a fine disregard for the niceties of language:

Let others tombes, which ye glad heires bestowes

Write golde in merble, greefe affects no

showes,
There's a trew harte intombed him, &
that beares
   A silent & sadd Epitaph writt in
teares.

Although the vestry has been rebuilt,
its door from the chancel shows that it
was a medieval chapel. This is confirmed by a long **squint** which is angled
up to emerge in the **sanctuary**. Across
in the s. wall there is a very worn C14
piscina which has faint traces of **crockets** and pinnacles, and nearby is the
dilapidated monument of Thomas
Tympley, his son Nicholas, and their
respective wives. Thomas died in 1593
and the little alabaster figures kneel in
pairs across prayer desks, with their
children grouped behind them. The
plinth and cornice are inlaid in colour
and there are three shields of arms on
the top. The C17 **communion rails** have
well-turned and very closely set **balusters**, and the panels that stand against
the side walls of the sanctuary may
well have formed part of the rood loft.

Hitcham, All Saints (B7): By the sign at
the s. end of the village a short lane
leads past an attractive late C15 house
which was once the Guildhall to a
spacious churchyard; its path rises
steadily to the large, handsome church
whose **Perpendicular** tower has heavy
buttresses reaching almost to the top,
making it seem even bulkier than it is.
There is a solid stair turret to the s. and
the bell stage, with its generous three-
light windows, has the look of an
addition to the original design. **Base
course** and buttresses are decorated
with **flushwork** chequer and the late
C14 w. doorway with small **headstops**
is flanked by niches under **crocketted**
canopies. On walking round, you will
find an early C14 n. door and the
remains of a **rood stair** just visible in
the angle between the n. **aisle** and the
chancel. The large two-storeyed **sacristy** with barred windows nearby has
recently been restored, and the chancel
was largely rebuilt in 1878 (look for the
photograph inside which shows it mi-

nus s. and e. walls). A little to the e.
there are two stones of the 1680s
carved with skulls, hour-glass and
death's sharp darts, while alongside is a
finely lettered modern headstone. In
the rebuilding, the C14 **priest's door**
was retained. Note the squat and
curious windows of the **clerestory**. The
C15 **porch** is so like Bildeston's that
one suspects that the same master
mason designed both – there is the
same lavish flushwork on the facade
and three particularly good niches;
they are tall and vaulted, with angels
below the stools and crocketted canopies formed by pairs of little **ogee**
arches. The parapet here, however, is
flushwork and instead of roses the
spandrels contain a **Trinity** shield on
the l. and **instruments of the Passion** on
the r. There is no sign of an upper room
here but the impressive inner doorway
is again of the Bildeston pattern, with a
double rank of deep mouldings set
with shields and crowns rising to an
angel at the apex; there are worn lion
stops to the **hood mould** and the tracery
of the doors was applied to new panels
when the porch was restored in 1882.

   Within, walls and C14 **arcades** are
brilliantly white above pale brick
floors and the narrowness of the aisles
suggests that they were designed for
processions rather than for additional
seating. All was re-roofed in the early
C17; this is interesting because the
form chosen for the **nave** was a double
hammerbeam – harking back more
than a hundred years in terms of
technique. The structure is familiar
but the detailing reflects its age, with
pineapple pendants below the **collar
beams**, grotesque masks against the
arch-braces, and **Jacobean** scrollery
behind the vertical struts. Instead of
the old-style angels, the hammerbeams
carry oval plaques with mainly secular
emblems – harp, thistle, and portcullis
on the s.; rose, crossed sword and
baton, and sun in splendour on the n.
The date is confirmed by a crowned
monogram for James I on the s. side and
another for Charles I at the e. end of the
s. aisle. The aisles feature interesting

bosses, including some faces, and look for the curling **unicorn** just e. of the s. door. On the wall below is possibly the best of the county's modern **Royal Arms** – a 1937 set of George VI's, pierced and carved in gilded and painted wood. The cover of the C19 **font** in the s.w. corner has a pretty coloured and gilt Gothic cover presented in 1943. The way in which the tower buttresses obtrude and allow the arcades to pass beyond them suggests that the tower was built separately and the nave extended to meet it. Below stands a pair of C19 churchwardens' stalls which are attractive and unusual, having hoods and desks. The medieval nave benches have fragments of beasts on the elbows and, repaired and restored, they were augmented by three C19 ranges at the e. end. A large C18 oil painting of the visit of the Magi by an unknown artist hangs on the s. wall, and in the aisle chapel the C14 **piscina** has unusual recessed **cusping** and a very deep drain. Over the n. door there is a fine and large demi-angel; I wonder whether it is a survivor from the previous **roof** or whether it has come from elsewhere. At the e. end of the n. aisle a tiny ogee niche is set in the **jamb** of the last arcade arch and opposite is an alabaster and **touchstone** memorial for Sir George Waldegrave, with fourteen lines of totally obfuscating genealogy. He died in 1636 and his wife, 'Laments her loss, and bids these lynes declare his piety … late faithful mate, now blissful soul (quoth she) though weeping for herself I joy for thee'. The syntax is as confused as his family tree, but it's the 'faithful mate' I rather care for.

The C18 pulpit is in plain panelled oak but its **tester** has a dark marquetry star on the underside. Close to it is the base of an early C16 **rood screen** and there are traces of painted figures in the panels which are a little unusual – they are all angels bearing Passion emblems. Set against a stippled background pattern, they have green wings, capes of ermine, and golden

crowns. Determined attempts were obviously made to disfigure them but they display from l. to r.: pincers, the pillar and cords, spear, possibly Christ's robe, (next panel half destroyed), sponge on cleft reed, nails, and a very indistinct but possible crown of thorns. The chancel is reached by no fewer than five steps, with two more into the **sanctuary**, and it is likely that such an extreme change in level was an 1870s alteration. The coved and panelled ceiling dates from then. Three **ledger-stones** bear indents of large **brasses** and two of them had fine canopies. In the sanctuary the C14 piscina lies below a large cusped and crocketted ogee arch, complete with **finial** and leaf stops.

On the n. wall the chaste tablet of shaped marble set on a mottled dark red back is by Thomas Woolner, a Hadleigh boy who went on to achieve considerable success as a sculptor and was a friend of the **pre-Raphaelites**. It commemorates John Stevens Henslow, who was rector here from 1837 to 1861. As botanist, geologist, and chemist he had international standing, and secured for Darwin the appointment to H.M.S. *Beagle*. His work at Cambridge did not mean a neglected parish, and his stand against local landowners on behalf of the poor made him powerful enemies but countless friends in the hungry 1840s. A lithograph portrait of this outstanding man hangs by the s. door and the porch was restored in his memory.

Holton St Mary, St Mary (E9): The squat tower was no doubt a good deal taller originally and now has low brick battlements, with a perky weathervane on one corner and a flagstaff on another. There are panels of **flushwork** at the base of the buttresses and a large glacial boulder is built into the base at the n.w.; a tall, two-**light Perpendicular** w. window was inserted later. The C14 **nave** has a n. door with worn **headstops** but it was blocked at some time and the top half glazed. The nave windows have **Decorated tracery**, and a small C19 **vestry** was added to the n. side of the C13 **chancel**, which has had all its windows renewed. Most of the **priest's door** on the s. side is apparently original and there is a Victorian s. **porch** whose benches incorporate medieval **poppyheads**. The inner doorway has large king and queen headstops and within, the nave and chancel lie under modern panelled pine **roofs** with **tie-beams** and **king-posts**. The C14 tower arch is tall and, beyond, the 1880s w. window glass by **Heaton, Butler & Bayne** displays better than average modelling in the Resurrection and Ascension scenes; cherub heads emerge from the angry clouds behind the two figures of Christ. The bowl of the C15 **font** has a **Tudor rose**, defaced shields, and a fleur de lys in the bowl panels, but note that there are sockets for shafts around the base, which belonged to a C13 predecessor. A dark set of George II **Royal Arms** hangs over the s. door, and to the r. is a very interesting painted wooden panel which has been well restored. It shows a youth wearing a tricorne hat, leaning on a spade, and holding a paper in one hand. The legend reads: 'Opened August 29th 1748' and flanking scrolls have: 'Not slothful in Business. Serving the Lord.' It once hung in the school, now a private house, by the churchyard gate, and the story is completed by the Revd Stephen White's epitaph on the n. wall:

> on April 12, 1773 being Easter Monday as he was officiating in the church he was suddenly called away from his labours to receive their Reward, and expired in that School which his Piety had raised.

A chancel s. window contains glass of 1899 by Heaton, Butler & Bayne with two pale musical angels, and the windows flanking the **sanctuary** have glass which may be by the **O'Connors** – figures of the **Evangelists** in agreeable colour, with their symbols in the lower panels. The small C13 **piscina** has an arch with shallow **cusps** and the shafts have ring **capitals** and bases. Plain

dropped-sill sedilia lie alongside, and in the n. wall there is an **aumbry** which was evidently fitted with a door. The odd thing is that its arch is cusped and not designed to be hidden.

Hoo, St Andrew and St Eustachius (F4): Standing by the Hall at the end of a lane, away even from the scattered houses of the hamlet, the church enjoys a memorably peaceful setting. In linking one of the apostles with a little known soldier-martyr, the unique dedication is one of the most curious. The leggy little brick tower dates from the early C16 and its parapet has been renewed relatively recently. It has a stair turret to the s., and makes use of an earlier w. window of about 1300 which matches the **chancel** e. window. The neat little plastered **porch** has a tiled **roof**, with medieval side timbers exposed within, and it shelters a C14 doorway which has a deep channel set between two mouldings.

The modest interior lies under a single plastered ceiling spanned by six heavy **tie-beams**, one of which carries the date '1595'. It seems likely that the body of the church needed strengthening just before the tower was built. The C15 **font** has four contented lions seated round the shaft, and in the bowl panels you will find angels holding shields which carry a **Trinity** emblem (n.e.), possible **Passion emblems** (w.), a crown, a large **Tudor rose**, and a rampant lion. Curiously, instead of an angel the s.e. panel contains a standing figure, possibly a priest, although, like the others, it is defaced. By the n. door with its replacement drawbar stands a deep C14 chest of poplar, reinforced with narrow bands and fitted with three locks. The **decalogue boards** above are probably early C19 like the plain benches with their rudimentary **poppyheads**. These extend well into the chancel area, there being no division to separate it from the **nave**, but the site of the **rood screen** is marked by the stairs which gave access to the loft. They rise from a window embrasure on the s. side and are a little unusual in that they proceed to the w. rather than the e. At first glance the niche in the chancel e. wall looks like a **piscina** but it is placed a little too high and there is no drain. Three-sided **communion rails** were a late C17 fashion but these are very austere and have the look of the early C18. They perform a double function on the s. side and have a book ledge which was probably for a little choir which sat on the low bench in the s.e. angle of the chancel. The **altar** is a small, almost square, late C17 table with unusual turned decoration on the legs, rather like a series of napkin rings.

Horham, St Mary (D3): The village street bends sharply to skirt the churchyard and an attractively clipped conical yew complements the handsome early C16 tower when seen from the w. The tower (well restored in 1984) is particularly impressive from this side, beautifully proportioned, with diagonal buttresses that have four **set-offs**, and two prominent **string courses**. The **flushwork base course** is badly mutilated to the n. and w. The w. doorway has slim attached shafts, fine moulding in the arch, and **spandrels** carved with the **sacred monogram** and an 'M' for the dedication. The doors themselves are original, and the wear on the r. hand side of the step shows that the entrance was heavily used for years. There are pairs of bell openings on three sides, but to the s. a substantial stair turret rises to the top, leaving room only for a single, wider window. Note that the flushwork on the buttresses is doubled at that level and that there are flushwork panels worked with emblems set below the windows. The most elaborate decoration is reserved for the battlements as if in celebration of the tower's completion, and although much of the heraldry is unidentified, with binoculars one can recognise the diamond-shaped buckles of the

Jernegan family, the three boars' heads of the Borretts, crowned 'Ms', and the sacred monogram. Although the **nave** was obviously heightened, it still looks low in relation to the tower, and on the n. side is the first indication of the church's true age. The blocked n. doorway is **Norman**, with a simple roll moulding resting on shafts which have volute **capitals**. The nave walls are plastered and the late C14 square-headed windows have simple **Decorated tracery**. By the mid-C19 the church was in poor state and there was a full-scale restoration. The architect was Augustus Frere and in 1879-81 he virtually rebuilt the **chancel** and gave it an adventurous e. window which has three **cinquefoils** within a circle in the head. The side windows were re-used, together with the **priest's door**, and above it is an interesting example of a **scratch dial**. It is incised on a square slab and the double rim is a complete circle with Roman numerals cut in the lower half. The small brick **porch** is probably C18 but within there is another Norman doorway, this time rather more elaborate, as befits the main entrance. There are pairs of columns with capitals matching those on the n. doorway, but here the roll moulding in the arch is joined by an outer double **chevron**.

The interior is attractively homely under a plastered ceiling, and the sturdy tower arch is completely panelled in. This is unusual and may have been done to reduce the draughts before the church was restored. There is a particularly interesting graffito about 6ft. up on the n. side: 'Be it knowne unto all ringers which doe assemble to this place [must] bestow somthing on the sixton'. Although unringable at the moment, the C16 and C17 bells are claimed to be the oldest ring of eight anywhere, and were popular with visiting bands (although someone obviously objected to the cash levy!). There are good examples of **consecration crosses** on either side of the tower arch – incised discoid crosses within painted circles. On the n. wall are C19 **decalogue boards** in good condition, and the substantial buff-coloured C15 **font** has squat, smiling lions around the shaft. Four of the bowl panels are carved with lions whose tails curl between their legs and up over their backs, and the remainder have angels holding shields. **Dowsing** was here in August 1644, and as he specifically mentions a **Trinity emblem** that he defaced on the font, he was no doubt responsible for the rest of the damage. The contemporary spirelet cover has well-carved **crockets** on the ribs which themselves retain some colour, and the excellent **finial** still has the ring which shows that there was once a counterbalance and chain to raise it. In 1963 the remains of the church's ancient glass were rearranged in the s.e. window of the nave. The top shield in the l. hand **light** is that of the Black Prince (although a lion in a roundel has been substituted for one quarter of it), and the shield below is Edward III's (with a fleur de lys inserted where the leopards of England should be); at the bottom is the shield of the De Veres. The Warenne shield is in the centre of the other light, with the arms of Ufford below it. Other C14 and C15 fragments include an errant leg and foot bereft of body in the l. hand edging. **Rood stairs** lie in the n. wall and although there is now only a low C19 **screen**, the beam above it is likely to have been the original rood beam. The nave benches are an extraordinary mixture. At the w. end there are stubby C15 bench ends with **paterae** carved on the chamfers and **poppyheads** (some are good copies); C16 **linen-fold panels** have been inserted sideways in the backs of later benches, and there are more farther e. Although much of the main range is C19, the benches stand on the old sills that raised them above the brick floor and left room for straw covering. Quite the most intriguing item is to be found under the 4th bench from the e. end on the s. side. It is a hand-carved wooden trough which is held by a dowel so that it may be swung out. It is 14in. long, 2in. deep, and 3in.

wide, with a hole drilled in the bottom. It looks a good deal older than the seat to which it is attached, and although it has been called a snuff box, I think it may have housed long churchwarden's tobacco pipes originally. The pulpit of 1631 is a fine piece – although much altered. The blind-arched panels have delicate strapwork and there are complementary carved panels below the canted book ledge. The door latch is a good original but the bas relief lamb is a later addition and the base is modern. Its backboard now stands on the floor by the modern lectern and the centre panel contains a boldly carved and dated shield. Although it is tempting to describe the other panel of C17 woodwork that lies between pulpit and backboard as part of a two-decker arrangement, I think it came from another source.

A recently acquired **Royal Arms** in stained glass hangs as a panel inside the chancel n. window. They are **Stuart**, set within an oval, and although the crest and helm are missing, the painting is good. The glass in the **sanctuary** side windows is by **Ward & Hughes** and shows all the defects of the firm's early work, although the arrangement of the figures on the s. side is interesting. Christ's head in the Ascension scene probably weathered badly and was replaced. The sanctuary has two remarkable chairs, the backs of which belong to the **Renaissance** period, with portrait roundels. The rest is a strange amalgam, with demi-figures in heavy wigs holding lambs at the front of the arms on the n. side, while the s. side chair has naked male and female supporters holding a 'W' and an 'H'. Twisted scrolls terminating in acorns frame the backs and are C19 work (like the acorns on the font cover). There is a typical example of an early C17 chest in the corner of the sanctuary, and a late C14 **piscina** with arches that do not match. The simple C17 **altar** table has turned legs and plain stretchers; its beautiful frontal was embroidered by a retired priest, John Cowgill, who had only one arm; more of his work is to be seen at Stradbroke. The church has a fine C14 chest which will soon (hopefully) be displayed. It is 7ft long, totally sheathed and banded in iron, and has six locks.

Horham may well be the only church which at present has its own beehives in the churchyard. The produce helps the funds and the project is a particularly nice idea. It makes a change from sheep.

Hoxne, St Peter and St Paul (C2): On the evidence of place names, some would have us believe that **St Edmund** was martyred at Hellesdon in Norfolk, but the strong and reasonable tradition is that he met his death here at the hands of the Danes in 870. The oak against which it is claimed he was pierced by arrows finally succumbed in 1848 and some of the timber was used in the church. A grassy walk leads from the ample **lych-gate** past weeping willow and spreading cedar to the s. **porch** and the eye is drawn inexorably to the handsome tower which, with the porch, was built in the mid-C15 by the De La Pole family. It has a delicate **base course** of **foiled** shields and a sturdy octagonal turret on the s. face rises above the stepped battlements. The w. door has **Tudor roses** in the **spandrels**, small **headstops**, and shields, mitres, and crowns decorate the mouldings. The pretty niches flanking the w. window are canopied, with minute heads at the end of the **cusps**, and they contain modern figures of the church's patron saints. The **put-log holes** used by the builders are outlined in brick and there are generous three-**light** bell openings. The long **nave** is tall, with elongated **Perpendicular** windows, and just above the w. wall of the porch you will see the **quoins** that marked the end of the building before the tower was added. The n. doorway is excellent small-scale work, with shields and **paterae** in the moulding and a delightful pair of headstops. The **aisle** buttresses on that side were renewed in brick at some stage and a brick

parapet takes a curving line along the top. The 1470s Lady chapel at the e. end is taller, and the **chancel** was largely rebuilt in 1880, with a small **vestry** set endwise against it on the n. side. This was the work of **Ewan Christian** for the Church Commissioners. A C19 embellishment was the male saint placed in a niche over the **priest's door**.

The s. doorway has good king and queen headstops that have been partially re-cut, and just inside is a C13 grave slab in the floor. The nave was restored in the 1880s under the direction of J.K. Colling, who had worked at Eye, and he designed the majority of the fittings. The low-pitched **roof** has decayed **tie-beams** and two more were inserted later at a lower level at the e. end. The **wall plate** is now coved on the n. side only. There is a low, late C13 **arcade** of six bays separating nave from aisle and the westernmost **hood mould** comes down to an angel bearing a shield – possibly added when the nave was extended to meet the tower. There are partially blocked **clerestory** windows on that side only. Like the **Evangelistic symbols**, the angels in the bowl of the C15 **font** have had their heads chopped away, but the heraldic shields are of more than usual interest. On the e. face are the arms of Bishop Lyhart of Norwich. He had been chaplain to William De La Pole, Duke of Suffolk, and died at his palace at Hoxne on Whitsunday 1472. The arms on the s. side are those of John De La Pole, 2nd Duke of Norfolk, who married Elizabeth Plantagenet, the sister of Edward IV and Richard III. That was in 1460 and so the font must have been installed between then and the bishop's death – a much more accurate dating than is normally possible. Seated monks and headless figures support the shaft, and the cover dates from 1879. Before moving on, note the **consecration cross** behind the font.

The wall above the arcade once displayed a most interesting range of early C15 wall paintings but, sadly, very little can be distinguished now. However, we know what they were,

Hoxne, St Peter and St Paul: Maynard monument detail

and there are some things which can still be identified (a bright day and binoculars are the ideal combination). Starting from the w. end, in the traditional place opposite the main door, is **St Christopher**, recognised by his massive staff. Then we come to the tree whose fruit are the **Seven Deadly Sins**. At the bottom, the face and tail of one of a pair of devils are clear and also the saw he is using to fell the tree. The sin of envy is top l., sloth is bottom r., and lust is just above it. The dragon on that side and traces of the red and green background can be seen. The series was balanced by the **Seven Works of Mercy** alongside in a series of panels with inscribed scrolls. There are outlines of the first six figures ministering (in order) to the naked, hungry, thirsty, imprisoned, sick, and the dead, but the end of the sequence was overlaid by an C18 memorial. The final tableau was a **Doom** of the sort more often found over

a chancel arch. Only the arc of heaven remains and two massive tie-beams secured by wooden pins emerge just to confuse things. In 1987 the n. aisle housed an excellent and varied exhibition illustrating the history of church and village. At the w. end is a huge late C14 parish chest, 8ft long and over 2ft wide; heavily banded, it has securing bars as well as six hasps. A group of bench ends has been re-used at the e. end of the aisle and the mutilated carving at the w. end of the range is the wolf guarding St Edmund's head, the only direct reference to the saint now to be found in the church. On the e. wall of the n. aisle chapel is the imposing memorial of Thomas Maynard who died in 1742. Its backing obelisk towers up nearly 18ft. It is one of two important monuments for the Maynard family by Charles Stanley (the other is at Little Easton in Essex and is even grander). Stanley's talents embraced stucco ceilings, chimney pieces, and even china, and here we have a life-size figure in complete Roman dress down to the sandals; he rests one arm on an urn and holds a book in his right hand. There is an exquisite bas relief miniature of women and children on the pedestal of the urn and the front of the chest has a beautifully cut Latin epitaph.

The steps that led to the **rood loft** are exposed below the arch leading to the n. chapel and there is a statue niche behind the pulpit. Close by the lectern there are two **brass** shields and inscriptions for Thomas Thruston (1606) and John Thruston (1613); one for another John Thruston (1640) is now on the wall by the door. In the chancel you will find what is the only listed work in Suffolk by Sir Francis Chantrey, but it is not signed and it is not typical – a plain tablet and elementary sarcophagus shape against a black background as a memorial for Sir Thomas Heselrige who died in 1817. The **reredos** and **altar** date from 1907 and the church's **mensa** has been restored to its rightful place. The s. chancel windows have stiffly conventional figures of the **Evangelists** which were inserted when the chancel was restored and the e. window glass of 1853 is by Thomas Baillie. There are four shapes containing scenes in blatant and sickly colour, and the rest is taken up with texts set against yellowy-green patterned **quarries**; not very nice. It is a relief to look again at the centre nave window – a rich design of Christ subduing the waves, possibly by **Heaton, Butler & Bayne**. The window to the e. of it has the two patron saints set against deep blue, with the remainder of the space taken up by patterned quarries, and may date from the 1850s. Nearer the door is the spiky Victorian Gothic memorial to Gen. Sir Edward Kerrison; he commanded the 7th Hussars at Waterloo and lived to remember that famous day for nigh on forty years.

Ipswich, All Hallows (E7): This, like St Thomas's and St Andrew's, was a church built in the 1930s to cater for the town's growing population. Stand-

ing on Landseer Road, it serves the area of the Gainsborough estate and was designed by **H. Munro Cautley** in 1938. Unlike his church of St Augustine, this was an economical exercise in red brick which followed a conventional contemporary line. Under a hipped roof, the **nave** has tall windows at high level and beyond the square **transepts** there is a short **chancel** whose blank e. wall has a cross outlined in smaller bricks. There is a **vestry** block to the s. and a slim n.e. tower, oblong in section. There are twin **porches** at the w. end and in the baptistery the solid octagonal **font** has a very nice cover which is arcaded like a miniature market cross and decorated with marquetry and veneers. The red brick of the walls is warm but not strident, and severity is relieved by small blind arches below the nave windows. The flat, panelled ceiling is tricked out in blue, red, and green. The transepts lie beyond two-bay **arcades**, and a miniature font stands in front of the **altar** on the s. side. Nearby on the wall is a portrait plaque of Sir William Smith, founder of the Boys' Brigade. Screened by heavy green curtains, the n. transept Lady chapel was re-furnished in 1951 and its **sanctuary** lies beyond a smaller version of the chancel arch. Cautley was fond of reproducing medieval-style **piscinas** and there is one here, complete with drain and **credence shelf**, set in the brick wall. The C19 nave benches came from Ely cathedral, but pulpit, reading desk, altar, and choir stalls are all veneered in walnut banded with burr walnut in the furniture style of the period. Even the cross that hangs below the chancel arch was made to match. The barrel **roof** of the chancel matches the nave, and the altar is backed by a plain hanging against which is set a striking cross formed from polished steel rods.

Ipswich, All Saints (E7): Consecrated in 1887, the church stands on Chevallier Street, part of the w. ring road, and the architect was Samuel

Wright of Morecombe, who submitted the winning design among eighty-five entries in a competition judged by **Ewan Christian**. There is a **porch** at the n.w. corner but the main entrance is in the base of the s.w. tower. This takes an octagonal shape at the second stage and there is a terracotta **sound hole** to the s., under tall bell openings. Above the parapet pierced with **quatrefoils** is a distinctive concave-profiled lead spirelet. The overall style is **Perpendicular** and the tall **nave** and **aisles** lie under double-pitched **roofs**. At the e. end of the s. aisle and on the s. wall of the **chancel** are low-level terracotta panels of intricate **tracery** rather like mock sound holes. There was once a medieval church dedicated to All Saints near Handford Bridge and its dedication stone is preserved in the redundant St Nicholas. A copy was made and inserted at the base of the tower here but it is now damaged and unreadable.

The architect's brief was to provide for a congregation of 800 at £7 a seat and the interior shows how successful he was in dealing with this level of economy without sacrificing aesthetics. Red brick and terracotta *en masse* can be overpowering but here, with plenty of light and a spacious setting, the feeling is comfortable and very pleasant. The **arcades** are particularly effective, their terracotta quatrefoil **piers** having simple **capitals** and bases, and the chamfers of the arches are slightly ridged. The nave roof is panelled out over braced collar beams and **tie-beams** and there are barrel roofs in the aisles, again with tie-beams. At the w. end there is a heavy stone **font** in restrained style, but a portable version in a light oak frame stands in the n. aisle. Nearby is an organ in a stripped pine case with gaily painted pipes, but the main instrument is housed to the s. of the chancel, separated from the s. aisle by a half-arch in the form of a flying buttress. This makes a distracting background for the **altar** in the Lady chapel. Wright designed the pulpit in 1905 and its rather stiff carving in conventional style incorporates two standing figures. The chancel lies under a barrel roof with a two-bay arcade each side, the easternmost bays being blind except for narrow entrance arches to **vestry** and organ, and quatrefoil **clerestory** windows. Shallow **sedilia** are set in the s. wall and Wright designed the **reredos** of 1896. A cross encircled by a text from the opening of St John's Gospel is flanked by **Evangelistic symbols** and vases of lilies and roses, with shallow **tabernacle work** and cresting; the carving was by Hatch & Sons, painted panels by Jewett, and decoration by Shrigley & Hunt – all Lancaster firms. The e. window glass by Campbell of London dates from 1947 and has Christ the King with figures of the **Blessed Virgin, St John, St Edmund**, and **St Thomas of Canterbury**, with an **Agnus Dei** in the tracery.

Ipswich, Holy Trinity (E7) The church stands on rising ground above Fore Hamlet and a line of dock cranes can be seen from the churchyard. Built in 1835, it was the first of the town's C19 churches and its indeterminate design is typical of the period. The architect was Frederick Harvey, a local man, and he chose to build a nave that is like many a nonconformist chapel, in plain Suffolk white bricks, with round-headed windows. To it he added a spindly tower complete with battlements. At some stage, outside staircases were built at the w. end to give access to the **gallery**, and they are boxed in and glazed in domestic fashion. In 1895 a **chancel** was added by Edward Bisshopp in matching style, although we shall see inside that he was more enterprising there. A large parish hall of 1891 stands to the s. linked to the church by a passage that would have been more comely in brick.

Do not be discouraged by the dull exterior for you will find that the inside of the church is remarkably attractive. A **font** stands in the base of the tower, with **decalogue boards** nearby, and there are replicas of the seals used by the old Holy Trinity priory reproduced in the w. window. The broad **nave** lies under a flat plaster ceiling pierced with round cast iron ventilators, and the slightly raked gallery has wings which advance on each side, supported on slim iron pillars. It is Bisshopp's shining white chancel in the style of the classical revival that lifts the interior from the mundane and makes it lively. The semi-circular chancel arch has pairs of fluted Ionic columns each side below rich cornices, and the design is continued on the flanks by smaller, matching arches; the **sanctuary** is panelled out in white up to a deep plaster frieze decorated with foliage. In a 1960s reorganisation the organ was moved to the s. side and the narrow chancel n. **aisle** became a Lady chapel, using the former **high altar** and its **reredos**. This is a 1919 painting by Leonard A. Pownall of the supper at Emmaus, and the bold profiles of the two disciples with the risen Christ are characteristic of an artist whose work included stained glass design. He was related to the vicar of the time and was chosen to carry out the splendid e. window, a memorial to those who fell in World War I. Christ in Majesty stands within a ring of angels above the Tree of Life; harpists are grouped below, and in the corners stand figures of a centurion, **St George**, a C20 soldier, sailor, and a nurse below orange and pomegranate trees. More angels drink from the River of the Water of Life as it flows into the distance, and around the figure of Christ there is a lovely gradation of colour from lilac through orange and cerise to gold. The only other stained glass is in a nave s. window and is not in the same class, a figure of **St Paul** with a roundel portrait below of a vicar who died in 1917. Nearby, however, is an excellent pulpit on a tall stem in C17 style; it has strapwork in the lower panels and Ionic columns at the angles, sheathed in **acanthus** leaves at their bases.

Ipswich, Holy Trinity: Leonard Pownall e. window

Ipswich, St Andrew (E7): Standing just off Britannia Road, this is one of three new churches built in Ipswich in the 1930s to cater for the growing population. Now, a burgeoning congregation requires a larger building, and by the time this is published a new church will have been consecrated adjoining the original. That was designed by **Cautley** in 1936, a simple hall in red brick, with a shallow **chancel**, to which a w. baptistery and entrance were added later. The old **nave** will be used for Sunday School and youth activities, with the chancel retained as a chapel, and the main body of the new church is a large square building under a hipped **roof** to the e. An entrance foyer links it with the s. side of the chancel and a further extension runs the length of the nave on the n. side. At the time of my visit, no more than the shell of the new work had been completed.

Ipswich, St Augustine of Hippo (E7): This is a church with a good deal of presence and it stands on a commanding site by a roundabout on the Felixstowe road. Designed by **H. Munro Cautley**, it is his one major work, carried out in the medieval style he always favoured. The walls are plain rough cast and there are tall two-**light** windows at high level in the **nave**, with gabled buttresses between them. The **aisles** are no more than narrow passages, presenting a blank wall on the s. side, with the n. aisle masked by a low slab extension which has domestic windows. A substantial tower rises above the centre crossing and there are tall **transepts**. War damage affected the s. transept and the problem was solved by adding flying buttresses down to the ground at the corners. It has a small projecting bay to the e. whose window matches the e. window of the **chancel**. There you will find a stone recording the gift of the site in 1926. A baptistery projects below the w. window and entry is by way of a small **porch** at the s.w. corner.

It has a quietly impressive interior and it is appropriate that a building in this style should give a home to a **font** that was saved from the ruined church of St Peter at Linstead Magna. This is of a typical East Anglian C15 design with four lions squatting round the shaft. Four more alternate with angels in the bowl panels who carry shields carved with a **Trinity emblem**, **Passion emblems**, and the cross of **St George**. One of the baptistery windows has stained glass of 1961 by Hugh Easton which illustrates a brightly coloured family group with the priest at the font, a guide to contemporary costume in the years to come. More of this artist's work can be seen at Bury St Edmunds (St Peter), Elveden, and Stowlangtoft [all Vol.1]. The walls above the low arches of the nave **arcade** are blind panelled and the **roof** is a handsome

exercise in the medieval forms that Cautley knew so well. The **tie-beams** have braces below them which rise to demi-angels, and there are collar beams below the ridge. Also typical of the architect are the matching pulpit and reading desk, made interesting in this case by the narrow panels of pierced foliage below the rims. The tall arches of the crossing enclose a stone vault with **bosses** at the rib intersections. The organ occupies the n. transept and in the **sanctuary** there are **piscina/sedilia** in plain recesses. The painted and gilt **reredos** has slim **tracery** panels, with shallow coving above the centre section. The glass in the window above by Horace Wilkinson portrays the ascended Christ with the disciples and the **Blessed Virgin** below, with miniature angels filling the tracery. The Lady chapel **altar** in the s. transept matches the pulpit, and in the window above there is attractive glass, again by Wilkinson, with the Blessed Virgin flanked by **St Augustine** and his mother **St Monica**. At the bottom of the centre panel there is a vignette of the church's great benefactor with his mother. His devotion to her explains both the dedication and the choice of subject for the chapel window. His name was Charles Bantoft and a tablet nearby reads: 'This church has been given by an Ipswich tradesman as a thank-offering to Almighty God for the blessing of a pious and affectionate mother'.

Ipswich, St Bartholomew (E7): The church stands in Newton Road, a massive building in red brick. It was designed by Charles Spooner and mainly built between 1894 and 1900, the w. end being completed in 1907. Its vast **roof** slopes uninterruptedly over **nave** and **aisles** and along the sides there are pairs of two-**light** windows in the **Perpendicular** style. The seven lights of the large w. window have minimal **tracery** and below it a broad and shallow **porch** has a wooden figure of the patron saint between the two doors. As at the town's other great red brick church of St John the Baptist, a tower was planned but never built.

Designed for Anglo-Catholic worship, the interior is spacious and beautifully appointed. Massive stone **arcade piers** continue up across the wall surface to support **tie-beams** which carry **king-posts** below the wagon roof. The aisle roofs have braced tie-beams with pierced tracery in the **spandrels**. The wall below the w. window is clad with linen-fold **panelling** painted in green and white as a backing for the attractive **font** of veined alabaster and green marble. Its tall panelled oak cover was added in 1944. The pulpit matches the font and stands on tall, shaped columns, and to the l. of the **chancel** arch there is a brass plaque in memory of Anna Frances Spooner, who endowed the church. Her husband's memorial to the l. bearing his shield of arms is a good example of a late Victorian **brass** and is signed 'Scott, Ipswich'. George Cobbold was the church's first vicar and served the parish for over twenty years. He died in 1915 and ten years later the chapel of the Blessed Sacrament s. of the chancel was dedicated as his memorial. Designed by **H. Munro Cautley**, a two-bay arcade in **Early English** style separates it from the chancel, and there are handsome oak benches with decorative roundels on the ends. A typical Cautley touch is the medieval-style **piscina** complete with **credence shelf**. The chancel lies under a barrel vaulted roof whose ribs and **bosses** are painted, and the **rood** on the beam above the entrance is a memorial to a curate who fell while serving as a chaplain in Italy in 1944. The beautifully proportioned **high altar** is backed by a rich fabric hanging designed by **Morris & Co.** It falls from the base of the rose window above whose tracery is a clever combination of pointed ovals. A suite of **sedilia** in oak stands on the r., excellently carved in C15 style with angel masks on the elbows and a pierced vine trail in the canopy.

Ipswich, St Francis (E7): The church stands on Hawthorn Drive and was built in 1958 to cater for the extensive development of the Chantry estate. It was designed by Basil Hatcher and is contemporary with his church at Chelmondiston. It is a tall, gaunt building under a single, shallow-pitched **roof**, with large, high-level windows between broad brick **pilasters**, and pebble-dash panels below. A slim, vaguely Italianate brick tower at the n.w. corner is pierced at belfry level, and the upper section is open below a double-pitched roof. With a large church hall to the l., the foyer leads into the w. end of the **nave**, a single hall under one roof, with a shallow **sanctuary** at the e. end. Concrete beams rise from the floor and arch over to carry a soft-board panelled ceiling, and between them the windows form a virtual wall of glass at high level. A door in the n. wall leads in to a chapel dedicated to the Holy Cross. This is a simple room with domestic windows and a flat ceiling – unadorned except for a colourful appliqué work **altar** frontal, but it has that essential quality of calm. In the nave there is a jolly display of tapestry hassocks and the **font** is a simple bowl set in a circular oak frame. There is no division except a step between nave and **chancel**, and there the matching pulpit and lectern have that concave board cladding which seemed to be obligatory in the 1950s. The sanctuary is narrower, and its side walls have a series of vertical concrete fins with reeded glass between them from floor to ceiling. The e. wall is blind and the brickwork is painted a dark green as a backing for a large cross in black and gold above the altar. Returning to the w. end, you will see a painting of **St Francis** over the w. door which shows him bearing the mark of the nail on his hand (one of the stigmata) which he received as the result of a vision of the crucified Christ; probably C19, the artist is unknown.

Ipswich, St Helen (E7): The church gives its name to the street and houses crowd up to the e. end, leaving only a very narrow passage round to the n. side. There has been a church here since **Norman** times but although the present building is medieval in character most of it is C19 replacement. Work was done in the 1830s when **transepts** were added, and then some twelve years later the rest of the church was practically rebuilt, apart from the tower and **porch**. In 1874 the tower was replaced and the **nave** was extended westward to the limit of the churchyard. The rather battered porch is therefore the only visible survivor of the old building. It has a very worn niche above the entrance and a restored sundial is set on the apex of the gable. There are angels in the **spandrels** of the doorway, **paterae** in the mouldings, and lion **stops** on the **dripstone**. The inner door has a very large medieval ring handle and there are remains of a **stoup** in the corner. The tower is built onto the w. side of the porch and becomes an octagon above the belfry; the parapet is pierced with **quatrefoils** and a short, rather bald spire rises above it. The s. wall of the nave with its **Perpendicular** windows was largely undisturbed by the rebuilding and has a simple **flushwork base course**.

Entry is now via the s. transept, and a vestibule leads into what was originally the **chancel**. At this stage one tends to feel somewhat disorientated because the interior has been completely rearranged. The chancel is now a Sunday School/activities area and entry to the nave is through folding screen doors under an organ **gallery**. The **altar** is now placed midway along the n. wall and chairs are ranged around to centre on it. It is flanked by the lectern and C19 **font**, and the pulpit has been relegated to the n.w. corner. One of the s. windows has stained glass of 1890 which may be by **Hardman**; a Resurrection scene spans the three **lights** and there are vignettes below of the **Annunciation**, Christ's baptism,

and Gethsemane. Close by is a tablet by James Drawater, a London mason of whom little is known. It is for Richard Canning, who was minister at St Lawrence's until his death in 1775. The epitaph is set in a beige frame between **pilasters** with coloured strips; the roundel at the top has three rather nice profile heads. Farther along there is a tablet of 1726 for another Richard Canning:

> who having served his country with unexceptional courage and conduct during the wars of K.William and Q.Anne retired to this town and through the resentment of Party, founded on misreported Facts died a private Captain.

I itch to know what happened to blight his career.

Ipswich, St John the Baptist (E7): The first church on Cauldwell Hall Road was built in 1857, a small building in **Perpendicular** style that never got around to being consecrated. Grander things were in store, however, and in 1899 **Sir Arthur Blomfield** designed the massive replacement that stands alongside. In rich red brick with stone dressings, it has **aisle roofs** that slope down from a **clerestory** in which triple **lancets** are set within semi-circular arches, with single lancets at each end. There is a gabled door at the e. end of the s. aisle and originally a substantial tower was planned to rise above it but was never built. The e. window has five stepped lancets under a single **dripstone** that has curly leaf **stops**, and mature cedars flank the **chancel**. There is a **vestry** at right angles on the n. side and a utilitarian extension beyond it. A polygonal baptistery projects at the w. end and, above it, the two-**light** w. window is flanked by lancets, with a double bellcote on the gable.

The interior is spacious and attractive, a prime example of the architect's skill in achieving maximum capacity with economy, without sacrificing good looks. The six-bay **nave arcades** rest on alternate octagonal and round **piers**, and the roof is a form of **hammerbeam**, with **tie-beams** and collars. The shaping of the main timbers and transverse braces gives an overall impression of scalloped curves. The attractive pendent light fittings in wood are reminiscent of medieval **tabernacle work**. The aisle roofs are quite elaborate, with **king-posts** standing on the cross-braces and small pendent **bosses**. There is a good pulpit of 1926 in C15 style and the same quality shows in the richly carved glazed screen that forms the entrance to the chapel at the e. end of the s. aisle. The chancel lies under a wagon roof, and the centre panels of the marble **reredos** are inlaid with mosaic in a woven lattice pattern as a background for the alpha and omega signs and the **sacred monogram**. Above it, there is attractive glass by Shrigley & Hunt, the Lancashire firm founded in 1874 and still in business today; the ten main panels contain an Ascension scene above the baptism of Christ, with surrounding figures of the **Evangelists, St Peter**, and **St Paul**.

Ipswich, St Luke (E7): This started life as a severely utilitarian low, rectangular building on Cliff Lane in 1954. Built in red brick, with corrugated asbestos **roof** and domestic windows, its only concession to style was a **porch** which continues upwards to form a substantial bellcote. However, in the mid-1980s, an extension has been added to the side and rear which has made a vital difference. One now enters via a new foyer on the l. under a pyramid roof, and beyond it is a single hall which capitalises on the awkward shape dictated by the available site. It is segmental in plan, tapering towards the e., and has a roof clad in pine with substantial **arch-braces**. There are plain oblong windows to w. and n. augmented by skylights and there is a polished wood-strip floor. To the r. of

the **sanctuary** a folding screen divides the new area from the old which can thus be brought into use as occasion demands. The sanctuary steps are angled in sympathy with the overall shape, and beyond the **altar** the three **lancets** of the original building have been re-sited and back-lit. This is to display the glass by Francis Stephens, a contemporary artist much influenced by Martin Travers. The figure of Christ the King raises his r. hand in blessing, with a book in the other open at the text: 'I am the Truth, the Way and the Life.' **St Paul** and **St Luke** kneel on each side, the latter bearing an ikon and a pouch to mark his traditional roles as artist and physician. This is certainly a church which cannot be judged from the outside alone and I liked it.

Ipswich, St Margaret (E7): Standing above St Margaret's Green and backed by the grounds of Christchurch Mansion, this is undoubtedly the town's most handsome church. There was a priory of the Holy Trinity here, and as the population grew around it this church was built for them to use about the end of the C13. The approach from the s. is through a manicured churchyard attractively set out with shrubs and flowers. The face of the impressive clock shows that it was made by Moore of Ipswich in 1778, although a stone below is dated 1737. The w. door is low and wide, and the belfry stage of the early C15 tower was elegantly rebuilt in 1871 when pairs of bell openings were inserted and the parapet decorated with **flushwork**. The early C14 n. door is unused now and the **aisle** windows on that side have typical 'Y' **tracery** of about 1300. The buttresses of the C16 n. **transept** are decorated with an 'MR' for the **Blessed Virgin** and the **Tudor** portcullis badge, and the s. transept is flanked by polygonal turrets with **crocketted** pinnacles. One of these housed the **rood stairs** and it has been suggested that the other served the same purpose on the n. side but was moved later purely for structural support. If that were the need, a straightforward buttress would have been as effective and much cheaper – a doubtful story, therefore. The s. aisle windows are C19 insertions but above them is a beautiful mid-C15 **clerestory**. Its windows fill most of the wall space and are separated by buttresses which rise to pinnacles between the stepped battlements. There is a good deal of shallow ornament carved in the **ashlar** and merchants' marks with donors' initials appear in the window **spandrels**. The solid C15 **porch** has very worn flushwork panels, with three canopied niches above the entrance, angels in the spandrels, and the remains of lion **stops**.

In a light and attractive interior, the early C14 **arcades** have their **capitals** nicely accentuated in red and gold. The late C15 double **hammerbeam roof** overhead is an interesting blend of faded colour. It was panelled in the 1690s and painted with a mixture of scenes and pure decoration. There are cut-out **cartouches** of arms fixed to the ends of the hammers, and tie-rods were inserted in the early C19 to combat the spread of the roof. There is pierced tracery above the hammerbeams and the **wall posts** are carved with figures (now minus their heads) seated below canopies. Within the tower there is an C18 or early C19 Table of Fees for the services of the clerk and sexton which is worth reading. Parishioners had the free use of the **bier** at their funerals but strangers had to pay for the privilege. The w. window has fine 1870s glass by **Ward & Hughes**, with figures of Faith, Hope, and Charity; the same firm provided the glass in the w. window of the n. aisle where six of the **Seven Works of Mercy** are illustrated. **Dowsing** was here in January 1643 but he relied on the promise of a churchwarden ('a godly man') to take down between twenty and thirty 'superstitious pictures'. He was probably responsible for mutilating the angels that hold scrolls in the C15 **font**

panels but the text on the one facing w. is still legible. This is a rare and most fortunate survival because it refers to a pre-**Reformation** practice which was part of the sacrament of baptism. It reads: 'Sal et saliva' and reminds us that salt was placed in the child's mouth, and its nose and ears were anointed with saliva during the ceremony. There is a **sanctus-bell window** under the roof ridge, and below it is a splendid **Royal Arms** of Charles II in an elaborate cut-out frame. The painting is in perspective and two cherubs peer over the dais on which the supporters stand. A large painting of the Prince of Wales's feathers, dated 1660, hangs above the s. door – which is rather strange because there was no such person at the time. Perhaps it was done to flatter the young Duke of Monmouth. A C13 tomb slab is clamped to the wall nearby and it is likely to be one of the few relics of the vanished priory of Austin canons. **Box pews** were removed from the **nave** in 1846 and **Henry Ringham** provided the new benches. They are typical of his solid style and have nicely varied **poppyheads**. **Hatchments** hang above the n. arcade, and from w. to e. they were for: Revd William Fonnereau (1817), Revd Mileson Gery Edgar (1853), Mary Anne Edgar (1835), and Mileson Edgar (1830). Halfway along the s. aisle wall is a niche which seems too low for a statue and too far away from the entrance to house a **stoup**. At the e. end there is an oblong recess that may have been a **reliquary chamber**, and nearby is the entrance to the rood stairs. There is another like it in the n. aisle and an opening to the side of the **chancel** arch, so the **screen** stretched right across the church. The area in front of the chancel arch has been newly paved in textured slate to form the **sanctuary** for a nave **altar**.

The transepts open into the chancel and the organ takes up the n. side. Below the s. transept window a slab reaved of its **brasses** lies within a recess which has a back of panelled tracery. This was once the Lady chapel, and in his will Sir William Roskin directed that he should be buried here in 1512 so this is likely to be his tomb. There is a **piscina** to the l. and two benches in the chapel have restored sections of a screen as backs. The chancel ceiling is panelled, with a modern coloured **celure** above the **high altar**. The C19 choir stalls have their **finials** carved as **pelicans in piety**, and there is attractive **reticulated** tracery in the n.e. window. Four more hatchments hang on the walls here; s. wall e. to w.: Thomas Neale (Col. of the Ipswich Volunteers, 1839), William Charles Fonnereau (1855), Revd Charles William Fonnereau (1840); n. wall: Revd Dr Claudius Fonnereau (1785). Although the tracery of the e. window is C19, the inner shafts show that it dates from the C14, and it is filled with pleasant glass of 1913 by Jones & Willis of Birmingham – Resurrection and Ascension scenes flanked by figures of the Blessed Virgin and **St John**.

Ipswich, St Mary at Stoke (E7) The church stands on Belstead Road, just above the s. bank of the river, and commands an extensive view across the docks and town. This was a simple country church dating at least from the beginning of the C14, but the expansion of C19 Ipswich flowed over the parish and major alterations were made in consequence. The building consisted simply of tower, **nave**, and **chancel**, but in the 1860s **R.M. Phipson** carried out a restoration which added a n. **transept**. Then in 1870 there was a major rebuilding by **William Butterfield**, who added a new nave and chancel, turning the old part into a n. **aisle** and Lady chapel. The unbuttressed tower is small in scale, with a **Perpendicular** window above a restored w. door. The bell openings were altered at some stage in the C19 and brick battlements were added. Beyond the large n. transept there is a **vestry** end-on to the wall of the old chancel. The Butterfield extension has bands of **ashlar** in the walls, with

flushwork chequer in the gables of chancel and organ chamber. The flintwork is dense, of high quality, and makes use of lots of white flint. The **porch** again has chequer in the gable, with a **traceried** circular window above the entrance. Some have found the effect of the new work harsh but it is sound and competent, and while it may not be wildly exciting it marries well with the old church.

One moves in to find a light and spacious nave and chancel which make the old n. side seem dark by comparison. The **font** is a C19 replacement and the nave **roof** is **arch-braced** with heavy tracery below the ridge. The principal timbers rest on stone **corbels** carved with foliage and the low, five-bay **arcade** has gilded **capitals**. Immediately to the r. of the entrance is a window with very nice glass of 1905 by **Heaton, Butler & Bayne** which has been well restored recently. It illustrates the young Christ sitting among the elders in the Temple and the overall effect is golden and glowing. There is more glass by the same firm in the next window to the e., a **Blessed Virgin** and Child flanked by the **Annunciation** and St Mary with **St John** by the cross. You will see by the list on the wall between the windows that the patronage of the church has rested with the prior and convent of Ely followed by the dean and chapter since 1300, and their arms appear at the head of the second window. In the n. aisle is a good **hammerbeam** roof which was restored under Phipson's direction by **Henry Ringham**. He replaced the figures on the hammerbeams who hold shields with **Passion emblems** and no doubt the demi-figures at the base of the **wall posts** as well. The roof continues through unbroken over the Lady chapel but there are no replacement figures there. Phipson's transept has been blocked off with a new door in the archway and now serves as a commodious choir vestry. Phipson also replaced the e. window with a new one in **Perpendicular** style which ignored the form of the original, and it is filled with glass of 1864 by **Ward & Hughes**. This is a very pretty, dense pattern of vine and oak foliage around shapes containing texts and a centre cross, with the **sacred monogram**, the Chi Rho (another version, based on the Greek initials), and the alpha and omega letters at the top. It is interesting that the design was by P.L. Burrell, who later became Lord Gwydyr; his brother's memorial is on the wall to the l. There is a C14 **piscina** under a **trefoil** arch to the r. With no arch between, the chancel is almost as broad as the nave. The corbels here are carved as musical angels and those over the **sanctuary** bear the **Evangelistic symbols**. There is a recess in the n. wall under an **ogee** arch, **cusped** and **crocketted**, which seems to be original C14 work; if that is so it must have been moved from elsewhere at the rebuilding. The stone **reredos** is panelled and painted with the arms of the diocese and of Ely cathedral, together with the Evangelistic symbols. The glass in the five-**light** e. window is fairly routine stuff by **Clayton & Bell** of 1871 – Christ's nativity, baptism, crucifixion, resurrection, and the coming of the Holy Spirit; apostles fill the tracery and there are vignettes from the life of Christ along the base.

Ipswich, St Mary at the Elms (E7): Although busy Elm Street is now right up against the **porch**, redevelopment has opened up a view of this most attractive little church from the w. There was an C11 church on this site called St Saviour's, but when it was rebuilt in the early C14 the present dedication was adopted and a reference to the nearby trees was added to identify it among the clutch of St Marys in the town. There was probably always a tower of some sort but the present one dates from the **Tudor** period, and it has been claimed that the bricks were imported by Cardinal Wolsey from the Netherlands for use in his projected college, only to be diverted here. There are patterns of darker

bricks in the walls, pairs of bell openings under wide **labels**, and stepped battlements. The polygonal buttresses have shallow **set-offs** and there is a heavy stair turret on the n. side. It is worth walking round to view St Mary's Cottage just n. of the churchyard. Recently restored as a meeting room with first-floor flat, it is the oldest occupied house in Ipswich and dates from 1467. Not long after that, the brick n. **aisle** was added to the church as a chapel, but the little **transept** to the e. of it dates from the C14 or even earlier. As at a number of the town's churches, there were extensive alterations here in the C19, and in 1883 the old **chancel** was absorbed into the **nave** and a new one added; **vestries** and an organ chamber came a little later. The **priest's door** in the s. wall led into what was then the chancel and we enter by the small C14 porch. There are three niches that once had canopies above the entrance, and within is the only remaining evidence of the earlier building. It is a **Norman** doorway, with single shafts alongside very worn **jambs**, and there is a **chevron moulding** on the outer rim of the arch. The door itself may be as old and certainly its ironwork is very early.

After the strident traffic outside the interior is beautifully peaceful and meticulously ordered. The attractive little tower screen is a World War I memorial and on the walls of the ringers' **gallery** hang **hatchments** and the **Royal Arms** of Charles II. The space below is furnished as a Lady chapel and the 1870s **font** is quite an adventurous piece by a Mr Ireland of Princes Street. The small bowl panels are carved with Gospel scenes, an **Agnus Dei**, and a **sacred monogram**, while figures of the four **Evangelists** stand round the shaft. There is a **stoup** by the entrance which is once again put to its proper use, and the 1860s restoration by **R.M. Phipson** included a good deal of **Henry Ringham's** work. The nave ceiling is C18 plaster and the first three bays of the **arcade** are C15, with the 1880s two-bay extension beyond. The aisle and transept **roofs** are C15, and at the e. end on that side is a beautiful window of 1907 by **Comper** (look for his strawberry signature). It commemorates Walton Turner, who was churchwarden here; he is portrayed kneeling in his civic robes at the bottom. Above, the two figures of the **Annunciation** flank Christ in Majesty, and there are lots of miniature angels in the borders. The nave windows are filled with glass of 1879-80 signed 'Taylor late **O'Connor**' – figures of Purity, Faith, Hope, Charity, and Mercy. The hatchment for Elizabeth Hamby hangs in the n. aisle and her memorial of 1758 is on the s. wall; an urn on a bracket and her shield of arms are set against a large oval of mottled marble. Farther along there is a **touchstone** tablet for Daniel Burrill which has an intricate alabaster frame carved with a fine selection of the emblems of mortality. The new chancel was by Edward Bisshopp, the architect of St Michael's, among other things, and it includes a fine arch with **paterae** and shields bearing **Passion emblems** in the mouldings. These are painted and gilt and so are the four angels at the base of the roof **arch-braces**. The monument on the n. wall is an interesting family group conceived on a small scale. William Acton died in the same year as Shakespeare and he faces his wife across a desk with a draped skeleton brandishing the arrow of death between them; a son and three daughters are ranged below them and their daughter-in-law Alice lies in a separate compartment below, with her elbow on a skull and a book in her hand. An alabaster roundel of arms decorates the top and, as on Burrill's memorial, there are symbols of death on the frame. The e. window has been blocked in and the space is filled with a mighty figure of Christ on the cross which dominates the chancel and compels the eye from the w. end. Walking back to the door, notice how the replacement tower does not quite line up with the nave.

Ipswich, St Mary le Tower (E7): This is an impressively large church in the town centre, hemmed in by buildings, with a churchyard that is also a colourful garden of flowers and shrubs. **R.M. Phipson** directed a series of restorations between 1850 and 1870 that gave it its present character and he designed the massive replacement tower which stands on the s. side. The pairs of tall bell openings are surrounded by distinctive **flushwork** chequer, and **Evangelistic symbols** almost leap from the corners of the pierced parapet. Above it, the handsome, **crocketted** spire rises to 176ft. Among other things, Phipson rebuilt the n. **aisle** on a larger scale, added a n. **chancel** aisle, heightened the **clerestory** and redesigned the **roof**. It is worth making a circuit of the building to admire the quality of the flushwork on the chancel and to examine the two niches in the e. wall, with their modern figures of **St John** and **St Mary Magdalene** sculpted by Pheifer. Like the one over the s. door, the niches were part of the medieval building. The C13 inner doorway was carefully preserved and given new **Annunciation headstops**.

An early C15 **font** stands just within, raised on three steps which have **quatrefoils** carved in the risers. The bowl panels contain chubby lions, there are two bands of vine below, and the lions round the shaft sit on human male and female heads. These are just like those at Helmingham and Grundisburgh (but in better condition) and there must have been a reason behind this little local oddity of symbolism. As part of the Victorian upheaval, wall tablets were collected together in corners, and there is a selection by the font. Of particular interest is the painted memorial for William Smart, M.P. for Ipswich, who died in 1599. Framed and glazed, the first letters of its verse spell out his name, and the epitaph is set in strapwork above the kneeling figures of William and his wife. A panorama of the town is painted along the bottom and a helpful key below identifies the landmarks. Smart's **ledger-stone** is clamped to the w. wall, and nearby there are two **brass** inscriptions; one is for Robert and Grisil Clarke (he was town clerk for 40 years and died in 1697), the other is for Robert Sparowe (1594). The fifteen main panels of the w. window make up a **Jesse tree** in 1860s glass by **Clayton & Bell**. Below it there is an excellent set of Charles II **Royal Arms**, pierced and carved in relief, and they are one of the very few whose maker is known – Jonathan Reeve was paid £15 for them in 1687. On either side of the doorway there are churchwardens' pews with modern coved hoods, but the C15 bench ends with their beast **finials** and seated figures came originally from the chancel. There is attractive 1870s glass by **Lavers, Barraud & Westlake** in the aisle w. windows and in two of the n. aisle windows; episodes in the early life of Christ fill the main **lights** with vignette scenes below. Phipson linked the C15 nave **arcades** to his new chancel arch with two smaller arches, and a band of red on the **capitals** is picked up on the ledge below the clerestory. The steeply pitched roof has **tracery** above the collar beams, and there are large demi-figure **corbels** below alternate principals. **Henry Ringham** worked on the aisle roofs and they are good solid designs, with pierced tracery in the **spandrels** and painted demi-angel corbels. The stained glass in the n. aisle is an interesting selection; from the e. end: an early design of 1844 by William Wailes, a Newcastle glazier who had worked with Pugin – the figure of Christ with the text 'My beloved is gone down into his garden to gather lilies'; another window by Wailes for Herbert Cobbold, who died young on an Hon. East India Company's steamer in 1852; an attractive Transfiguration and Good Shepherd of 1862 by **O'Connor** with features slightly eroded; Christ's first miracle illustrated above the scene with Martha and Mary, in glass of 1865 by an unidenti-

fied glazier. Phipson designed a screen for the chancel but this now stands at the e. end of the n. aisle masking the organ beyond. The pulpit is an impressive but rather ponderous late C17 piece on an 1860s stem. Its raised marquetry panels have wreaths of flowers above them and there are coarse swags at the corners. A marquetry **sacred monogram** decorates the backboard and the **tester** is a solid octagonal hood whose **ogee** curves rise to a gilded dove finial. The curving stairs are exceptionally nice, with delicately turned and carved **balusters**, and **acanthus** trails decorating the risers of the steps.

This has always been the town's civic church and there are two sword and mace rests on the nave pillars, with corporation pews which have the lion and ship emblems on the bench ends. The s. aisle window glass is a sequence by Clayton & Bell, and at the e. end there is a **piscina** which C19 alterations reduced to floor level. Beyond a **parclose screen** of 1906, the chapel has carved panelling to windowsill height with memorials which, in some cases, are eccentrically painted to look like pieces of parchment. The heavy **reredos** is richly coloured and gilt, and the centre triptych contains a painting in C14 mode of the supper at Emmaus, flanked by Moses and Elias. A C14 arcade separates the chapel from the chancel, and there one finds that the back ranges of the choir stalls are medieval and have simple **misericords**. The centre section of the screen in front of the organ is C16 work and the rest, together with the bulk of the choir stalls, is high quality work by Cornish & Gaymer, with statuettes by Pheifer. More monuments were collected together on the walls of the choir **vestry**, including a fine tablet for John and Elizabeth Robinson (1666 and 1694); nicely posed figures kneel facing each other within a frame flanked by **touchstone** columns; three children are grouped below, two of them offering the skull and posy emblems of death and rebirth. There is a brass text by the vestry door, but the church's main collection of four brasses lies under the chancel carpet and inspection is not encouraged. The **high altar** is backed by a rather splendid reredos of about 1900 in which the centre Crucifixion group is flanked by panels crowded with angels, all painted on a **gesso** ground in very slight relief. There are figures of the Evangelists with their symbols, and the panels of the **sanctuary** are painted with the figures of East Anglia's saints: **St Osyth, St Erkenwald, St Edmund, St Ethelburga, St Felix, St Ethelbert**, and **St Etheldreda** – to these are added **St Augustine, St Edward the Confessor**, and **St Alphege**. Phipson designed an exuberant suite of piscina and **sedilia**, all painted and gilt, with quatrefoil polished marble shafts and nodding ogee arches.

Ipswich, St Matthew (E7): Busy Civic Drive now runs to the e. of the church and the development has given it a more spacious setting. Like others in the town, it was considerably altered in the C19 and a **porch** disappeared when the s. **aisle** was widened in 1845. **R.M. Phipson** added the s. chapel with its small projecting porch in 1860 and the e. wall was rebuilt six years later. The n. **aisle** was widened and extended by **Sir George Gilbert Scott** in 1876, and in 1884 7ft was added to the tower and the s. aisle was refaced and given new windows and buttresses. The s. wall is worth studying as an example of the very high quality of Victorian rebuilding in the medieval style.

The widening of the aisles has made them each equal to the **nave** and, as a result, the interior is extremely spacious. The **arcades** are superficially alike but you will see that there are differences; the s. range with small **paterae** in the **capitals** dates from the C14, while the **piers** of a century later on the n. side have concave faces. All the **roofs** are Victorian but those in the aisles are particularly good, with pierced **tracery** above the braced **tiebeams**. The C15 **font** stands in the n.

aisle, and although considerably retouched, it is a most interesting example which differs significantly in style from the average. Six of the bowl panels have delicately carved scenes, each beneath a pair of **crocketted ogee** arches; clockwise from the n.e. they portray: the **Blessed Virgin** enthroned, her coronation, the **Assumption**, the visit of the wise men, the **Annunciation** – a sequence which matches the Joyful Mysteries of the rosary. Another panel has the baptism of Christ and the last pair contains a conventional **Tudor rose** and foliage. The attractive gilded cover is modern. The w. end of the n. aisle has been curtained off to form a chapel and at the e. end a screen incorporates six interesting panels that belonged originally to the early C16 **rood screen**. They are painted with the figures of four bishops, and the first on the l. is probably **St Thomas of Canterbury**. The fourth may represent **St Eligius**, but **St Erasmus** is more likely because there was a **guild** here under his patronage. The remaining panels are filled with lay figures who were undoubtedly the donors and probably members of the guild. The men kneel in front and the leader has a heavy purse which may indicate that he was master or treasurer. Apart from manuscripts there is little left to illustrate guild activities and this is a rare survival. A modern rood group hangs within the **chancel** arch, and on the n. side there is a long **squint** aligned with the **high altar**. A simple **piscina** and shelf are arranged within it to serve the altar that stood nearby. The other openings into the chancel and s. chapel date from 1860. The good 1890s screen between the s. aisle and the chapel was designed by John Corder and made by John Groom (whose carving may be found in a number of Ipswich churches), and the **communion rails** beyond incorporate three etched glass panels illustrating India, Ethiopia, and St Matthew's. They commemorate an Indian priest who was curate here in the 1970s. The chapel e. window has an interesting example of glass from the beginning of the Victorian revival; it was designed by Frank Howard and made in 1853 by George Hedgeland, the glazier of the great w. window of Norwich cathedral. There is glass by **Ward & Hughes** in the window to the r. and more of their work can be seen in the centre window of the n. aisle. The glass in the third window from the w. end in the s. aisle is by W.H. Constable of Cambridge. The C14 chancel roof is a **hammerbeam, arch-braced** design with gilded angels below the principals, and there are two substantial monuments on the n. wall. To the w. is the memorial for Anthony Penning who died in 1630. There are reclining **putti** on top with skull and hour-glass, and the figures kneel before shallow arches flanked by polished **touchstone** columns. The similar monument alongside is for Richard Cock who died in 1629. Here the effigies are much stiffer and there are garlands on the frame with a swag of fruit below. The brass altar rails with a heavy square top rail came from Hart & Co. in the C19, and gates were added to match in 1946. Beyond them is the high altar and **reredos** designed by Corder. Its three painted bas relief panels of the Magi and the shepherds at Bethlehem are set within a richly gilded tracery frame, and figures of **St John** and **St Matthew** stand each side. Above, the e. window glass of 1894 by Ward & Hughes has a figure of Christ in Majesty surrounded by a host of Old and New Testament figures.

Ipswich, St Michael (E7): C19 Ipswich was thriving and so populous that the central parishes had to be subdivided, and in the 1870s the new parish of St Michael's was formed. A site was acquired in Upper Orwell Street, cleared of slum cottages, and the foundation stone of the new church was laid in 1880. The architect was Edward Fearnley Bisshopp and, although he was concerned in a number of restorations and extensions, this is his only complete church. Both site and funds were restricted but his solution was creditable. The exterior cannot be viewed as a whole although the w. front speaks for its general style – **Early English** in the main, in red brick relieved by narrow bands of terracotta and stone facings. There was not room for a tower and the centre section of the w. wall is carried up in a wide and shallow buttress to form a double bellcote on the gable. The **aisles** are lit by pairs of **lancets** and the **clerestory** takes the form of dormer windows. The **nave** was extended eastwards and **transepts** were added in 1884, with the shallow **chancel** following in 1890.

One should not be deterred by the rather down-beat exterior because within is a beautifully spacious setting for worship in the C19 Evangelical tradition. The red brick glows warmly, and bands of darker brick enliven the **arcade** arches and w. wall. The sturdy drums of the arcade **piers** are faced with Bath stone and carry square carved **capitals**, while a band of multi-coloured glazed bricks links the triple lancets of the dormer windows. Between the aisle windows there are curious little adjustable ventilators, and the **font** in the n.w. corner is highly individual – concave panels under **trefoil** arches in the bowl panels, with spiral columns and leafy capitals at each angle. The s. transept window has a centre panel of **St George** with his foot on a scarlet dragon, the glass by W.H. Constable of Cambridge. There are plain pitch pine pews in the nave but the pulpit has a range of small panels which were beautifully carved by Philip Groom with foliage in which there is a beast biting its tail, another eating grapes, and a vigorous dragon. The chancel is rather more lavish than the nave, and its arch has **dogtooth** ornament and leafy capitals above triple stub **responds**. The **roof** is panelled out and curves to match the line of the arch. There are large pierced **cusps** on the principal timbers, and a little arcaded cornice stretches below the plain coving. The e. window has three tall lancets contained within a single arch, each divided into three narrow traceried **lights**. The outer sections are filled with glass by John Underwood & Sons, and there are figures of **St Andrew, St Peter, St Matthew, St Luke, St John**, and **St Paul** set within **tabernacle work**; wreaths enclose **Passion emblems** below and a painting at the w. end of the church shows how the design should be completed. By 1903 Bisshopp had gone into partnership with **Cautley** and one or other of them designed the **altar** and **reredos**, again carved by Philip Groom. An **Agnus Dei** is set below a pendent central arch and the cornice is a thick band of vine.

Ipswich, St Peter (E7): Standing on Stoke Park Drive, this church was built in 1975 to serve the mass of new housing that has developed along the e. of the Belstead Road. It stands well, on slightly rising ground, with a view across to Bourne Park, and is clearly identified by the large wooden cross standing in front. The building was designed by Marshman, Warren & Taylor, and consists of a main hall, an ancillary block projecting on the s. side, and a two-storeyed section at the rear. The main area is wedge-shaped and the side walls are stepped to take tall, narrow windows. Viewed from the road, the long slope of the **roof** comes down to a heavy beam section stretching across the frontage, below which there are curtained windows across the whole width. The heavy chains which are suspended from the lintel at each end serve to direct rainwater into the concrete drums below in place of conventional fall pipes, a mildly eccentric architectural conceit. Entry is from the rear, and the foyer leads into a spacious hall that can accommodate a congregation of 250. Decoration is minimal, with white-painted brick walls under a pine boarded ceiling. The e. wall is virtually all glass, and semi-transparent curtaining serves to provide an effective backing for the **altar**. This is a large pine slab set on an iron frame, with a

centre panel recess – carved with a cross and the loaves and fishes – an interesting mingling of Christian symbolism which is repeated on the lectern in front. Plans are already in hand to provide additional accommodation for church activities, and eventually there will be an extension eastward to form a **sanctuary**. St Peter's attracts people from a broad spectrum of traditions and this austere yet attractive setting seems particularly appropriate.

Ipswich, St Thomas (E7): As the town grew in the C19 and early C20 its parishes had to be divided, and in some cases divided yet again. All Saints' was carved out of St Matthew's only to prove too large itself, and a new parish of St Thomas was created alongside the Norwich road. A little corrugated iron building was used initially, but in 1937 the foundation stone for a new church was laid by the donor of a site on Bramford Lane. The architect was N.F. Cachemaille Day and his design contains faint echoes of the familiar East Anglian **Perpendicular** style. The basic material is greyish brick, but he used expanses of **knapped flints** on the w. gable and walls, and introduced **flushwork** panels round the doors and between the **aisle** windows whose arches are a rounded version of the **Tudor** shape. The church's most striking feature is the bulky four-stage tower placed at the s.e. corner. There are paired belfry windows and bell openings above them, and the clasping buttresses rise to square corner turrets which are linked by a leggy openwork parapet. Balance is maintained overall by a large n. **transept** aligned with the tower.

The interior is low key, unfussy, and quietly attractive, with all the surfaces in plain, cream-coloured plaster. The arches of the **arcades** echo the window shapes, and from the pillars, ribs rise to form smooth braces under the nave **roof**. On either side, a low **clerestory** wall is pierced by small rectangular two-**light** windows, while the aisles lie under flat roofs. At the e. end the organ is sited below the tower and the n. transept forms a spacious chapel, with another in the s. aisle. The ribs of the **chancel** roof are placed diagonally and the zigzag form of the e. wall is given additional emphasis by the use of exposed brickwork. Small **lancets** are set in the angles right at the top and their brightly coloured glass is remarkably effective. The **sanctuary** is bounded by a low brick wall which drops down in steps and curves round to meet a set of simple **communion rails**, with **sedilia** incorporated on the s. side. The **high altar** is tremendously long, but in this setting the proportions seem entirely natural and right.

Kenton, All Saints (D4): With a population of only 150, this village has done wonders in restoring its church over the past few years; it is a place of rest, refreshment, and beauty in simplicity. The w. door of the late C14 tower is small, and the two-**light** window above it has **ogee** shapes in the **Decorated tracery**, echoed by the bell openings farther up. The curious **flushwork** roundels in the battlements may or may not be original. **Edward Hakewill** was the architect in charge of a major restoration in 1871 when all the window tracery was renewed. He designed the n. **porch** and rebuilt a great deal of the C13 **chancel**, inserting a rather harsh triple **lancet**-and-roundel e. window, and remodelling the **priest's door** on the s. side. The wide lancets in the side walls seem largely undisturbed, although the small Decorated window to the s. is partially blocked (its position suggests that it was once a **low side window**). From the e. end the line of the old **nave roof** shows up clearly above Hakewill's replacement. The s. **aisle** is entirely in mellow red brick, with an unobtrusive pattern in blue and characteristic **Tudor mullioned** windows. It was endowed as a **chantry chapel** dedicated to **St John** by Lord of the Manor John Garneys in 1524, and he made provision for a priest to serve it. The outer arch of the tall C15 s. porch displays **fleurons** and crowns in the mouldings, but despite their worn appearance, the **headstops** are likely to be C19. The roof timbers are original and one **wall plate** is carved with a little leaf trail. To the r. a handsome brick doorway with a well-worn step gives access to the Garneys chapel, but the main entrance is straight ahead and that shows that the early (possibly **Saxon**) church was rebuilt in the late C12. The style is **Transitional**, with single shafts and leaf **capitals**, one of which is a replacement; the arch has a roll moulding between deep hollows. Kenton has plenty of **scratch dials** – there are three on this doorway and you may have seen two more outside, a faint one on the centre buttress and another on the s.w. corner of the nave.

The medieval s. door still has its closing ring and opens on to a nave cheerfully enlivened with modern hassocks. Beyond the plain tower arch you will see attractive C19 **bosses** under the belfry ceiling, and there are sections of lead from the old tower roof framed on the n. wall. They were cast in 1714 with names, including 'W.Lord Churchwarding' and Jane Garneys (the family continuing here). Below stands an interesting Elizabethan pew, with a range of slim **balusters** at the front; the top rail has 'K.G. 1595 M.S.' There are two C15 bench ends with **poppyheads** nearby and seven **consecration cross** roundels are spaced round the walls (there is original paint on the one by the door). The octagonal bowl of the **font** is C13 **Purbeck marble**, with sharply canted sides and traditional pattern of blind arches; the shaft and steps are by Hakewill. When he replaced the roof, one **tie-beam** across the nave was retained, and there is a plain niche in the embrasure of one of the n. windows. The other has a tall arch access to the **rood stairs**, but the medieval **screen** has gone and so has the old chancel arch – which has been replaced by a rather fussy model with multiple shafts and intricate capitals.

The plain C17 pulpit has been largely remodelled, with Victorian Gothic tracery applied to the panels. Behind it is an attractive C15 niche which has a **Trinity** shield in one **spandrel** and **St George's** cross in the other and there may have been a nave **altar** here. A two-bay **arcade** replaced the s. wall when the chapel was built, and there are three rather odd little brackets below the capitals. The chapel has a small, plain **piscina** and the C15 shaft of the font has been moved here to carry a modern statue of the **Blessed Virgin**. The niche to the l. was probably designed for a statue of St John, and there is another with traces of stencil decoration between the side windows. The almost flat roof was undisturbed in the C19 and a blocked w. window suggests that the porch had an upper room, possibly for the chantry priest. John Garneys was undoubtedly buried in the chapel and there is a fine and important **brass** for him and his wife Elizabeth. He wears an heraldic tabard, she bears the arms of Sulyard on her cloak, and there is a rare remnant of a Crucifixion between them. Unfortunately, it can only be seen by appointment and one hopes that some day it will be placed on display. Hakewill must have enjoyed redesigning the chancel. Apart from its arch, he used a **cusped** arch and slim shafts to frame the e. lancets, and raised the altar on three steps which show off the jolly pattern of the **encaustic tiles**. The glass in the windows is by **Lavers & Barraud** – small figures of the Blessed Virgin, **St Paul, St Peter, Gabriel**, two angels, and Christ the King in the top roundel.

Kersey, St Mary (C8): In one of Suffolk's loveliest villages the steep street, followed by a flight of steps, leads up from a watersplash to the church on the hill. It is a fascinating building which shows, perhaps more clearly than most, the way in which it evolved over the years. In the C14 an ambitious reconstruction began which enlarged

the **chancel**, added a sumptuous n. **aisle**, and made a start on a new tower. Then came the **Black Death** in 1349 which brought everything to a standstill. Work did not begin again until at least half a century later when the **nave** was heightened, new windows were inserted on the s. side, and the **roof** was rebuilt. The position of the tower shows that a s. aisle was part of the C14 plan but this was never built and the C15 s. **porch** was built directly onto the nave, with another added to the n. aisle. The tower was not finished until 1481 and the only other major alteration came in the 1860s when the chancel was rebuilt and a **vestry** added on the n. side.

The triple **base course** of the tower has squares of **flushwork** and continues round the n. aisle, confirming the unity of the C14 design. The w. doors have weathered **tracery**, a vine trail decorates the edges, and the **label** of the arch has lion **stops**. Above is a **transomed** window with slim, **cusped**, and **crocketted** niches each side within an **arcade** of flushwork. The two **lights** of the belfry windows are separated by a flushwork panel and there is a very deep band of flushwork at battlement level which displays a distinctly individual pattern. A stair turret on the s. side rises to the very top and, with its four **set-offs** and prominent **string courses**, the tower has fine proportions and is very handsome. The s. porch is lovely and has all the panache of a showpiece. The triple base course is decorated with flushwork diamonds, **quatrefoils**, and arcades, and there is more diamond embellishment on the battlements; the buttresses are stepped and gabled, with niches at the upper level, the facade is panelled with flushwork overall, and a canopied centre niche has tiny figures at the top of its flanking buttresses. The carving in the **spandrels** is intriguing but the subject is obscure. To the l. there is a tree with two fish (one with another in its mouth), and to the r. a foliage design that looks more like seaweed than anything else. The porch roof is a stunning piece of work and probably owes its fine condition to the fact that it was plastered over for ages and only uncovered in 1927. Measuring a mere 13ft by 11ft, it is divided by heavily moulded beams into a lattice of sixteen square panels, each lined with a lacy cresting and carved with four panels of varied tracery. The C15 alterations made the nave tall for its length but the proportions of the n. aisle are impressive and so too is its decoration. Its e. window has **Decorated** tracery, with quatrefoils within **reticulations**, the stepped and gabled buttresses all have niches at the upper level, and the battlements are ornamented with flushwork chequer and crocketted pinnacles. There are large **gargoyles**. The n. porch matches the s. in style but lacks the flushwork embellishment, and its roof is not in the same class. It is interesting to note, however, that mortice holes show where carved **bosses** were applied to the heavily moulded beams. The inner doorway is finely moulded with vestiges of **headstops** and the base course shows on each side as a reminder that the porch was built later than the aisle.

Within, the aisle fulfils its promise of luxuriance despite the terrible mutilations exacted after the **Reformation**. Just inside the door is a **stoup** which has had its **corbel** base cut away and farther along there is a large niche in the n. wall under a wide **ogee** arch with pinnacles, crockets, and **finial** shorn off; there are stumps of angels inside it which show traces of colour, and a large alabaster **Trinity** group is now displayed there. It has been defaced but the drapery-covered knees of God the Father flank the outline of a cross and a remnant of Christ's figure. The wall has sections of painting in dark red and one figure is recognisable to the l. of the blocked window. Part of the stem and bowl of the early church's **font** was found doing duty as a cottage doorstep in 1927 and now stands in the centre of the aisle, and a section of the late C15 **rood screen** is nearby. The panels are painted with three Old

Testament prophets and three kings, one of whom is **St Edmund** with his arrow emblem. Two of the prophets hold parchment scrolls and all the figures wear ermine-trimmed cloaks. The robes are curiously stiff and bulky, reminiscent of contemporary illustrations of mummers in a mystery play. The two large niches flanking the e. window were barbarously treated by the despoilers and all the frontal decoration was hacked off, but a portion of delicate **groining** with a small head corbel survives on the l. and there are traces of colour. In that niche is a headless seated figure in a golden gown holding a book, still with its lettered page, and this must represent **St Anne**. To the r. stands a beautiful suite of **piscina** and **sedilia**. It is tall, with heavily cusped ogee arches, and close panelling fills the spaces below the straight top. The priest's stall was planned with a groined canopy and the deacons' stalls are decorated overhead with cusping and centred heads. You will see that the carving above the piscina and first stall was never completed; this must have been where work came to an untimely halt in 1349 or just after. There is a **squint** through to the **high altar** above the piscina bowl and the windows at the back of the sedilia were evidently renewed during the 1860s rebuilding and may have been altered. The scale and elaboration of the aisle suggest that it was perhaps planned as a parish church in miniature for use while the rest of the ambitious rebuilding went ahead. Over its **sanctuary** the roof was covered in the late C16 or early C17 with four **stucco** panels – crosses within lozenges decorated with **Tudor roses** and the arms of the Sampson family. There are three good wooden centre bosses at the e. end and the roof itself is an interesting design. Basically a lean-to, extra timbers are framed in from the arcade side to give the impression of a cambered roof. Below it, a cornice of clunch (a soft limestone) was carved from end to end with figures, some of which can be

Kersey, St Mary: s. porch

recognised as angels. All is terribly mutilated but **Cautley** thought that it might have a been a sequence of the **Seven Works of Mercy**. The graceful seven-bay arcade has tall, closely spaced arches with very attractive **hood moulds** carved as vine trails, and the octagonal **piers** have deeply moulded **capitals**. The w. bay shows again how work on the decoration was apparently interrupted. Above the arcade on the n. side are three **hatchments**; from e. to w. they are for: Sir Thomas Thorrowgood (1734), Katherine Thorrowgood (the last descendant of this important family, whose memorial you will see elsewhere), John Thorrowgood (1734).

The belfry floor in the tower is carried on heavy corbels and the bells, having been augmented to eight and lowered, are now rung from the ground floor. The early C15 **font** is squat, the deep bowl panels carved with angels and circular designs; one face is blank and probably stood against an arcade pillar originally. The 1970s oak cover is thoughtfully designed, with shaped ribs rising to a finial. There is a section of painting on the s. wall of the nave which was apparently a **St George**, and within it can be seen the hook that once supported the **tester** of a pulpit. The C17 arrangement of **box pews** grouped around a pulpit well down the nave lasted here until the 1880s. Overhead, the C15 roof has alternating **hammerbeams** and **arch-braces** with the hammers carved as angels – now minus their heads. Those at the e. end carry shields carved with **Passion emblems** and the e. bay is a **celure** with curious bunched ribbon decoration painted in white on the main timbers. **Rood** and screen have gone (except for the section in the n. aisle) but the stair to the loft is in the s. wall and the small opening above the arcade shows that it probably connected with another screen in the n. aisle. The stem of the worn C15 wooden lectern is hexagonal

(very like the one at Aldham) with little flying buttresses and miniature image stools. The handsome and very upright eagle on top is later – possibly C16. The C19 rebuilding included a wooden chancel arch resting on large stone figure corbels, and the spiky **reredos** has gabled and pinnacled side niches which have been effectively complemented by vivid little perspective paintings.

Kesgrave, All Saints (F7): The church stands by the side of the busy Ipswich-Woodbridge road and looks a conventional enough building, but there are surprises in store. The base of the tower has angled buttresses, a blocked w. doorway, and a window above it with 'Y' **tracery** that dates from about 1300. Having collapsed or become ruinous by the early C16, it was restored to its full height in red brick patterned in dark blue and topped with stepped battlements. The large early C14 n. **porch** has **ball flower** in the **dripstone** of the outer arch with an ample niche above it, and there are small windows at high level in the **nave** wall on either side. The C13 **chancel** is lit by side **lancets** and an unusual e. window. Its three stepped lancets lie under one arch, and in the space above them there is blind **plate tracery** – pairs of **trefoils** and **quatrefoils**, with a sexfoil at the top. Moving round to the s. side, one finds that the picture changes dramatically, for in 1980 a large extension designed by Derek Woodley was added that has changed the character of the church significantly. In red brick, it stands at right angles to the nave, and the sloping e. wall is hung with tiles in Kentish fashion. There is a large dormer on that side, and the shaped s. wall is broken by slit windows; **vestry**, cloakrooms, and kitchen continue back to join the tower.

The new work has transformed the interior and given it an exciting new dimension. From within, the form is like that of a giant's upturned boat

Kesgrave, All Saints, modern extension

attached to the old nave, with massive ribs encased in pine above exposed brickwork. The **high altar** is now placed off centre below the dormer window with the seating formed in a hollow square around it, the old nave making up one side. And what a pleasure it is to have total carpeting and comfortable chairs! The **communion rails** are of welded iron with a beech top to match the altar, and the architect's award-winning designs for lectern and candlesticks were carried out by Hector Moore. The altar is backed by a lovely appliqué hanging made by Isabel Clover on which four musical angels swirl around a golden globe, illustrating the theme of Psalm 150. Overhead, a black quadrangular cross is suspended, bearing the symbolic nails of the Crucifixion. The **hatchment** on the n. wall of the tower was used at the funeral of George Thomas, a high sheriff of the county who died in 1820, while that for

Rebecca Thomas hangs opposite and dates from 1770. Late C18 Creed and Lord's Prayer boards flank the arch and a well-restored set of George III **Royal Arms** hangs on the s. wall. The **font** was made by a Woodbridge mason called Smythe in 1843. Overhead, the **roof** is a false **hammerbeam** with **king-posts** above the **arch-braces**, but remedial work had to be done when the extension was built and the central timbers were replaced by steel and boxed in. When he was here in January 1643, **Dowsing** ordered that eighteen cherubim be taken down and these would have been the carvings that once decorated the ends of the hammers. The chancel is now divided from the nave by a full-height glazed pine screen and has become the chapel of **St Francis**. The old **rood beam** remains just inside, and some of the C19 benches from the nave have been installed. The **decalogue board** of the set hangs on the n. wall, and in the **sanctuary** there is a large early C14 **piscina** with attached shafts and ring **capitals**.

Before leaving, have a look at the coffin-shaped tomb e. of the entrance to the churchyard. It was originally for Rosabella Chilcot who died in 1837 and her epitaph begins:

> Stop traveller and drop the sympathetic tear . . .

Then her brother John died in 1851, also in his twenties, and the following was added:

> Meek resignation did his mind display
> While pale disease consum'd his life away.

He had been a horse dealer, and to the r. of the verse there is a bas relief of him displaying a likely nag to a prospective buyer (the same mason was probably responsible for the carving on Abraham Easter's stone at Woodbridge [Vol.3]). The top of the tomb bears the epitaph of John's niece, Repronia Lee, a gypsy queen who also died young in 1862. The family evidently favoured the parting verse and this one is in the ripe tradition of Victorian sentiment:

> Put your arms around me mother,
> Draw your chair beside my bed,–
> Let me lean upon your bosom,
> This poor weary aching head.
> Once I thought I could not leave you,
> Once I was afraid to die,
> Now I feel 'tis Jesus calls me,
> To his mansion in the skies.
> Why should you be grieving mother,
> That your child is going home,
> To that land where sin and sorrow,
> Pain and weakness never come.

Kettleburgh, St Andrew (F4): Church Lane winds up to finish at a pleasant pair of cottages and access is through the kissing-gate in their back yard. The C14 w. tower has a simple **base course, flushwork** in the buttresses, and modern stepped brick battlements. The w. window is **Perpendicular** but the bell openings have **Decorated tracery**. The n. door is blocked and farther along the shape of a large archway in the wall shows where there was an entrance to a side chapel; the **trefoil piscina** that served its **altar** is still in place. The

siting of the chapel may have been the reason why there are **clerestory** windows of three sizes below the eaves to give extra light for the **nave**, for strangely enough there are no other windows on that side. The **chancel** has a narrow Decorated window farther along and the e. window is Perpendicular. A heavy C18 to C19 brick buttress sits hard up against the small C14 **priest's door** and the s. facade has varied windows scattered with charming abandon. Again there is a clerestory (with no associated **aisle**), and the tall and wide **Tudor lancet** in the chancel is quite unusual. The low C14 **porch** has a minuscule base course and the inner door retains its original closing ring and strap hinges.

A rather nice set of Queen Anne **Royal Arms** stands on the tower screen; the background is a dusky pink with drapes and there are cut-out **acanthus** scrolls each side. The C15 **font** is a familiar design, although it now lacks the lions round the shaft. There are seated lions in the bowl panels, alternating with angels bearing shields whose heraldry belongs to the Charles and Ramsey families. Sir Thomas Charles married Alice Ramsey and when she died a widow in 1463 she may have left money to provide the font. The low C17 cover is in good condition, with arched supports rising to a centre shaft and ball **finial**. There were restorations here in the 1880s and 1890s and it looks as though the **arch-braced roof** was at least partially replaced then. Steps leading to the vanished **rood loft** rise from a s. window embrasure and three bells that have been lowered from the tower now stand below. The tenor was cast by William Brend of Norwich in 1592, but the second is anonymous and undated, having only the inscription: 'Sancta Maria ora pro nobis' (St Mary pray for us). The treble came from Robert Phelps's Whitechapel foundry in 1711 and bears the names of rector and churchwardens. **Cautley** was scandalised by the **screen** which was installed in 1891 but I find it a light and acceptable pastiche of the **Jacobean** style, with pierced tracery and acorn pendants, and it happily accommodates some original C17 panels in the base. The pulpit has some more and so has the lectern. There are four low C15 benches of two sizes in the chancel, and the large pair are so like those at Earl Soham that I believe them to be from the same workshop. On the n. side there are remains of a man astride a lion, and the lower benches have parts of three small figures and a castle which has a face peeping from its tiny window. Overhead, the medieval archbraced roof has its main timbers partially obscured by plaster, and the **wall plates** are **embattled**. The original of Murillo's *The Two Trinities* is in the National Gallery; the church has an C18 copy which hangs on the chancel wall. Also of interest at an entirely different level is the little coloured map of the village on the opposite wall which was produced by the W.I. as their contribution to the Jubilee celebrations in 1977. Also on that side there is a tablet by Sanders of Fitzroy Square for George Turner who died in 1839, having been rector for thirty-two years; not in itself remarkable, but further along a Gaffin tablet commemorates another George Turner who died in 1871 and who also served the parish for thirty-two years. Like father, like son indeed! The two sections of the **communion rails** are C17, and their style suggests that they once formed part of a three-sided set like those at Cretingham and elsewhere. The **altar** beyond is a very light-weight **Stuart** table, set on blocks with a large top added, and in the s.e. corner lies a C13 coffin slab with the double omega sign on top. A pair of excellent **decalogue** panels painted on canvas hangs on the e. wall. They date from the early C18 and are well lettered within frames with flanking scrolls, of a standard rather higher than the similar set at Saxtead. A slab on the n. side of the **sanctuary** bears 2ft **brass** effigies of Arthur Pennyng and one his wives (1593). He wears a ruff and gown and the lady has a fashionable hat and brocaded petticoat. The figure of the second wife is missing, as it was when Cautley made his notes in 1934, although he had seen it in the church chest some time before. He vented his feelings by supposing that 'some vile sacrilegious pilferer' had pinched it – as no doubt they had.

Layham, St Andrew (D9): The church dates from the late C13 or early C14 but its tower was replaced in 1742, in red brick and probably to the same scale. The w. door, belfry window, and bell openings are outlined in yellow brick, and the top stage looks as if it was rebuilt in 1861 when there was a general restoration (the date pierced in the weathervane gives the clue). There is a yew tree hard up against its s. wall reaching almost to the top which was probably planted to commemorate Queen Victoria's coronation, and a smaller one hugs the n. side. The small C14 n. door is blocked and all the windows were renewed as part of the 1860s restoration or during another in the 1880s. At that time a **vestry** was added on the n. side. The **priest's door** in the **chancel** s. wall has rather nice little male and female **headstops** and when the s.w. **nave** buttress was rebuilt a **scratch dial** was moved down almost to ground level. Just round the corner there was quite a large window in the w. wall which may have been blocked when the tower was rebuilt.

Beyond the C19 s. **porch**, the wide nave is spanned by a new **roof** with **scissors bracing** and you will see that the original w. arch was filled in and a small C18 door inserted. **Cautley** believed that the recess in the wall to the l. was a shelf where bread for the poor was placed and it may well have been used for this purpose, although it is obviously the embrasure for the blocked window. The C13 **Purbeck marble font** is unusual in being hexagonal but, apart from that, it has the typical shallow lead-lined bowl with canted sides. The pairs of arches in the panels have lost some of their detail and it rests on a centre column and six shafts. A simple **piscina** under a **trefoil** arch shows that there was a nave **altar** on the s. side and there is a **squint** cut through the **respond** of the chancel arch nearby. The odd thing is, however, that it does not align with the **high altar** but is cut e. to w. Beyond the pulpit on the other side of the nave there are four tall panels which were once part of the base of the C16 **rood screen**. The tablet above commemorates members of the Norman family and was the work of Edward J. Physick, a London sculptor and Royal Academy gold medalist – although one would not have guessed it from this design. Like the benches in the nave, the chancel stalls are Victorian but they have very elaborate **poppyheads** carved with vines, holly leaves, and thistles for the patron saint. The early C14 double piscina in the **sanctuary** has no drains now and is partly obscured by the end buttress of the stone **reredos**. This dates from 1904 and is quite elaborate, with gabled and pinnacled niches each side containing roundels against a deep blue background; the centre panels have Christ in Majesty flanked by **censing** angels, **St Andrew**, and **St John**, all in mosaic. The 1880s e. window glass, with its heavy and intricate **tabernacle work**, may be by a pupil of **Clayton & Bell** – Christ's baptism, crucifixion, entombment, and the martyrdom of St Andrew. Anne Roane's memorial on the s. wall of the chancel is most unusual because it is in the form of a canvas **hatchment**, although I doubt if it was used as such. Her coat of arms has flourishing yellow and red mantling, the epitaph is painted on a simulated drape, and although she died in 1626 it is dated 1736.

Leavenheath, St Matthew (C10): A C19 church that is by no means typical and, for that reason, interesting in a mild way. It was designed by G. Russell French in 1835, a time when the demand was for uncomplicated buildings in economical materials and the heady passions of the **Ecclesiological Society** had not yet been kindled. And so we find a simple hall of brick like many a nonconformist chapel. Buttresses were provided to give it some respectable solidity, a wooden w. porch, and instead of the prevailing 'Gothick' **lancets**, the windows are in **Tudor** style complete with **labels** – except, that is, for a w. lancet which has lion **stops** to the **dripstone**. Its character changed in the 1880s when the architects Satchell & Edwards added a red brick **chancel**, s. **aisle** and tower, and the combination viewed from outside is faintly eccentric. The chancel has four e. lancets and its **roof** is carried down on the s. side to cover a **vestry**; the aisle with lancet windows has its own gabled roof and standing at its w. end is the squat and solid tower with a large w. door under a heavy arch; there are three slits for bell openings on each face and the pyramid roof is capped by a lead spike like an unfortunate afterthought.

In contrast, the simple interior is quietly attractive and the feeling is much more C20 than C19. A s. **arcade** on octagonal brick **piers** matches the chancel arch and at the e. end of the aisle an arch leads to what was presumably a family pew which opens off the chancel. The chancel fittings are solid and sensible and the **nave** gained a suite of oak pews in 1963. At the w. end stands a small octagonal **font** that would have been supplied with the original building and, ranged on the wall nearby, seven Flanders crosses with photographs of the young village men who marched away and never came back.

Letheringham, St Mary (F4): The tower can be seen from a distance along the lane that leads from Easton to Hoo but access is a little convoluted, through the yards of Abbey farm. A priory of Augustinian canons was founded here in the 1190s and this small building is the remains of their church. Apart from the C16 gatehouse to the s.w., little else survives although there are traces of a doorway in the n. wall which may have led to the cloisters. Following the dissolution of the priory in 1537, a long sequence of neglect, spoliation, and decay set in so that when Horace Walpole visited in 1755 he found the church 'very ruinous though containing such treasures'. These were mainly the monuments and **brasses** in the spacious **chancel** and by 1780 they too were pillaged, broken, and battered. In 1789 the parish was told to put things right and, perhaps in desperation, the churchwardens gave the whole of the chancel to a Woodbridge builder in exchange for a rebuilt **nave** and new e. wall. The monuments went for road ballast, the **font** disappeared, and many of the slabs that once bore brasses were used to pave the nave. Against all odds this tiny building has emerged triumphant from its trials and is beautifully cared for by the faithful few. The C14 tower has recently been restored and there is **flushwork** on buttresses and stepped battlements which have new lions seated at the corners. The blocked w. door is partially below ground level and there is **Decorated tracery** in the w. window and bell openings. A boundary wall joins the tower at the n.w. corner so that one cannot circle the building, but there is a semi-circular sundial dated 1609 to be found at the top of a nave buttress. The low red brick **porch** also carries a date, 1685, below the quirky gable whose straight sides develop convex curves in the lower half.

The **Norman** s. doorway is almost the only visible survivor of the original building and its single attached shafts have scallop **capitals** below an arch with zigzag and **billet** mouldings. Various fragments are displayed in the porch – the body of a feathered angel, the bust of a man with a club, a defaced alabaster head of a woman, and an alabaster block carved with two female figures – possibly a mother and daughter. The tower arch is tall and there are sections of Norman zigzag and slim

jamb shafts that were re-used by the C14 builder. On either side, rudimentary niches have been made to house the kneeling figures of William Naunton and his wife. He died in 1635 and after his monument in the chancel had been destroyed the statues were used as garden ornaments. They are of high quality and the inscriptions that were originally below them are now set in the n. wall beyond the font. That is a plain cauldron shape on a drum shaft and presumably came from elsewhere to replace the one that was lost at the rebuilding. A set of naively painted **Hanoverian Royal Arms** hangs above the s. door and on the n. wall is the fine brass of Sir John de Wyngefeld of 1389 set in a new wooden frame. It is just over 5ft tall and is an excellent illustration of the armour of the period. The leather coat or jupon that was worn over the armour has the wings of the family badge and they were originally inlaid with colour. The stone in which it was first set has migrated to the w. end of the nave. There are no windows to the n. and those in the s. wall are early C14 like the e. window, which was probably saved from the chancel. Floors are brick with a number of slabs reaved of their brasses, and there is a small suite of late **Georgian box pews** in deal at the e. end to match the plain panelled pulpit. The large shield with about forty quarterings on the n. wall retains some of its colour, and below it are **touchstone** tablets for High Sheriff Thomas Wingfield who died in 1609 and Sir Anthony Wingfield who died four years earlier. The church's only other brass to survive is fixed to the e. wall. It is for Sir Thomas Wyngfeld who died in 1471 and was probably made in the same workshop as the Taylboys brass at Assington. 3ft long, it displays a mixture of Yorkist and Tudor styles of armour, and was filched from the church by a collector in 1786. It eventually found its way to the Ashmolean Museum in Oxford and by good fortune is now on permanent loan. With it is one of the shields that really belongs to Sir John's brass. On the wall above is a fragment of Sir Robert Naunton's memorial. He died in 1635 and was 'sometime principal secretarie and after Master of the Wards and Councillor of State to our late King James of happy memorie and to our now Sovereign Lord King Charles'. James, his only son and heir, had died when only 2 years old in 1624 and was even then given the title of esquire; his epitaph on the s. wall reflects the parents' grief at their loss:

Here lyes the Boy whose infancie was such
As promised more than parents durst desire.
Yea frighted them by promising to much
for earth to harbour long;

The **altar** is a C17 table and is set within a set of very slender three-sided **communion rails**, a late example of that fashion dating from the late C17 or early C18. The American organ may seem unremarkable but it does have the charming refinement of 'patented mouse-proof pedals', just like the one at Westley [Vol.1]. When leaving don't overlook the group photograph of Letheringham's Home Guard in the porch. Not to be parted from their dog, they are a cheerful company with forage caps at all angles.

Lindsey, St Peter (B8): In a quiet upland situation, this is an unobtrusive early C14 church with a good deal of character. By 1836 the tower had partially collapsed and it was taken down, a new window was inserted in the rebuilt w. wall, and a wooden bellcote was placed on the gable. On walking round, you will see that the **nave** has an unusually large and elaborate window on the n. side and there was another w. of the blocked n. door. The w. end of the s. **aisle** is lit by an attractive little single-light window with **Decorated tracery** and the **chancel** has a wide **lancet** to the n. The e. window is C19 but may repeat an original design, and there is one with 'Y' tracery of about 1300 on the s. side. The **priest's door** with **headstops**

Lindsey, St Peter: C14 porch

to the **dripstone** is now blocked and a **scratch dial** can be seen on the r. hand **jamb**. The outer arch of the open-sided C14 **porch** is gnarled and seamed like driftwood, with eroded **cusps** to the barge board of the gable, and there is a braced **tie-beam** above the small C14 doorway.

Within, there are heavy **arch-braced** tie-beams and **king-posts** under plaster ceilings, and in both nave and chancel the parallel **wall plates** have a plaster cove between them. The square early C13 **font** must have been made for an earlier building, and although it now stands close to a **pier** of the C14 **arcade**, the bowl decoration shows that it was not always so. The varying arch designs are raised in unusual fashion on flat surfaces and the C17 **cover** is distinctly individual – a plain board carrying a centre post which is support-ed by eight turned struts splayed at a low angle. Creed and Lord's Prayer boards stand at the w. end, and above the outline of the blocked window in the n. wall there is a set of **Royal Arms**. They are **Hanoverian** and naively painted on board. The benches are C19 unstained pitch pine but against the n. wall there is a suite of plain C18 **box pews**. The window on that side is intriguing. It is much larger than one would expect to find in this situation and the beautiful tracery is unusually elaborate, with fragments of its original glass surviving. Not only that, but large canopied niches were formed at the inner corners of the embrasure and the one on the r. had a tall pinnacle. It must have had a special significance and may have been associated with the village **guild** of St Peter which, in the next century, was given a house so that the master and brethren could keep the annual feast in style. A small C17 chest is now used as an **altar** in the s. aisle and mortice slots in the arcade piers at that end show that there was once a **parclose screen** for the chapel. The piers are worth examining closely for another reason. They are thick with medieval graffiti and the bishops' heads on the s. side of the easternmost pier are of particular interest because they illustrate horned mitres of the C12, implying that the stones came from an earlier building. Above and to the l. on the s.w. face there is a lovely little **Tudor rose** in a circle. On the pier by the font there is a scratch dial that was either drawn for fun or else the stone must have come in from the outside of the earlier church, and on the s.e. face is an elongated bird. Below it there are some very strange devices. They seem to represent basketwork objects with handles and cross **finials** and there is no way of telling their real size. Possibly related to some ancient religious ceremony, they are enigmatic and mysterious.

The stair to the **rood loft** remains in the n. wall and the base of the **screen** still stands, albeit precariously. The two panels on the n. side still have their colour and by them the pulpit is a C19 reconstruction in which the panels and three of the ledge brackets are C16. The

benches on the s. side of the chancel have heavy, worn ends with remains of **poppyheads** and the front panels are likely to have formed part of the rood loft. The organ with its early C19 case largely obscures the monument to Nicholas Hobart who died in 1606. The **touchstone** tablet has cherub heads and swags of flowers each side, there is a **cartouche** of arms in the **pediment**, and a skull nestles in a swag at the bottom. A plain lancet **piscina** lies beyond **dropped-sill sedilia** and the altar is enclosed by a very nice set of three-sided late C17 **communion rails**. Pale in colour, they have delicately turned **balusters** with clusters of four at the corners.

Little Bealings, All Saints (F6): This is one of a number of churches in the area which have towers to the s. of the **nave** doing duty as rather grand **porches**. All Saints' unbuttressed tower is very uncompromising, built in the C14 but with bell openings and parapet reshaped relatively recently and the s.w. corner repaired in brick at the top. Decoration is limited to **paterae** on the single **string course**. Nave and **chancel** date from about 1300, judging by the form of the window **tracery** and the **priest's door**, although there is one window with **Decorated** tracery on the s. side of the chancel and a late C15 brick section with a two-**light** window was inserted in the s. wall of the nave, probably to give additional light to the **rood screen**. A n. **aisle** was added in the 1850s which has a w. window to match the nave and small brick **lancets**, and just beyond its e. end you will find the grave of James Hogger, a village blacksmith who died in 1857. He chose a version of the well-known epitaph for those of his trade, but unfortunately it has been largely masked by the footstone being moved up against it and I could only read the first two lines:
My sledges and hammers lie reclined,
My bellows too hast lost their wind . . .

The interior is plain and simple, with plastered ceilings hiding the medieval **roofs**, although there is still a **wall plate** to be seen in the chancel. The three-bay C19 **arcade** rests on octagonal brick pillars, and the C18 **reredos** now hangs on the aisle wall, its panels painted with the **decalogue**, Creed, and Lord's Prayer. The C15 **font** was very roughly treated by C17 image breakers and only one of the **Evangelistic symbols** and a single angel survive in the bowl panels; the angels below the bowl and the lions round the shaft are but remnants. There was a **Stuart** pulpit, but having fallen on hard times it was skilfully reconstructed by a local carpenter in 1925 so that only a tithe of what you see is original. The glass of 1899 in the e. window is by Albert L. Moore, a designer for **Powells** in the 1860s. It is not unpleasing, with Gethsemane and Resurrection scenes flanking the Crucifixion, and trumpeting angels above the canopy work – there is another of his windows at Dallinghoo.

Little Blakenham, St Mary (D7): This little church sits attractively on a bank above a steepish lane and the garden of the old rectory reaches right up to the e. wall. In consequence, a circuit of the outside is not practicable, but just by the wicket gate into the garden there is a **scratch dial** to be found on one of the **quoins** of the s.e corner of the **Early English chancel**. All the walls are plastered and a **Perpendicular** window was added to the s. side next to the **priest's door**. The unbuttressed tower has a small w. window with **Decorated tracery** matching the bell openings and the windows in the **nave**. The s. **porch** has lost the tracery in its side windows but there is a fine modern statue of the **Blessed Virgin** and Child in the niche above the low C14 outer arch.

The octagonal C14 **font** has no decoration whatsoever and within the tower a little chamber organ fits snugly onto the **gallery. Royal Arms** of James II hang opposite the door and they are an excellent set, vigorously painted on

board and dated 1685. The solid pews with doors and the pulpit were no doubt part of the enthusiastic mid-C19 restoration. On the s. wall is a tablet for the three infant children of John and Sarah Cuthbert who died between 1841 and 1858:

> My Lord hath need of these flowers gay
> The reaper said, and smiled …

In the chancel e. wall there are three C12 stepped **lancets** within a single arch but the flanking niches with **trefoil** heads were either heavily restored or added in the C19. They once framed paintings of the **Assumption** and **St John the Baptist** but, having been repainted, they have now vanished. One wonders why. The deep splays of the lancet in the n. wall are painted with full-length figures of Christ and a woman cradling a dove; they follow the curve of the arch to the top and peer down benignly. They were repainted in 1850 and it would be interesting to know how close they are to the C13 originals. There is an undistinguished version of Holman Hunt's *The Light of the World* in the e. window centre lancet and the **piscina** has a multi-**cusped** arch under a square head. Although I could find no trace of him, Samuel Hardy was a late C18 rector here who was a prolific author and scholar of some standing. He published a number of works on the Eucharist and edited a Greek Testament that ran to three editions.

Little Cornard, All Saints (B10): Approached via a farmyard and a grassy track, this little church is set most attractively on the ridge above the valley of the Stour. The w. window of the tower is early C14, the bell openings have recently been renewed, and on top there is a small early C19 circular wooden cupola; by using binoculars the names of rector and churchwardens can be picked out on the lead-covered base to the s.e. The C14 n. door is blocked but note the masses of graffiti of all ages cut in the soft stone of the **jambs**. A C17 two-storeyed **vestry** lies alongside the **chancel** whose **Perpendicular** e. window has **headstops** turning towards each other. There is a small, plain **priest's door** on the s. side and to its l. a two-**light Decorated** window has had its **tracery** cut short at the top. The s. **porch** has large, open brick windows and the C14 inner doorway is flanked by a pair of modern plaques carved with doves set in the wall.

There is a neat interior, with modern **roofs**, pine pews, and pulpit. The w. window glass of the early 1920s is by **Heaton, Butler & Bayne** on the theme of the Good Shepherd, and a late C15 **font** stands in the base of the tower. Its stem is panelled, four of the bowl panels have window tracery patterns, and the rest have shields – **St George's** cross, the chevrons of either the Cornhead or the De Grey families, the cross with serrated edges of the Peytons, and a shield with a star which was probably borne by a member of the De Vere family. The glass in the modern window on the s. side of the nave featuring the figures of Christ, the **Blessed Virgin**, and **St John** looks like the work of **Clayton & Bell**, and in the window on the n. side there is a C15 roundel of an angel bearing a scroll in yellow stain. Both windows at the e. end of the nave have dropped sills and this indicates that there were probably **altars** nearby – the church certainly had one dedicated to the Trinity before the **Reformation**. There is no longer a **screen** within the tall chancel arch and the **vestry** is open to its full height on the n. side and now houses the organ. Nearby stands a C14 wagon-topped chest heavily banded with iron and fitted with four hasps. The priest's door is blocked and the window to the r. has a dropped sill; this, and its position, suggests that it was used as a **low side window**. The **piscina** in the **sanctuary** lies under a **cinquefoiled ogee** arch with a renewed base, but the interesting thing is that a C19 bas relief of Christ presiding at the Last Supper has been set in the back (there is a similar

but more elaborate treatment at Market Weston [Vol.1]. There is a C19 stone **reredos** and a tall renewed niche by the e. window which is filled with a late example of Charles Clutterbuck's glass. With **Hardman** and the **O'Connors**, he was one of the artists who began the Victorian revival of stained glass, and having moved on from C13 forms, here he used larger figures, with a central Christ in the style of Murillo surrounded by typically Victorian angel heads. Our Lord as the Good Shepherd and the True Vine stand on either side and both are badly eroded. All are set within dense foliage patterns with texts and are by no means as pleasing as his early work.

It is surprising to find a new and very attractive parish hall in the churchyard just w. of the tower; it replaced one which was flattened by the fall of a mighty elm tree. In such a pleasant spot it is salutory to remember that once this was a place of desolation. The court rolls of one of the village manors record the first known instance of the **Black Death** in East Anglia; between January and June 1349, sixty people died and twenty-one families left no heirs to claim their goods.

Little Finborough, St Mary (B7): The short drive to Hall Farm leaves the minor road at a sharp bend, and beyond the attractive cluster of house and outbuildings the way to St Mary's is along a rough track. Tiny and unpretentious, the early C14 church lies among open, rolling fields, with a heavy cedar to the n. and a scattering of pine and holly and a windswept hedge towards the road. There is no tower and restoration in 1856 replaced a lath and plaster w. end with a blank pebble wall banded at intervals with dressed flint. There are angle buttresses and a single bell turret sits on the gable. The **nave** was at least partially rebuilt and cement rendered, retaining two early **Perpendicular** windows to the s. and another to the n. The **chancel** is a mixture of flint and **septaria** and the e.

window has intersecting 'Y' **tracery**. The **set-off** e. of the nave window on the n. side, combined with faint outlines on the wall within, shows that there was once a **rood loft stair** here, and just by it in the churchyard stands an old shepherd's hut on fat little cast-iron wheels. Before going in, have a look at the C18 headstones by the path. They carry baroque scrolls and varied cherubs, with one weeping by an urn. A double stone commemorates the four children of William and Ann Cross who died between 1789 and 1802 aged 3 years, 1 month, 2 years, and 11 months. 'Ah! why so soon just as the flower appears ...' cries the epitaph.

Beautifully kept, the interior lies under a plaster ceiling with some of the timbers of the **roof** exposed, and one of the **tie-beams** has rustic **arch-braces**. Another divides nave from chancel and probably supported the **rood**. The **tympanum** above it is plastered and there hangs a handsome set of George III **Royal Arms** painted on board and dated 1767. The plain C14 **font** stands on a wide step and the sides of the bowl are slightly canted. There are no signs of original **porches** but, unlike the entrance, the little n. doorway retains its simple shape and leads to a C19 **vestry**. Benches and **encaustic** floor tiles date from the 1860s and so does the rather odd pulpit and reading desk. Both are square and built as a unit featuring pierced **Decorated**-style tracery shapes. In the **sanctuary** the cast-iron **communion rails** take the form of 'Gothick' arches and there is a **piscina** recess with no drain. The openwork **altar** has one of those Victorian eccentricities – a brass inscription set in the bevelled edge of its top to Charlotte, widow of W.M. Townsend, 1895. The **reredos** must be of about the same period and the panels are painted with sacramental sentences flanking the Lord's Prayer in a style beloved of the late C19 – florid Gothic, with multi-coloured initials. Under the glow of candles and oil lamps, Evensong in this endearing little church must be as balm in Gilead.

Little Stonham, St Mary (C5): Very pleasantly situated at the end of Church Lane. The handsome tower with sharp **drip courses** has a polygonal turret to the s. which goes right up to the stepped battlements; these are decorated with a deep band of lovely **flushwork** which features monograms of the **Blessed Virgin** and there are **Evangelistic symbols** midway between the corner pinnacles. There is **Decorated tracery** in the twin bell openings and flushwork on the buttresses and **base course**; the w. doorway has worn lion **headstops, paterae** in the mouldings, and **quatrefoils** with arms of the Crane family above it. The doors themselves have excellent tracery – tall **crocketted** pinnacles over pairs of Decorated arches. The **nave clerestory** is **Perpendicular** and its gable, like the **chancel's**, is crow-stepped. The C14 chancel has **reticulated** tracery in its e. window and was restored by the rector in 1886 when a new **priest's door** was inserted beneath a buttress, like the one at Yaxley. A chapel rather like a short s. **aisle** was built onto the C15 s. **porch** and the **dripstone** of the inner doorway is carved with paterae and rests on large male and female headstops.

Within, an C18 **gallery** stands on very slim iron columns and the panels of the C15 **font** contain unusually interesting carvings – w., a Crucifixion; s.w., a Sacred Heart within a crown of thorns; s.e., a crowned 'MR' for the Virgin; n.e., a **Tudor rose**; n., the Crane monogram. Four battered lions round the shaft stand below a deep band of angels with linked hands. The nave **roof** is quite lavish for this size of church – a double **hammerbeam** in which short **king-posts** rise to the ridge from the collar beams, and mutilated figures sit under canopies against the **wall posts**. All the **spandrels** are carved and the ends of the hammers retain the tenons that once secured angel figures. The hammerbeam against the wall at the e. end of the s. side had to be replaced in the C17 and was decorated with scrolls and grapevines in the style of the period – a notable addition to a good roof. Over the s. door hang the **Royal Arms** of Anne painted on canvas (pre-1704 and without her usual 'Semper eadem' motto). The **touchstone** tablet, in alabaster frame with skull and hour-glass, on the n. wall is for Gilbert Mouse, sometime servant of two lord chancellors and one lord keeper of the Great Seal. He died in 1622 and was buried in St Margaret's, Westminster, but his roots were here and there are details of his local charities. It is notable for the portrait engraved at the head of the tablet as though it were a **brass**. The restrained **Stuart altar** table in the s. chapel shows how heavy timbers can no longer being used for legs – slabs were added to increase the girth before the bulky sections were turned. 'T.G. 1703' painted on the wall is probably the record of a repair with churchwarden's initials. C19 benches stand on brick and **pamment** floors and by the pulpit the wall recess may have been a **piscina** but the panelling masks any possible proof. The chancel restoration included an **arch-braced** roof which rests on stone **corbels**, four of which are carved with Evangelistic symbols. Above them are sizeable oak figures under canopies and there are two rows of demi-angels on the **wall plates**. The same bout of restoration included the angle piscina and **dropped-sill sedilia**.

As one turns w. and sees the gallery and organ again, it brings to mind the extraordinary confrontation in 1872 between a curate and a choir – or at least one member of it. It provided plenty of juicy copy for the *Ipswich Chronicle* and ended unprofitably for all concerned at Quarter Sessions. Ronald Fletcher's *In a Country Churchyard* tells the tale.

Little Waldingfield, St Laurence (B9): This was an important village in the heyday of the Suffolk wool trade and the handsome church reflects this. There was a building here at the time

of the Domesday survey but this was replaced in the C14 and the tower still has **Decorated** bell openings and a stooled niche in the s. wall at ground-floor level. The buttresses have four **set-offs** and there are three well-defined **drip courses**. There are regularly spaced **put-log holes** n. and s. and below the renewed **Perpendicular** w. window the edge of the C15 door is carved with a band of **quatrefoils**; headless angels stand at the corners of the stepped battlements. C15 and C16 wealth allowed for extensive remodelling and all the **aisle** and **clerestory** windows lie under **crocketted labels** which have a shallow **finial** at the centre and terminate in masks which are full of character. The most distinctive feature of this period is the pair of octagonal **rood stair** turrets which rise to crocketted spires on either side of the **nave** gable, and they originally gave access to the **roofs**. The **Tudor** brick n. **porch** is a most interesting design and has a series of steps which are **weathered** like buttresses and rise above the arch to a deep niche whose heavy octagonal pinnacle matches those at the corners. The windows are deeply moulded and now that it has become a **vestry** the outer arch is blocked. At one time there was a chapel on the n. side of the **chancel** and the outlines of **piscina, aumbry**, connecting door, and low roof remain in the outer face of the wall. The C17 five-**light** e. window has a high **transom**, and round the corner is a very small **priest's door** under a square **label**. The walls of the C15 s. porch are attractively striped in brick and flint, the windows have stepped transoms, and the **dripstone** of the inner doorway matches the aisle windows. It has angel **stops**, however, and the mouldings are distinguished by very large **paterae** carved with masks, a centre crown, and a crowned woman's head.

Two of the charity boards under the tower specify that loads of wood are to be delivered to the poor, and by the arch stand two chests. One dates from about 1300 and its curved top is eaten

*Little Waldingfield, St Laurence: C15
chest*

away with age between the broad iron
bands; the other is a C15 example
whose entire front is carved with
shallow Decorated **tracery** and there
are four small masks in the heads of the
ogee arches. Between stands a late C14
font and all the figures round the stem
have been destroyed. However, four of
the panels are deeply carved with
Evangelistic symbols and the others
contain seated figures of monks. These
are unusual and although they have
been defaced, a lot of interesting detail
remains. They are seated on benches
reading, one has a pen and inkhorn by
his side, two have double-sided lec-
terns, and one wears a cope as opposed
to the capes of the others. The chancel
arch and those of the elegant nave
arcades all have crockets and finials
that match the window exteriors, and
the clerestory embrasures are enlivened by little **headstops** that angle
downwards. A **string course** dotted
with paterae is picked out in cream to
match the arcades below and contrasts
well with the pale blue of the plastered

chancel ceiling. Overhead, a heavy
cambered **tie-beam roof** with alternate
arch-braces in unstained oak spans the
nave, and in the s. aisle there is a line of
centre **bosses** which includes a **green
man** and a modern gridiron symbol of
the church's patron saint. At the e. end
you will find a small **Stuart Holy table**
and there is a plain piscina nearby.
Over in the n. aisle there is another in
the e. wall next to the rood stair door.
Fragments of medieval glass in the
aisle e. window include a small
crowned head and most of a monk's
tonsured head. The pulpit is a good C17
example resting on a heavy turned
stem. It has distinctive scrolls and
acorn pendants below the body and the
panels are carved with shallow blind
arches and diagonal crosses. The
canted book ledge is adventurously
carved and rests on bulky scrolled
brackets. It is more than likely that it
was made by the same craftsman who
supplied pulpits to nearby Milden and
Edwardstone, and the boxy reading
desk here is from the same workshop.
There are three interesting **brasses** in
the n. aisle: at the w. end are the 20in.
figures of Robert and Mary Appleton.
He was lord of one of the local manors

and died in 1526. He is shown in Tudor armour, with his wife wearing a **kennel head-dress**, and there are also three shields, one of which bears the punning or canting device of three apples. This probably came from the same workshop as the famous De Bures brass at Acton [Vol.1]. In the centre of the aisle is the 29in. effigy of rich clothier John Colman. This is a fine brass; he wears a cloak with heavy sleeves and has a large pouch slung at his hip. There is an inscription and separate plates showing his six sons and seven daughters. For years all the components of this brass were loose in the vestry, together with the effigy of John's wife Katherine which disappeared long ago, but in 1977 they were fixed to an unmarked slab. The third brass lies at the e. end of the aisle and is for another clothier, John Wyncoll, who died in 1544. His 'picture' (as he called it in his will) shows him wearing a flowing gown left open to display his doublet and the inscription is immediately below.

A long **squint** gave a view from the s. aisle chapel through to the **sanctuary** and there you will find late C17 **communion rails** and a C19 Minton tiled floor. There is a plain piscina and **dropped-sill sedilia** and, like the door to the vanished n.e. chapel, the priest's door is blocked.

Little Wenham, All Saints (D8): Isolated churches have a fascination all their own and this is no exception. A turning off the minor road between Capel St Mary and Great Wenham soon becomes a rough farm track, but after half a mile or so the reward is to find the church perched on a hillock behind Hall farm. Although the official dedication is to All Saints, it is known locally as St Laurence's and it is now in the care of **the Redundant Churches Fund**. In such a setting, with an Elizabethan tithe barn nearby, it is easy to imagine what Suffolk was like long ago. To the s. the battlemented tower of Little Wenham Hall rears sturdily be-

yond the farm buildings. Built in the late C13, that is one of the earliest English country houses and the church was built at about the same time. This is most clearly seen in the **chancel** where the e. window has three plain circles of **plate tracery** above three **lancets** separated by delicate **mullions**. The tracery actually has shallow, pierced **cusping** but it is visible only from inside. The tall lancet in the n. wall has a **low side window** below it in the form of a plain slit. Other windows have 'Y' tracery, there is a **priest's door** on the s. side, and the buttresses are gabled. The one on the **nave** wall not only has an old sundial pointer but below it are three earlier **scratch dials**. The C15 tower has a **base course**, a **Perpendicular** w. window with a small niche above it, and little belfry slits. The bell stage was rebuilt in brick, probably in the early C16. The C15 s. **porch** has a brick base but the upper framework is attractively weathered timber, with three simple niches cut in the planks above the outer arch; turned **balusters** were inserted in the open sides early in the C17. Slots in the frame indicate that there was a lift gate to keep out stock at one time (like the one at Badley, another isolated church in the care of the Redundant Churches Fund).

On entering, notice the deep drawbar holes in the stonework of the doorway and the small **stoup** recess just inside. A late C18 or early C19 **bier** stands in the tower, and on the wall is a delightful photograph of a man in a billycock hat who may well have been a sexton who used the bier later in the century. Two **tie-beams** span the **nave** under the single-braced **roof**, and a **sanctus-bell window** lies behind the rafters at the w. end. The early C14 **font** is a large, plain octagon resting on a centre drum and eight polygonal shafts. At least half of it has been replaced by new stone but the rest shows that it was painted originally. An C18 Lord's Prayer board hangs on the n. wall opposite, and below it are displayed a door and section of

Little Wenham, All Saints: Brewes monument

panelling from a **Jacobean** pew. In the traditional place opposite the main entrance are the remains of a large C15 **St Christopher** painting. The head of the saint with its curly chestnut hair is clear, and the Christ child with hand upraised has a dark halo, but the rest has gone except for part of the lozenge border. The rear benches have good **linen-fold** backs, and beyond the large late-Perpendicular window, the brick steps up to the vanished **rood loft** remain complete in the n. wall. In the s. wall of the nave there is an elaborate late C14 tomb. Its chest has four shields within **quatrefoils** on the front, and the tall recess lies under a multi-**cusped** arch; above that, a **crocketted ogee** flanked by blind panelling and pinnacles reaches up to an elaborate **finial** at roof level. All is in very good condition and probably restored. The **screen** consists now of solid 5ft walls, over 1ft thick, and one wonders whether it was like Bramford's originally. There are

oblong plastered panels each side which no doubt framed painted **reredoses** for nave **altars**, and one of the **piscinas** for them remains on the s. side (the shapeless recess by the stair doorway on the n. may be the remains of the other). The C18 pulpit has a rudimentary marquetry **sacred monogram** in one of its panels, and the little curving stair with its twisted balusters is very attractive.

On the s. side of the chancel there is a section of medieval glazed tiles which were probably saved by having a C17 **box pew** placed over them, and in the centre is one of the church's treasures. It is the **brass** commemorating Thomas Brewse and his wife Jane. He died in 1514 and the remains of the inscription begin: '... Brewse Esquyer onetyme lord of this maner and patron of this churche...'. The brass measures 87in. by 36in., with 28in. effigies, and has the only complete and undamaged double canopy in Suffolk. His armour is an excellent example of the **Tudor** period and his wife's dress is opulent, with fur collar and cuffs, a long veil over her **kennel head-dress**, and a pomander at the end of her girdle. There are separate plates engraved with the little figures of two sons and three daughters, the latter with hair down to their waists, showing that they were unmarried at the time. A most unusual feature of the design is the pair of portrait heads within roundels in the canopies which may represent the **Blessed Virgin** and **St John**. The four shields were originally inlaid and all feature the Brewse heraldic lion coupled with families connected by marriage. Pride of lineage even extended to his great-grandfather's wife's family of Stapleton! A late C13 or early C14 burial slab rests against the n. wall and note that the low side window has a deep sill that could be used as a seat. Over the priest's door there is a fine marble **cartouche** for Alice Walker who died in 1683; cherub heads rest in a garland at the top but the verse below the Latin epitaph is very roughly lettered. The late C17 **communion rails**

are sturdy, with twisted balusters, and
in the s. wall of the **sanctuary** one
section of the **Early English sedilia**
remains, with a **trefoil** arch and attached shafts. The rest of the space on
that side was appropriated for John
Brewse's monument in 1585. In stone
and multi-coloured marble, it has a
classical **pediment** and flanking
Corinthian columns above the tomb
chest, with a small round-headed
niche at the back. This contains a little
kneeling figure in perfect condition,
the armour completed by large metal
spurs. Colour has been well restored
and there are four shields of arms and
an **achievement** at the top. On the n.
side of the sanctuary there is a tomb
chest with shields in lozenges on the
front, and the late Tudor arch above
has two ranges of **paterae** and is
panelled within. Above it there are
shallow blind panels with six shields
left blank and, in the centre, a vigorous
bas relief of the Brewse arms on a tilted
shield, with helm and Saracen's head
crest. The recess may well have been
used for an **Easter sepulchre** originally,
but in 1785 a tablet was placed there for
John Brewse, Col. Commandant of the
Corps of Engineers. When **Dowsing**
was here in 1643 he broke down 26
'superstitious pictures' (stained glass,
one assumes) and left orders about six
more, but although he says that one of
them was of the Virgin Mary, the
remarkable thing is that there is a
painting of her on the e. wall which has
survived. It is part of an important
series on either side of the e. window
which dates from the time that the
church was built, and it is possible that
in Dowsing's day it had been covered
up. The Virgin and Child stand on the
n. side and the robes are now blue-
green and pale brown, with hands and
faces oxidised to black. The chestnut
hair is thick and curly, and the infant
Christ reaches across his mother for
the branch she holds in her right hand.
Above them there was an elaborate
canopy of which only the green leaves
of the crockets show clearly. On the s.
side of the window there are three tall

figures in attitudes typical of the late
C13. They stand within painted niches
which have cusped and crocketted
arches, above which are steep gables;
across the top, a line of two-**light**
windows under sharp gables and a roof
line give the effect of a church facade.
Again, the colours are blue-green and
pale brown for the robes but more
detail of the folds has survived. Here
we have three favourite female saints,
each with brown hair peeping out from
under a veil: on the l., **St Margaret** (see
the dragon's head at the bottom), in the
centre **St Catherine**, on the r. **St Mary
Magdalene**. This was work of high
quality and the artist may well have
belonged to the Colchester abbey
group.

Mellis, St Mary (B3): The village greens
are extensive and the church lies on
the edge of them to the w. of the main
railway line. There was a tower
originally but it collapsed in 1730 and
two large buttresses were roughly
shaped from the remains. Between
them is a large window outline above a
modern lean-to shelter. The wide **nave**
and **chancel** have a continuous
flushwork base course and at the e.
end a frieze of flushwork panels continues across the **vestry** wall on the n.
side. Extensive repairs to the chancel
were evidently necessary in the C17 or
C18 and large red brick buttresses
support the e. end. It was probably then
that the side windows were blocked
up. The **rood stair turret** shows
externally between the chancel and
the nave on the n. side.

Entry is by way of the early C14 s.
porch and note that although they are
blocked, the side windows still display
attractive **Decorated tracery**. The nave
is spacious and the tall **Perpendicular**
windows have stepped **transoms** and
shafts at the inner corners of the
embrasures. The w. doorway is small,
with a plain round arch, and this
suggests that the tower was either
Saxon or **Norman** and may have been
round. The C15 **font** is similar to

nearby Thrandeston's, with its **Evangelistic symbols** and fat **Tudor roses** in the bowl panels and dumpy lions squatting round the shaft. One point of difference here is the **quatrefoil** tracery on the step. The **Royal Arms** on the w. wall are painted on board and dated 1634; one of five sets in the county from the reign of Charles I, they are well designed and worth restoring. A door in the s.w. corner opens to reveal a stair which one would have thought led to an upper chamber in the porch – but it turns the other way and presumably gave access to the tower. By the C19 pulpit there is a tomb which once had **brasses** on top and an inscription on the bevel. It is anonymous now but the shields in the lozenges along the front would have been painted with the arms of Richard Yaxley who was buried here in 1570 together with his wife. An unidentified tomb of the same period is set in the wall nearby, and overhead the window contains quite a lot of C15 glass. There is a range of eight figures but the paint is very worn and only **St Jude** can be recognised by his boat emblem (3rd from l., lower rank). A C17 chair was placed by the pulpit when I visited; it had a lively carving of the sacrifice of Isaac in the back panel, complete with the ram caught in a wispy thicket. The handsome C15 **rood screen** has been repainted and gilded and the flattened **ogee** arches of the main **lights** are backed by panel tracery. The coving has been restored and has three attractive tracery panels. The chancel has a low-pitched cambered **tie-beam roof** and the stalls below are fronted with ranges of C17 **balusters** which were the original **communion rails**. The **altar** table is of the same period and has nicely fretted top rails. There is a plain **piscina** and in the opposite corner a most interesting **Easter sepulchre** recess. The arch is decorated with **paterae** and below there are five blank and shallow niches which were once **groined** and canopied. **Cautley** suggested that they symbolise the **five wounds of Christ** and this is not unlikely.

Mendlesham, St Mary (C4): Fronted by limes, this lovely church stands on rising ground at the end of the village street within a large churchyard, and its noble tower can be seen from some way off. Built in the 1480s and 1490s, its **base course** displays **flushwork** roundels worked in **mouchette** and **quatrefoil** patterns interspersed with shields, but those flanking the w. door are cut in stone for emphasis. There are shields of the Botecourt and Knyvet families in the **spandrels** of the doorway and the **Perpendicular** w. window, with **ogee tracery** shapes, is unusually small for such a tower. In contrast, the large double bell openings are linked by a deep **label**, with a panel of flushwork between. Above them are stepped flushwork battlements crowned with pinnacles. The s. **aisle** windows are early C14 with flushwork and crowned 'Ms' and 'MRs' for the dedication set either side of a canopied niche. The entrance arch rests on decayed lion **stops** like those at Wetheringsett and there were six pinnacles on the parapet originally. The **chancel** is largely C15 and in the n. aisle you will see late C14 windows and a **Tudor** brick **rood stair turret**. The tall **nave clerestory** has windows which match the w. window of the tower, and note how the **sanctus-bell turret** was enclosed within a later parapet on the e. gable (with a bell recently installed). Entry is via the late Perpendicular n. porch and this is decidedly lavish. The elaborate flushwork facade has side niches under nodding ogee arches, and the larger version over the doorway has a beast mask below the image stool. The arch itself has an angel with a shield at the apex and decayed shields in the spandrels. The upper chamber is lit by double windows and there are unusually good crowned lions and **woodwoses** at the parapet corners. The porch builders retained the inner C13 doorway but they cut into it on the r. when constructing the stair to the room above. By it stands the little **font** from

Mendlesham, St Mary

the redundant church at Rishangles. It was made about 1600 and it is rare to find the bowl of a post-**Reformation** example carved with **Passion emblems** and **Evangelistic symbols**, with figures in contemporary costume filling the shaft niches. Restored to the extent that it looks quite new, it now serves as a **stoup** (it must be said that both **Cautley** and **Pevsner** had doubts about its antiquity).

The church within is bright with light and beautifully kept, a blaze of colourful hassocks lining the benches. Buttresses of the later tower encroach on the C13 **arcades** and its tall arch has a nice 1930s screen with turned shafts in the doors. Beyond hangs an unidentified **hatchment** bearing the arms of the Cresacre/Marshall families. The arcade **piers** are circular but the easternmost bays are separated from the rest by square sections which must have either supported a central tower or marked the entrance to **transepts**. It

is curious that the shape and decoration of the **corbels** on the w. faces of these piers differs – tapered fluting to the n. and oblong **dogtooth** to the s. In an 1860s restoration by **Ewan Christian**, the nave **roof** was replaced, the tower arch re-opened, and the fine C15 benches restored. These have large **poppyheads** and an enterprising selection of tracery on all the ends, with a number of grotesques on the elbows (look for the **wyvern** at the n.w. corner of the centre range, and there is a figure holding an initialled shield at the front on the s. side). The pews in the aisles with simpler poppyheads came from Rishangles and blend well with the rest. There are other migrants on the wall of the s. aisle, this time from redundant Southolt – a good set of George III **Royal Arms**, and the **brass** of Margaret Armiger wearing a Paris cap and lacking one shoulder. Below her is an inscription for Robert Armiger, who 'departed out of this transitory world' in 1585. The s. aisle roof was untouched by the Victorian restoration and is remarkable for having **king-**

Mendlesham, St Mary: C17 font cover

posts on the **tie-beams**, with traces of stencil decoration at the e. end. The s. porch was restored in 1926 and has been converted for use as a chapel of the Holy Cross. The roof has angels at the base of the braces and the large wall paintings by Cyril Fradan were commissioned in the 1970s. A fascinating miscellany has been marshalled at the w. end of the n. aisle – a C16 wooden clock weight barrel and windlass, an early C18 clock frame, a simple late C18 **bier** in pine, and (a rarity, but there is another at Brundish) a matching child's bier in lovely condition. The plain C15 font has a cover which was made by John Turner of Mendlesham in 1630, a remarkably fine piece. Restored in 1908, it is raised on four columns, with brief turned pendants at the other angles of the cornice, and a fat fruit trail runs just above the flattened arches; there are steep broken **pedi-**

ments while spiky **finials** stand in front of a second storey which repeats the first on a smaller scale. Above that, curved sea-horse brackets support the centre shaft and ball finial. The lovely pulpit is also by this gifted joiner and its style is more elaborate than most of that period, with some **Renaissance** motifs. The familiar blind arches in the main panels have centre pendants and they are carved with deep foliage scrolls instead of the usual strapwork. The upper range is filled with flowers and birds with seeds in their beaks and at the base the moulded panels have double-acorn bosses.

Medieval glass panels from Southolt have been hung inside the aisle windows (including a figure that has been given a lion's head!). The s. aisle e. window contains a small dove of the Holy Spirit in ruby glass inserted in 1982 and the solid **altar** block made up of medieval fragments supports the church's original **mensa** in which new **consecration crosses** have been cut. The **piscina** nearby lies within an ogee **trefoil** arch and there are plain **dropped-sill sedilia**. In the n. aisle Lady chapel the altar is a good early C17 table – Doric capitals and **acanthus** leaves on the legs and shallow carved top rail. The C14 piscina is in the windowsill to the l. and the Perpendicular e. window design is unconventional. The lower half of the centre **light** contains a niche to house a figure of the **Blessed Virgin**. The **cusping** of the round arch has been chopped away, along with the ogee **hood mould** and side pinnacles. It now contains a 1960s Virgin and Child. The glass is a World War I memorial and was designed in 1921 by T.F. Curtis of **Ward & Hughes**. To the r. are the capacious stairs that led to the vanished **rood loft** and there is now a modern rood group above the chancel arch. The limed oak altar below was designed by Jack Penton and made by Barrie Chester in 1982. To the e. of the pulpit lies the brass of John Knyvet who died in 1417. Worn very smooth, the 4ft 7in. figure is a fine example of the Lancastrian period; the large feet rest on a recumbent lion and there is a dragon's head crest on the helm behind the head; it is unusual to see the beard displayed outside the armour. Knyvet was Lord of the Manor and both his father and father-in-law were lord chancellors of England. The chancel roof and e. window date from the 1860s restoration (although the C13 shafts of the latter were retained) and the fine panelling on the e. wall came a century later.

The church has few monuments but there is one to Richard Chilton (1816) on the n. wall of the chancel which is worth studying. The shallow sarcophagus with a small flaming urn on top and Grecian ornament is by Charles Regnart, a competent sculptor whose work can be found in many counties. One of the most interesting features of Mendlesham is the parish armoury, housed since 1593 above the n. porch. All communities had to provide a stock of weapons and armour for the militia, but few collections have survived. Dating from 1470 to 1600, it includes a rare Elizabethan longbow, helmets, breastplates, and powder horns. Access is normally by appointment only.

Milden, St Peter (B8): This is one of the highest points in Suffolk and across the valley to the n.w. the tower of Lavenham shows proudly on the skyline; a seat by the gate combines with a gap in the hedge so that one can view it comfortably. The sixty-year-old avenue of laburnums leading to the s. **porch** has recently been renewed with young saplings and should soon provide a springtime swathe of blossom once again. The tower was badly damaged by lightning in 1827 and taken down in 1840; the remains were used to rebuild the w. wall, new **lancets** were inserted and a bellcote was placed on the gable. The lancet in the s. wall of the **nave** and the s. door identifies this as a **Norman** building. The **chancel** windows are C13, with triple lancets at the e. end, and there

are two large renewed windows in the nave. The small **porch** has a little **cusped** lancet each side and the arch of the Norman doorway is carved with a bold zigzag moulding.

The C14 n. doorway is simply moulded and, like the main entrance, it has slots cut in the **jambs** to house a security drawbar. In the 1860s **vestry** beyond hangs a most unusual portrait of William Burkitt, who was rector from 1678 until 1702. It is engraved but scraps of fabric have been applied to represent his surplice, gown, and bands. He crops up again on the benefactions board at the w. end of the nave, from which we learn that he left money 'for learning all the poor children to read and for buying them Bibles and Catechisms'. The square Norman **font** stands on a drum shaft and four columns with circular **capitals** and bases, and to the s. there is a range of rustic C17 benches. The end of the front one is boldly lettered 'Churchwarden' and its back has: 'August 24 1685 William Stud Junr.' There is no chancel arch, the ceilings are plastered, and on one of the two **tiebeams** is a crude C14 **king-post** with four-way struts. The plain glass of the n. window affords another fine view across the valley to Lavenham and on the s. wall there is the attractive monument for bachelor John Canham who died in 1772. His arms are displayed in a **cartouche** on the **pediment** and there is a pair of pretty cherub heads at the base; coloured marble frames the epitaph: 'His only sister Mary placed here this memorial of that sincere affection with which they were mutually endeared to each other, and happily lived together for more than 50 years.'

A whole range of C13 decorative painting was discovered on the nave walls in 1987 and there are large areas of simulated masonry, with sections of a dado on the s. side and a **consecration cross** below the Norman lancet. Standing on a modern base, the **Stuart** pulpit has a canted book ledge supported by scroll brackets and the carving of the blind arches in the upper panels is very shallow; those below are incised with diagonal crosses and there is so much similarity between this and the pulpits at Little Waldingfield and Edwardstone that they were probably made in the same workshop. In the **sanctuary** there are **Commandment panels** painted on the e. wall and a plain lancet **piscina**. Against the n. wall of the chancel a modern canopy encloses the tomb of James Alington who died in 1627 and whose charity you will have noted at the w. end. It was originally much more elaborate but sections were apparently dispersed into private houses earlier this century. Luckily the fine alabaster effigy is intact, apart from the feet. He is shown in armour with left hand on breast, his frogged and taselled cloak beneath him, and his head rests, most unusually, on a Bible and prayer book. On the wall behind are his arms in a roundel and there are two **touchstone** panels in oblong alabaster frames very delicately carved with bones, coffins, pick, and spade – all interspersed with fruit.

Monewden, St Mary (E4): The C14 tower has a simple **base course**, a doorway with blank shields in the **spandrels**, and **Decorated tracery** in the window above. There is a nice variation in the **flushwork** of the stepped battlements. Two **lancets** in the **nave** show that it dates from the **Norman** period, but the rest of the windows both in nave and **chancel** are from the early part of the C14, like the low **priest's door** on the s. side. The brick early C16 **porch** has three small niches above the outer arch and its **roof** rests on a cambered **tie-beam** and **kingpost**.

Beyond the C14 inner doorway there is a modern wagon roof over the nave, and the chancel roof is nicely panelled out and decorated with flower **bosses** – all dating from a restoration in 1906. The unassuming C15 **font** has a panelled stem and plain shields hung on little rosettes in the bowl panels. You will see that the Norman lancets lie in deep splays and that for some reason the heads were altered to a pointed shape. The **rood loft stairs** have a handsome entrance in a n. window embrasure and hinge lugs survive in the stonework. There is a shallow niche to the r. and over on the s. side is a much larger one. Nearby stands a wooden cross brought back from the grave of a soldier who died a prisoner in World War I. The front range of benches is plain C15 with heavy **poppyheads** of varying designs but has the virtue of being virtually intact. There is now no **screen** and the modern wooden chancel arch comes down to pretty canopied niches which rest on stone **corbels** carved with demi-angels. The C14 **piscina** in the **sanctuary** lies below a **trefoil** arch, and there is a nice chunky **Holy table** with shallow carving on the top rails. To the r. is a **brass** in the wall commemorating the Revd Dr Thomas Reve, who died in 1595. It is set within a shallow stone arch on which there were once three small shields, and his **achievement** and figure are engraved on the one plate. He kneels before a small table on which an open book is set, and there is a thirteen-line inscription below. He was the son of William and Rose Reve; their brass has been moved from the nave to the e. wall on the other side of the **altar**. There were once effigies but now only a shield and two verse inscriptions remain. The e. window glass takes the form of a World War II memorial, a conventional Crucifixion group, but the shield on the l. at the top is interesting because it is medieval and displays the arms of the Black Prince. Before leaving you may like to pause at the tombstone with semi-circular top which stands e. of the chancel and rather nearer the boundary hedge. The inscription is somewhat worn but it records that William Pitts died in 1819: 'Having once sailed round this terrestrial Globe, thou little knows what I have seen. To have learnt the liberal sciences thoroughly softens such men's manners and suffers them not to be brutal.' That somewhat gnomic turn of phrase is explained by his adventures. The son of a local farmer, he travelled as assistant to William Gooch, the astronomer attached to Capt. Vancouver's expedition which surveyed the w. coast of America in 1791. Gooch was murdered by the natives of Hawaii and Pitts was eventually sent home by the commander with his despatches. In the fullness of time he succeeded to his father's farm and rural quietude but, understandably, did not wish his circumnavigation to be forgotten.

Monk Soham, St Peter (D4): Remote from the village, the church enjoys a beautifully spacious setting. The tower with its modest w. doorway dates from about 1300 and has narrow **lancets** at ground and middle levels. There is pretty **Decorated tracery** in the bell openings and the battlements are chequered with **flushwork**. On walking round, you will find that, as at Sproughton and elsewhere, there are massive boulders used as foundation stones at the s.w. corner of the tower and under the e. buttresses of the **chancel**. They may have been pagan cult stones which were transferred to the service of the new religion. The **nave** has **Perpendicular** windows but the blocked n. door is the same age as the tower, and so is the long chancel with a **priest's door** to the s. and lancets which have pointed **trefoils** in the tracery. The wide five-**light** e. window is most attractive and has intersected tracery enlivened by **cusps**. The large C15 s. **porch** is sadly decayed, with niches each side and above the archway which shows traces of a double row of **fleurons** in the mouldings. There are the remains of flushwork and the **ashlar** of the corner buttresses is cut with shallow patterns. Before going in, don't miss the **scratch dial** on the s. buttress of the nave.

The inner doorway is narrow by contrast and its **jambs** have recesses to take a heavy security bar. The tower screen would not be remarkable but for the fact that it makes use of two varying sections of C14 tracery which were probably saved from the **rood screen**. Close by are a few medieval benches with **poppyheads** and an excellent C14 chest of quite eccentric proportions – 8ft long but only 18in. wide; encased in iron bands, it has an abundance of locks and bars. The **font** is one of the **Seven Sacrament** versions peculiar to East Anglia and although the carvings in the deep bowl have been grievously defaced, the subjects can be identified. Clockwise from the e. they are: mass, confirmation, Crucifixion, ordination, Extreme Unction, matrimony, penance, and baptism. The bulky figures round the shaft are cowled like monks but they must have represented the **Evangelists** because their symbols stand between them. Traces of green paint remain and the overall design is so like the font at Hoxne that it is likely to date from 1460-70. At first glance the nave **roof** looks like a standard **hammerbeam/arch-braced** design but note that the hammerbeams are only for effect; the braces rise from the back. **Wall plates** and hammers are decorated (although they have lost their angels or shields) and there are **embattled** collars below the ridge. There is an additional **tie-beam** above the font and the **rood beam** remains in place at the e. end. At least, it is generally assumed to be the rood beam, but you will see that the stairs to the rood loft emerge at a lower level on the n. side and the hook for a **Lenten veil** remains embedded in the apex of the chancel arch. This makes me wonder whether the rood was at a lower level and the beam is merely a structural support like the one farther w. A simple **piscina** on the s. side shows that there was a nave **altar** and the delicious little niche in the window embrasure above would have housed a statue of the dedicatory saint. It is shallow, with curly **crockets** to the arch, flanking pinnacles, and **paterae** on the bevel moulding. The pulpit is rather odd. The upper range of its plain panels is pierced with roundels and one angle is dated '12 May 1604' – it is not at all typical of the early C17. Beyond the wide chancel arch the **hood moulds** of the side lancets are linked with a moulding, and the eye is drawn to the mighty e. window which fills virtually the whole of the 14ft width. The contemporary piscina must have been beautiful in its youth but sadly all the arch, with its mouldings and **finial**, has been hacked away although the stone **credence shelf** remains. The church had a tradition of long-serving rectors in the C18 and C19 and one of them, Robert Hindes Groome, served for forty-four years. He was a great friend of Edward Fitzgerald, the famous translator of The Rubáiyát of Omar Khayyám; his children all have bronze plaques in the chancel but I didn't come across his memorial. Like the pulpit, the **Stuart** altar table is not a typical design but has square legs with recessed panels and a modestly decorated skirt below the front rail. The **sanctuary** is peaceful enough now but on Sunday 17 April 1636 it was the scene of an extraordinary disturbance. Bishop Wren was busy enforcing the **Laudian** order that communion should be received at the rail, but Daniel Wheymond violently disagreed with the change and, backed by his family and others, paraded up and down and round the parson while he attempted to administer the sacrament. For this 'indecent, prophane and unseemly' behaviour they were haled before the high commission the following month.

Naughton, St Mary (C8): The village green is secluded and the churchyard, ringed with trees and a secretive stream, makes a beautiful setting for this little church built about 1300. The unbuttressed tower has a single **drip course** below **Decorated** and 'Y' **tracery** bell openings; the **Perpendicular** w. window is restored. All the windows to the n. are renewed and the top half of the C13 n. door is now glazed. A

priest's door is to be found on that side of the **chancel** and although the e. window is renewed, the one round the corner to the s. has **plate tracery**. The **cusped** outline of C14 barge boards remain above the **porch** door and a bowed, moulded **tie-beam** spans the little plastered ceiling. There are remains of **headstops** to the **hood mould** of the doorway and, beyond it, a simple rustic interior. The **nave** is brick floored with a range of pitch pine pews, but at the w. end there are clumsy low C17 benches. Some of their seats and backs are warped endearingly and one rail is carved. The nave has a C14 **roof** whose heavy, cambered tie-beams are braced from **wall posts**, and above them **king-posts** rise to a ridge beam that runs from end to end below a plastered ceiling. The **Norman font** now stands in the n. doorway and the corners of the square shallow bowl were lopped off in the C15 or thereabouts when a moulding was worked below. Part of a **St Christopher** painting was uncovered in 1953 on the n. wall and, although indistinct, one can see that the saint had the Christ child on his right shoulder and there was a stencil decoration in the background. Another small fragment discovered over the n. door is unidentified but the shapes suggest two angels facing each other with an animal of some sort in the upper r. hand corner. There is now no **screen** but half of a doorway and a vestige of the steps of the **rood loft stair** remain in the n. wall, and the mark of the loft shows to the l. of the chancel arch. There was also a nave **altar**, and its C14 **piscina** in the s. wall has a cusped **trefoil** arch and deep drain. Both pulpit and wooden eagle lectern are C19 and the chancel is spanned by heavy C14 tie-beams resting on moulded **wall plates**. The priest's door has been sealed off and in the **sanctuary** is a large piscina of about 1300. The chamber organ of 1777 has a very nice mahogany case and there are delicate frets enclosing the heads of the pipe clusters.

Nayland, St James (C10): In this most attractive village, houses nestle around the church on three sides, with lanes to the s. and e. so that there is open churchyard only to the n. It was one of the most important centres of the Suffolk cloth trade with a population of nearly 400, and rebuilding in the C15 and early C16 made the church large enough to hold them all. The C14 unbuttressed tower, with its two strong **string courses**, was left alone until the early C19 when the top was rebuilt, and it carries a short spire. The bell openings have 'Y' **tracery**, there is a C19 clock to the w., and lower down the belfry is lit by **lancets** under **ogee** arches with **finials** and **headstops**. Four steps lead up to the w. door and it is notable that levels vary curiously throughout the church. William Abell was one of Nayland's wealthy clothiers and, like others of his time and station, he chose to build a new **porch** in 1525 as his memorial, but lack of space on the s. side meant that it had to be sited at the end of the s. **aisle** facing w. – a unique arrangement, as far as I know. There are three very worn **groined** and canopied niches in the frontage with blind panelling and **crocketted** pinnacles above, and there is an angel holding a shield above the **Tudor** inner arch (the interior vaulting and panelling date from a rebuilding of 1884). Towards the e. end of the late C15 s. aisle an octagonal brick and flint **rood stair turret** juts out and its stone cap with the remains of a finial rises above the **roof** line. Round the corner in the angle between aisle and **chancel** there is a **priest's door** under a little porch, and the door itself is interesting because above the **linen-fold panelling** is carved: 'John Foum'. The list of known vicars is incomplete, and this may be the name of the priest who had the door installed. The e. window of the C14 chancel has attractive flowing tracery which has been renewed, and there is a n.e. **vestry** which was originally a chapel. The n. aisle has a large niche in the n.e. buttress and although the large side windows are

Perpendicular, the w. window retains the intersected tracery of the earlier C14 building. The main entrance now is through the early C15 brick n. porch (three steps down) and there is an ogee niche over the inner C14 doorway. The doors are carved with good linen-fold panelling set within a bold vine trail and they have been sensitively renewed.

The interior is beautiful, wide and open, with elegant **piers** to the six-bay **arcade**; shafts rise above them to divide the **clerestory** windows into pairs and the 'wall of glass' effect continues over the chancel. The **nave** roof is almost flat and every other **tie-beam** is braced with carved **spandrels**. There are centre **bosses** and the one w. of the pulpit is carved with the head of a **green man**. The **font** stands by the n. door and is either C19 or totally re-cut; the bowl panels are deeply carved with **Evangelistic symbols** set within rays, plus two shields and two large chalices. The 1940s oak cover by R.Y. Goodden is a simple design – almost flat, with gabled segments and a centre finial. The plain but stylish C18 w. **gallery** happily accommodates the organ and against the w. wall below there is an early C16 screen, with its three wide **lights** blanked off. The church has two sets of **Royal Arms**: a large and rather dim one over the n. door on canvas is C18 but it had William IV's initials added later, and a lively little post-1816 **Hanoverian** set on the front of the gallery – three-dimensional, with the painting and gilding beautifully restored.

There are a number of **brasses** to see and the first two lie just within the n. door – parts of a canopy dating from about 1440, and remnants of an 1475 inscription which show that it was for a man called Sekyn and his wife Joan. Of more interest are the two in front of the gallery. The first is for a Mr Hacche and his wife and dates from about 1485 but only the upper half of her effigy and its delicate canopy survives; though worn smooth, it shows her in **butterfly headdress** with a book under her arm.

Alongside is a brass of the early C16, with 3ft. figures of a couple under a double canopy – he in fur-lined gown and she with a **kennel head-dress**. The same style of dress is to be found on the brass in the n. aisle for Richard and Joan Davy. He was a local clothier who died in 1516 and, apart from the 18in. figures, the interest lies in his merchant's mark on a shield; it bears his initials and a pair of tenterhooks which were used to hold the cloth when it was stretched and dried. To be on tenterhooks was obviously a painful experience. Another example of them can be seen in a window at Stoke by Clare [Vol.1], where they figure in the arms of the Clothworkers Company. A window nearby contains a memorial for Gilbert Warwick, a vicar who died in 1960 – a tall thin panel portraying Christ holding the chalice and wafer, with the priest and people below celebrating the Eucharist (I have not been able to identify the artist). The aisle w. window is filled with glass of 1908 by **Kempe & Tower** (see Tower's symbol of wheatsheaf and castle low down on the l.) – a fairly standard design with typical figures of the **Blessed Virgin, St John**, and **St Luke**, but enlivened a little by the six small angels who hold up the background drapery on ribbons. A particularly lovely s. aisle window of 1921 commemorates Edith Caroline Farmiloe and her life work among women and children. The artist was Robert Anning Bell, a Scottish teacher and designer much influenced by the **Arts and Crafts Movement**. Christ the King is shown with a group of old and young villagers, some with faces that are demonstrably portraits.

Farther along is the door to the rood loft stair and from the position of the upper opening you will realise that the loft spanned the whole of the church. There is a **consecration cross** nearby, and on the wall overhead are panels which originally formed part of the late C15 **rood screen**. They carry the outlines of canopies and are terribly defaced, but enough is left to identify most of them. From l. to r.: **St Cuthbert**

with the head of **St Oswald**, **St Edmund**, **St Gregory** (who had his papal tiara and staff specifically mutilated in Henry VIII's reign), Henry VI ? , **St Edward the Confessor** (the best preserved, shown with the ring he is supposed to have given to St John when the latter was in the guise of a beggar), a king who might be the Emperor Charlemagne, an unidentified king, and an archbishop who was probably **St Thomas of Canterbury**. The e. wall of the n. aisle has a window at high level and the recessed ledge behind the **altar** was probably fitted with a **retable**. To the r. is a C14 **piscina** with a roll moulding to the arch and the curious little recess above it may have been used as an alternative to a **credence shelf**. Four steps lead up to the vestry door in the chancel and the headstops on the **hood mould** boast luxuriant moustaches. Farther along, a tabernacle for the Blessed Sacrament is set within what was originally a **squint** – proving that the vestry beyond was once a chapel. There is a heavily cusped piscina opposite but the eye is constantly drawn to the painting behind the **high altar**. Set in the centre of a C19 **reredos**, it is by John Constable and portrays Christ blessing the bread and wine of the Last Supper. Commissioned and paid for by his aunt who lived in the village, it was painted in 1810 before he became successful, and his father described his activities at the time as 'pursuing a shadow'! Patently, he was hardly doing that. It is one of three altarpieces by him, the others being painted for Brantham and Manningtree in Essex. The e. window is filled with stained glass whose maker has not been identified; there are four panels with scenes of the life of Christ and one of the stoning of **St Stephen** – it has strangely ungainly figures with staring eyes and the panels are set within bright interlace designs. Its garish restlessness points up the tranquillity of the altarpiece below.

William Jones, vicar here from 1777 to 1800, was a learned divine and a leader of the old High Church party.

Known as 'Jones of Nayland', his work inspired Wesley on the one hand and the youthful Newman on the other, anticipating in many ways the work of the Oxford Movement by a generation. He would, one trusts, be pleased with the way in which this church is now used jointly by Anglicans and Roman Catholics taking advantage of similar modern liturgies to combine in worship.

Nedging, St Mary (C8): The lane climbs steeply to this pleasant spot where a few houses keep the small church company in a neat, spacious setting, and there is a view across the valley to the church of the Magdalen at Bildeston. The w. window and bell openings of the tower have **Decorated tracery**, and so too has the s.w. window of the **nave** in more elaborate form, with four **quatrefoils** centred over a pair of **ogee**-headed **lights**. The rest of the windows date from about 1300, and both doorways are **Transitional**. Their round arches contain roll mouldings punctuated with thick rings and the main entrance has an additional **dogtooth hood mould** resting on head **corbels**. The **capitals** of the plain shafts are carved with varying leaf shapes. The n. doorway is blocked, its upper half filled with an C18 'Gothick' window which matches the one in the little **vestry**, and the **chancel** parapet seems to date from the same period. The C17 brick **porch** is now plastered and although its w. window is blocked, the other is fitted with a cunning set of wooden louvres that are controlled by a centre rod.

Within, all is neat and simple. The Decorated tower arch fades into the **imposts** and below is a plain C15 **font** with canted bowl. Its low **Jacobean** cover has rustic scrolls supporting a centre post carved with rudimentary leaves. Floors are paved with humble **pamments** and the C15 benches at the w. end have **poppyheads** and crested elbows. The inner range once carried carved beasts but those by the walls are

Needham Market, St John the Baptist: nave roof

little towers, and on the n. side one has a man's head resting curiously upon a pillar. C14 **roofs** have survived in one or two churches in the area and this one has heavy, braced **tie-beams** supporting **king-posts** which are braced four ways at the top. Above them is a boarded C19 ceiling. The main range of pews and pulpit are Victorian and, although there is now no chancel **screen**, you will see the doorway and two steps of the stair to the **rood loft** in the n. wall. The chancel ceiling is plastered and in the **sanctuary** the simple C14 **piscina** has a hint of the ogee in its arch. On the s. chancel wall a tablet records how, in the 1880s, the rector lost six of his sons in eight years, two of them at sea.

Needham Market, St John the Baptist (C6): From the outside this is a rather dull, ungainly building with scarcely a hint of the glorious surprise within. Created a parish church in 1901, it began as a chapel of ease for nearby Barking and was built between 1458 and the end of the century. One of its oddities is that it is aligned s.e. and n.w., parallel with the street, and there are lanes on the other three sides. Thus there is no graveyard and the limits were set so close that the n.e. buttress had to be pierced to allow processions to circle the chapel within consecrated ground. The bishops of Ely were patrons of the Barking living and there are two worn shields carved at the top of the **priest's door** in the **chancel** s. wall – the arms of the diocese on the l. and those of Bishop Grey on the r. (which pins down the building date). But there was evidently a local benefaction involved because a stone some 12ft above the door is inscribed:

Pray we all for grace
For he yt hav holpe ys place
God reward he for her ded
& heve' [heaven] may be her meed.

Depending on how one interprets the English of the day, that could refer to **guild** members who used the church or to a single benefactress. It is interesting that C19 restoration work uncovered the foundations of an earlier chapel and the **dripstone** of the priest's door is a survival from that building. The wall line of **nave** and chancel is continuous and the buttresses on the s. side have niches under worn **crocketted** canopies with, above them, inscription panels which form: 'Crist **I.H.S.** have merci on us'. One of the buttresses on the n. side carries a similar legend and another combines with an exterior **rood stair turret**. The shallow **clerestory**, with its small windows, adds to the oddity of the building's appearance, looking rather like the cabin top of a large Victorian yacht. The low **vestry** at the w. end was added in 1909 but there are door and arch outlines on the wall above that suggest that there may have been a tower. In 1879 the building was declared unsafe and closed for a major restoration under **John Hakewill** and C.H. Mileham. The nave **roof** was reconstructed, the chancel roof lowered and replaced, and a bellcote removed from the w. gable. In 1883 H.W.Hayward designed a replacement porch that suits the building quite well, but then went on to add a clock turret and small spire in a bizarre combination.

The s. door has **tracery** within oblong panels that are similar to Barking's w. door, and one enters a spacious nave dominated by a roof which has no parallel in England. With a span of 30ft, a double **hammerbeam** under a conventional ridge might have been expected, but here is a variation of the single hammerbeam design whose technical audacity takes the breath away and stands as the supreme example of the carpenter's art. The hammers are immensely long and half their length is masked by a coved double cornice decorated with angels and **paterae**. The posts on the hammerbeams stretch right up to the low-pitched roof and are braced, first

by cambered **tie-beams** e.-w., and then by heavier tie-beams n.-s. Above that, the frame is locked together by a timber clerestory with small windows. Immediately above the cornice, vertical posts backed by boards form a false wall from which springs a canted roof so that the whole upper airy space takes on the form of a clerestoried nave with narrow aisles. Prior to the C19 restoration there was a plaster ceiling 16ft below the roof and all but two of the hammerbeams had been cut off. This demanded a virtual rebuilding and all of the lower timbers and the angels are new. There had originally been clerestory windows on the s. side only and those on the n. were added at that time.

Below this splendid *tour de force* of a roof the church is spacious but undemonstrative. Its length is broken only by the **rood screen** of 1953 which, perhaps wisely, did not attempt to fill the space with tracery but carries the figures on a false **gallery** front supported only by two plain central posts. There is a large unidentified Madonna and Child painting (C18?) above an **altar** at the w. end and the plain C15 **font** is painted blue, red, and gold, with an **Agnus Dei** carved in the e. bowl panel. The n. door is blocked and in front of it stands what appears to be a section of a **Jacobean** court cupboard. The doors to the original rood loft stair remain in the n. wall and there are two **aumbries** in the chancel – one in the n. wall and another in the n.e. corner. Some fragments of medieval glass have been collected in the **sanctuary** window on that side.

Nettlestead, St Mary (C7): A trim and secluded little church which was badly damaged by enemy action in 1940 and restored to use ten years later. The unbuttressed tower has a stair turret to the s. where fragments of **Norman arcading** show haphazardly in the stonework – they were found, I suspect, during restoration. Its Norman origin is confirmed by a small **lancet** in the n. wall of the **nave** which has similar decorative detail in the arch – minuscule bands of interlaced arches, scrolls, and beads. There is a blocked C14 n. door and the **Perpendicular** windows on that side have lion **stops** to their **dripstones**. The e. window has attractive renewed **Decorated** tracery with a **cinquefoil** and two **trefoils** over three **lights**. The low C16 brick **porch** has a semi-circular gable with a shield of arms above the entrance, and the mouldings of the inner doorway are embellished with large **fleurons**. The early C15 **font** is notable in that the stem is supported by four crowned lions and the bowl is much shallower than usual; its panels are carved, not only with the familiar **Evangelistic symbols**, but also with a king, a bishop, a face with tongue rudely out, and, to the n.w., **St Catherine** crowned and seated with her wheel alongside. This is interesting because **Dowsing** noted her specifically when he came in 1644, and although images of six apostles, **St George**, **St Martin**, and **St Simon** have disappeared, she escaped more or less unscathed.

The nave was re-seated to celebrate Queen Victoria's Jubilee in 1897 and plain **tie-beams** span it below a coved plastered ceiling. Halfway along the s. wall there is a small puzzle to ponder over. By the side of the Perpendicular window there is a small **squint** which emerges at an angle in the embrasure. It aligns roughly with the pulpit so there may have been an **altar** there, but what was outside? It seems an unusual place for an **anchorite's** cell but nothing else comes to mind. In the centre of the nave there is a 17in. **brass** of a man in Tudor armour. The inscription has gone but the Wentworth family were Lords of the Manor in the C15 and this might mark the grave of Sir Richard – sometime high sheriff of Norfolk and Suffolk and present at the Field of the Cloth of Gold in 1520. The **Royal Arms** of George IV are well painted and unusual because the lion and unicorn don't support the oval shield heraldically but emerge from

behind it. The **Stuart** pulpit stands on a new stone base and is very compact, with conventional strapwork and blind arch carving in the panels. The position of the door and seat show that it has been turned round. There is no **chancel** arch but there was once a **screen**; the stairs to the **rood loft** remain in the s. wall. The choir benches have **poppyheads** and C19 Evangelistic symbols added to the elbows on the s. side, although a lion on the n. side seems original. All the e. window tracery is moulded, the **mullions** are shafted, and there is a smaller blank arch each side painted terracotta, most effectively. Stone **decalogue** tablets flank the altar and the Creed and Lord's Prayer above them form a complete set. The square-headed **piscina** has a multi-**cusped** arch with flower and leaf in the **spandrels** and there are **dropped-sill sedilia** alongside. On the opposite wall the handsome C17 alabaster busts of Samuel and Thomasina Sayer hold hands over a skull and rest on a modern ledge; his arms are displayed in an oval overhead and their epitaphs are on a separate slab below, but the rest of the monument has gone. Stephen Jackson's memorial of 1855 in the n.e. corner of the churchyard will appeal to those with a taste for Victorian extravagance. It is like a **preaching cross** but the shaft is triangular and so is the base, with three large gables festooned with fat **crockets** and **ball flowers**.

Newton, All Saints (B10): Nowadays the **chancel** is the parish church and the rest of the C14 building is cared for by the **Redundant Churches Fund** – a happy arrangement whereby everything is beautifully maintained. The w. window of the plain tower has been renewed but the **headstops** are interesting; one is a C14 woman and the other is a devil's mask superimposed upon a second. There is new **tracery** in one of the bell openings and the battlements are of brick. The n. door is blocked with its upper half

Newton, All Saints: Boteler tomb

glazed, but it was part of an earlier **Norman** building. The shafts have scalloped **capitals** and the deep roll moulding of the arch is set between bands of **chevrons**. The inner one has an unusual variation, with little truncated pyramids pointing inwards from the chevron intersections. On walking round, you will find more good C14 headstops, including a pair of jovial men on the n. side of the **nave**, a man and a snarling dragon above the modern n.e. **vestry**, and two more on the **dripstone** of the shortened window in the s. chancel wall. A stone just e. of the chancel marks the grave of Amos Todd, who died in 1822 and was an officer in the early days of the yeomanry. It reflects the zeal of the movement:

He commanded for many years the 1st Regiment of Suffolk Yeomanry Cavalry and was so much respected by the Colonel and the

Members of the Troop that they have caused this Stone to be erected as a lasting Proof thereof. Churchyards are often blessed with fine trees and here there is a rare mature specimen of a small leaved lime, to be found n.e. of the large oak e. of the **chancel**. The sides of the wooden s. **porch** are now glazed and the **roof** renewed, but the C14 **tie-beam** and **king-post** are still in place above the contemporary doorway with its large, worn headstops and pilgrim cross cut in the r. hand **jamb**.

Within the spacious, uncluttered nave a C15 **font** stands in front of the n. door. It has a shallow bowl with pairs of **quatrefoils** in each face and is uncharacteristically gawky. A C19 **bier** can be found under the tower and a C20 horse plough at the w. end of the nave. In 1967 an interesting sequence of large C14 wall paintings was discovered on the n. wall; it was restored by Miss Eve Baker in the 1970s. The left section illustrates the

Annunciation; the centre is badly
damaged but is the Visitation with an
angel to the l. and the Blessed Virgin
and St Elizabeth embracing to the r.
The 3rd panel is the Nativity, with the
babe lying between the heads of ox and
ass and the studding partition of the
stable showing below. In front of the
painting the C15 pulpit has good
tracery in the heads of the panels and
an inscription cut below to commemorate the donors: 'Orate p. aia Richi
Modi et Leticia [consortis suae]' (Pray
for the souls of Richard Mody and
Laetitia his wife). A tomb recess in the
wall opposite contains the effigy of a
woman which was found under the
nave floor in the C19. It is probably
back in its rightful position and con-
ceivably commemorates Christina de
Moese, whose second husband was
Lord of the Manor. The face of the life-
size figure has been destroyed but
considering its history it is in good
condition, the hands at prayer and
dainty feet showing below the long
gown. There are matching piscinas
under ogee arches at the e. end,
marking the sites of two nave altars,
and the chancel arch is now filled with
a simple glazed screen.

The parish church in miniature is
now entered by the priest's door and an
abutment e. of the nave/chancel junction may mark the position of a rood
stair. There are solid modern oak
benches and the wooden lectern is an
interesting C17 example from a period
when few seem to have been made. It
has a turned and carved stem and the
decoration of the oblong desk, with its
elegant, sinuous brass candle-holder,
was old-fashioned from the beginning.
A brass inscription on the n. wall
commemorates Maria Weatherall who
died in childbirth in 1624. Her husband
was rector here but her epitaph
reminds posterity that her father, John
Domelaw, was vintner to Queen Elizabeth and James I. The tomb on the n.
side of the sanctuary is one of the finest
in the county for its period and almost
certainly commemorates Margaret
Boteler, who was Lady of the Manor

from 1393 to 1410. The effigy, in a cloak
with large rose brooches, lies within a
recess under a cusped and crocketted
arch, and the richly panelled spandrels
are topped by a straight frieze. There
are eight shields in the spandrels, five
on the chest, and an extra large one
held by an angel beyond the effigy. All
have been re-coloured by members of
the Suffolk Heraldry Society and a
helpful key is provided. On the s. side
is a handsome early C14 suite of
piscina and sedilia. The piscina is like a
small Decorated two-light window and
was obviously designed for two drains
although there is only one now. The
contemporary e. window has reticulated tracery with considerable remains
of C14 glass, including a number of
shields. They are: top row from l. to r.,
the families of Deane, Seymour (St
Maure), Bottevilleyn; the bottom row
has the arms of England and France in
the centre, Peyton on the l. and Peach
on the r. There are sections of C15 glass
in the s. windows, including a lion
roundel (St Mark?).

Oakley, St Nicholas (C2): The church is
isolated, along with the rectory, and to
the n. the fields drop gently down to
the Waveney, giving a pleasant pros-
pect across to Scole and Billingford. A
large oaken lych-gate of 1908 forms the
entrance to the spacious churchyard.
The buttresses of the tower extend in
line with the e. face of the tower to
make it seem wider, but those to the w.
are angled, with a tall two-light Decorated window between them. There
are four set-offs with a single string
course below the Decorated bell openings, and the battlements are faced
with flushwork. The n. wall of the
nave is plastered, with a small blocked
door and Perpendicular windows, and
a box-like little early C19 vestry is
attached to the n. side of the chancel.
The handsome Perpendicular e. window has a castellated transom above
the ogee tracery of the four lights, and
the dripstone rests on bishop and king
headstops. The line of nave and

chancel is continuous, but notice that
there are **quoins** showing at the join,
which proves that the original chancel
was narrower. The early C15 s. **porch** is
quite lavish and the whole of its
frontage is decorated with flushwork,
including the buttresses in which are
set crowned initials – one of them an
'N' for the patron saint. The arch·is
flanked by niches and the shields in
the **spandrels** bear the arms of the
Crane family, who were presumably
the donors. A canopied niche stands
between two windows which once lit
an upper room and there is a later
sundial below the battlements. Prominent **gargoyles** survive on either side
and there were probably standing
figures on the corner pinnacles. A
lozenge in the e. window of the porch
contains an attractive little C15 **St
Christopher** in yellow stain, and there
are lots of interesting fragments of
medieval glass in the window opposite,
including the head of a bearded man
and three heraldic hooks. Many **stoups**
were smashed after the **Reformation** as
symbols of superstition but Oakley's
still has a complete bowl below a **trefoil**
arch.

Within, the **tie-beams** of the nave
roof are braced down to **wall posts**,
some of which rest on tiny wooden
figures. There are deep castellated **wall
plates** and flower **bosses** (which were
possibly renewed during the 1870s
restoration, when the chancel roof was
replaced). The church contains some
interesting Victorian glass and the w.
window is by **Heaton, Butler & Bayne**,
showing the angel appearing to
Cornelius the centurion in a vision
(Acts 10: 1). There are four bench ends
with **poppyheads** at the w. end, and the
one nearest the door is carved as an
angry mask with its tongue out. The
font is a very rough octagon on a short
round shaft, and in the n. wall there is a
very strange arrangement of two
niches side by side, one taller than the
other but matching in most respects.
They have deeply moulded **crocketted**
ogee arches, with **paterae** in the spandrels and cresting over one of them.

They would have contained statues
and one wonders which saints were
paired thus (but perhaps one was
originally elsewhere). Farther along,
the **rood stair** is boldly cut in a window
embrasure and continues within the
wall to emerge level with the spring of
the chancel arch. On the s. side there is
a **piscina** under a trefoil arch, with
dropped-sill sedilia alongside, marking
the site of a nave **altar**. The wooden
eagle lectern on a turned stem dates
from 1908. In the s. chancel window,
1870s glass by Heaton, Butler & Bayne
portrays Christ and Simeon with the
Blessed Virgin and St Anne; a rich but
restrained treatment of colour which is
very attractive. Much less so is the
glum trio of **St Nicholas, St George**, and
St Edmund opposite, but the full
display of St Nicholas's symbols gives
the window some interest. The s.
sanctuary window is of the same
period and portrays, with **St Stephen**,
two saints rarely seen – **St Longinus**
and **St Denys**. There is a large C14 angle
piscina nearby and the large trefoil
arch has leaf carving in the spandrels,
with a smaller, matching opening to
the w. There were dropped-sill sedilia
originally but the space was taken in
1611 by the large tomb of Sir William
Cornwallis. Unusually austere for the
period, its only decoration is an
alabaster **achievement of arms** in deep
relief on the end; it was coloured
originally. There are some well-carved
modern **poppyheads** on the choir stalls
(one displaying peacocks) and on the
n. side of the sanctuary a marble
credence shelf is backed by a gilded
wooden bust of St Nicholas in low
relief within a wreath; there are three
cherub heads at the top, and below the
shelf the saint's emblem of three
golden balls lies within attractive
scrollery. The 1880s e. window displays scenes of the Nativity, Crucifixion, Resurrection, and the **three Marys**,
and there are **Passion emblem** shields
and musical angels in the tracery. The
painted stone **reredos** of 1882 has the
scene of the Last Supper backed with
gold mosaic, flanked by panels of

ancient sacrifices, and the rest of the wall is filled with tiles and mosaic, mainly in a dusky pink – very pleasing.

Occold, St Michael (C3): The early C15 tower has a panelled **base course** with flint below a shallow **ashlar arcade**. There are fragments of carving in the **spandrels** of the w. door, **fleurons** on the square **label**, and more of them along with crowns in the mouldings of the arch. There is a three-**light** w. window and the bell openings have **Decorated tracery** below the stepped **flushwork** battlements. On the n. side of the **nave** is a small C14 door, and the shape of a **rood stair** shows against a later brick buttress. The **sacristy** n. of the **chancel** is small in scale but had an upper room originally, and a **Norman lancet** peeps out just to the w. of it. The intersected 'Y' tracery of the early C14 chancel e. window has been renewed, and on the s. side there is a small **priest's door**. Nearby, an early C14 **cusped** lancet is decorated with **ball flower** and the **dripstone** has shallow mask **headstops**. The simple s. **porch** has had part of its C14 outer arch encased in brick and plaster and there is a small, plain inner doorway.

Within the base of the tower you will find a very unusual painted memorial board for Stephen Humfrey who, in 1598, 'departed this life Very old and full of Daies'. His descendants are listed down to 1638 but the last two did not have their dates added – the family either died out or laid the custom aside. The n. door is blocked and above it are the **Royal Arms** of Charles II, simply painted in pale colour with no shading. The C15 **font** has plain recessed bowl panels and now stands in front of the n. door, with blue and buff C19 tiles decorated with the **Evangelistic symbols** around the base. The e. splays of two nave windows contain pretty Decorated niches which vary in design. Both have surface carving on the cusps below **crocketted ogee** arches, but the one on the s. side is flanked by pinnacles and the n. window displays delicate **jamb shafts** with miniature

capitals. There is some **Jacobean** panelling against the n. wall and farther along you will see that the vanished **rood loft** could evidently be approached from both sides. There is the shape of a door on the n. side (where the stair shows outside) and steps lead up from the s. window embrasure through a little arch. By it stands a fine **Stuart** pulpit on a low stem. The blind arches in the panels are vigorously carved (with some careful restoration) and there are pierced brackets to the book ledge. The remains of the backboard, initialled and dated 1620, are now inside the pulpit and the **tester** has turned pendants and well-carved panels below the cornice. Behind the pulpit there is a C14 **piscina** in the s. wall and it looks as though the chancel was deliberately offset to the n. to allow enough space for a nave **altar** here. The church's only **brass** is in the centre of the nave where there are 27in. effigies of William and Joan Corbald of about 1490. Their slim figures are well worn and he has long hair and wears a fur-trimmed tunic, a pouch, and a heavy rosary. She has an early form of **kennel head-dress** and the chequered pavement they stand on was once inlaid. There are large male and female head **corbels** to the chancel arch and beyond, four panels of the old **rood screen** have been incorporated in the choir stalls which have some original **poppyheads**. The lancet on the s. side contains a C14 painted figure in the embrasure and there is a trail of ivy leaves in the arch moulding – all that remains of what was probably an overall scheme of decoration. The original sacristy door survives, with ring handle and key escutcheon, and large **paterae** decorate the arch moulding. Opposite, the priest's door has a little inner porch, with **dropped-sill sedilia** and piscina to the e. The **reredos** is C19 but there is a single stall in the **sanctuary** with a good **misericord** carving of a crowned woman supported by angels. Unfortunately, there are only unidentifiable fragments of medieval glass and the reason is to be found in **Dowsing's** journal entry for August 1644: 'Divers superstitious pictures were broke. I came, and there was Jesus, Mary and St Laurence with his gridiron and Peter's keys'. Horrid man.

Offton, St Mary (C7): The unbuttressed C14 tower has two shallow **set-offs**, with **Decorated tracery** in the small w. window and the bell openings. Below the **flushwork** of the battlements two of the **gargoyles** are purely ornamental and have no spouts. The windows of **nave** and **chancel** display an interesting variety of placing and design in **lancet**, Decorated, and late **Perpendicular** forms, with a C19 e. window set in a flint wall which contrasts with the plaster of the rest of the church. There is a C15 **priest's door** on the s. side and in front of the **porch** is an interesting and unusual tomb. Robert Wyard of Castle farm was returning to the stables one morning in 1867 when he fell dead and his horse stood guard until he was found. The scene is sculpted on top of the tomb; the farmer's body lies beneath a blanket while a young woman stands at the horse's head. The late C14 wooden porch has **cusped** barge boards over the entrance arch, and pierced tracery each side above **mullions** that were renewed when it was restored in 1956.

The simple inner doorway with thin **imposts** indicates that the church was begun in the C12, and within there is a fairly startling floor in a tartan pattern of red, black, and yellow tiles which was laid to celebrate the 1887 Jubilee. The w. window of 1861 is filled with richly coloured glass (probably by **Lavers & Barraud**), illustrating Christ's presentation in the Temple, and above the arch to the nave is a small **quatrefoil sanctus-bell window**. The C15 **font** is a nice specimen of a familiar type in yellowish stone. The angels in the bowl panels have shields slung round their necks, with the arms of **St Edmund** carved on one of them, and they alternate with seeded roses, a knot of foliage, and a leaf shape; the

masks of the lions round the shaft have been cleverly restored. By the s. door, the bowl of the **stoup** is quite undamaged and this is unusual, particularly as **Dowsing** is known to have visited in 1644 and given orders for various things to be defaced – including a 'holy water font in the chancel'. Overhead, C14 **tie-beams** rest on little **wall posts** with shafts that curl under at the base and the **spandrels** are carved; roughly moulded **king-posts** with four-way struts stand below a plastered ceiling. Two nave windows inserted in the early C17 are placed high, and the undersides of their arches are panelled – one more elaborately than the other. There is no chancel arch but the **rood stair** lies hidden in the n. wall behind a C19 door. Fragments of C15 glass remain in the tracery of the s.e. nave window, and opposite you will see a C14 shield of the De Bohuns, who were Lords of the Manor from 1312 until 1377. The C17 pulpit contains familiar blind-arched panels, with scrolls in the range above, and the base is modern. The very upright wooden eagle is Victorian and so is the boarded panel ceiling of the chancel. The three-**light** e. window is filled with glass by **Hardman** in C13 style; parents and children are grouped under steeply gabled canopies and the girl with Christ in the centre looks uncommonly like Tenniel's Alice. There are bright angels and an **Agnus Dei** in the tracery, and some of the painting of the main figures is now grainy and fading. The n. lancet contains a figure of the **Blessed Virgin** matched by a Christ in Majesty on the s. side, and there is a pale and attractive **Annunciation** in the two-light s. window (it would be nice to know whose glass it is). Half of what was the base of the **rood screen** forms the back of a bench in front of **dropped-sill sedilia** in the **sanctuary**, and the rest is similarly treated under the tower.

Old Newton, St Mary (B5): The church stands above the level of the village street and the excellent **Decorated tracery** of the C14 **nave** windows catches the eye immediately. The centre one has a single large **reticulation** shape, and the pair to the e. have the same motif tight against the **ogee** arch enclosing two **quatrefoils** and two **mouchettes**. The fine mouldings of the early C14 doorway are uninterrupted by **capitals** and the **priest's door** in the **chancel** is a smaller version but with worn **headstops** to the **dripstone**. A **scratch dial** can be traced on the s.e. nave buttress and the s.e. corner of the chancel has an odd arrangement of two buttresses at right angles with a third diagonally between them. A heavy C17 or C18 brick buttress supports the n.e. corner so there may have been a history of structural weakness. On the n. side, there is more beautiful C14 tracery in the chancel, and on the nave a **drip course** runs up and over buttress and door. The tower was built around 1300 and has a small plain w. door, **lancets** n. and s. at ground level, and 'Y' tracery in the belfry windows and bell openings; there are angle buttresses to the w. and **flushwork** battlements. The **porch** windows have been blocked and over the inner door there is an image niche which has tiny headstops to the **crocketted hood mould**.

There were late C19 restorations here, and the plain **tie-beam** and **kingpost roof** of that time lies under a coved plastered ceiling. There is a small door to the tower and over it a sharply raked C19 **gallery** rests on slim cast-iron pillars. It is worth exploring to see the mouchettes of the side windows at close quarters and to examine the seating. Apart from two crude C17 benches at the back, there are backless forms for children on each step and, by the centre rail that divided boys from girls, two spaces with rudimentary arm-rests were reserved for master and mistress. The **Jacobean** benches at the rear of the nave have **finials** with scrolls and rosettes and there are only moulded back rails for support. The two rear ranges are angled to provide space round the C15 **font** which has

lions and angels bearing shields in the bowl panels. Headless lions and **woodwoses** support the shaft and the lack of a step makes it appear rather squat. A glass case in the blocked n. doorway contains a faintly eccentric war memorial in the form of a Moorish facade cut delicately in fretwork, with the names applied to the lower panels. The only other church fretwork that comes to mind is a Lord's Prayer which was an apprentice piece to be found at Cringleford near Norwich. A large set of George II **Royal Arms** painted on board and in good condition hangs on the n. wall and C19 pitch pine pews fill the nave – not all that attractive but a lovely timber sample. Fragments of the original C14 glass can still be seen in the heads of some of the windows. Although there is no **piscina**, stepped **sedilia** confirm that there was a nave **altar** and the C17 pulpit nearby is very plain, with shallow moulded frames to the panels and a later base. The tall chancel arch rests on half-octagon **jambs** and capitals, and in the **sanctuary** there is an attractive piscina with **cusped** ogee arches. The sedilia columns are free-standing and the mouldings appear to be later than those of the piscina. The e. window has late C13 shafts with ring bases but the arch is later and the four **lights** have no tracery. The tall niches each side match the sedilia but have remains of crockets, finials, and pinnacles which must have made them very attractive in their salad days.

Otley, St Mary (E5): A narrow tree-lined drive leads up to the e. end of the church from a rather secretive frontage, but there are open fields to the w. and the handsome early C15 tower can be seen from some way off in that direction. The flint work of its walls is dense and it is rather strange that the **flushwork** filling of the narrow **base course** has all disappeared. The w. door has been handsomely restored and it looks as though three of the carved figures are original. The doorway has leaves carved in the **spandrels** and a line of **tracery** shapes lies below the three-**light Perpendicular** window. The stepped battlements are in brick and the bell openings below them are but one sign that a lot of money has been spent recently on restoration. On walking round, you will find a C14 n. **porch** with plain oblong windows and there is a section of brick walling in the **nave** on that side where the old **rood stair turret** was removed. The walls had to be raised in the C15 when the new **roof** was constructed, and the join shows just under the **clerestory** windows.The **chancel** was largely rebuilt in the C19 and a new **vestry** added along its whole length. However, on the s. side there is a tiny little **priest's door** dating from about 1300, and there are late Perpendicular windows with deep **labels** in the s. **aisle**. Its e. wall is completely blank, but that may be the result of having the organ moved up against it inside. The canopied niche over the C14 s. porch entrance was almost hidden by rambler roses when I visited, and the moulding of the archway below is carved with hung shields, a motif that can be seen again on the inner doorway.

After passing the remains of a **stoup**, you will find that the interior gives an impression of hard whiteness – from walls and from the panels between the main timbers of the C15 roof. This is a **hammerbeam, arch-braced** design, but unfortunately the recumbent angels have lost their heads and have suffered the indignity of having iron tie-rods thrust into them to counteract the spread of the walls. In front of the tall tower arch stands a battered C15 **font** with angels and lions alternating in the bowl panels and familiar lions round the shaft. The fine late C14 **arcade** which separates nave and aisle has **quatrefoil piers**, and their **capitals** are carved alternately with bands of leaves and demi-angels. The arches are almost semi-circular and I wonder whether they were amended when the clerestory was built. The C19 **deca-**

logue boards on the s. wall have frames enlivened with gilt rosettes, and across the nave you will see that a window as well as the n. door has been blocked up, together with the rood stair entrances farther e. The **Stuart** pulpit is a very good piece, with carvings of vines in the top panels, blind arches below, and composite mouldings in the bottom panels; the base is modern. The nave benches date from 1879 but there are some interesting survivors from earlier sets. Those ranged along the walls of the s. aisle are C15 and have excellent tracery below their **poppyheads**. Placement makes them a little difficult to see, but there are also initials that spell out the word 'Prepare', and the message may have been longer in the original layout. One bench by the entrance is C17, and there is another at the front of the nave on the n. side, its end carved from a 4in. plank, complete with fleur de lys **finial**; the large shield below displays the arms of Beauchamp and FitzAlan. Original C15 panels form part of the low **screen**, and beyond it on the l. a tall blank arch is filled with a bright, abstract embroidery/collage on the theme of 'Let there be light'. Just by it stands a tiny little C15 bench, again with lovely quatrefoil tracery carved in the solid on the ends, and the choir stalls incorporate more work of the same period. Although the vestry has been rebuilt, the low door of about 1300 in the n. wall shows that there was either a predecessor or a chapel on that side early on. The priest's door opposite has been plastered over, and the Victorian alterations placed the **Early English piscina** right in the corner of the **sanctuary**. The restored roof presents a very odd appearance, for, under a steeply sloping plaster ceiling, fantastically shaped braces curl up to **tie-beams** which have pairs of scrolls above, and the whole design is like a cardboard cut-out when seen from the nave. The **Stuart Holy table** is particularly interesting because it has been cunningly adapted for modern use. No one would dare do it today but, probably around the turn of the century, a clever joiner extended it by 12in. at either end by introducing two matching legs on the front and inserting repeat sections of carving. He fooled **Cautley**. A tablet for Anne Russell on the n. wall is very delicately lettered; she died aged 87 in 1836 and the C18 convention of using Mistress (shortened to Mrs) for maiden ladies lingered on in her epitaph. On the sanctuary n. wall there is a **touchstone** tablet and flanking columns under a modest **pediment** for John Gosnold. He died in 1628, having been a minor figure at the courts of James I and Charles I; colour has been restored to the shields of arms and there is a helpful key to the heraldry below. Opposite is a plain tablet with Latin inscription which mentions nobody by name and uses only initials, but it should on no account be overlooked. It commemorates Paul Storr, probably the greatest English silversmith and goldsmith of the Regency period. He neither lived nor was buried here, but it so happened that his second son Francis was instituted as the rector in 1837 and Storr became interested in the church. He made a replica of its Elizabethan chalice, with a paten to match it, and paid for a new e. window shortly after. By way of compliment, Francis planted the avenue that leads up to it outside, and when his parents died he had them remembered here. The glass in the window is a rare and important example of the period, although the maker is unknown. Remarkably attractive, in orange, yellow, red, and a touch of sky blue, it has three texts in the tracery, finely painted borders, and delicate leaf patterns on the **quarries**.

Pettaugh, St Catherine (D5): The stream that runs under the road to form an attractive eastern boundary to the churchyard meanders across country to join the infant River Deben. The C14 unbuttressed tower has two **string courses** and there are **Perpendicular** bell openings below the stepped

flushwork battlements. On walking round, you will find that there is a **Decorated** w. window but no door below it, and a plain brick stair to the n. Two of the **nave** windows were replaced and others restored in 1863 (when the vicar doubled as architect), but the low n. door is C14. The plastered **chancel** has a large modern **vestry**/organ chamber to the n., with new brick buttresses each side of the e. window; that has intersected 'Y' **tracery** of the early C14 and small **headstops**. The **priest's door** has been re-shaped and there is a small and simple C19 **porch** in brick and flint leading to a plain C14 s. doorway.

The tan-coloured C15 **font** is the common East Anglian type, very worn lions alternating with shields in the bowl panels, battered angels underneath, and seated lions round the shaft. The plastered ceilings of nave and chancel are divided unobtrusively by the chancel arch, with no **screen** below it. The blocked n. doorway now houses a display centred on a small **brass** of about 1530. It probably commemorates Thomas Fastolfe, his wife Anne, and their daughters Pannel, Agnes, Elizabeth, and Dorothy (the inscription and the plate that pictured their sons is lost). A shield identifies the family and the women wear **kennel head-dresses**. The engraving is coarse, but it is interesting because when the brass was moved it was found that part of it had once belonged to the figure of an early C14 knight. The back of the daughters' plate is engraved with a portion of a surcoat like that worn by Sir Roger de Trumpington on his brass at Trumpington in Cambridgeshire. The nave benches and pulpit are modern, but the prayer desk in the chancel incorporates two **Jacobean** bench ends dated 1615. Their **poppyheads** are rather like rams' horns and the carving is rudimentary. The choir stalls of 1930 were designed to match. The remains of a **pillar piscina** set below a narrow recess in the **sanctuary** suggest that the original building was **Norman**, and there was certainly a church here at

Pettaugh, St Catherine: e. window detail

the time of the Domesday survey. On the s. wall is an undistinguished tablet by Robert Wills of London for the Revd Edmund Bellman who died in 1843, and opposite is the memorial for Charles William Tucker. He was young when he died at sea in 1861, and the models of the Crimea and Sebastopol medals sculpted at the top mean that he was a victim of that campaign.

The lovely glass in the e. window is the only work in Suffolk by **Caroline Townshend and Joan Howson**. Installed in 1936, the three scenes form a thick swathe of rich and vibrant colour across the window; Christ as the Good Shepherd stands in the centre, Lazarus rises from the dead surrounded by his family on the l., and Christ speaks to Zacchaeus in the sycamore tree on the r. Panes of striated glass fill the rest of the window, with the wheel of St Catherine at the bottom and the shields of East Anglia, St Edmundsbury, and Canterbury at the top.

Pettistree, St Peter and St Paul (G4): The churchyard is spacious and the Greyhound Inn's age and position suggest that it may have started life as the Church House where village **guilds** met and church ales were held. The C15 tower has a handsome w. frontage but the e. face extends across buttresses which project beyond the width of the **nave** and this gives it a curiously bald appearance when seen from that side. There are lozenges and chequerwork of flint in the **base course**, on the buttresses, and in a double band below the battlements, where there are corner **gargoyles**. Above the small **Perpendicular** w. window there is an unusually ornate belfry window which has traceried **ashlar spandrels** under a **label** that forms part of a **string course**. It looks as though it was designed as a niche for a statue. The nave has late Perpendicular windows but above them on each side are four **quatrefoil clerestory** windows which have been blocked. There is no sign that there were ever **aisles** and they were perhaps inserted to give additional light for the earlier C13 or C14 nave. In the tower e. wall just above the present low-pitched **roof** you will see a small window which was probably a **sanctus-bell window** inside the church before the roof line was lowered. The **chancel** dates from about 1300 but it was largely rebuilt in 1894 and an organ chamber was added to the n. The nave n. door is blocked and as far as one can see there have never been **porches** – which is unusual in a church of this size.

Within, below an almost flat plastered ceiling, most of the seating is modern but there are four low medieval bench ends with shallow **tracery** at the w. end on the n. side, and the **poppyhead** by the entrance is an interesting carving of a crouching lion with a mask on top. On the w. wall hangs a very decorative charity board of 1717 in black and gold, cut to a silhouette with fat flanking scrolls. Bread was to be provided for 'such poor of this parish as shall here religiously and constantly joyn with ye Congregation in ye Publick Prayers of ye Church' – wording which could, I suppose, have provided a number of excuses for being uncharitable. Half a century later the **Royal Arms** of George III were painted and they hang now on the n. wall, dark and sombre. At the e. end of the pews on the n. side is a bench made up of medieval sections. It has unmatched ends and the poppyhead next to the aisle is exceptionally well carved, while the range of panels below the seat could well have been part of the front of the **rood loft**. The stairs that led to it are still in the n. wall although the lower entrance has disappeared. Below there is a **piscina** with a **cusped** arch that would have served a nave **altar**, and there is another one to match on the s. side. Just above it the head of another arch may have been part of an image niche, although a simple recess for a statue is provided in the **jamb** of the adjoining window. There is now no **screen**, but the chancel arch has slot marks which show where a **tympanum** was fitted. The stone for Francis Bacon and his wives Elizabeth and Mary is fixed to the s. wall and bears 18in. **brass** effigies. He wears a fur-trimmed gown, both wives have Paris caps, and one displays an embroidered petticoat below her farthingale; the inscription remains although three shields have gone. There is some medieval glass on this side; look in particular for the very decorative little C15 **pelican in her piety** in the s.w. window, and the rare

(albeit murky) example of C13 **grisaille** glass in the s.e. window above the C14 arms of Ufford. The C14 **angle piscina** was preserved in the restoration and the four-**light** e. window has 1880s glass by **Clayton & Bell** which is typical of their work for the period. On the n. wall a roundel against a black ground tells how Ann Carter died in childbed in 1790:

> How dear the Purchase! how severe the Cost!
> The Fruit was sav'd, the parent Tree was lost!

Playford, St Mary (F6): The church stands on the hill above the village and the little River Fynn; there is a **lychgate** at the bottom of a steep path and attractive steps lead up to the churchyard. Like a number of others in the area, the late C14 tower stands to the s. of the **nave**. The substantial outer arch has large crowns in the mouldings and an angel holding a shield at the apex; judging by the shields in the **spandrels**, the tower was built by Sir George Felbrigg whose **brass** you will see inside. Just above is a nicely canopied and **groined** niche with flanking panels of **flushwork**, and the upper stage has a pair of widely spaced bell openings with a C19 cross set between them. They are **Perpendicular** in style, but the others are **Decorated** and it is likely that the arrangement on the s. side is all Victorian. On walking round, you will find that there is a three-**light** Perpendicular w. window, a blocked n. door, and a rebuilt **chancel** in early Decorated style which was designed by **R.M. Phipson** in 1873. The massive obelisk that stands s.w. of the tower commemorates Thomas Clarkson who died in 1846 and was erected eleven years later 'by a few surviving friends'. He achieved fame as 'the friend of slaves', having devoted most of his life to the cause and helping to achieve the Emancipation Bill of 1833. He lived at Playford Hall and is buried with his wife and son just outside the **priest's**

door in the chancel. The grave is worth examining because not only does it retain its cast-iron railings, but they incorporate oval marble plaques set in cast-iron frames, a most unusual feature. Close by, a group of Airy family stones is enclosed within a cast-iron fence that also has distinctive components – a plaited top rail and a plate on the gate bearing a text.

Within the porch the **jambs** of the inner doorway are scored with a mass of C17 and C18 graffiti, and above it on the nave side hang the **Royal Arms** of George III painted on canvas. The **roof** was replaced in celebration of Queen Victoria's Jubilee in 1897 and the **font** is C19 too. On the n. wall is a memorial for Sir George Biddell Airy, an astronomer royal who died in 1892, having restored to that office the authority and prestige it had lost in the C18. It takes the form of a fine bust by F.J. Williamson and the head is set in a dished oval with a loose collar lapping over the frame onto the grey marble surround. The chancel arch is tall, with **castellated capitals**, and beyond it on the s. wall is another bust portrait, this time in profile, of Thomas Clarkson, sculpted in 1878 by Sir Hamo Thornycroft, well known for *The Kiss* in the Tate Gallery and his statue of Cromwell at Westminster. Fixed to the wall opposite is the fine **brass** of Sir George Felbrigg who died in 1400. Lord of the Manor, he was an esquire-at-arms to Edward III and lieutenant of the Court of Chivalry. Although there is now no trace of it, his tomb was in the n. wall of the nave where there was a **chantry** founded by him. The 4ft. 9in. brass is a good illustration of the armour of the period, and the heraldic lion, the helmet cords, and the sword scabbard were originally inlaid with colour; there are remnants of a canopy and marginal inscription. Above it is a lozenge-shaped panel with four coloured shields of arms and good lettering for Sir Anthony and Dame Anne Everard, placed there in 1657 by their son who 'desirous to be layd here with my parents have erected this memorial

as wel for them as my selfe'. Retracing your steps, note that Sir George Felbrigg's shield occurs again (back to front!) in C15 glass in the tracery of a nave n. window.

Polstead, St Mary (C10): The church stands on a hill-top by the Hall and there are open views to the s., with a scaled-down replica of the Whitehall Cenotaph as a war memorial on the e. boundary of the churchyard. Seen from the gate, the outline of the church is a little stark, with a flat **chancel roof** behind a plain parapet and a **nave** gable that is sliced off at the top. To make amends, the early C14 tower had an attractive spire added later which has small gabled windows at two levels – the only surviving stone medieval example in Suffolk. There is 'Y' **tracery** in the bell openings and a **lancet** is set above the small red brick w. doorway. Tie-rods with large 'S' braces are signs of a later structural problem. Although some of the windows are **Perpendicular**, the **aisles** were replaced in the C14 and the e. window of the s. aisle has **reticulated** tracery. There is a **priest's door** on that side and traces of **Norman** lancets in the chancel wall are the first indication of the true age of the building. There is a restored s. **porch** but the main entrance is on the other side and there are two steps down into the early C14 n. porch. The side windows contain fragments of medieval glass and, on the e. side, two roundels of C16 Flemish glass; one of them is a lively scene of Jesus being arrested, in which Judas kisses him and Peter strikes at Malchus with his sword, while the other depicts the Magi. The C14 doorway has large, worn **headstops** and above is the shield of the Lambourne family, who were Lords of the Manor when it was built. The door itself still retains its original strap hinges and the remains of a central closing ring.

Once inside, the true age of the church is confirmed. The nave **arcades** are Norman with oblong **piers** which have pairs of shafts towards aisle and nave and varied **capitals**. The real interest lies in the arches which are brick with a scattering of tufa, a dark volcanic stone which was probably filched from a ruined Roman building. The bricks, however, are the wrong size and shape to be Roman and are very like those used to build Little Coggeshall abbey in Essex which have been dated about 1200. This means that these at Polstead may well be among the earliest surviving English bricks. The chancel arch matches the arcades and there are blank, roughly shaped **clerestory** windows of the same period which were covered by the roofs of the later aisles. Judging by the w. arch on the s. side of the nave, the C14 builders began to replace the arcades but the work was taken no further. Their tower, however, was placed against the Norman w. front without disturbing the original doorway and it can be seen from within the tower – fine and broad, with bands of heavy **chevrons** in the arch and three shafts in the **jambs**. The dark set of **Royal Arms** on the n. wall carries the initials of one of the Georges but it belongs to the reign of Queen Anne, although her 'Semper eadem' motto is not used. There is a C14 tomb recess below and, nearby, a fragment of wall painting that can still be recognised as the figure of a bishop. The large expanse of wall-hanging to the w. is made of crimson Italian silk velvet, embroidered with a repeat design of **sacred monograms** within crowns of thorns. In the s. aisle, the octagonal brick bowl of the **font** is difficult to date but it rests on a C13 base with centre shaft and four columns with ring capitals and bases. The cover could, perhaps uncharitably, be described as an amorphous pancake of green fibreglass with a stylised and spiky handle representing a dove; scenes of the healing of the paralytic, the blind man, and Christ's encounter with the woman of Samaria are roughly incised on the top; it was designed by a nun of Oxford. On the wall beyond, two **consecration crosses**

are placed unusually close to each other. There are a number of **hatchments** here for members of the Brand family and although the one above the arcade is unidentified, the others are for: Jacob, who probably died in the early C18 (above the font), another Jacob (w. wall, top), William, who died in 1799 (w. wall, r.), and his widow Anna Mirabella Henrietta who died in 1814 (it must have been pleasurable to call the banns!). The nave is lit by three small dormers on the s. side and below the plaster ceiling there are rough C14 **tie-beams** and heavy octagonal **king-posts** which are strutted to a runner under the ridge. At the e. end of the s. aisle is a long, low C14 chest and on the wall to the r. a **touchstone** tablet framed in marble for Charles Vincent who died in 1700 – curiously old-fashioned for its period. The e. bay of the n. aisle roof is panelled with centre **bosses** and formed a **celure** for the **altar** below. It still has a lot of its C16 colouring and some of the gilded stars are cast in lead. By the pulpit is an anonymous **brass** of about 1490, with figures of a man wearing a heavy rosary, his wife with a veil head-dress but with her face erased, and a group of five children. A small monument in the angle to the r. of the chancel arch is for Lord of the Manor Jacob Brand who died in 1630. It is coloured and he kneels within an arch with his hand on the head of his son Benjamin, who is said to have fallen to his death from a window in the Hall.

Just within the chancel there are a pair of benches of curious design – spiral back posts and steeply cranked arms. They appear to be C18 or early C19 and may have been used as **housel benches** like those at Shelland [Vol.1]. The church's other brass is now fixed to the n. wall of the chancel and is a mid-C15 18in. effigy of a priest – one of only four in the county which are shown wearing eucharistic vestments. **Dowsing's** journal records a visit here in 1643 when he broke over forty 'superstitious pictures' and little remains of the church's medieval glass.

However, there are fragments in the s. chancel window, including a bishop holding a cross and what might be the handle of an auger. If so, it probably represents **St Leger**. The **communion rails** are a handsome three-sided set with shapely **balusters** and it is interesting that the design was varied by using twisted columns at the ends and corners. The **Stuart Holy table** is unusual in having a thick centre stretcher which carries two slim turned posts. Behind it stands a modern oak **reredos** in **Jacobean** style but the three centre blind arches appear to be original.

Many visitors come to Polstead expecting to find some trace of poor Maria Marten but, like the Red Barn, nothing remains of her gravestone; it was by the tower.

Raydon, St Mary (D9): The church was built in the late C13 to early C14 and had a tower until it collapsed in the C17, bringing down four bells with it. Now, the single bell is housed in a diminutive annexe with a tiled pyramid **roof** built on to the w. end. The windows have an enterprising mixture of **Decorated tracery** and there are some very good **headstops** which include two dames at the w. end. The **rood stair** turret is set within a buttress angle on the n. side, and the **chancel** is of exceptional quality for a church of this size. It is all early C14 but the details are varied and inventive. The buttresses on the n. side are triangular (like Thorpe Morieux [Vol.1]) with headstops on the **dripstones**, but those to the s. have very steep **weatherings** and **cusped** gables under the eaves. Each corner buttress continues upward as a traceried octagonal shaft, to finish in a flourish of densely **crocketted** gables and a pinnacle. There are quite large masks sculpted on the weatherings and little devils sprout around the gables. They were comprehensively restored in 1988; note the large dragon with a curly tail that crouches at the base of the n.e. pinna-

Raydon, St Mary: early C14 chancel

cle. The **low side windows** either side of the chancel are equally lavish in their way. Each is tall, split by a **transom**, and set within broad and shallow mouldings; the upper section is a cusped **lancet** below a **trefoil**, and the lower lancet is now blocked. The **priest's door**, with its slim shafts and large ring **capitals**, is on the s. side, and the church clock is placed above the e. window – unusual but eminently sensible. A **scratch dial** with a heavy rod in the centre hole can be seen on the s.e. **nave** buttress.

Passing through an open wooden porch, one enters via a plain C14 doorway which has very worn headstops to the dripstone. To the r. is the remnant of a **stoup** and a cracked C13 grave slab serves as a threshold. Within, there is a small door in the w. wall that once led to the tower, and the peculiar **font** is probably C19 – a small octagonal bowl on a **baluster** stem, all now picked out in brown and cream. A full-scale restoration in the 1880s provided benches, roofs, a new e. window, and the **vestry** beyond the nave n. door. This now has new doors presented by members of the 353rd Fighter Group of the American 8th Air Force, who were stationed nearby during World War II. There is no longer a **screen** between nave and chancel but the position of the **rood beam** is indicated by the two wooden brackets which are still in place above the arch. The steep stair to the loft can be seen in the n. wall and there is a **piscina** with a finely moulded trefoil arch on the other side of the nave marking the site of an **altar**. The remnants of two **brasses** are nearby: an inscription for Thomas Reydon, and an 8in. figure of Elizabeth Reydon which now lacks its top half and **butterfly head-dress**; both date from 1479. Seen from within, the low side windows lie in deep embrasures and there are grotesques at the w. end of the arches. Behind the organ, a large tomb recess probably marks the resting place of the founder; the sharply angled arch has headstops and the deeply recessed moulding is cusped within. The bottom sections of the chancel side windows were plastered up at some time and they contain fragments of C14 and C15 glass, including some delicate leaf shapes on the n. side. The **sanctuary** floor was raised in the C19 to the detriment of the early C14 double piscina. This is fine and large, constructed like a complete window head with all the tracery moulded and pierced. The design matches the side windows and the piscina was doubtless made along with them. On the n. wall opposite there is a **touchstone** tablet set within an alabaster frame enriched with skulls wearing wreaths of laurel. A flaming urn sits in the broken **pediment** and the memorial commemorates John Mayer, a 'faithful & laborious servant of God', who was twenty-two years at Little Wratting before serving thirty-three years here. He died at a good age in 1663 and had been no simple country parson; as the epitaph says, 'he wrote also for ye

publick good these most useful books', and proceeds to list them (a rare example of a bibliography preserved in stone!). Bible expositions in many volumes were followed by an *Antidote Against Popery*, and *Ye History of the World from ye Creation to 1648*, amongst other things. There's confidence!

Redlingfield, St Andrew (D3): A small and simple church just to the s. of the hamlet, it is easily seen from the road and a footpath leads directly to it alongside Hall farm. The tower has a red brick base with fragments of blue patterning, and the second stage is plastered below a gabled **roof**. From the inside you will see that there is the outline of a C14 window in the w. wall of the **nave** and it is more than likely that there was no tower until the C17. A Benedictine priory was founded here in 1120, endowed with the manor, and from the outset was assigned the parish church for its own use – an unusually early example of appropriation. Its fortunes fluctuated and there were scandalous revelations at a bishop's visitation in 1425 when the prioress was forced to resign. Thereafter, life was blameless until its dissolution in 1536 when its prioress, seven nuns, two priests, and twenty-one servants were turned out into the world with very little to bless themselves with. It is interesting that at that time the dedication was listed as 'The Blessed Virgin and St Andrew' and the demise of the nunnery may have prompted the change. There was some rebuilding in the C14 and a blocked door of that period lies in the centre of the n. wall; above it there is the faint outline of a **lancet** which is the only visible reminder of the original building. Farther along is a C16 brick **mullioned** window and the **chancel** appears to have been rebuilt in C18 or early C19 brick. However, the **Decorated** e. window with its **reticulated tracery** was re-used, and so was the **priest's door**. Nearby, a memorial slab with a shield of arms for Joannis Garneys who died in 1697 has been set in the wall. There are Decorated windows on the s. side of the nave and one of the **headstops** is a mask with its tongue lolling out. The angle buttresses at the w. end are another indication that the medieval building had no tower. The **porch** has blocked 'Y' tracery windows and its steeply pitched roof rests on **arch-braces**.

Moving to the simple interior, you will see the **Royal Arms** of George IV hanging on the n. wall – painted on board, with a surprisingly good unicorn. The C15 octagonal **font** is rather battered and this may be because **Dowsing** came here in April 1643, although his diary has no direct reference to it. There are **woodwoses** and lions round the shaft, and angels below the bowl whose panels are carved with **Evangelistic symbols** alternating with angels bearing shields; the emblems of **St Edmund** (s.) and the **Passion** (n.e.) are recognisable. The nave roof is arch-braced, with **collars** under the ridge, and naive carved busts were added to the base of the **wall posts**, probably in the C17. The benches and pulpit are modern and may have come in when there was a restoration in 1873. A C14 **piscina** is to be found on the s. side at the e. end of the nave, and a pair of C15 bench ends survives in the chancel. Susanna Everard has a good **ledger-stone** of 1670. It lies partly under the **altar** and is a simple representation of a fashionable architectural tablet. Before you leave, note that there is an interesting modern version of a tithe map by the door. Drawn in 1977, it gives all the field names in the parish and vignettes of various buildings, and even identifies the mobile library halt!

Ringshall, St Catherine (C7): Attractively placed at the head of a little lane on rising ground, the church has a very solid **Norman** tower. A low **drip course** runs just above the tiny **lancets** set in the n. and s. walls of the ground floor

and there are shallow **set-offs** farther up. The w. window of about 1300 has 'Y' **tracery**, and there are lancet bell openings and a much more recent brick parapet. The n. wall of the **nave** had to be massively supported with brick buttressing in the C18 or early C19 and there is an early C14 doorway on that side. The side windows are all **Perpendicular** but the **chancel** e. window tracery is **Decorated**, displaying two **mouchettes** and the remains of **headstops** on the **dripstone**. The **priest's door** on the s. side dates from about 1300 and two **scratch dials** can be found on its e. **jamb**. Apart from the restored Perpendicular window on the s. side of the nave, a single Norman lancet has recently been given a new frame. Note that the line of an earlier **roof** is marked on the e. face of the tower and that two **tie-beams** emerge through the wall to be secured by large wooden pins – a most unusual feature. **R.M. Phipson** directed a restoration in 1878 and his oak **porch** is a very satisfactory reproduction of a C14 model. The doorway was inserted about 1300 but on going in you will see that the inner arch is round-headed and so it may have replaced a Norman original.

The tower was remodelled at that time and its arch to the nave is tall, with the plain chamfered mouldings merging into the jambs without **capitals**. Have a look beyond it at one of the little lancets and see the thickness of the walls. Octagonal C13 **fonts** in **Purbeck marble** must have been mass produced for their design seldom varies – pairs of arches carved in low relief on each face of a canted bowl. This one has had its supporting ring of shafts replaced. There is no chancel arch, and the open **roof** has exceptionally low tie-beams on which rest two tall and slender **king-posts**. They support a ridge which runs below the rafter braces and there are little **castellated** wall shafts. Hanging lamps were used at one time and their pulleys are still in place above the nave. As well as the Norman lancet already noted, there are two in the n. wall, differing in size and now blocked. All the furniture dates from the 1870s restoration and Phipson repaired the roof. The **hammerbeams**, **wall plates**, and carved **spandrels** of the C16 roof in the chancel look as if they too were restored. One normally finds a **piscina** in the s. wall of the **sanctuary** but here it is in the e. wall and has the unusual feature of a **trefoil** drain, with a wooden **credence shelf** above it. The e. and s.e. windows are filled with 1870s glass by **Clayton & Bell** in typical style – the Resurrection and Christ with **St Mary Magdalene** in the garden in one, and Christ as the Good Shepherd and the Light of the World in the other.

Rushmere St Andrew, St Andrew (F7):
This is an interesting building, combining as it does ancient, Victorian, and modern work. William Cadye died in 1497, his wife Katherine in 1521, and they left money for a new tower on condition that it was built 'in like fashion, bigness and workmanship as is the steeple of Tuddenham'. Its buttresses and stepped battlements are decorated with **flushwork**, and the **Evangelistic symbols** at the corners have been renewed. The w. door and window are C19 and the latter has quite extraordinary **tracery**, with six **quatrefoils** and a centre shape around a figure of the patron saint. This was part of a massive rebuilding directed by **E.C. Hakewill** in 1861 when he replaced the **nave** and **chancel** on the old foundations and added a n. **aisle**. The only sign that a church has stood here for 900 years is the fine **Norman** doorway which Hakewill retained in the s. wall. It is broad and low and has two bands of broad **chevron moulding** above flanking shafts decorated with a spiral pattern. The style of the Victorian work is **Early English**, with tall **lancets** on the s. side of the nave, and the **roof** slopes right down on the n. side over the aisle. Then in 1967 a major extension was added to the e. end of the **chancel** which, in effect, forms a second nave

with aisles of unequal width. It was designed by George Pace, an architect who has several modern churches to his credit and who was responsible for the rebuilding of Llandaff cathedral. The broad slope of the C19 roof is repeated, with the addition of a dormer on the top of the ridge facing n. and a taller version on the other side lower down. There is a large hall/meeting room at right angles linked to the s. side of the chancel and a flat-roofed **vestry** block was added n.w. of the nave.

Inside it is rather dark at the w. end, with an organ blocking the tower arch; Hakewill's square block **font** stands below it. His two-bay **arcade** has a drum shaft and overweight **capital**, and there is glass by **Lavers, Barraud & Westlake** in the aisle lancets – Noah and his wife with the dove, Solomon in the Temple, and the sacrifice of Isaac. The same firm filled the nave s. lancets with scenes of Christ's baptism, His entry into Jerusalem, and the Crucifixion. Medieval timbers were re-used in the nave roof and William Polley of Coggeshall provided a lovely range of benches with infinitely varied **poppyheads**. He placed delicately carved angels on the elbows and the pair at the w. end cradle models of the tower and the chancel. There are birds and beasts in the aisle and the Evangelistic symbols are used at the e. end. Close by them is the **ledger-stone** for William Seely who died in 1660 (note the spelling of the village name). The old chancel has become the setting for a new limed oak central **altar** flanked by elegant metal candle stands. Overhead, the roof timbers are painted a deep red and the Victorian **sedilia** have been backed with panels to match the rest of the **sanctuary** furniture. The window glass behind them commemorates Hakewill and he gave the carving of **St Andrew** bringing **St Peter** to Jesus which is now set in the wall on the n. side. The Ascension panel above dates from 1889. A s. chancel window has good glass of 1860, again by Lavers, Barraud & Westlake; jewel-like leaf patterns surround panels of Christ with St Peter and St Andrew and the martyrdom of the church's patron saint; the arms of William Schreiber are displayed below. The new e. nave has a high-pitched, cleverly braced roof whose shape and density is taken up by the wide e. window. Bulky rough-cast conecte beams provide the framework, and while these do not jar, the coarseness of the unadorned stock bricks of the walls does – simplicity should not cancel out quality. That said, and ignoring the typically uncomfortable chairs that architects delight in, this is a bold and stimulating setting for worship.

Saxtead, All Saints (E3): For those with a taste for the precise, it is on record that Saxtead's tower fell on 8 July 1805, but whether from decrepitude or thunderbolt we know not. The w. wall was duly repaired and, typical of the period, a window with wooden **tracery** bars was inserted. A circuit of the outside reveals a C13 n. door and farther along, a square window in domestic style complete with opening quarter light. There is a single **lancet** in the the n. wall of the C14 **chancel** and the lovely three-**light** e. window has **ogee** shapes in the head which enclose an oval, itself divided by tracery. There is more **Decorated** tracery in the windows on the s. side and a minuscule **Tudor priest's door** in red brick. The C15 **porch** is faced with **flushwork**, there is a small canopied niche above the entrance, and a dragon and a lion sport among writhing foliage in the **spandrels** of the arch. The **wall plates** of the **roof** are delicately carved and, as at Athelington, the village stocks have found a home in the porch. Saxtead's, however, are a rather superior version and have a central whipping post as well. Not only that, the three sets of holes for the legs are graded in size to take both young and old, and an inscription reads 'Fear God and Honour the King' as though blasphemy and treason were the particular crimes in question.

Beyond a **Perpendicular** doorway with **fleurons** in the moulding is a neat and immaculately maintained interior which, despite its smallness, boasts a C15 **hammerbeam** roof over the **nave**. The deep wall plates are crested and there is pierced tracery behind the **arch-braces** and above the collars under the ridge. The roof was well restored in 1986 and there are interesting photographs of the work in progress displayed at the w. end. The bowl panels of the C15 octagonal **font** are decorated with plain shields within **quatrefoils** and it seems rather squat, probably because the floor level has been raised, masking the step. The C17 cover is a plain panelled pyramid. The carved seated figure on the n. side rear bench is very similar to one in the same position at Tannington, and other bench ends have traces of figures on the elbows so that the same craftsman may have been at work here. Most of the seating, however, is modern. A **consecration cross** is to be found on the nave s. wall and on the other side the **rood loft stairs** rise well to the w. of the chancel arch. Looking e. you will see that Saxtead has an example of a **weeping chancel** – to the s. in this instance. There are a C19 pulpit and C20 choir stalls, and in the chancel with its plastered ceiling there are two more consecration crosses on the walls. The late C17 **decalogue** panels are rather splendid and very well preserved. On canvas, they have painted architectural surrounds and pendent swags. Also painted on canvas are the fine **Royal Arms** of George II which hang over the priest's door. The late C17 **communion rails** are satisfyingly solid, with well-turned **balusters**, and the C14 **angle piscina** has a slender corner shaft with ring **capital** and base and **cusped** ogee arches. The style is repeated in the e. window which has small **headstops** to the **hood mould**. Below stands a small **Stuart Holy table**, and the chest with marquetry inlay which stands in the corner is probably continental work.

Semer, All Saints (C8): This little church has a captivating setting, lying as it does secluded in the valley of the Brett well away from the few houses and Manor farm. One can appreciate how it was that someone reported the C16 rector Edward Kettle to the bishop, 'because he worketh in harvest tyme in byndinge of oats without any hatt on his head, or dublett on his back, but onlie his hose and shirt'. There was a wholesale restoration here in the 1870s when the **chancel** was rebuilt and given a solid **porch** for the **priest's door**. A **vestry** was added beyond the n. door, and the ridge of the **nave roof** was sliced off, leaving the old line showing on the tower. Although the **Perpendicular** w. window of the tower was restored, the bell openings have fragments of **Decorated tracery** and indicate its age. The s. porch was sensitively rebuilt in 1899, making use of the original C15 barge boards and **jambs**, and the C14 inner doorway houses a medieval door which has had a whole selection of lock positions over the years.

Two **tie-beams** span the nave under a plaster ceiling and above the tower arch there is a set of George III **Royal Arms** on canvas. Within the tower is an interesting charity board, and either side of the arch hang C18 **Commandment boards** in unusually rich frames. Oddly, they do not match; the one to the l. has a cherub head and scrolls on top. The square and massive C14 **font** is fitted with a pleasing little **Jacobean** cover which has four scrolls against a turned and carved post, with knobs for lifting. There are C19 benches and pulpit, and a brass lectern whose inscription not only tells us that, along with the **screen** and reading desk, it was given by the rector in 1897, but also advises us to ponder Psalms 42, 23, and 84, and not to overlook the collect for the second Sunday in Advent. The chancel arch was part of the rebuilding and the new roof has heavy **arch-braces** resting on **corbel** angels bearing musical instruments and **Evangelistic symbols**. On the n. wall a 1660s memo-

rial for Rector John Bruning is nicely composed in alabaster and **touchstone**. The tablet is flanked by scrolls below his arms within a broken **pediment**, and a small scrolled oval beneath is capped by a skull. Opposite there is a pair of tall, matching C18 tablets (and a third behind the organ) with **cartouches** of arms over them and graceful lettering, for the Revd Thomas Cooke and his wife Sarah. The paintings of Moses and Aaron which flank the **altar** seem to have been made to accompany the Commandment boards at the w. end, and in front stands a fine pair of brass candle stands of the type recommended by the **Ecclesiological Society**.

The setting invites a leisurely tour of the churchyard and n. of the chancel Maria Elizabeth Archer lies in a table tomb. She died aged 18 in 1786 and her epitaph is reminiscent of one of Fanny Burney's characters: 'This amiable young woman was blest with an uncommon sweetness of disposition, a refined and highly cultivated understanding, and a most striking urbanity of manner.' By the s. porch lies the recent grave of a baby boy ('our little man') and, just as one has sometimes seen favourite horses carved on an old farmer's stone, so this stone has a teddy bear – the cherished companion.

Shelley, All Saints (D9): This is a lovely situation for a country church, in the little valley of the Brett with a house or two nearby and meadow land beyond. Judging by the blocked **lancet** in the s. wall of the **chancel**, it was built in the C13 and in the early C14 a tower (which also serves as a **porch**) was added to the n. The s. **aisle** is of the same period and one of the windows has intersected **tracery**, although you will see that its w. window was replaced in the early C19 with a 'Gothick' model in an iron frame. Just below it a glacial boulder stone peeps through the plaster and a number were used in the foundations. Indeed, some have thought that they were pagan cult objects that were ritually cleansed and re-used deliberately by the church. The tower bell openings are tall **cusped** lancets e. and w., with a wider one to the n. which has the remains of tracery. It was a very pleasant surprise to find that the clock not only worked but the bells chimed the quarters – a rare thing in the country these days. The steep entrance arch of the tower is finely moulded but now has a small wooden door set within it, and there is a straight-headed late **Perpendicular** four-**light** window in the n. wall of the **nave**. Beyond it, the Tylney chapel in **Tudor** red brick juts out from the chancel, with token octagonal buttresses at the corners. A coat of arms in a small stone panel lies between two windows in the n. wall and there is the outline of a third window in the gable. It is interesting that the C16 builder still used diminutive **headstops** on the brick **dripstones**. The e. window and the **priest's door** were renewed in the 1880s and, except for the tower, all the walls are plastered. The s. porch has a timber frame on a brick base with stone seats and is now the principal entrance. The doorway belongs to the C13 building and has a continuous roll moulding down to the floor.

Just inside to the l. hangs a set of George III **Royal Arms** painted on canvas, and there is a small C19 **font** in the nave. The C14 **arcade**, with its octagonal **piers** and wide **capitals**, leans gently outwards. On the n. wall are two **hatchments**: one undated for Mary Kerridge to the w., and the other for Thomas Kerridge who died in 1743.There are brick floors and C19 pine benches, whose front ranks incorporate oak **linen-fold panels** that match those in the stately Elizabethan pulpit standing on a centre pedestal. At the base of the n. nave window stands the tomb of Dame Margarett Tylney who died in 1598. The chest has an alabaster epitaph panel set in strapwork and the flanking columns are made of a prettily mottled marble. The edge of the slab is

moulded and picked out in yellow but her effigy is all in black, with a high-necked gown and ruff; only the nose and fingers have been mutilated. The stained glass in the aisle window is by **William Warrington** and the figures in uncomplicated colours have little animation. But it is of more than usual interest because it commemorates Henry Partridge, one of Warrington's apprentices, who died in 1864 aged 21. In the chancel, the choir stalls have two excellent **griffins** holding shields carved with the Tylney arms and a tomb chest is set in the n. wall of the **sanctuary**. There are three shields of arms within shallow niches along its front, and on the top, set in strapwork, stands a large coloured shield with many quarterings. With the two smaller shields, it really belongs to Dame Margarett's tomb, and that itself may originally have stood in the large recess in the chancel wall which is now clad with panels of linen-fold and other C16 motifs. The plain **piscina** has one drain and a dish scooped out beside it which may have been a way of providing a double version cheaply. A plain painted door in the recess on the n. side of the chancel leads into the Tylney chapel and an elaborate version of their family arms is carved in relief within a stone panel on the facing wall. Unfortunately, the supporting griffins have lost their feet but a cute little leaf trail up each side sprouts more of the beasts. The strangest thing in the chapel is the 10ft post with a 'T' bracket at the end which stretches out from the w. wall just below the ceiling. It is carefully moulded, with a wrought iron stay, and was used to display a tabard, a surcoat embroidered with the family arms. The C18 **decalogue boards** below are in rather poor condition and would have been in the chancel originally, while the plain panelling came from **box pews** discarded during the 1880s restoration. On the s. wall, however, is more good C16 linen-fold and (yet again) the Tylney arms carved on a panel.

Somersham, St Mary (D7): This early C14 church has a simple unbuttressed tower whose outline is varied only by a single **string course**. The w. window has **cusped 'Y' tracery**, and at the upper level there are cusped **lancets** n. and s. and windows with **Decorated** tracery e. and w. The top half of the blocked n. door has been glazed and a 1780s gravestone is clamped lower down – has it been there all the time? There is 'Y' tracery of about 1300 in the window farther along. Note the oblong shape of the **rood stair turret**, and beyond that, a late **Perpendicular priest's door** with eroded **paterae** in a broad moulding. Like the e. window, those on the s. side of the **chancel** have Decorated tracery. The outer arch of the **porch** is formed from two massive slabs of timber and **Cautley** thought that it could perhaps be the earliest in the county, dating from the late C13. The open sides display prettily cusped tracery but you will see that the carving is on the inside only. This suggests that they originally formed part of the **rood screen** and were used to decorate the porch when the screen was destroyed. The modern device for housing the **bier** in the **roof** on hinged bearers is both neat and effective. The C14 inner doorway is simple and the door itself still has its original strap hinges and the boss of a closing ring.

The mouldings of the narrow w. arch fade into the **imposts** and there is a modern **gallery** within the tower. To the l., a well-painted set of Charles II **Royal Arms** has coarse strapwork on the edge of the frame, and a single **hatchment** hangs opposite – unidentified but connected with the Bacon family. Lower on the wall, a glass case contains one of those curiosities that sometimes find a home in churches for want of a better. This one is an unexploded bomb dropped by a Zeppelin in World War I, looking rather like a small old-fashioned milk can (another is similarly preserved at Acton [Vol.1]). There is no chancel arch and below the plastered ceilings there are four rugged **tie-beams**. The wooden pegs on the

wall plate at the w. end may have been used to hang the garlands called crants for maidens who died young, but this is not as certain here as the example at Walsham le Willows [Vol.1]. The plain octagonal **font** has a pyramid cover that probably dates from the C16, and there is a fragment of C14 wall painting on the s. wall of the **nave**, but only a pair of legs can be distinguished. Nearby, a long and shallow oblong recess in the wall is puzzling. It has a moulded frame and I can only think that it was made for a **brass** or possibly for an inscription. A second set of Royal Arms hangs above the pulpit and this time they are **Hanoverian**, cut to a silhouette. The tie-beam overhead no doubt served as the **rood beam** and the one in the chancel still carries the stocks for a **sacring bell**. This is a rare survival and the only other Suffolk instance that comes to mind is at Hawstead [Vol.1]. The **communion rails** are late C17 and some panelling dated 1601 has been inserted behind the **altar**. To the r., the tall **piscina** arch is **ogee**-shaped with lightly carved cusps and a **Jacobean** chest stands in the **sanctuary**. C18 **decalogue panels** with Lord's Prayer and Creed are framed on the side walls, and there are large paintings of Moses and Aaron on the e. wall that were given to the church in 1750. Painted on board, they are unusually good and are obviously the work of a competent artist – though who he was is not known. Apart from the usual smashing of glass, **Dowsing's** depredations in 1644 included the removal of a **stoup** and defacing an inscription on the outside of the priest's door: 'Jesus, sancta Maria, Jesus'. He left untouched the pilgrim's cross cut in the stone just inside the doorway on the r.

Sproughton, All Saints (E7): The building dates from the early C14, but there was a heavy restoration in the 1860s and **chancel aisles** were added shortly after. The unbuttressed tower has two narrow **set-offs** above the belfry and the 'Y' **tracery** of the bell openings points to a completion date of about 1300. As at nearby Washbrook and Bramford, glacial boulders can be detected in the footings and they may well have been pagan cult objects that were cleansed and re-used in the service of the new religion. There is a broad **Perpendicular** window by the blocked C14 n. door, but the others on that side have angular **trefoils** in the heads of 'Y' tracery. There is a n.e. **vestry** and the Perpendicular e. window has five **ogee**-headed ligh.'s. There are interesting **headstops** on the **dripstone** of the chancel s. window and the C14 **priest's door** is in the s. aisle wall. Within the **porch**, there is a fine C14 doorway, with pairs of shafts set within a broad moulding under close-coupled ring **capitals**.

The C19 **reredos** has been relegated to a spot just inside, and beyond there is a **font** of the same vintage but in C15 style. The lovely C14 **arcades** match the doorway, and the **quatrefoil piers** have intermediate plain shafts. The steep chancel arch, however, with its plain chamfers fading into the **imposts**, is likely to be slightly earlier. There is a tall **clerestory**, with three windows a side and a small one over the chancel. The **nave roof** was repaired and stained as part of the C19 restoration and the angels on the alternate **hammerbeams** have had their heads and wings replaced. This may have been the work of **Henry Ringham**, who provided the excellent range of benches below. There are **embattled collars** with short **king-posts** below the ridge of the roof and the braces at the e. end are painted as a **celure** for the vanished **rood**. By the s. door there is a generously proportioned tablet for Metcalfe Russell who died in 1785, and above it, a large draped urn stands against a black obelisk. This is undoubtedly the work of a London sculptor and there is a graceful epitaph provided by his 'natural and elected heir Michael Collinson' – a deliciously ambiguous phrase on which to ponder. At the e. end of the aisle is a C19 **piscina** in

Gothic style but note that it was placed over an original drain, showing that there was a medieval **altar** nearby. In the n. aisle there is another but this time it is the original, beautifully proportioned and matching the arcades. There are seven C15 bench ends with **poppyheads** incorporated in the choir stalls and they were used by Ringham as his models for the rest of the seating. In the **sanctuary** the C14 piscina arch has pierced tracery which matches the aisle windows, and on the n. wall there is a large monument for Elizabeth Bull who died in 1634. Her kneeling figure is dressed in a long black cloak and two stiffly posed angels draw curtains aside. Pairs of shields and obelisks adorn the cornice and much of the original colour remains. A similar design is used for Edward Lambe's monument at East Bergholt and, as they were relatives, one mason may have carved both. The tablet alongside commemorates Lieut. William Collinson of the 37th Bengal Native Infantry who fell in action on 13 January 1840 (unless he survived to die again on 30 January as the omnibus family memorial above has it). The door to the vestry has small, angled headstops, and there is a **squint** to the e. of it which shows that it was originally a chapel. A small stone in the chancel floor records that Joseph Waite the rector died in 1670, but the **touchstone** tablet on the s. wall is a neatly amusing memorial for the same man. Engraved with the **Chi Rho** symbol, and a winged hour-glass on a skull, it carries the text 'Behold I come' (Revelation 16: 15); below is engraved 'I. Waite' (Job 14: 14), taking advantage of the fact that Js were always printed as Is in those days.

The church has an extensive array of modern glass, and apart from two windows, all of it was installed by Gibbs, the prolific firm of London glaziers, during the 1860s restoration. The e. window displays a varied colour range and the centre panel has Christ holding a chalice and wearing a rich purple robe; there are separate panels for each of the twelve apostles (it was probably a later repair that gave **St Philip** two left feet!). The chancel chapel s. window has glass by **Ward & Hughes** of 1881 which is a sentimental and terribly insipid version of the **three Marys** at the tomb. For better things, move to the n. aisle where there is a fine **St Christopher** window. The central figure, in dark, sombre colours and grainy texture, is by **Christopher Whall** and was installed in the year of his death. He had used the design in a church elsewhere, and his daughter Veronica combined it with four vignettes of her own to provide an integrated composition.

Stoke Ash, All Saints (B4): A neatly kept church clearly visible across a field to the e. of the A140. The bell openings of the C14 tower have **Decorated tracery**, there is a later w. window, and a substantial stair turret rises on the s. Walking round, note the flint pebbles lying in courses in the n. wall, and the round arches of the low, blocked **nave** door and **priest's door** in the **chancel** - all showing that the church was begun in the **Norman** period. The three-**light** nave window has pleasing Decorated tracery with four petals within a circle and **mouchettes** either side. The e. window is a C19 replacement and there are tall, thin **Perpendicular** windows to the s. **Flushwork** diamond crosses are worked on two nave buttresses and may have been **consecration crosses** although their high position is unusual. The homely late C15 brick **porch** has a niche over the outer arch and there is the vestige of a **stoup** by the inner door. The windows in Decorated style were probably inserted when **R.M. Phipson** carried out a big restoration in 1868. The Norman inner doorway is entirely plain and is only 6ft high and 3ft 6in. wide.

Phipson stripped out plaster ceilings to reveal a **scissors-braced roof**, with heavier **arch-braces** in the chancel coming well down the walls; the benches are to his design and the stalls in the chancel incorporate fine medieval **poppyheads**. The tower arch is tall and thin and at the base stands the crown of a bell, affording an opportunity to examine a medieval founder's work at close quarters. It was cast at the earliest foundry that has been traced in Bury St Edmunds, between 1460 and 1480. The inscription was applied upside down and on that account it may have been one of the unknown craftsman's first efforts. The wording is apparently unique for a bell: 'Credo in Deum Patrem omni potentem' (I believe in God the Father Almighty). Over the s. door hangs a very dark set of **Hanoverian Royal Arms**, re-labelled for William IV in 1836; they are painted on board and have a pedimented top. There is now no chancel arch or **screen** but the stairs which led to the **rood loft** rise within the window embrasure on the n. side. The early C17 pulpit close by has the familiar pattern of blind arches in the panels and although the carving is shallow, it is lively, with bird beak forms in the scrolls; the lower panels are renewals. The little priest's door lies within a much larger and later pointed arch (puzzling) and in the n. wall of the **sanctuary** there is a plain and fairly large recess. Its depth suggests that it was an **aumbry** but it has chamfered edges and is therefore unlikely to have had a door - perhaps an **Easter sepulchre**? The **decalogue** is painted on C19 zinc plates on the e. wall and, without its drain, the **piscina** recess is now meaningless. In the window alongside there are C15 glass fragments but a single hand in one place and a book in another are all that mean very much. The 1750s **ledger-stone** of Elizabeth Bedingfield lies before the priest's door and it is a pity that the Victorian sanctuary floor cuts short her epitaph: 'She was taken away lest wickedness should alter her understanding or deceit beguile her ...'. Completion of it might form the basis for a cosy competition in one of the more cultivated journals.

Stoke by Nayland, St Mary (C10): In one of Constable's loveliest pictures this grand church gleams atmospherically below a rainbow, standing proudly on the hill. Garden land falls sharply away from the broad sweep of gravel on the s. side which leads to the main village street and the combination of half-timbered houses, **lych-gate**, and mighty tower when viewed from the w. is irresistible. To all intents and purposes the church was rebuilt in the C15 – the **nave** and **chancel** were probably completed by 1440, the tower by 1470. And it is the tower which sticks in the mind. There seems to have been a local burst of enthusiasm for towers with corner turrets (one thinks of Eye, Redenhall, and Bungay particularly) but here the material is brick except for the **base couse** and the pinnacled parapet. A further difference is the most unusual addition of diagonal buttresses to the octagonal turrets, and at each of the four stages they are enriched with two niches under nodding **ogee** canopies. The w. facade is particularly impressive, with a broad band of grinning lion masks in the moulding of the doorway and fearsome devil **headstops** from which rise triangular shafts supporting seated beasts. Shields of the Howard and Tendring families show who paid for the work, and the arch is **crocketted** with a **finial** – a motif repeated in the four-**light** window above. The large belfry windows and the bell openings above them are set within wide, sloping embrasures. There is a low, early C16 brick n. **porch** with blind **arcading** below the battlements and the tall **clerestory** has square-headed two-light windows which were replaced as part of an extensive restoration in 1865. There is a faint **scratch dial** to be found e. of the **priest's door** and a rather better example on a s. **aisle** buttress. The wide s. porch has windows with **Decorated** tracery and formed part of the early C14 building. Restored in 1870, it has an upper room with a turret stair tucked in the corner to the w. and there are **bosses** on the

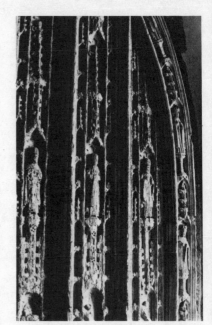

Stoke by Nayland, St Mary: s. door

centre line of the vaulting within (the innermost could be an **Annunciation**. The lovely C15 doors are perhaps the finest in the county – silvery grey, with much of their intricate detail intact. Each has three narrow panels and, in the upper half, eight figures stand within canopied niches. Another twelve fill the niches in the border and if the worn figure carved at the top of the centre spine is the **Blessed Virgin**, the whole design may be identified as a **Jesse tree**. On that assumption, the figure top l. with a harp would be King David.

Within, the impression of spaciousness and height is sharpened by the incredibly elongated tower arch reaching to the **roof**. At its foot the base course decorated with shields in **foiled** circles reappears , and the high w. window seems almost lost in the vastness. It is filled with the rich, dark colours of 1860s glass by the **O'Connors**

– figures of Faith, Hope, Mercy, and Charity below the four Evangelists, all standing in front of drapes. The superb **piers** of the nave arcades, with their tall bases, have eight miniature shafts, all with enriched **capitals**, and the **hood moulds** come down to headstops. Above the line of arches is a **string course** carved with demi-angels and **paterae**, and the **wall posts** of the almost flat roof rest on stone **corbels**. Most of these were replaced in 1865 but eight at the w. end are original and it is worth using binoculars to study the **pelican in her piety** on the s. and what I take to be the ram caught in a thicket on the n. (the sacrifice of Isaac). The w. area has been cleared of benches and provides a generous setting for the fine C15 **font**. Its substantial base is stepped and four platforms project in the form of a cross, with shields set below them – w., the Howard/Tendring arms, s., cross of **St George**, n., **sacred monogram**, and e., the Sun in Splendour badge of Edward IV – which gives us a date 1461-83. The short stem has nodding ogee arches reaching up to a sloping band of demi-angels, and apart from the conventional **Evangelistic symbols** and an angel, the bowl panels are carved with three mysterious figures – s.w., a woman in a cowled head-dress bearing a scroll, with a tree or bush to the r., s.e., a man with a sack on his shoulder pointing to a volume standing on a bookcase with a staff resting against it, n.e., a man with a scroll by a lectern. What can they be? At the w. end of the s. aisle there is a range of late C14 stalls, all of which had **misericords**, and there are two more single stalls – one in each aisle. The large and rather murky **Hanoverian Royal Arms** over the s. door were updated by adding Queen Victoria's initials.

A small chapel dedicated to **St Edmund** opens off the n. aisle and was a **chantry** established by John de Peyton or Peydone around 1318. Its windows were replaced as part of the great C15 rebuilding but its position seems to indicate that the original church was as large as its successor. There is now no **rood screen** but the chapels that flank the chancel have matching screens to the w. which **Cautley** thought were not in their original position; dating from the C15, their delicate ogee arches are **cusped** and crocketted. The pulpit was part of the 1860s refurbishing and stands on a typical stone and marble base, but the oak lectern is much better – a shaft in **Early English** style carrying a muscular eagle with strongly curving neck and head. The clerestory stops short partway along the chancel and the **sanctuary** is lit by tall side windows. Its floor is paved with black and white marble that is probably C18 and there were **communion rails** along the frontage e. of the present set. The stalls on either side are interesting because their backs were once part of the original rood screen. The tracery retains some of its colour and there were painted figures originally; ends with half **poppyheads** were added and the desks in front have wide ledges, traceried fronts, and poppyheads. The tall C14 **piscina** has a cusped ogee arch but the canopy has been hacked away. The chancel roof seems to be all C19 and the elaborate marble and stone **reredos** of 1865 is now hidden behind a curtain. Above it, there is more glass by the O'Connors in the e. window – stagily posed figures in a Resurrection scene across the top five lights and a Crucifixion below, with heavily striated skies behind. The glass in the e. windows of the side chapels is more interesting as an example of the work in a totally different style and colour range which was imported from the Continent during the same period. Dated 1868 and 1869, it is by John B. Capronnier and is his only work in the county, although he had many commissions elsewhere, notably in Yorkshire. In the n.e. chapel there is a painterly composition of the Holy Family with **St John the Baptist** as a child and two groups of angels against a classical landscape; in the s.e chapel, the window illustrates the episode of Christ raising the widow's son to life and both designs employ canopies with riotously curly cusps and willowy angels in the upper tracery.

In the n.e. chapel there is a C13 piscina which was evidently re-used; the hood mould continues down to the base and the deeply moulded arch rests on detached shafts with large ring capitals. Partially blocking a window in the n. wall is the tomb of Sir Francis Mannock who died in 1634. The base, with its heavy swags touched with gilt, is identical to one by **Nicholas Stone** elsewhere and this is likely to be his work. The effigy in pink-veined alabaster is in fine condition and there are eight coloured shields grouped round the tablet above; polished columns of **touchstone** carry small, well-carved figures each side and the semi-circular arch above is crowned with a **cartouche** of arms. If Stone was responsible for the monument he may well have provided the **brass** and **ledger-stone** for Sir Francis's wife, Lady Dorothea, which is in the floor towards the chancel. It is an excellent piece which shows her wearing the fashionable calash or voluminous hood, with elaborate lace collar and cuffs on her gown; the 7ft stone is engraved with an architectural niche design that encloses the effigy, the large inscription plate, and a shield of arms. Next to it, all that remains of a 1590 brass commemorating an earlier Sir Francis Mannock and his family are two plates engraved with the figures of his ten children, a Latin epitaph, and two shields.

In the s.e. chapel behind the organ is the impressive brass of Sir William Tendring, the Lord of the Manor, who probably died about 1420. It is set in a stone more than 10ft long which originally lay in front of the **high altar** and it once had canopy, shields, and marginal inscription; the 6ft effigy is a good illustration of the period when chain mail gave way to plate armour and both sword and belt are highly ornamented. He is shown bare-headed, with a forked curly beard, and his helm has what is known as a 'panache' of

feathers as a crest. The lion under his spurred heels is remarkably amiable – which is more than can be said for his wife Katherine's expression. Her brass is nearer the chancel and shows her wearing a cape held by a tasseled cord over a gown whose close-buttoned sleeves reach to her knuckles. Their grandson became the first Duke of Norfolk and his wife, Lady Katherine Howard, has her brass below the chapel e. window. The inscription and three of the shields are lost but it is a fine effigy engraved some eighty years after her death in 1452. That is why she wears a **kennel head-dress** and heraldic mantle of the later period, which must have been impressive when all the inlays were coloured; it is worth noting that she is wearing her rings – something seldom seen on brasses. She and Sir John were forebears of three queens of England – Anne Boleyn, Catherine Howard, and Elizabeth I. The large tomb on the s. side is for a later owner of the manor, Lady Anne Windsor, who died in 1615. In alabaster, with traces of colour, it shows her lying in a voluminous fur-lined cloak caught up and folded over her farthingale; she has a striking hair style of tiny curls above a steep ruff, and two daughters kneel behind her head while her fashionably dressed son kneels at her feet. The elaborate back incorporates a lengthy epitaph, a winged skull crowned with laurel, and a selection of shields. To the w. the small alabaster wall monument is for Lady Anne's mother, Lady Waldegrave, who died in 1600. The e. end of the chapel is crowded with tablets for members of the Rowley family, of which one in the n.e. corner is by **John Bacon the Younger** for Admiral Sir William Rowley (1768) and Vice-Admiral Sir Joshua Rowley (1790); it has a sarcophagus topped by draped flags, an anchor, and a flaming urn, and two sets of arms in shallow relief on the front. Just in front of the priest's door is an interesting ledger-stone engraved with the figure of a **chrysom child** and on the way out of the churchyard you will pass a Calvary war memorial by W.D. Caröe – a far cry from his pyrotechnics at Elveden [Vol.1].

Stonham Aspal, St Mary and St Lambert (D5): A number of Suffolk churches have C14 towers which also serve as **porches** and this one is distinguished by a unique weatherboarded bell stage crowned by a little cupola and pointed pinnacles. Squire Theodore Eccleston was so keen a ringer that he substituted ten bells for the original five in 1742 and provided a new bell chamber large enough to house them. The **nave** w. window and those in the **aisles** are C14 and much of the **tracery** is attractive. So too is the e. window, but that was part of **E.C. Hakewill's** 1870s restoration. He provided a peculiar **priest's door** on the n. side, which has a steeply gabled porch. Niches flank the e. window and there is a **scratch dial** on the buttress to the l. of the other priest's door in the s. wall, with two more on the next buttress – one of which has a double outer circle. The n. porch is unused now except to house a Victorian **bier**. The most striking feature outside is the **clerestory**, whose windows have **quatrefoils** in the **spandrels** and are separated by traceried buttresses; over them, a line of stepped battlements is decorated with little **flushwork trefoils**, shields, and crosses. Before going in, pause at Anthony Wingfield's tomb just s. of the **chancel**. He died in 1714 and it was sculpted by Francis Bird, a craftsman who had worked under Grinling Gibbons and whose fame rests on his 'Conversion of St Paul' in the great pediment of St Paul's cathedral. There are precious few C18 gentlemen to be found taking their ease so elegantly in a country churchyard.

Within the tower there is a **stoup** recess and one passes through red baize doors into the body of the church. The C13 **font** is an uncommon design in that the bowl panels are shallow trefoil arches outlined with a roll moulding, and it stands on a shaft carved with tracery of the following century. As with the entrance, the early C14 inner arch of the n. door is broad and shallow and above it hangs a dark set of George III **Royal Arms**. Below, the pulpit **tester** of 1616 has been made into a table and to the w. lies the **brass** of John Metcalfe who died in 1606. He was rector here for over thirty years and the 18in. effigy illustrates the preaching gown and scarf of the post-**Reformation** period; it lay originally in the chancel. The **hatchment** over the s. door is for Nathaniel Lee Acton who died in 1836. The **Jacobean** benches at the w. end have rosettes on the **finials** and bands of gouge cuts down the ends, and the main range of benches, though extensively and cleverly restored, has some interesting carvings: 4th from the w. end in the centre is a **basilisk** whose tail is itself a dragon, and on another the wolf guards **St Edmund's** head. There are praying figures too, but what is the one 2nd from the w. on the s. side holding? According to **Cautley** the n. aisle chapel alone rather than the whole church carried the dedication to **St Lambert** and the s. chapel was dedicated to **St Anne**. There you will find a **piscina** with a deeply moulded arch, and the construction of the **arcade** at that end shows clearly how the C15 remodelling of the nave encroached on the C14 aisle. The pulpit is a nice pale golden colour, with strapwork in the top panels above conventional blind arches. It was once a **three-decker** and it is unfortunate that it was separated from its tester when it was dismantled and moved. **Dowsing's** deputies played havoc here in 1643 and smashed most of the stained glass but some of the remains are remarkable. Apart from **Tudor roses** in the e. clerestory windows and shields of arms in the aisles, the slivers of tracery in the e. and w. s. aisle windows contain extraordinary little beasts. Three at the e. end have secondary heads emerging from their bellies and the fourth has a pair of eyes on its

Stonham Aspal, St Mary and St Lambert: Wingfield tomb

rump which, with the tail, form a face; the tail continues under the body to finish with a head just like the basilisk on the bench end. The upper doorway of the **rood loft stair** is on the n. side and the tall **Decorated** windows on that side of the chancel are now unglazed and open into the organ chamber. Hakewill designed a pleasing range of choir stalls for his restored chancel and the traceried panels of the 1907 **reredos** enclose a C17 section behind the **altar**. The latter dates from about 1640 and its turned and carved legs have small volute **capitals** (the top extensions are modern). Overhead, the e. window is filled with excellent 1870s glass by **Lavers, Barraud & Westlake**. Ten panels in good clear colour illustrate scenes from the life of Christ and the figures of **St Peter**, **St Paul**, and the **Evangelists** stand under canopies below. Hakewill provided a large recess in the n. wall for the stone figure of a late C14 Aspal knight. His dress of short tailored doublet and extensive chain mail is unusual and the bosses on

his belt once held jewels. More or less complete to the waist, his head and the remains of his legs were found in the rood loft stair when it was re-opened.

Stowmarket, St Peter and St Mary (B6): For most of its life this church has had a spire which beckoned visitors from every direction. The first decayed in 1674, its successor blew down in 1703, and the third lasted until 1975 when all but the stump had to be dismantled. Hopefully it will rise again. The double dedication is inherited from two separate churches – the C11 St Peter's and a chapel of St Mary which stood a little to the s.e. A will of 1453 talks of 'the new tower', but it has **Decorated tracery** in the belfry windows and tall bell openings. With its heavy buttresses it stands right on the street corner and this probably explains the placing of doors n. and s. which would have allowed processions to circle the building without leaving consecrated ground. Only a small round window pierces the lower w. face and there are three more in the w. wall of the n. **aisle** – strangely placed below a window with Decorated tracery which has **mouchettes** within two large **ogees**, and fanciful shapes in the head. The n. **porch** of the 1440s is faced with simple **flushwork** and the aisle windows continue the Decorated theme, the n.e buttress housing a large niche. The bulky **vestry** n. of the **chancel** was extensively restored in 1986 and its second floor was originally living accommodation for a priest. The 1980s work involved stabilisation and partial rebuilding of the chancel e. wall, whose window contains **reticulated** tracery. The C14 window over the **priest's door** is very attractive and there is more interesting tracery of the period in the s. aisle windows, some of which have been replaced. Flushwork **arcading** at the base of the tall C15 s. porch reaches out across the buttresses and there are diamond chequer patterns higher up. A **stoup** is set by the outer arch, three decayed niches stand in the facade, and a large sundial is set on the gable.

The main entrance is now the tower s. door and recent cleaning and limewashing have made the spacious interior light and fresh. The **sanctusbell window** in the tower is unusually large and its tracery is the same period as the Decorated **nave** arcades (the s. range remodelled a little later). Arches and **piers** lean outwards and above them the broad expanse of wall is pierced by tall C15 **clerestory** windows. The dark wagon **roof** with spindly divisions and **bosses** is part of the work carried out in the 1860s by **R.M. Phipson**, who was so determined to rid the church of its C18 fittings that he destroyed a great deal of value. The C18 spire **finial** and weathervane now rest on the n. aisle w. window ledge and a C13 grave slab is clamped by the s. aisle w. window. In front of it stands a heavy octagonal **font** whose almost flat cover incorporates C15 cresting on the rim salvaged from a **screen**, and uses part of a **poppyhead** as a finial. The font once stood centrally and by the entrance there is a small octagonal section of stone with C14 tracery in its panels that was probably a stoup. Dr

Thomas Young was vicar here 1628-55 but is better known as one of John Milton's tutors. He introduced Milton to Latin poetry and was gratefully remembered in the poet's 4th Latin Elegy. His portrait hangs by the s. porch door, and on the other side there is a small translucent alabaster roundel of the **Blessed Virgin** and Child – probably C19. The s. aisle originally housed the Lady chapel but the **altar reredos** is now a war memorial, the work of Eleanor Gribble. The angels of Self-sacrifice, Fortitude, Victory, and Peace flank a group of the Holy Family with the Magi, and their pale colours are set against a gold ground. Details of wings, jewels, and ornaments are raised in **gesso** and, despite its harking back to the **pre-Raphaelite** style, it is fine work of high quality. A memorial **cartouche** for Charles Blosse (1724) is on the wall to the r. and the pulpit frame, lip, and panel centres are all C15 fragments salvaged from **parclose screens** that were removed in the C19. Most of the seating is pitch pine but two traceried bench ends remain at the e. end of the nave, with a well-preserved lion and monkey on the elbows. The range behind carries two angels which have been varnished and have the feel of modern work.

In the n. aisle wall there is a C14 tomb recess and, close by, an unframed **hatchment** for the Revd Charles Tyrell, the rector of Thurston, who died in 1811. The arms have fierce leopards as supporters – a distinction seldom awarded to commoners. The Tyrell family were Lords of the Manor of Gipping and had their private chapel there, but this was their mortuary. On the wall is the monument for Margaret English of Westminster and her brother and sister, Thomas and Mary Tyrell. A crowded group of little figures kneel in a recess, with Margaret facing eight men and four women. Repainted, they front blind arches containing shields, and gold ribbons decorate the square **pilasters**; a roundel of arms from the top rests in the pew alongside. John de Carle of

Norwich carved the memorial for Edmund Tyrell on the e. wall in 1799 – an urn like an Easter egg traps drapes which lap over the tablet, and the lettering is the firm's usual good quality. Ann Tyrell was only 8 when she died in 1638 and her little shroud **brass** is on the wall here. The large plate below it is engraved with a fine epitaph which begins:

Deare Virgine Child Farewell thy mothers teares

Cannot advance thy Memory . . .

– well worth reading. The entrance to the **rood loft stairs** is to the r. and above it is a large and impressive monument of 1641 to William and Dorothy Tyrell. Their painted alabaster busts turn towards each other and his hand rests on a skull between them; **touchstone Corinthian** columns support a broken **pediment** on which mourning women lie, and below the parents are the figures of the three little children – Penelope kneels in the centre while Mary and the baby (who must have died before baptism) lie folded in gold-fringed shawls on scrolled couches.

The last bay of the n. arcade contains a tomb whose top is now at floor level but which was once just below the canopy. The brasses were probably torn up when **Dowsing** visited in 1643 but the indents show that there was a 3ft image surrounded by twelve 7in. figures and three shields, and it is likely to have been for Lady Margaret Tyrell, who died in the early C15. The ogee arches of the canopy are **crocketted** and panelled with **quatre-foils** and there is a crouching lion **corbel** to the e. with the remains of a dragon to the w.; **spandrels** on both faces are carved with **sacred monograms** and 'MRs' for the Blessed Virgin. The top of the rood stair is e. of the chancel arch and below it is a tablet by Robert Brown of London for Samuel Hollingsworth, C19 vicar and local historian. There is now no chancel screen but the stalls at the w. end have C15 panelled ends displaying a ram on the n. and a hound on the s. The late C15 door to the vestry has **linen-fold**

panelling and a folded leaf border, while above it Vicar Richard Shute's tablet of 1686 has fat flanking scrolls and a broken pediment and cartouche of arms. Dowsing broke much medieval glass in 1643 and the parish had to pay out 16 shillings the following year for re-glazing. Then in 1875 the great Stowmarket gun cotton explosion blew in the e. window and the glass was replaced by Camms of Birmingham. The main **lights** contain quite good figures of Christ flanked by the **Evangelists**, their symbols below, and Our Lord in Majesty within the centre tracery. The s. window glass of 1878 is by **Clayton & Bell** – six attractive Passion scenes in C13 style under sharp, crocketted gables. The high altar and reredos are typically solid designs by **Cautley** in the C15 idiom, well carved by Edward Barnes of Ipswich. Although removed during the 1987 redecoration, a rare example of a wig-stand normally hangs on the chancel wall. Unlike Kedington's [Vol.1], this is in wrought iron with '1675' and 'T.B.' worked in the circular back plate. That stands for Thomas Blackerby who was sheriff of London and Suffolk's high sheriff; you will find his **ledger-stone** just in front of the sanctuary step.

Stowupland, Holy Trinity (C6): Until 1843 the village was regarded as part of Stowmarket, but then a growing population called for a separate parish and that required a new church. It was a time when the demand was for simple buildings in economic materials and the missionary fervour of the **Ecclesiological Society** had not taken hold. In consequence, the architect Thomas Marsh Nelson plumped for Woolpit white bricks and a plain rectangular **nave**, with a token **sanctuary** at the e. end flanked by twin **vestries**. A w. tower with a broach spire sheathed in copper, **lancet** windows throughout, and gabled buttresses were his concessions to popular notions of what a church should look like (even at the time the local press didn't think that he had quite mastered the **Early English** style!). The n.e. vestry door now leads to a small church hall completed in 1985; extending eastward, the design by Alan Noble uses window shapes and materials which blend successfully with the original.

There are stairs in the base of the tower which lead to a **gallery** resting on **quatrefoil** cast-iron columns and very shallow braces. The **Royal Arms** of **Hanover** (after 1816) adorn the front and are a handsome iron set in bright colour. To the r. stands a plain C14 **font** which belonged to Creeting, All Saints, a church which was demolished in 1801. By 1843 the stem was being used as a birdbath in Ringshall rectory garden but, united with its bowl once more, it was presented to Stowupland and used within a week of the consecration. The rear benches are part of the original furniture but the rest were designed by **Cautley** in the 1950s, as were the three ranks of choir stalls. Behind these, the wall panelling has cresting, **paterae**, and inset **tracery** panels, with an incised inscription picked out in blue. The corners of the square-topped ends are cut back to take sweet little cherub heads and the panelled, pierced fronts match the **communion rails** – a solid, typical Cautley design immaculately crafted by Edward Barnes.

The base and stem of the pulpit return to the wall in precisely the same way as Battisford's but its panels and the exuberant caryatids at the angles are unlike anything to be found elsewhere in the county. How they came to the church is unknown but the work is probably Flemish late C16. The panels are carved with bas relief scenes set within scrolls and some match incidents in the life of Christ. From the n.: the Holy Family; the Circumcision; a figure holding a cross and book that has been called **St John the Baptist** but which is demonstrably female; a group which could be the visit of the wise men except that there are only two; and on the door, a puzzling tableau of a woman proffering a child, with an elderly man at the back, while a third figure kneels and touches a vase – presentation of Christ in the Temple? The village war memorial takes the form of a painted board by the **sanctuary** arch, with the names excellently lettered on a natural wood insert. Its small **tympanum** contains a bas relief of two angels supporting a stone: 'They held their lives dear' and I believe it to be the work of Ellen Mary Rope (1885-1934), who sculpted the Nativity panel in Bury St Edmunds All Saints [Vol.1]. It is a pity that the lettering of the World War II panel is less than professional. There are doors to both vestries in the e. wall and beyond the tall arch the prevailing lancet shape is used again for pairs of **Commandment boards**. The **altar** was made by John Pamment of Norton in 1982 and the shaped, carved skirt in yew blends very uneasily with the thick oak slab and trestle frame. Before leaving, try to fathom the symbolism of the carving on the large 1860s obelisk by the path – a snake coils round a fallen torch and dips its head over the chalice above.

Stradbroke, All Saints (D2): The village sign portrays a famous son of Stradbroke, Robert Grosseteste, the most formidable scholar of his day and the combative bishop of Lincoln whose diocese in the C13 stretched as far as Oxford and Hertfordshire. Despite his clashes with Henry III and the pope, he was a man whose holiness was enlivened by humanity and whose recipe for healthy living was a simple combination of food, sleep, and merriment. The church in which he was baptised was not the present building – even the **font** has been replaced, but the connection is worth recording.

What we see in the spacious churchyard by the village street is a church whose tower, **nave**, and **aisles** are C15, and whose **chancel** was originally C14. Over all lies the hand of **R.M. Phipson**, the architect whose restorations in the 1870s were nothing if not thorough. He was enthusiastically backed by the vicar, Canon John Ryle, a leading Evangelical who went on to be bishop of Liverpool. The tower is impressive, with a strong stair turret rising above the battlements like the one at Hoxne. There is a narrow **base course** of shields in **cusped** squares, the angled buttresses have **flushwork** panels, and there are three **set-offs** emphasised by **string courses**. Canopied niches flank the tall and thin w. window, and the doorway mouldings are enlivened with foliage **paterae** and leopard heads – a reminder of the arms of the De La Poles, who probably financed part of the work. Above the two-**light** bell openings the battlements are panelled in flushwork. The n. **porch** was restored by Phipson, but look for the initials in the doorway **spandrels** which refer to John Pype, who paid for the work in 1489. The chimney which rises from the back may be necessary but it is bald and ugly. Near the aisle wall is the grave of James Chambers who called himself an 'Itinerant Poetaster'. Born in 1748, he was a pedlar with a gift for acrostics and rustic verse, and he was buried here in 1827. The epitaph is notable. The n.e. **vestry** was added in the 1870s and the e. window is a Phipson design of 1878, when the chancel was largely rebuilt. The **tracery** is elaborate and very attractive, with cusps so sharply defined that they look positively prickly. The C14 side windows were re-used and so was the **priest's door**, although the new flint cladding of the s. aisle chapel partially overlaid one of the **headstops**. The high quality of the work by Grimwoods of Weybread and Vines of Eye shows on the s. aisle particularly, and also on the s. porch, which was taken down and rebuilt, using a white facing flint in meticulously **knapped** squares. There are C19 headstops to the inner doorway, but at high level it is flanked by C15 niches.

Passing over an Evangelical doormat ('Guide our feet into the way of peace'), one enters a well-kept and spacious interior. However much the passing of **box pews** and **three-decker pulpit** may

be regretted, I cannot but admire the quality and integrity of Phipson's pews and other furnishings, including a tall tower **screen**. He carefully restored the steep nave **roof** and the **castellated tie-beams** are boldly lettered with texts, with another banding the new chancel arch. **Wall posts** rest on small stone **corbels** carved as angels and the arms of Ryle and his wife are displayed on shields at the e. end of the roof. The **Decorated arcades** are beautifully proportioned, and above them, the **clerestory** is arranged with pairs of windows above each pillar, and singletons at each end. The tower w. window is filled with attractive glass by the **O'Connors** – grisaille patterns with centre panels of lily, rose, and grape. Having seen it, do not neglect the very good photographs below of the church in 1867, 1871, and 1874. The glass in the w. window of the n. aisle is skilful work which was moved from the previous chancel e. window and commemorated Queen Victoria's coronation. It contains several panels of stained and enamelled glass – shields and crests, with an incomplete **Royal Arms** in the centre. The C15 font was moved nearby in the 1870s and much of the stonework was re-cut. It is a typical East Anglian design with **woodwoses** alternating with lions round the shaft, and angels holding shields share the bowl panels with the **Evangelistic symbols**. Anti-clockwise from the n.e. are: **St Matthew**, Norwich diocese, **St Luke**, **Passion emblems**, **St John**, three chalices, **St Mark**, **Trinity emblem**. The beautifully clear inscription cut in the step is particularly interesting because it identifies the donors: 'Johannes Smyth et Joanne Rouse hunc fontem fieri fecerunt' (John Smith and Joan Rouse had this font made). Just by the n. door is a wide niche which by its shape suggests that it framed a **retable** or sculptured group to back an **altar**, possibly for a **guild**. Close to the font under the arcade, the **ledger-stone** of Nathaniel and Lydia Cook has a poignant text. Aged 25, they died within days of each other in 1802 'leaving two children too young to be sencible of their loss'. The benches at the e. of the n. aisle were clearly designed for children, and although it now contains the organ the n. aisle chapel retains its **piscina** and **aumbry**. In the s. aisle is a typical 1890s window by **Clayton & Bell**; Christ is flanked by **St Peter** and **St Andrew**, with three Gospel vignettes below. The upper entrance to the **rood loft** is in the wall nearby, and its position shows that it passed via a **parclose screen** round the chapel to the chancel arch.The s. aisle chapel roof is the only one to retain most of its original timber and a pleasing screen of 1957 separates it from the chancel. Altar frontal and hangings were exquisitely embroidered by John Cowgill, a one-armed priest who retired here and whose golden jubilee in the ministry was celebrated by the re-ordering of the chapel as a Lady chapel.

The side arches of the chancel were part of the 1871 restoration, together with the roof which rests on positively fungoid corbels. The 1878 **reredos**, altar, and pinched layout of the **sanctuary** reflect Ryle's austere taste, and there is a fine display of Minton floor tiles with a portcullis and rose pattern. The piscina is a replacement, but the **dropped-sill sedilia** have original and curiously placed shallow niches each side. The only remains of the late C15 **rood screen** are two panels which are now mounted on the wall above the priest's door. They have been well restored and the painting is above average quality. They portray two seated Old Testament kings, Ahias and Abias, and their golden robes are intricately folded; a fragment of the tracery survives. The 1879 e. window glass is untypical Clayton & Bell, and the design was obviously dictated by the current churchmanship – which makes it all the more interesting. Panels portraying a helm, shield, crown, sword, and breastplate are echoed below by font, lectern, cross, pulpit, and chalice/paten, thus neatly illustrating **St Paul's** message to the Ephesians listing the Christian's spiritual armour. The chancel showpiece is undoubtedly the lavish niche in the n. wall of the sanctuary. Its generous size, intricate canopy, and mock vaulting suggest that it was designed as an **Easter sepulchre** (the **acanthus** carving at the base is Phipson again). Note a Gaffin memorial on the n. wall which is much better than his endless and rather tedious tablets. For Elizabeth White who died in 1840, it has a graceful standing figure leaning on a sarcophagus with palm frond in hand. The epitaph is in English, but a year later her husband, the vicar, must needs have Latin for his tablet below, also by Gaffin. Passing the Phipson pulpit on the way out I was reminded that from it Sir Alfred Munnings once treated a congregation of one, Adrian Bell, to an impromptu sermon on life.

Stratford St Mary, St Mary (D10): The A12 swoops by, and these days travellers catch only a fleeting glimpse of the church standing down by the old road at the Ipswich end of the village. The building has seen many changes over the years, and the first major alteration came in the C15 when the **nave** was rebuilt and a s. **aisle** was added which ran the full length of the building. A n. aisle was built late in the century, a n.e. chapel followed in 1530, and the n. **porch** in 1532. There things rested until the 1870s when a full-scale restoration and rebuilding was put in hand under the direction of Henry Woodyer, a Guildford architect. He rebuilt the upper stage of the tower and added a rather eccentric stair turret that projects on the n.w. corner. The remainder of the tower was encased in flint to match the rest of the church, and the initials of the rector who financed the work and those of his wife can be seen alongside the w. bell opening. The whole of the s. aisle was rebuilt and the new windows in the side wall have rather wilful and untraditional **tracery**. The e. wall of the **chancel** and all the **clerestory** were also dismantled and rebuilt. Despite this new work it is important to study the church from the outside, and the n. frontage in particular. The n. aisle was built by Thomas Mors, a prosperous clothier, and it displays an extraordinary range of inscriptions and devices. By the 1870s they were damaged and fragmentary but the restoration was carried out judiciously. The **base course** inscription (interrupted by the later porch) reads: 'Orate pro animabus Thome Mors et Margarete uxoris ejus qui istam alam ffieri fecerunt anno dni mccccxviiii' (Pray for the souls of Thomas Mors and Margaret his wife who had this aisle built in 1499). There are **sacred monograms**, Mors's merchant's mark, and a crowned 'T' and 'M' with the letters 'P.B.A.E.S.'. These stand for 'Propitiemini beati ad eternam salutem' (Be propitious, ye blessed to eternal salvation), addressed to the donors' patron saints **St Thomas** and **St Margaret**. Halfway up you will see all the letters of the alphabet in an **ashlar** band that stretches across wall and buttresses. This is a unique survival and, bearing in mind that it is close to the roadside, it is probably connected with a breviary ritual used by devout travellers in the Middle Ages. When they could not pause for services they were enjoined to say the Lord's Prayer and an Ave Maria, followed by the letters of the alphabet and this prayer:

> O God, who out of twenty-six letters didst will that all the sacred scriptures of this breviary should be composed, join, disjoin and accept out of these twenty-six letters, mattins with lauds, prime, terce, sext, none, vespers and compline, through Christ Our Lord, Amen.

Farther up there is a sacred monogram with 'est amor meus' (Jesus is my love), although the last word is now round the corner on the w. wall. Mors's son added the n.e. chapel specifically to match the layout on the other side of the church, and the base course inscription reads: 'Praye for the soullys of Edward Mors and Alys hys wyfe and all crysten sowlys Anno Domini 1530'. Note how the use of flint had changed between the building of the aisle and its chapel – the stones of the latter are squared and much more regular. The n. porch is the replacement built in 1532. Margaret Mors had left money for it but it bears the initials and merchant's mark of another clothier, John Smith. It extends right to the roadside and the frontage is blind panelled to the full height each side of the entrance. There is a central canopied niche and small shields decorate the parapet; the tracery of the side windows was inserted in the C19.

The interior is spacious, and the arches of the tall **arcades** have a vestigial **ogee** shape at the top. Shafts continue up on each side of the large clerestory windows, and the low-pitched nave has angels bearing scrolls in pairs along the ridge, carved by a Mr Vinnell as part of the restoration. A large w. **gallery** was removed in 1850 and the painted decoration on the smaller version in the tower arch is relatively modern. The bassoon that hangs on the wall nearby is a reminder that, like many another, the church had its own little orchestra in the C18 and early C19. The **font** below is an extraordinary confection of 1858 in stone and coloured marbles, with delicately carved little tableaux that have suffered some damage in the bowl roundels. The few remnants of the church's medieval glass were rearranged in the n. aisle w. window. There is a nice figure of **St Jude** with his ship in a centre panel, and two dark and discoloured C14 shields (one of the Black Prince's arms, the other of the De La Pole family). The little roundels at the top of the side **lights** contain sets of Thomas Mors's merchant's mark and initials, and the six headless figures with scrolls in the tracery seem to be Old Testament characters. The Mors family were buried as they directed in their new aisle, and the grave slabs bereft of their **brasses** must be theirs. Only two of the church's brasses have survived, and one is hidden under the nave carpet – a simple inscription for William Smithe who died in 1586, the son or grandson of the porch donor. The other, of 1558, commemorates Edward and Elizabeth Crane and is mounted on a board on the n. aisle wall. He wears a fur-trimmed gown, and it is noticeable that the 20in. figures show no signs of wear at all and can never have been walked over. They probably formed part of a wall monument. John Constable made a watercolour sketch of the church in 1798, and a reproduction is displayed by the entrance. An engraving of 1848 hangs on the s. aisle wall, and together they show what the building looked like before Woodyer's restoration. One can but wish that he had left the tower alone.

The s. aisle chapel has modern **parclose screens** but there are fragments of the original **rood screen** tracery fixed to the wall just inside the entrance. The chapel **altar** is a time-worn **Jacobean** table with coarsely turned legs which have shallow carving to match the top rails. In the corner lies an early C14 grave slab with a raised cross of Lorraine on the top, and above it there is an elaborate C19 gabled recess in the wall. The tall stone pulpit in **Perpendicular** style is a good Woodyer piece and he donated the alabaster panels between the many buttresses. His too is the chancel arch, with its purple marble triple shafts. The n.e. chapel now serves as an organ chamber and **vestry**, and although the builders matched the dimensions of the s. aisle chapel, you will see that the two arcades do not match exactly. The **piscina** with its large drain lies under an ogee arch, and on the other side of the **sanctuary** the C19 **credence shelf** is a copy of the one in All Souls' chapel, Oxford. The e. window is a memorial to Henry Palmer, the rector who restored the church, and the glass of 1898 is an excellent example of **Powell's** work. Encased in **tabernacle work**, the four scenes from l. to r. are: the **Annunciation**, the visit of the wise

men, Christ's presentation in the Temple, and His being found there by His parents. The spaces below are filled with sprays of vine against red and green grounds, and angels hold shields with **Passion emblems** in the tracery. The Black Prince's shield has been repeated at the top and is matched by the arms of Queen Victoria. There is an interesting variation in decoration on the wall above the chancel n. arcade. Three large scenes are painted on canvas and portray: King Melchizedek offering Abraham bread and wine (Genesis 14: 8), Moses striking the rock for water at Massah (Exodus 17: 1), and the supper at Emmaus (Luke 24: 30). They date from the early years of this century and were apparently painted either by the rector of the day or one of his family.

Stuston, All Saints (B2): The church stands secluded at the end of a green lane with the old rectory nearby, and the outside is trim and neat – due in large measure to the wholesale restoration, rebuilding, and extension that took place in the 1860s and 1870s. Apart from the C14 octagonal belfry stage, the round tower has few distinguishing features but could possibly be **Saxon**, with its plain pointed arch within.

There is an unmutilated **stoup** in the s. **porch**, and note that the socket for the old drawbar of the door emerges in the window embrasure to the w. The n. porch was converted into a **vestry** with a window inserted in the outer arch, and both n. and s. inner doors are in medieval lapped boards. There is a plain C14 octagonal **font**, and plaster has been removed to reveal arches in narrow red bricks over the windows on the n. side of the **nave**. They can be seen again round the upper opening of the **rood stair** which climbs steeply within the wall farther along. The wagon **roof** and pews are C19 and the octagonal pulpit in C14 style was made by a Revd Braham Johnson (one of a number of Suffolk parsons who were gifted amateur woodworkers). To the s. of the **chancel** step there is a **piscina** with a small, plain image niche in the window embrasure nearby – a sure sign that there was a nave **altar** although there is now no chancel **screen**. The Victorian restoration included a new chancel arch, and the contemporary partiality for multi-coloured brick was seized with rather more enthusiasm than taste. There are bands of pink, yellow, and black, and the same brash theme is repeated in the arches of the 1860s n. chapel, chancel windows, and **priest's door**. The e. window glass by **Heaton, Butler & Bayne** is of the same period and is a fine example of their early work, using clear colours and bold design – hieratic figures of **St Peter** and **St Paul** flanking Christ with a lamb in his arms, and an **Agnus Dei** and **pelican** in the upper **lights**. On the n. side of the **sanctuary** is the monument to Sir John Castleton and his wife Bridget. He died in 1727 and their well-modelled busts stand on a ledge above the large inscription panel, he in full wig and she in décolleté gown; their three young children are portrayed in bas relief roundels and the architectural frame is in mottled grey marble, with two flaming urns and coloured **cartouche** of arms completing the design.

Swilland, St Mary (E6): Pevsner called the top of the tower 'an extraordinary Victorian contraption' and did not at all approve, but I find it beguiling and would miss its half-timbered eccentricity, all those gables, dormers, and the perky lantern. It was designed in 1897 by John Corder, the architect who rebuilt Hepworth [Vol.1] in much more conservative fashion the following year. Below it, the tower is in C16 brick with diamond patterns in darker colour, and the sturdy stair turret has a little window at the top shaped like a slanting oriental eye. There are small eroded shields carved with initials in the **spandrels** of the w. doorway, and on the door itself one can just trace the

outline of **linen-fold panelling** that has been worn away by the weather. A brick and tile shed has been tacked onto the w. wall and part of the blocked n. doorway peeps out from behind it. There are C13 **lancets** in the **nave**, together with a single **Decorated** window on the s. side, and the **roof** continues uninterrupted over the **chancel** which was shortened in the C19 and given a new brick e. wall. Note that a blocked **low side window** is still set in the s. wall, and to its l. there is a **scratch dial** on the s.e. corner of the nave. The light-weight glazed wooden **porch** protects a **Norman** s. doorway which looks as though it lost its flanking shafts early on. The clue is that a section was cut out some time in the Middle Ages so that a **stoup** could be added. That too has gone, but it is very interesting that below it there is the original scratch dial which was replaced by another to the r. when the stoup got in the way. The outer rim of arch decoration is largely replacement, but within it is a thick **chevron**, a deep channel moulding, and a double band of diaper work. There are scalloped **capitals** but the **tympanum** has been filled with plain brick.

The neatly kept interior lies under a **false hammerbeam, arch-braced** roof which has **embattled** collars, **king-posts**, and a **tie-beam** at the w. end. This is matched by another at the chancel entrance which probably served as a **rood beam**. The Victorians covered the plain C14 **font** with painted patterns and texts which are now fading away and they provided the cover. The oak benches with **poppyheads** date from the same period, and their solid competence makes me wonder whether **Ringham** was responsible. The contemporary glass in the nave windows is quite pleasing, featuring the **Blessed Virgin, St Felix, St Edmund**, and **St Richard** (an unusual choice dictated by the name of the vicar commemorated). The last is possibly by **Clayton & Bell** and shows the saintly bishop richly vested. The **Royal Arms** of Queen Anne that are framed

Swilland, St Mary: Royal Arms of Queen Anne

on the wall by the organ are undoubtedly the best for their period in Suffolk. Measuring only 27in. by 22in., they are carved in stained lime, pierced and deeply undercut; the detail is exquisite and apart from a little worming the condition is excellent. Nice to have them at eye level. The **Stuart** pulpit has conventional panel work of the period and may well have had a back and **tester** to match originally. A small Russian ikon stands at the centre of the **altar**, and behind it is a fine **reredos** in the **Comper** or **Bodley** manner (although I have not traced the designer). There are twenty small gilt figures of apostles and Evangelists ranged in three ranks about a centre Crucifixion, and the decoration is in muted blue and gold.

Syleham, St Mary (C2): Girt with trees, the church lies secluded in the water meadows close to the Waveney and is almost a mile from its village. It requires some effort to imagine the scene, but apparently the Baron Bigod swore submission to Henry II here in the church in 1174 and surrendered his castles of Framlingham and Bungay. The **nave** roof was replaced in the C19 at a much lower level, but the **chancel** was left alone so that a large bite seems to have been taken from the profile. The plain **Norman** round tower with its coursed flints seems to have earlier work at the base and there is some **long and short work** at the n.w. angle of the nave, both indications that the original church was **Saxon**. The **lancet** bell openings and the **flushwork** panels in the upper stage of the tower may date from the C19 or they may be restored C14 work. The n. doorway is blocked and two of the original lancets of the C13 chancel survive on the n. side. The e. window is a Victorian replacement and those in the nave are **Perpendicular**. Just under the eaves on the s. side there is a plate which reads: 'These leads were repeard. E. Backler churchwarden 1737.' The outer arch of the **porch** is decorated with **fleurons** and crowns, and the inner doorway has plain shields in the mouldings, two that bear arms in the **spandrels**, and the remains of seated lions as **stops**. The C13 plate for the closing ring and the keyhole escutcheon still remain on the door and there is a **stoup** recess to the r.

The tower arch within was remodelled at some time and the nearby **font** is both small and entirely plain – probably C14, but it stands on a base with heavy scrolls at the corners which belonged to a C12 predecessor. The rustic cover is like a small candle-snuffer and is dated 1667. The C13 chest is haphazardly banded with iron and has five locks. C18 **decalogue boards** hang over the n. door, and the nave seating is C19 although there are one or two medieval bench ends in the church. Only the top panels of the C17 pulpit are carved but there was probably more decoration originally. Two tall door shapes in the n. wall close by show where stairs once led to the **rood loft** above the vanished screen, and a **Stuart Holy table** stands against the chancel n. wall. The **communion rails** probably date from the late C17 and have attractive corkscrew **balusters**. C19 restoration raised the floor level of the **sanctuary** so that the wide and plain **piscina** is now low in the wall. Its drain is offset so it probably dates from the late C13 when two drains were briefly in vogue. Set in the floor below is a **brass** inscription for William Fuller who died in 1634 and his wife Anne. In the opposite corner is another, for Anthony and Elizabeth Barry, dating from 1641. There is a nice turn of phrase in the 1730s epitaph for Bridget Lambe and her sister Anne: 'They were two Worthy religious ladies and like

the Wise Virgins in the Gospel had always oil in their lamps.'

Tannington, St Ethelbert (E3): Standing well back in an open churchyard, the building has rather a bald, hard look, with a continuous tiled **roof** over **nave** and **chancel**. The tower has a flint chequer **base course**, and although there is **Perpendicular tracery** in the bell openings the stone **mullions** of the w. window have been replaced by wooden glazing bars. There were once shields in the **spandrels** of the doorway below but they are unidentifiable now. Set in the cement-rendered n. wall of the nave you will find a **Transitional** doorway with a prominent roll moulding in the arch and single shafts (one replaced in wood) with carved **capitals**. Farther along there is a very pretty C14 **lancet** with a pair of **mouchettes** at the top. The intersected 'Y' tracery of the chancel e. window dates it at about 1300, although the side windows are C15 insertions, and a drain-pipe hopper carries the date of the full-scale restoration that took place in 1879. The facade of the attractive C15 **porch** is covered in **flushwork**, with a central niche and large roses in the spandrels of the arch.

A bright, neat interior awaits, and there is a showcase at the back of the nave full of odds and ends of memorabilia, including a village constable's staff of 1779. The bowl of the **font** is the familiar C13 **Purbeck marble** design that must have been produced on a factory basis – a shallow octagon with pairs of blind arches on the slightly canted sides. It rests on a narrow C12 shaft that probably belonged to something else altogether. The nave's wagon **roof** is likely to be C14 and is unusual because it has a boarded **celure** in honour of the **rood** that once stood below. It has been nicely restored in red, white, and gilt, and there are **sacred monograms** and roses painted on the panels. The church's most interesting feature is its series of C15 bench ends in the w. half of the nave. They share the distinction with those at Wilby of including parts of sacraments and sins sequences, and it is more than likely that they were carved by the same craftsman. Despite terrible mutilation, some of their subjects can be recognised. The bench at the w. end on the n. side differs from the rest in having the remains of a seated figure in the top half and an animal below. Very little is left to go on but the cloven hoofs suggest an ox, which means that the saint was probably **St Luke**. Next to the e. you will find the remnants of a Gluttony figure from the **Seven Deadly Sins** sequence, and on the other side of the **poppyhead** is the headless figure of Avarice shovelling coins (as at Wilby). Next are the remaining illustrations of the **Seven Sacraments**, that of the mass (headless priest and deacon behind an altar) and penance (penitent kneeling before the priest, both lacking heads). On the s. side the rear bench has the remains of one figure by the wall and panelled tracery in the back. The 4th bench along has a little scene in which a woman pushes a man through a doorway and could perhaps stand for lust. Beyond it there are two gaping hell's mouth masks facing upwards with the remains of figures in them. **Dowsing** and his deputy came here in April 1643 and although he writes only of breaking pictures I suspect his hand in the damage done to these little carvings. On the s. wall of the nave are the **Royal Arms** of Elizabeth II painted by M. Moore on copper in 1966, and farther along on the stairs to the old **rood loft** rise in a window embrasure. Across on the n. side the nice C14 lancet has vestiges of **headstops** to the **hood mould**, and by the modern pulpit there is a monument by Robert Blore, who was a prolific if rather uninspired sculptor. Complete with affecting verse, it is for Jane Barker (1820) and has a mourning figure in bas relief draped over a sarcophagus, with column and urn on top. Her **hatchment** hangs above. The two-**light** window on the n. side contains glass of 1976 (maker unidentified) in which there

are consciously archaic figures of sower and reaper; birds and animals abound, with church and house in the background, and the general effect is uncomfortably close to a 'painting by numbers' exercise. The monument on the n. wall of the **sanctuary** commemorates Thomas Dade and his relations, 1612-24; in alabaster, its twin panels are flanked by no fewer than twenty coloured shields and there is a coloured **achievement** within the broken **pediment** on top. Those mentioned in the epitaph also have **brasses**, and Anne Dade's 21in. figure is just below wearing a Paris head-dress and ruff. Inscriptions and shields for Thomas and Mary are on the s. side below the simple angle **piscina** of about 1300.

Thorndon, All Saints (C3): The early C14 tower also serves as a s. **porch** and there are heavy buttresses up to a single **set-off** at the second stage. The bell openings have lost their **tracery** and the battlements were renewed in brick. Within the angle by the outer arch there is a **stoup** beneath a worn **trefoil** arch and overhead is a single niche. A steep wooden stair leads up to the belfry and beyond it the inner doorway shows that the tower was stitched on to a **nave** dating from the early C13. Lying within a blank arch matching the entrance, it has a plain chamfered moulding and simple **capitals**. The nave windows, with hoods like a lady's head-dress of the period, have stepped **embattled transoms**, and on walking round you will find a C13 tomb recess in the s. wall hiding behind a C19 table tomb. There is a grave slab in the bottom, and when it was opened in the C18 a coffin was discovered 4ft down. This is likely to be the resting place of Nicholas de Bockland, the C14 builder of the **chancel**. The **priest's door** is flanked by a handsome pair of buttresses and the three stages of recessed **flushwork** panels have **ogee** decoration and small blank shields. There are larger, worn shields lower down and the one on the

l. was carved with the arms of the Earl of Ufford (seen again on the n.w. buttress of the tower). Above the priest's doorway itself, a spacious blank niche with a **finial** is framed in lozenges of red brick. **R.M. Phipson**, architect of Great Finborough [Vol.1], carried out a big restoration here in 1870, and in renewing the **roofs** he added a characteristic conceit in the form of large **crockets** on the chancel ridge. I suspect that the e. window was his too. On the chancel n. side, the thick walls of the large **vestry** are pierced by C13 **lancets** and the blocked n. doorway is a worn version of the main entrance. The w. window had been largely bricked up but in the 1860s it was re-opened and new tracery inserted. Below it, the **Perpendicular** doorway **corbels** are seated, rather benign lions, with crowns and shields set in the moulding. There are damaged shields in the **spandrels** – the one on the r. looks like a **Trinity emblem**.

Within the church there is no division between nave and chancel and the line of Phipson's wagon roof is broken only by an **arch-brace** resting on large demi-angels above the chancel step. By the door stands the C15 **font** of the type so often found in East Anglia – four lions round the shaft, demi-angels at the angles of the bowl, and, in the panels, angels holding blank shields alternating with lions, their tails rampant. They are deeply cut; note that new faces were provided for some of the figures in the C19. One of the pews to the w. has a small brass plate in memory of A.E. Read of Bungay – an ex-chorister who obviously loved his time here: 'This is where I always sat to give my prayers and thanks to God every Sunday. My favourite hymn: "All things bright and beautiful".' A fine 1822 set of George IV **Royal Arms** on canvas hangs in the n. doorway and on the wall to the e. is a **brass** which has been moved from the redundant church at Rishangles. Comprising an inscription and two shields, it is for Edward Grimeston who died in 1599:

By twice two kings and queens his life was gract,
Yet one religion, held from first to last . . .

Opposite, his son's brass reads:
The sonne paied to his fathers parts increase, wittie and wise he was . . .
Wher truth hath writt that envie cannot blott
The name of Grimston cannot be forgott.

A nice thought. The early C17 pulpit, with new book ledge and base, has three ranges of panels – scrolls in the top, blind arches in the centre, and plain with centre bosses below. There is no **screen** but there once was; the **rood loft stairs** remain in the n. wall. The lectern presented by a rector in 1873 is an excellent example of the Victorian woodcarver's ability to reproduce C15 styles. Its double-sided hood top is pierced with lovely tracery and three substantial lions support the triangular base.

The stained glass arranged in the n. chancel window is an interesting mixture. There is an example of a C14 heraldic border displaying the leopards of England and the castles of Castile, a tiny C15 dove of the Holy Spirit in the l. hand **light**, with an angel holding a crown of thorns and a small **St Peter** bottom l. The C16 roundels of Flemish glass portray a Crucifixion and the stripping of Christ, in which the two thieves sit naked and bound, a carpenter bores holes in the cross with an auger, and there is a group of mourners in the background. Against the priest's door is a long, plain chest on which rests a fine Bible box. It has strapwork and leaf designs on the sides, brass lockplates, and a large 'S.B.' with flourishes carved on the lid. On the window ledge nearby stands a C19 brass-bound wooden barrel with handle, and the hoops are engraved: 'One Lord, One Faith, One Baptism'. Presumably for baptismal water, it is unique in my experience. The **sanctuary** was paved with Minton tiles as part of the restoration and their familiar

Evangelistic symbols are set in front of the altar. On the e. wall are painted zinc decalogue panels and Phipson designed the oak reredos. Given by a poet laureate, Robert Bridges, it was carved by Abeloos of Louvain – a three-dimensional Last Supper under a deep, low canopy which is all spiky gables and pinnacles; the two side panels have an Agnus Dei and a pelican carved at the centre of diaper backgrounds. Like the rood stairs, the piscina with an ogee arch and slim side shafts was uncovered during the C19 restoration.

Thornham Magna, St Mary Magdalene (B3): Set just within the park and affording a pleasant view across to the big house, the church stands in a churchyard studded with sentinel evergreens. The C14 tower has a broad and flat e. face, and no window above the w. door, giving it an unusually blank appearance for its size. A stair turret rises to the bell stage on the s. side and the battlements have corner pinnacles. There was an extensive mid-C19 restoration with a number of window replacements, and a vestry was added beyond the old n. door. There is a priest's door in the s. wall of the early C14 chancel and the windows of the Perpendicular nave retain earlier reticulated tracery. The tall C15 s. porch has flushwork panels, large gargoyles, and crocketted ogee niches each side of the entrance; above the arch the principal niche is more elaborate – canopied and groined, with a little mask below the image stool. The plain parapet has short corner pinnacles and note that there are large consecration crosses on the corner buttresses. Similar crosses at Stoke Ash and Wickham Skeith show that this was a local fashion, but these are formed from a pattern of shallow lozenges cut in the ashlar rather than the more common flushwork.

The nave roof is a late hammerbeam and arch-brace design and collars below the ridge have centre bosses, with others split over the main

intersections. Tenons protruding from the ends of the hammerbeams show that they originally carried angel figures. The set of George II Royal Arms high on the w. wall is, I think, painted on canvas but is very dark (it is nice to hear that there is a possibility of its being cleaned and restored). The font is medieval in form but is either a C19 reproduction or entirely re-cut. The church possesses seven hatchments, but in 1987 redecoration was in progress and they were stacked in the vestry. Normally hung in the nave, they commemorate: Elizabeth, 3rd wife of the 2nd Duke of Chandos (post-1803, coronet and otter supporters); Elizabeth Major, wife of the 1st Baronet, died 1780 ('Deus major columna'); her husband John, died 1781 ('In coelo quies'); Emily, wife of 2nd Baron Henniker, died 1819 (baroness's coronet); her husband John, died 1821 ('Deus columna' on an all-black ground); John Minet, 3rd Baron Henniker, died 1832; Mary his wife, died 1837 (stag and otter supporters).

One of the most attractive things in the church is the s.w. nave window in memory of Albert Edward Henniker who died in 1902. It is by Morris & Co., from the period when Dearle was running the firm, but the three large figures are unaltered pre-Raphaelite designs by Burne-Jones – two versions of the Blessed Virgin flanking a St John at prayer. Set against drapery backgrounds, the rich colours alternate – blue on red, red on blue, and green on red; green foliage fills the panels below and the heads of the main lights above the drapery, while the tracery quatrefoils contain typical angels. Farther e. on the s. wall is an 1870s window, and stretching across three lights in heavy colour, the picture shows the sorrowing group at the sealed tomb before the first Easter Day. Three other nave windows have bright C19 glass with lots of patterns framing small and undistinguished figures. Most of the furnishings are C19 – pews with excellent poppyheads and paterae on the end chamfers, an over-fussy pulpit

Thornham Magna, St Mary: Morris &
Co. window detail

with openwork reading desk, and a good reproduction of a tall C15 **screen**. The stairs for the original **rood loft** remain in the n. wall. On the s. wall of the nave is a handsome wall monument of 1842 by William Frederick Woodington. He was a successful C19 sculptor and painter, best known for the great bronze relief of the battle of the Nile at the base of Nelson's Column in Trafalgar Square and the panels in St Paul's which combine with Stevens's Wellington Monument. This one is martial too and commemorates the Hon. Major Henniker, who was a captain in the 2nd Life Guards. His

plumed helmet and sword rest on a sarcophagus below an elaborate, draped cloak.

Just beyond the chancel screen on the n. side is a decorative little **cartouche** for Brig. Gen. Robert Killigrew, who fell at Alamanza in 1707 and who in his youth had been a page of honour to Charles II. The C19 roof overhead has perky angels on its short hammerbeams, and in the **sanctuary** is a fine **Decorated angle piscina**. The slim side columns have ring **capitals** but the quatrefoil corner shaft has foliage; **finials** and tightly curled crockets decorate the **trefoil** ogee arches. Opposite is the lavish memorial to John Henniker Major, Lord Henniker, and his wife Emily. Its sculptor Josephus Kendrick must take the blame for the awful tomb of Sir William Myers in St Paul's but this is one of his more restrained works. Large figures of Hope with her anchor and Piety (or Prudence) with her stork rest negligently against a pedestal carved with the family arms. All is entirely redeemed by the fine profile portrait heads in shallow relief on the large central urn.

If the tower is open, have a look at the peal board which celebrates a long length of Treble Bob Minor rung in just over five hours – and the photograph nearby of 'The ringers what rung the long peal'.

Thornham Parva, St Mary (B3): This is a small church of outstanding interest, beautifully maintained. **Nave** and **chancel** lie under reed thatch which was renewed in the 1970s and the pyramid cap of the little tower is thatched too – a happy conjunction. The tower dates from the 1480s and was probably based on the design at Thorpe Abbots in Norfolk. The masons were Richard Cutting and John Mason and although they were sued for defective work it has lasted well enough. As will be seen later, the church was **Saxon** originally and the regular coursing of the flint pebbles in the n. wall is evidence of **Norman** work, as are the doorways. The s. doorway was apparently the main entrance then and its arch, with a roll moulding, rests on single plain shafts and simple **capitals**. Farther e. on that side is a small **lancet** of the same period, followed by a **Decorated** window with curvilinear **tracery**. The **priest's door** on the n. side of the chancel has a sharply pointed arch and dates from about 1300, as do the windows each side of the **sanctuary** – although the e. window has the slightly later **reticulated** tracery.

Entry these days is through a tiny Norman n. doorway – less than 3ft wide and devoid of ornament. The first thing that attracts attention is the extraordinary range of wall paintings whose restoration was begun in 1980. They are rare survivals of no later than mid-C13 and include the most extensive illustration of the legend of **St Edmund** and scenes from the life of Christ. The predominant colour is the familiar dusky red, and one needs in many cases to get as close as possible to appreciate the detail that can still be recognised. The St Edmund sequence is, at least in part, the later story of how the wolf brought the martyr's uncorrupted head to Bury abbey, where the monks reburied it with the skeleton. The most surprising revelation is that what was for a long time taken to be the wheel emblem of **St Catherine** above the n. door actually belongs to a large farm cart, while to its r. are four small figures with a coffin. To the r. of the doorway, in faint but clear outline, is the wolf with a tip-tilted nose, and farther r., four larger monks – slightly pop-eyed and faintly smiling. To their r., two more support the king's head over a skeleton. The paintings on the s. wall were restored in 1984 and the e. section is probably part of the St Edmund sequence – a seated queen with a boy king in her lap reading a book, a man possibly offering a basket, and the head of another figure. In the first scene on the w. section, the angel visits two shepherds who stand with their sheep on a green hill. Above and to the w. of the

doorway is the Nativity, the head and neck of an ox peering out above the swaddled Christ child. The ass is to the l. but difficult to see. The picture of the **Blessed Virgin** and **St Elizabeth** embracing at the **Visitation** is by the end of the **gallery**. Below each panel there was a chevron border and a masonry pattern decorated with red and white roses, while scroll borders were added above and below, interrupted by **consecration crosses**, of which four can still be seen. The bow-fronted C18 gallery rests on two slim iron columns; access is via the r. hand door to the tower and it should not be overlooked. The neat stair is the same period and on a platform beyond the first short flight stands the **tester** of the church's early C17 pulpit. There are two levels of seats in the gallery; note how sections fold over both the outer door and the inner screen when they are closed in a neat arrangement that provides maximum seating (a similar thought occurred to the designer of Battisford's gallery). Once aloft, the wall paintings can be seen to advantage, particularly the heads of St Mary and St Elizabeth. The round window with its deep splay high in the w. wall is the best evidence of the church's Saxon beginnings, and either side hang **Commandment** and Lord's Prayer boards.

The early C14 **font** is simple but it is interesting that its bowl panels repeat some of the tracery shapes to be seen in the church. In the lower panels of the nearest nave s. window there is a memorial to Lady Osla Henniker-Major, who died in 1974, by Laurence Whistler, renowned for his engraving on domestic and celebratory glass. Birth and death dates are placed in the centre of a flower design and the second roundel displays a typically idealised Whistler landscape framed in delicate fronds of seeded grass or oats, within a finely lettered quotation from Shakespeare's 33rd sonnet:

Full many a glorious morning have I seen

Flatter the mountain tops with sovereign eye.

Thornham Parva, St Mary: C14 retable detail

The single Norman lancet is close by, with moulded **jambs** to the deep splay. The low pulpit is all C19 work or later but above it, note the plastered stumps in the n. wall which are the remains of the **rood loft** floor beam and the **rood beam** itself. The square-headed early C15 **screen**, with its wide unadorned lower panels, has been extensively but sympathetically restored and once through it, one's eye immediately focuses on the church's prime treasure – a **retable** whose high quality and remarkable condition is outstanding. It dates from the first twenty years of the C14 and mirrors the style of the East Anglian school of manuscript illuminators. In a highly sophisticated composition, eight figures flank a Crucifixion, and apart from the outer pair, their stance and draperies undulate langorously. From l. to r. they are: **St Dominic**, St Catherine, **St John the Baptist, St Paul**, the Blessed Virgin, Christ, **St John, St Peter**, St Edmund, **St Margaret**, and **St Peter Martyr**. Apart from the cleaver set in his skull which is his normal attribute, St Peter Martyr has a great wound in his chest, and St Margaret's horrid red-eyed dragon is pushed down at her feet; the Baptist holds a large roundel with an **Agnus Dei** against a red ground. The patterned background of each panel is the best example of **gesso** work in the county; five panels are all gold and the rest are a chequerboard, with fleur de lys on the black squares. The designs impressed in the gesso vary – the lozenges behind St Peter and St Margaret have pairs of birds, St Paul has rampant lions, the Baptist has Agnus Deis, and the two outer figures are set against **quatrefoils** embossed with spread eagles. The frame is contemporary with the painting and in equally good condition; the **trefoil** arches rest on half-round columns painted in alternate sections of red and green, decorated with small fleur de lys and roses, while roses and oak leaves fill the **spandrels**. The history of the retable is curious. It was discovered in 1927, having come from Rookery farm, Stradbroke, owned by the Fox family in the C18. They were Catholics and had bought it in a sale. The combination of St Dominic and the Dominican friar St Peter Martyr suggests that it once belonged to a house of that order – perhaps Ipswich, Sudbury, or Dunwich. The C17 panels below the retable are the right size to have come from the pulpit whose tester lies in the tower. In the n.e. corner of the **sanctuary** stands a plain C14 chest, with wagon top and broad iron bands, and by the priest's door a Bible of 1640 is well displayed.

Before leaving, visit the grave of Sir Basil Spence, O.M., architect of Coventry cathedral. It lies s.e. of the chancel and the two massive slabs are incised with a series of lines and arcs, as though a trace had been taken from his drawing board.

Thrandeston, St Margaret (B3): The tower is handsome, with well-defined **drip courses** and **crocketted** pinnacles at the corners of the battlements. The bell openings have stepped **transoms** and the one on the n. side is offset to make room for the stair turret. Three shields are carved below the w. win-

dow – one with the Cornwallis arms and another with 'Sulyard' on the label. The C13 **chancel** has later **Perpendicular** windows and the **vestry** alongside has a tiny window high in the n. wall which suggests that it originally had an upper room.

Entry is via a large s. **porch** and you will find a **scratch dial** on the e. buttress which has been moved so that it now faces s.w. Within, there is a four-bay **nave arcade** with octagonal **piers** below a Perpendicular **clerestory**, and the **roof wall posts** rest on stone **corbels** carved with large heads that look more like C19 work than C15. The **hammerbeams** are hidden by coving decorated with painted shields and **paterae**, and there is a single **tie-beam** halfway along. A poorly painted set of Victorian **Royal Arms** hangs over the chancel arch. The C15 **font** was restored in 1846 and is in nice condition; it has **Evangelistic symbols** and fat **Tudor roses** carved in the panels, there are demi-angels below the bowl, and four dumpy lions support the stem. The crocketted conical cover is of the same period. The nave benches retain their medieval ends adorned with **poppyheads** and the range opposite the door has buttressed ends with crude figures – **St Peter** and a crouching veiled figure on the s., **St John** (identified by the chalice he holds) and a woman on the n. bench. At the e. end of the s. **aisle** is a **piscina** under a **trefoil** arch, and in the n. aisle wall a tall image niche has a crocketted **ogee** arch set around with paterae and houses a modern figure of the Good Shepherd. The nearby window retains a pair of C15 stained glass canopies and some miscellaneous fragments which include some vigorously crowing cocks. Farther along, the **rood stair** has a slit window on the aisle side.

The chancel arch **capitals** are crisply carved with vines and ears of wheat, with a dove nestling on the s. side – all C19 work. The C15 **rood screen** has had its coving chopped away above the capitals of the supporting columns and it is strange how the lower panels are out of step with the divisions above them. Looking e., you will see that here is an extreme example of a **weeping chancel**, with the centre line offset sharply to the s. The C15 choir stalls have handsome applied **tracery** in the heads of the front panels and there are two quite extraordinary female figures carved on the n. side stall ends, with hoods falling in waves to their feet at the back. One has her skirt rucked up to display a knee and holds what may be an owl, while her companion cradles a possible cat. It is tempting to think of them as witches. Two **hatchments** hang on the wall above, the one on the r. being for John and Elizabeth Blakeley, who died in 1810 and 1822 respectively. The other is probably for their son William who died in 1842. They look as though they were painted by the same hand. The church has two medieval **brasses** – a shield and inscription in the chancel floor for Prudence Cuppledicke who died in 1619, and an inscription for Elisabeth Cornewaleys who died in 1537; the latter was returned to the church in 1847 and is now on the chancel s. wall. A little farther to the w. is a brass inscription for Thomas Lee French who died in 1909, having been rector for sixty-four years; he was the last surviving freeman of the borough of Eye. Behind the simple **Stuart holy table** is a lumpish C19 stone **reredos** with the **Agnus Dei** and **pelican** in panels, but it is redeemed by the attractive tiles on the side walls of the **sanctuary**. The vestry door is original and on peeping through you will see that there is now no upper floor.

Thwaite, St George (C4): –This is a tiny church set in a bosky graveyard, with an attractive plank bridge spanning the boundary ditch on the way to the s. **porch**.The bricked-up small n. doorway is plain and, together with the tall **lancet** in the **chancel**, is evidence of the building's late C12 origins. There is **cusped** 'Y' **tracery** of the early C14 in three side windows and the w. win-

dow, with **Decorated reticulated** tracery in the e. window. Two of the **nave** windows have attractive patterns of the same period, with roll mouldings both inside and out. There was a small tower at the n.w. corner but it collapsed early in the C19 and the rubble was used to build the pair of cottages that stand at the entrance to Church Lane. The church's w. wall and much of the chancel was rebuilt in the restorations of 1846 and 1871, and a bellcote was added. With its eaves cutting into the adjacent window, the C16 porch in homely red brick has a tiny sundial over the arch, and its **arch-braced roof** rests on large carved wooden heads. Lolling tongues are familiar features of the period but the face on the e. side here curls his up to his nostrils for a change. It is strange that one of the **jambs** of the little inner doorway has been replaced in wood – the door itself retains one medieval strap hinge with chevron decoration.

The roof of the church is quite elaborate for its size and is an unusual mixture of **hammerbeams** and **tie-beams**. The tie-beam marking the division between nave and chancel no doubt served as a **rood beam**, and the hammerbeams to the w. show clearly the remains of tenons which secured demi-angels. However, four of the beams at the w. end do not, and one can only presume that they originally stretched across the roof space (very odd). The deep **wall plates** and the collars below the ridge are **castellated** and there are three grotesque wooden **corbel** heads each side. The nave benches are gnarled, and in the n.w. corner a tiny **Norman** door no more than 2ft wide once led to the tower. In front of it on a plain shaft stands a late C14 **font**, with window tracery patterns in the bowl panels as at nearby Wickham Skeith. The 1846 w. window is a memorial for Dame Letitia Sheppard and the glass is by the painter-turned-glazier   Charles Clutterbuck. He was, with **Hardman** and the **O'Connors**, one of the artists to begin the Victorian revival of stained glass. Here, in C13 style, lozenge patterns of brilliant green and yellow enclose roundels and pointed ovals containing the figures of Christ and the **Evangelists**, with a dove at the very top. Other examples of Clutterbuck's work can be found at Little Cornard and St Mary's, Bury [Vol.1]. The C15 pulpit on its coved stem is lovely. There is a crest under the lip, and each panel contains a pair of **crocketted ogee** arches with tracery behind them. At the bottom, and below a band of foliage repeats, pierced **quatrefoils** have shields at their centres, and all the angles are adorned with crocketted pinnacles. The surfaces seem to have been filled and it is likely that it was painted originally. At the base lies a **gargoyle** from the old tower which was discovered recently in the wall at the w. end. Opposite is a strange reading desk which, apart from the base and ledge, seems to have begun life as part of an early C17 court cupboard, with **Renaissance** detailing in the panels. The chair behind it is a little older. In the **sanctuary** the **piscina** is unusual only in that it has a square raised lip, while fixed inside the bottom of the e. window is a panel of C15 glass – **St John the Baptist's** head with an **Agnus Dei**. Robert Reve's **ledger- stone** in the n.e. corner of the sanctuary has excellent, slightly idiosyncratic lettering, and his epitaph is precise to the very day about his age at death in 1688.

One should not leave Thwaite without pausing at the cast-iron cross just e. of the chancel that marks the grave of Orlando Whistlecraft, who died aged 83 in 1893. Apart from the delicious euphony of his name, he was that singular phenomenon, a 'weather prophet and poet'. A small fund was raised to enable this Suffolk worthy 'to pass his declining years in a greater degree of comfort than his needy circumstances would permit'. Originator of the enduring and no doubt invaluable *Whistlecraft's Almanac*, he published *The Climate of England* in 1840, a proper acknowledgement of our national obsession with the weather.

Tuddenham, St Martin (E6): It is quite a pull up the street from the bridge over the little River Finn but the effort is rewarded by a nice view over the village roofs from the churchyard. Money was left in the 1450s to build the slim tower and it was well enough thought of locally to be used as the model for the one at Rushmere. **Flushwork** decorates the buttresses and battlements, and although the bell openings have been restored, the lion **stops** and the shields of arms in the **spandrels** of the w. doorway are almost worn away. Coming up from the street, one's eye is taken by the fine **Norman** n. doorway which has bold **chevron moulding** in the outer arch. There are pairs of attached columns and two of them are carved in spiral form. The n.e. **vestry** dates from 1920 and was designed by John Corder, the local architect who gave us that splendidly eccentric belfry at Swilland, but here he only allowed himself decorative barge boards and a band of carving below the gable. The **chancel** e. window dates from 1861 and there is another C19 window in the s. wall. Corder also designed a comely timber s. **porch** for the late C15 s. doorway.

Inside you will find that the tower arch has been blocked above the level of the ringers' **gallery**, which has a stolid front carved by **Henry Ringham** in 1843. Below it, the glazed screen designed by **Cautley** and probably carved by Ernest Barnes is quite lively by contrast. The **font** is one of those that can be dated by the inscription on the step. It is very worn but records that Richard and Agnes Silvester (or it might be Schuster) were the donors in 1443. The carving was aggressively re-cut in the C19 and most of the figures have new heads if nothing more, but the imagery is of more than usual interest. Round the shaft stand priest and deacons vested for the mass, with acolytes between them carrying bread, wine, a book, and a basin. Under the .

bowl there are carvings associated with the church's patron saint – his cloak, and a hand alongside a corpse on a bed which reminds us that he was credited with raising a woman from the dead. The bowl panels contain the **Evangelistic symbols**, three angels, and the kneeling figure of a woman. She probably represents the **Blessed Virgin** at her devotions. There is a tiny angel squeezed into the top l. hand corner of the panel. The **crocketted** pyramid cover with painted and carved texts is Victorian. The **nave** lies under a good C15 **hammerbeam roof** which has a ribbed coving above the **wall plate**, **castellated** collar beams, and **kingposts**; there are mutilated demi-figures at the base of the **wall posts**. In the 1840s the village had its first resident vicar for many years, Mecan Thomas, and he energetically set about reversing the tide of neglect and decay. He secured the services of Henry Ringham, and the nave benches are one of the best examples in the county of that craftsman's skill in saving old work and matching it. It is very difficult to differentiate the one from the other, but you will see that he spliced on new bases for the pew ends, all the standards against the s. wall are his, and the top of the second bench end from the front on the n. side is his. The ends are carved with attractive **tracery**, there are lovely little sinuous beasts on most of the elbows, while others carry preachers in pulpits, **pelicans**, and a cock for **St Peter** on the s. side w. of the font. The church has an interesting and attractive selection of modern glass and the first to look at is in the s.e. nave window. Dating from the early years of the century, it is by Percy Bacon, and the figure of **St Martin** vested as a bishop holding a sword is flanked by **St Edmund** and **St Felix**; there are creamy colours with splashes of rich brocade. Other work by this artist can be found at Coddenham and Haverhill [Vol.1]. Opposite is a window of the early 1920s by Christopher Webb, who was one of **Comper's** pupils. A band of three panels across the centre illustrates the

story of the prodigal son, well drawn and finely coloured. The rest is filled with obscured glass within bird and leaf borders, except for the **Agnus Dei** and **sacred monogram** within **cartouches** and four texts. The stairs that led to the **rood loft** remain in the s. wall, and on the n. side there is a tall smoothed-out niche. This may well have contained a statue of **St John the Baptist** because there was a C14 **guild** dedicated to him here which maintained a chaplain and kept a taper burning before his image. Close by is a lovely late C15 pulpit standing on a modern base. Its panels have crocketted **ogee** arches whose shafts are carved in a curious stepped pattern. There are miniature figures in niches at the angles and the door is formed of one-and-a-bit of the body sides. It probably stood farther away from the wall originally. The n. panel is realistically carved as a door complete with portcullis and lock. Below the plain chancel arch stands a **screen** of 1947 designed by Cautley in his typical style. It made use of timbers from Ashfield and Earl Soham windmills and was carved by Ernest Barnes. The **altar** is from the same hand, but the choir stalls are another example of Ringham's ability to match old with new. The popularity of stained glass in the mid-C19 encouraged expansion in the trade and one of the new generation of glaziers was Frederick Preedy who had worked for George Rogers at Worcester before setting up his own business. He provided the good demi-angels in C14 style in the s. chancel window, set in grey, patterned **quarries** within flower borders. The e. window glass of 1860 with its six brightly coloured panels is also his work and commemorates an East India Company midshipman who died aged 15. The C14 **angle piscina** is at floor level now, and although this was no doubt affected by the introduction of **sanctuary** steps by the Victorians, the original chancel may well have been below the level of the nave. On the n. wall of the sanctuary Richard Keble of

Tuddenham, St Martin: Christopher Webb window detail

Roydon Hall has his memorial of 1653. A large **touchstone** oval lies within a heavy alabaster wreath, and above it is his coloured **achievement of arms** in relief. To the l. is a brass plate recording the dedication of the vestry in 1922 'by the Lord Bishop of Suffolk' (well, we all make mistakes) and beyond there is a tablet for Sydney George Cox who died in 1948. He has his little niche in history as the solicitor who acted for Mrs Simpson in Ipswich crown court prior to the abdication of Edward VIII.

Washbrook, St Mary (E8): This little church is hidden away in a fold of the country, remote from its village, and approached by a sunken winding lane. There is an arch of yew within the gate and the churchyard is exquisitely peaceful. Two small **Norman lancets** in the **nave** walls date its beginnings and at the base of the w. wall of the tower there is a large glacial boulder. As at Bramford and other churches in this area, stones like this were probably used in the foundations to cancel their pagan associations and secure allegiance to the new religion. The tower has a flint chequer **base course** and **Perpendicular** w. window, and in the nave and **chancel** the windows have C14 **Decorated tracery** involving curved **mouchettes**. On the e. wall you will see the outline of a large window that probably matched, but a smaller version was inserted as part of a C19 restoration. At that time a n.e **vestry** was added, a baptistry was built on to the n. door, and the **priest's door** on the s. side of the chancel was replaced. There is a **scratch dial** on the buttress to its l. The Victorian open **porch** shelters a C14 doorway whose **dripstone** has large male and female **headstops**.

Just inside, there is a simple **stoup** recess and an C18 or C19 **bier** rests against the wall beyond the tall and plain tower arch. A decorative set of Victorian **Royal Arms** is placed above the entrance to the baptistry, three-dimensional in coloured and gilt plaster, and the **font** beyond is an excellent C15 example. In the bowl panels there are four angels holding shields, three pomegranates, and a splendid **Tudor rose**; demi-angels decorate the underside, and snooty lions strain back against the stem. The C19 stained glass has an appropriate theme although it is badly eroded, but there is a very handsome window on the n. side of the nave. Installed in the early years of this century, it commemorates the life of Queen Victoria, with her arms and crest set in **quarries** decorated with the royal monogram; roses, thistles, and shamrocks form a border. A tall wrought iron **hour-glass stand** rests on a new stone **corbel** above the monolithic C19 pulpit, and the **roof** overhead is a C14 **tie-beam** and **king-post** construction. The chancel is a lovely, coherent essay in the Decorated style, and unusually lavish for such a small church. On both sides the walls are lined with six stalls, each in its niche below **cusped** and **crocketted ogee** arches. There are delightful miniature headstops above the shafts, and a **string course** connects the arcade with the window embrasures to the w. where there are matching blind arches. On the s. side it continues to link up with a **sedile** and **piscina**, and to the n. the scheme is completed by a beautiful **Easter sepulchre**. The arch of its tall, shallow niche is elaborately cusped and the combination of sinuous curves is quite Islamic. The 1860s glass in the e. window combines the sacrifice of Isaac with a Crucifixion and is badly eroded, particularly the figure of Christ. Looking w. you will see the Walsingham family arms in the tower window – again C19. The church's only medieval **brass** is an inscription for Edmund Knappe (1609) which is now in the window embrasure on the s. side of the chancel (there is another behind the organ for the Revd Joseph Clarke who died in 1653 but it is a modern reproduction). Within the vestry, the **tester** of a **Jacobean** pulpit has been converted into a table top, and in the corner is a very strange little chest. It is wedge-shaped and heavily banded with iron, with a hinged half-lid; the top is covered with strapwork in a dense scroll pattern which is C13 in form, but whether the chest is as old as that is doubtful.

Westerfield, St Mary Magdalene (E7): The tower was rebuilt in the early C15 but a fragment of **Norman** stonework survives just above the plinth at the s.e. corner. The w. doorway has **paterae** in the mouldings and roses in the **spandrels**, but its most interesting feature is the l. hand **stop**. It is very worn, but portrays a figure kneeling alongside a mass of foliage within which there seems to be the remains of a small head – all above a little palisade. It must once have had a quite specific significance but the other stop is too eroded to provide a clue and this remains, for me at least, an iconographical mystery. The bell openings have been much altered and there are **flushwork** battlements above. Until 1986, an 1840s schoolroom of little merit adjoined the n. side of the **nave**, but to celebrate its 900th birthday the church replaced this with a square **vestry**-cum-meeting room linked by a foyer to the n. door. With flint pebble walls and a hipped **roof**, it blends very well with the medieval building, and has an attractive arrangement of windows – bays to the e. and w., three bay-**lancets** to the n. The nave windows have 'Y' **tracery** of about 1300 (some are C19 replacements) and in the n. wall of the **chancel** there is a C13 lancet. The e. window, with intersecting 'Y' tracery, has bishop and queen **headstops** and the **corbel** heads at its base are modern replicas. Round the corner on the s. side there is a blocked lancet with a **trefoil** head next to a **priest's door** in **Tudor** brick. For some unexplained reason, a restoration in 1867 did away with a Norman s. doorway and replaced it with a window, but the **stoup** remains in the wall to mark its position.

Entry is via the w. door and the

narrow base of the tower. It has a very tall arch and there are dark C18 **decalogue boards** on the side walls. The glass in the w. window is by **Morris & Co** and dates from 1867, a prolific period for the company. It embodies no new principle of design or composition but repeats a tried and tested formula. Apart from the red and white roses by Philip Webb in the tracery, all the figures are by Morris, with four musical angels in white patterned with gold around a central figure of **St Mary Magdalene**. She wears a yellow brocade dress, bears her traditional emblem, and her very masculine face is framed in a mass of flowing hair; an 1865 version of the same design can be found at Antingham in Norfolk. The background **quarries** are patterned with pomegranates and the whole window has a lukewarm feeling about it. A set of George III **Royal Arms** painted on board hangs above the tower arch. The C15 **font** displays **Evangelistic symbols** in the bowl panels, together with angels bearing shields (n.e.**Trinity emblem**, s.e. three chalices for the Blessed Sacrament); very upright lions guard the shaft. Pieces of **chevron moulding** from the old Norman s. doorway survive in the arch and **jambs** of the window that replaced it, and (unusually) there was another stoup in the inside wall. The **roof** is a rare example of a C15 **hammerbeam** design that stretches uninterruptedly over nave and chancel, the division marked only by a heavy, **castellated rood beam**. Built on a more intimate scale than most, the roof merits careful study and strategically placed spotlights are a help. Its most striking feature is the series of demi-figures on the ends of the hammers and at the base of the **wall posts**. Some are renewals dating from 1901 but the majority are original and they are remarkable survivals. **Dowsing** does not record an image-smashing session here, and for a village church so close to Ipswich to go unscathed (at least in this respect) suggests that there was someone locally

with powerful friends. In the chancel the figures are of angels but in the nave kings and queens bear shields displaying a fine set of **Passion emblems**. On the s. wall is an attractive pictorial map of the village that won the local W.I. first prize in a 1977 county competition, and one **light** in a window opposite contains glass by Morris & Co. of 1921 – a figure of **St Michael** which is a typical production of the firm's latter days and a far cry from the **pre-Raphaelite** beginnings. There is a portion of the stairs to the vanished **rood loft** in the s. wall, and the crucifix on the pulpit came from Oberammergau in 1951. The glass in the n. chancel lancet is interesting because it is one of Burne-Jones's designs for Morris & Co. Although it commemorates Mary Jane Drage who died in 1850, the figure of Christ bearing a banner dates from 1873 and is a repeat of an 1871 window in Kirkbampton church, Cumberland. Nearby is a tablet commemorating **Henry Munro Cautley**, the diocesan architect whose name occurs so often in these books, and the bas relief roundel portrait at the top betrays more than a passing likeness to Rudyard Kipling. Cautley's father was rector here and he himself read the lessons here for most of his life. Appropriately, he designed the lectern and the **reredos**. The latter dates from 1938 and has small-scale pierced tracery, with a central canopied niche for the altar cross; small statuettes stand under canopies each side, and the rest of the e. wall is taken up with six shallow seat recesses under intricate tracery and a heavy cornice. His other work in the church is the war memorial by the n. door, which confirms me in the belief that he was never any good at this sort of thing. There are **dropped-sill sedilia** on the s. side of the **sanctuary** and a **piscina** lies within a square recess. On the n. wall there is a memorial for Major John Whitefoord of the 15th Hussars who was severely wounded at Waterloo and fell victim to a shooting misadventure in 1825. It is probably an exaggeration to say that the family was accident prone, but Lady Deborah Whitefoord's death in 1829 was 'occasioned by her clothes taking fire in consequence of which dreadful accident she languished in extreme agony for eight and twenty days'. The sad tale is set forth on a large tablet by Matthias John Crake of London; it has a bas relief urn against an obelisk on top. Round your visit off by visiting Cautley's grave near the kissing-gate s.w. of the tower.

Wetheringsett, All Saints (C4): Entry to the spacious churchyard ringed with trees is by way of a footbridge from the village street. The first thing one notices is that the C15 tower has a lofty w. arch that is completely open, with dainty mouldings uninterrupted save for small half-**capitals**. This strange feature can be seen again at Cotton not far away, but here there is no window in the inner wall – only a stooled niche. There is no doubt that the tower was built onto an earlier **nave** but the reason for the open plan is obscure. **Flushwork** chequer decorates the thick w. buttresses to the top and they have stooled niches to match the one over the w. arch. The overall style of the church is **Perpendicular**, with stepped **embattled transoms** in the **aisle** windows, and **clerestory** walls that are practically all glass. However, note that the s. aisle retained a **Decorated** window with **reticulated tracery** at the w. end, while the n.e. **vestry** has a **lancet** in its e. wall, and the C13 n. door has slim attached columns below wide and shallow ring capitals. The **chancel** was practically rebuilt in the C19. The face of the C15 **porch** is enhanced with minor flushwork and, as at Thorndon, the arch rests on lion **corbels** with crowns and shields in the moulding. Like that on the n. side, the s. door is part of the older building and the **dripstone's** curly **stops** match those on the **priest's door**. Note the pilgrim crosses incised on the **jambs**, and mind your head as you enter through the low

postern door.

There is a small **sanctus-bell window** at the very top of the w. wall, and the bowl panels of the **font** below contain lozenges and shields – plain except for arms on the n. side which feature the knot of the Staffords; the earlier C13 stem is ringed with shafts. This is a wide, light and airy interior where the main attraction is the late C13 **arcades**, generously proportioned with **quatrefoil piers** and deep ring capitals. They were heightened in the C15 to support the new clerestory, and overhead there is a C19 **roof** in which the space above the **tie-beams** is filled with panel tracery between the **king- and queen-posts**. On the n. aisle wall is a large benefactions board dated 1715 which has been restored (it says rather oddly 'made & written by C.A. Dilloway of Brockford 1960'). Nearby is a small iron-clad C15 chest. The main range of pews is sound C19 work but at the w. end there are some C15 benches with wide ends and **poppyheads**. By the organ in the s. aisle there are stairs which led originally to the loft of a **parclose screen** enclosing a chapel. In 1521 there was 'an altar to Our Lady in Master Richard's chapel' and this is likely to have been the site of his **chantry**. The chancel arch matches the arcade and although there is no **screen** now, the **rood loft stairs** survive to the s. Strangely, the panels on top of the organ and the roughly formed screen behind its console appear to be remnants of the vanished **rood screen**.

The panelled roof of the chancel is almost flat, and in the **sanctuary**, handsome stepped **sedilia** line the s. wall. The **Purbeck marble** columns support **trefoil** arches whose **cusps** and **hood moulds** have leaf terminals; the short end shafts rest on male and female heads which face one another. The plain **piscina** is small and unusual only in that its drain is square (like Thwaite's but without a raised lip). Two stalls with plain **misericords** stand opposite, and in the s.e. corner of the vestry is the interesting remnant of a double piscina with stiff-leaf carving below the bowl. This proves that it was used as a chapel in the late C13 or early C14. Returning down the nave, pause to read Dorothy Sheppard's epitaph; she died aged 19 in 1752 and is buried with her mother under the black **ledger- stone**: 'Reader if aught can fix th'attentive eye . . .'.

One of Wetheringsett's rectors was that eminent Elizabethan geographer Richard Hakluyt who, like Shakespeare, died in 1616. He is said to have been assiduous in his parish duties but one must remember that, apart from being secretary to the ambassador in Paris at one stage, he held prebends at Bristol and Westminster and was much in demand for advice to adventurers when Drake's circumnavigation was the topic of the day. His *Principal Navigations, Voyages and Discoveries of the English Nation* was first published in 1589 and he came here in 1590 with an international reputation. The greatly enlarged 2nd edition of 1598-1600 is an intriguing mixture of history, diplomacy, economics, and tales of daring. He was buried in Westminster abbey.

Whatfield, St Margaret (C8): There are picture-book thatched cottages in the lane that leads to the churchyard and the church itself is attractive despite cement rendering all over. The tower has a **Perpendicular** w. window under a square **label**, a stair turret to the s., and at some time the top was reduced and capped with a tiled pyramid **roof**. A modern **vestry** leads off the n. door and the **chancel** on that side has one 'Y' **tracery** window of about 1300 and another with **Decorated** tracery. The e. window has been renewed but the **reticulated** tracery is likely to have repeated the original C14 design. It is flanked by large marble tablets with side scrolls and one carries a mellifluous epitaph for Mary Church who died in childbed in 1741. There are Decorated windows and a **priest's door** on the s. side; w. of them, a **rood stair turret** under a tiled roof nestles against the

nave buttress. The outer arch of the small C16 brick **porch** is flanked by low-level recesses and the copper sundial of 1984 replaced a wooden version dated 1844; that is now above the inner doorway whose **hood mould** has the remains of **headstops**.

Watch for the two steps down into the nave and then have a look at the rare and lovely little C13 **stoup** just to the r. It has attached columns with ring **capitals** and there is **trefoil cusping** in the narrow arch. The early C18 **gallery** rests on iron posts and the bobbin and baluster turning in the balustrade is very attractive. The organ on it was rebuilt in 1952 in memory of George VI, who is credited with the royal title 'Defender of the Faith' – normally only seen on coins and abbreviated to 'F.D.' these days. There is perhaps a connection with the plain tablet on the s. wall for Sir George Falkener who was His Britannic Majesty's ambassador to Nepal after the war. There are **pamment** and brick floors, C19 seating on the s. side, and on the n. plain C16 benches with heavy roll mouldings on the backs and square ends. The one at the back is cruder and probably earlier than the rest and has a shield on the end: 'John Wilson 1589' plus '53' – his age perhaps? Over the C13 n. doorway hangs a well-painted set of **Hanoverian Royal Arms** and C17 hat pegs line the wall. The C14 **font** is a plain octagon resting on a centre shaft and ring of octagonal pillars, while overhead is a typical C14 **tie-beam roof**. The **archbraces** spring from little shafts on the **wall posts**, **king-posts** rise and are braced to a ridge beam which runs the whole length of the nave below a plastered ceiling. At the e. end on the s. side the monument of 1699 for William Vesey is most attractive. Against a shaped black background the substantial tablet is flanked by free-standing columns in mottled marble and pierced fronds; swags of fruit support an **achievement of arms** on the front of the cornice and there is a smaller **cartouche** at the base. The square recess underneath was once part of the entrance to the rood loft stairs. The pulpit opposite is tall and plain but its C17 back board is carved with a blind arch, and the hexagonal **tester** has pendants and a carved skirt. There is a cambered tie-beam spanning the chancel and above it is a fine C15 wagon roof, panelled with slender ribs and flower **bosses** whose centres contain animal masks and three kingly heads along the ridge. The **balusters** of the late C17 **communion rails** match the legs of the table in the vestry – so that was no doubt the **altar** of the period. In the **sanctuary** there is a tall and deep C14 **piscina** with a multi-cusped arch, and the grave slabs of two C13 priests lie in the corners – one with a plain cross and the other with the double omega symbol.

Whitton, St Mary (E7): Church Lane is a turning off the old Norwich road and the church is to be found at the very end, right on the edge of the housing development. It was rebuilt almost in its entirety in 1852 under the architect Frederick Barnes, who remodelled the **chancel** and provided a **nave** and n. **aisle**. Ten years later the tower and s.aisle were added by **R.M. Phipson**, incorporating stone from the ruined church of Thurleston which had not been used since the C16, except as a barn. It is an oddly shaped building from the outside, with n. aisle and nave flush at the w. end, and the small-scale tower set at the s.w. corner, complete with stone **broach spire** reminiscent of Lincolnshire. The s. aisle is built onto the e. wall of the tower and there is a flat-roofed **vestry** at the e. end of the n.aisle. Outside, the only identifiable survivor from the old church is the doorway re-set in the tower which, although it has been restored, is largely late C13, with ring **capitals** to the slim shafts and a deep roll moulding in the arch.

The interior is attractive and made more so by a new and sophisticated lighting scheme. For some reason Phipson did not match his **arcade** with

that of Barnes but used drum pillars instead of octagons, and the **roofs** of nave and aisles are all boarded, panelled, and painted above the plain brick floors. The C19 **font** has been moved from the w. end to the e. end of the n. aisle and is an attractive design using C13 forms; the drum bowl has an arcade of **trefoiled** arches, and there are four columns set around the centre shaft. A **lancet** nearby contains glass of 1922 by **Morris & Co.** which is quite unlike the firm's earlier style. It is a half-length **Blessed Virgin** and Child against a dark background, set within elaborate **tabernacle work**. Of more interest is the glass of about 1867 in the nave three-**light** w. window by **Hardman & Co.** A demi-figure of Christ is set at the top, and above and below three large angels across the centre there are six of the **Seven Works of Mercy** in shaped panels; Celtic scroll work fills the rest of the space and it is a fine window, C14 in feeling, with good colour. The 1860s glass in the s. aisle window is also by Hardman – a Resurrection scene in one light and the Ascension in the other. It commemorates Charles Steward 'by whom this church was mainly restored'. The e. wall of the s. aisle only has a high-level **quatrefoil** window and below it hangs a painting (probably C19) of the Virgin and Child; two mysterious figures, a man and a boy, lurk in the background. The **altar** here is a small and chunky C17 table. The C14 cross-braced framework of the chancel roof survived the restoration and the plaster behind the timbers is now painted a deep blue. Below, more medieval work may be found in the form of two **misericords** in the priest's stalls which came from a Sudbury church. The one on the n. side has a head carved below the seat, and the desk fronts have intricate and varied **tracery**. The choir stalls would seem to be all C19 work. There is more Hardman glass in the chancel s. window of 1865 – two mailed knights above kneeling angels, with the shield of faith in the top roundel; the e. window was supplied by the same firm a decade later – a stylised Last Supper across three lights, with demi-angels bearing the elements of the Eucharist above. Altered levels in the **sanctuary** have brought the C14 **piscina** close to the floor and the **cusps** of its arch have been broken away. In 1969 the window to the r. was re-glazed and now contains figures of **St Paul** and **St Peter** in pointed ovals above larger paintings of Christ and the Blessed Virgin. The four panels are set in plain **quarries** and date from the mid-C19.

Wickham Skeith, St Andrew (B4): A lane leads off the village street to the church and it is attractively placed. The stubby mid-C14 tower is unusually bulky and the absence of a w. window accentuates this. There is a decayed niche over the plain w. doorway and the w. buttresses, chequered with **flushwork**, have **consecration crosses** of the same size and pattern as those at Stoke Ash and Thornham Magna. The n. **porch** is tall, with side **gargoyles**, and both front and buttresses are decorated with flushwork panels. A band of crowned 'Ms' for the **Blessed Virgin** within stars lightly cut in **ashlar** are set above the outer arch below a central **groined** and canopied niche. The C15 **nave** windows have stepped, **embattled transoms** and the e. window of the **chancel** matches them. The narrow side windows of the chancel are also Perpendicular although the **priest's door** on the s. side was saved from the earlier building. There is a **scratch dial** on the r. side of its arch and three more can be traced on the s.e. nave buttress. A will of 1459 mentions money for the compact s. porch and it is interesting that its small side windows have **Decorated tracery** and are likely to have been salvaged and used again. There is flushwork up to the top of the arch and a tall **lancet** overhead once lit an upper room. The access stair shows in the angle with the nave on the w. side but the floor has been removed and the porch is open to the **roof**. The C16 inner

door has **linenfold** carving but access is normally through the tower, past the ropes of the ground-floor ring of bells.

The inner door is unusual in having tracery on the w. side. Like many others in East Anglia, the octagonal **font** has window tracery designs cut in the bowl panels, including **reticulations** to the s., but the figures round the shaft have been terribly mutilated. They were **Evangelistic symbols** at the angles with **woodwoses** between them and traces of the creatures' hairy coat survive on one only. The plain and dark **hammerbeam roof** has embattled **wall plates** and rests on interesting stone **corbels**. One on the n. side seems to hold a scourge and another opposite a Sacred Heart. The **rood stair** in the n. wall has a very tall bottom doorway and the upper opening faces w. Beneath the latter there is a triplet of niches with **trefoil** heads by the late C18 or early C19 pulpit. On the other side of the chancel arch is a wide niche under a **cusped ogee** arch and the chamber organ in front of it has a beautiful C18 mahogany case. The 'Gothick' detailing round the pipe clusters is excellent and there is a deep, pierced frieze below the cornice.

The chancel arch springs from large corbels which face inwards – a male and female head of considerable character. Below a plastered ceiling and heavy embattled wall plates, there are tall late C17 **communion rails** and a simple Elizabethan **Holy table** decorated with chip carving on rails and stretchers. On the e. wall is a C19 stone **reredos**, with Creed and Lord's Prayer on flanking panels. The tall **piscina** has flowers in the **spandrels** of the trefoil arch and in front of it is an interesting group of **ledger-stones**. Jane Harvey lies in the centre (she died in 1644 and was a Le Hunt of Little Bradley), with husband and son on either side; pairs of straps and buckles incised in the stone link the family in what seems to me to be a charming conceit. The church's seating poses interesting questions. Nine of the nave benches at the w. end are demonstrably medieval but all the bench ends in nave and chancel have **poppyheads** of early C17 design. However, the tracery in the fronts of the chancel choir stalls matches the front of the w. **gallery** and one would judge that to be C19 – good solid work that was probably part of the 1857 restoration. Under the **gallery** hangs a delightful photograph of David Mayes with his scythe. He died in 1949, having been sexton for many years, and he must have often used the Victorian **bier** on its sprung undercarriage that stands close by.

Wilby, St Mary (D2): The church stands close by the village street and the beautifully proportioned tower dates from about 1460. It has four **set-offs**, with **flushwork** panels in the angle buttresses, stepped flushwork battlements and corner pinnacles. There are shields in the **spandrels** of the w. doorway, one for the **Trinity** and the other carrying **Passion emblems**. The flushwork **base course** is simple and the w. window has stepped **embattled transoms**, with a niche on each side. In the tower's n. wall, by the angle of the n.w. buttress and about 7ft. from the ground, there is a large flint which, when it was **knapped**, revealed the fossilised outline of a bird's head with a hooked beak–like a small eagle. On walking round, you will see that all the windows are **Perpendicular** and there is a **clerestory** on one side only above the s. **aisle**. The flintwork in the wall of the aisle is a C19 restoration. For a small church the s. **porch** is quite lavish. The angle buttresses have niches and decorative stone panelling, and the mouldings of the outer arch are studded with **fleurons** with two masks at the top, while the shield of the Wingfields is carved in the spandrels. Panels of the base course are carved with 'Ms' for the **Blessed Virgin** and there is a **sacred monogram** on the e. side. Nine small niches graded in size stand over the entrance, and although the top is now squared off it was more

elaborate originally. Like the w. door, the inner doorway spandrels contain Trinity and Passion emblem shields and there are lion **stops**.

Just inside the door is a large monument for members of the Green family which looks as though it has been rearranged. On the front of the large chest is a beautiful rococo panel with winged cherub heads in deep relief and crisp foliage, while beyond on the wall a large double panel by Bedford is surrounded by lively scrolls and commemorates members of the family 1825-76. The three black marble slabs on top of the tomb are for Thomas (1730), George (1739), and Jane (1744) Green, and although the excellent portrait bust on the l. hand wall is not labelled it probably portrays Thomas. The nave **roof** was restored and re-leaded in 1966 and four old panels of 1657, 1742, and 1874 with churchwardens' initials were saved and are framed on the wall nearby. By the tower arch hang two massive Union Flag battle ensigns; they probably flew from the flagship H.M.S. *Duke of Wellington* on station in the Baltic during the Crimean War. The niche in the n. wall is likely to have been an **aumbry** associated with the **font** so that the oils, salt, and cloths could be stored conveniently to hand. The font has obviously been moved because it stands partly on a **ledger-stone** of 1678. The odd thing is that another stone with the same date, age, and name lies to the e. and was presumably provided in recompense. The font's bowl panels are very deeply cut and conventional angels with shields occupy four of them. However, the other four are more interesting because they contain figures representing the **Evangelists** (with curiously abundant hair styles) and they have their emblems at their feet. There are figures round the shaft, with **St Paul** to the w. and possibly **St James the Great** to the e. The attractive **hatchment** to the l. of the tower arch was used at the funeral of Thomas Green, a barrister who lived in the village and died in

Wilby, St Mary: bench end carvings of penance and extreme unction

1825. Also at the w. end of the nave is a **brass** for a man who died about 1530. The inscription has been lost so we don't know who he was, but a separate plate is engraved with a sheep so he was probably a clothier. Over the blocked n. door, in the traditional place opposite the main entrance, is a large wall painting of **St Christopher**. A good deal has been lost but fishes swim in the river round his feet, his staff is massive, and the hermit's hut is plain. An Elizabethan text on the s. wall by the door has largely gone. The simple but attractive **arch-braced nave** roof has embattled **wall plates**, small flower **bosses** at the main timber intersections, and transverse braces under the ridge. The s. aisle roof is medieval too but the fine angels at the base of the **wall posts** were carved by Archdeacon Darling in 1938 – another example of the woodworking skills to be found among the old-style clergy. A s. window in the aisle has glass of 1938 by Horace Wilkinson – figures of Christ, St Paul and **St Barnabas** in uncomplicated and conventional style. The aisle e. window glass dates from 1919 and is by **Hardman**. The presentation of Christ in the Temple is illustrated across three **lights**, with lots of steely grey tints setting off dark, rich colours. Below, the **altar** carries the church's original **mensa** set in a wooden frame. It had been demoted to a paving slab in the C16 but is now fulfilling its proper function once again. Note the thick stone **credence shelf** in the **piscina** recess close by. The pulpit is luxuriously carved, with centre rosettes in the body panels within flat-arched surrounds, elaborate **tester** and back to match, and the style suggests late C17. By it stands a massive C13 iron-clad chest, much eaten away, which was originally a good deal longer. The C15 glass in the tops of the nave windows has been restored but had not all been replaced when I visited in 1988. The fragments in the n.w. window include an angel playing a lute, and in the next window there is a headless figure at the top playing a psaltery. The 3rd window contains three deep, beautiful canopies with an eagle, a sweet little lion, and an angel with a cross bandeau as finials; above them on the r. is a headless **St Catherine** with a sword as well as her customary wheel. The last window has shorter canopies with tiny figures in the niches. On the l. is **St Osyth** with her keys, on the r. is an unidentified man in yellow hat and gown, and, in the centre, there are three musical angels. Binoculars are helpful here, and when all the glass is back you should be able to identify **St Barbara**, **St Helen**, and **St Margaret**.

Although they have been terribly mutilated, Wilby's C15 bench ends are the church's most interesting feature, mainly because they include part sequences of the **Seven Deadly Sins**, the **Seven Works of Mercy** and the **Seven Sacraments**. They are so like Tannington's benches that they were probably carved by the same man. At the e. end on the n. side of the nave the first bench illustrates penance, with Extreme Unction on the other side. The head of the priest behind the bed has gone but the scene is clear, with a chrismatory containing the holy oils being held by an attendant at the foot of the bed. Next to the w. you will find baptism and confirmation (a chrismatory again), and farther along an eagle stoops on its prey. **St John the Baptist** holds the **Agnus Dei** on the bench end next but one to the font, and on the 3rd to the e. St Barbara stands in her tower. Mutilated but still recognisable, with her hands joined in prayer, it is strange that she faces away from the aisle. At the e. end of the s. aisle are the acts of mercy of burying the dead (with a cross boldly carved on the coffin lid) and feeding the hungry, followed by the sacraments of marriage and the mass (with the stump of the priest's body behind the altar, a large paten upon it, and the outline of the base of the chalice). There is a musi-

cian on the 5th bench end from the w. end, and the last one has the sin of usury illustrated by the money-lender stuffing coins into a bag, and gluttony by a drunkard supping from a small barrel. **Dowsing** came to the church in 1643 smashing many things, and it may be that he was responsible for the damage to the pews. The rest of the benches are good C19 work with some nice carvings on the elbows in sympathy with their medieval predecessors. The medieval shields of arms in the n. chancel window belong to the Sullyard family, including Sir John, master of the rolls and an active supporter of Queen Mary. The large piscina recess in the **sanctuary** still has its wooden credence shelf and there are **dropped-sill sedilia** alongside. Part of the large stone figure of the Blessed Virgin and Child which stands on a pedestal in the corner was discovered in the churchyard ditch in 1935 and has been nicely restored. There are more brasses in the chancel, but inscriptions only: a Latin verse for Rector William James (1569), and another with a punning translation for one of his successors, Joseph Fletcher (1637), both on the s. wall; two with shields in the floor on the s. side of the sanctuary for Elizabeth Bayles (1588) and Joane Bayles (1620), and two more, also with shields, on the n. side for Lucy Bayles (1638) and John and Thomas Bayles (1639). The e. window glass of 1904 is a very nice example of the work of **Clayton & Bell** – Christ flanked by the Blessed Virgin and **St John**, with small figures of the Evangelists and angels in the tracery, and the **three Marys** with the two apostles at the tomb in the bottom panels. The colours are rich but subtle, the drapery very involved.

Willisham, St Mary (C7): From the churchyard there is a broad vista over the rolling countryside to the s., with Offton's C14 tower emerging from trees in the valley bottom. This building, however, is purely Victorian and was designed by Herbert Green in 1878. It cost only a little less than his church at Darmsden but there is not so much to show for the money. There is no tower and a tall bellcote rises above a little triple blind **arcade** resting on **corbels**. The w. door has its own shallow gable and the formal disposition of the **lancet** and two-**light** windows is broken only by a s. **porch** which has pairs of **quatrefoils** each side rather like portholes. Within, there is a **roof** of boarded panels and light **arch-braces** above pitch pine benches. On the n. wall an interesting engraving shows St Mary's as it was in 1844 and I wonder what became of the two C13 grave slabs that are illustrated below – very like those in the chancel at Whatfield. The C15 **font** is the only thing that was saved from the old building and it is a good example of a familiar East Anglian type. Angels with shields alternate with blank shields hung on pegs in the bowl panels and all the chamfers are decorated with **paterae**; demi-angels with partially re-cut heads spread their wings below, and four squat lions sit round the shaft gazing benignly heavenward. The openwork pulpit on its stone base, the matching reading desk, and the stalls with **poppyheads** are all in oak – possibly by Cornish & Gaymer. The **Commandments**, Creed and Lord's Prayer on the e. wall are not the usual painted set but are engraved on brass plates framed in alabaster. A similar style is used in the two matching memorials for members of the Boby family of Willisham Hall and the e. window has the same commemoration. The crucified Christ occupies the centre light, with two of the **three Marys** on one side and **St Peter** and **St James** on the other. The smaller panels below portray the Nativity, **St Mary Magdalene** anointing the Lord's feet, and the women at the tomb. This is fine glass (probably by **Heaton, Butler & Bayne**), with a fruit and foliage backing to the main figures which is strongly **pre-Raphaelite**. There is a style contrast in the lower panels where the drapery detailing is particularly good

and the tears on the women's cheeks remind one of the Virgin at Gipping.

Wingfield, St Andrew (D2): Although there was an earlier church on this site, the genesis of the present building was the foundation of Wingfield college under the will of Sir John de Wingfield in 1361. A provost and nine priests were to say daily masses for the repose of the soul of the founder and his heirs and they were housed in the building to the s. of the church. The church itself needed to be larger and more commodious in its new role and was rebuilt, with more additions and alterations following in the C15. A number of churches made provision for the parson's or the squire's horses in the C18 and C19, and by the n. gate there is a small brick and tile stable, with a wooden mounting platform nearby. Wingfield's tower is squat, with heavy angle buttresses, a stair turret to the s., and **Decorated tracery** in the bell openings (the w. window is a later **Perpendicular** insertion). On walking round, you will find that the windows of the n.e. chapel have flowing tracery with **mouchette** shapes, and the great e. window has stepped **embattled transoms**. The s.e. chapel was being built in 1415 and is an interesting example of old and new tracery forms being used together. The attractive four-petalled flower motif, used in the s. aisle fifty years earlier, reappears with the **ogee** shape alongside strong **mullions** and embattled transoms. There are Perpendicular **clerestories** over **nave** and **chancel**, the latter having seven closely-set windows a side linked by a running **label**. The s. **porch** was part of the work carried out by Michael De La Pole, 1st Earl of Suffolk, who had married the Wingfield heiress, but the inner doorway is part of the C14 building. Heavily moulded, with slim attached columns, it has large **headstops** inclining inwards, the one on the r. a knight's head in helmet and the chain mail collar called a 'camail'. Within, the mid-C14 nave **arcades**

have octagonal **piers** and are neatly married with the leading edges of the tower's e. buttresses. From this one would guess that the tower was part of the earlier church. The **font** is a typical East Anglian design, with lions seated round the stem, and four more in the bowl panels alternating with angels bearing shields. It was given by the 2nd Earl of Suffolk about 1405 and the arms e. and w. are De La Pole/Wingfield, n. Wingfield, s. Stafford. The cover incorporates sections of C15 **crocketting** that perhaps came from part of the **rood screen**. By the C19 the building was in a poor state and major restorations were carried out from the 1860s to the 1880s. The nave **roof** was stripped of its medieval decoration and colour was even removed from the four small angels which carry shields below the **arch-braces**. The pleasantly carved benches date from 1880. The rood screen stretched right across the church and the stairs which led to the loft remain in the aisle window embrasures. On the n. side, just below the top doorway, the stump of one of the floor beams remains embedded in the wall, and the heavily restored base of the screen stands below the chancel arch. The pulpit is modern but carved **spandrels** have been used in fours to fill the square panels and they were probably part of the screen originally. The shield carries the arms of William De La Pole, Duke of Suffolk. To the s. of the chancel arch is a large blocked **squint** that aligned with the **high altar**.

What is now the organ chamber was a chapel dedicated to **St Margaret** built about 1430 and the niche high in the e. wall has **groining** and traces of colour although the canopy has been chopped off; below is a small **piscina**. The chancel roof was virtually replaced in the 1860s and all the stone **corbels** date from then. The layout of the stalls follows the usual pattern for collegiate churches, with some backing onto the screen, and they all have **misericords** – plain pendent centres with leaf supporters. The attractive **parclose screens** to n. and s. have groined coving

on both sides. The large recess in the n. wall, with its handsome **cusped** and crocketted ogee arch and tall side pinnacles, was almost certainly an **Easter sepulchre** and not the original setting for the figure it now contains. This is the effigy of Sir John de Wingfield, the founder of the college and the Black Prince's chief of Council, who died in 1361. In smooth stone, the head of the armoured figure rests on the remains of a helm, with a lion at the feet. It was once richly coloured and at the back of the neck **gesso** work resembling chain mail survives. Sir John's grandson died en route to Agincourt and his son, William De La Pole, rebuilt the chancel in his memory and extended it eastwards in the 1430s. The De La Pole **chantry** was the chapel of the Holy Trinity (now the **vestry**) and its upper chamber has two squints to give a view of the high altar. The vestry doorway, with its finely moulded arch, was part of the rebuilding and to the e. of it is the fine tomb of John De La Pole, Duke of Suffolk, who died in 1491. His wife was Elizabeth Plantaganet, sister of Edward IV and Richard III, and their alabaster figures were once richly coloured. Even now there are traces in the folds of her dress and on the Saracen's head helm under his head. Both wear narrow jewelled coronets and, apart from the loss of her arms and chipped noses, the figures are complete. The buckles, straps, and rivets of his armour are meticulously detailed, one of the best examples of the period, but he has been sadly treated by graffiti addicts over the centuries – his chest has 'TS 1672' and his shoulder 'JLW 1906'. Above the tomb is a painted wooden helm with huge Saracen's head crest and the remains of two supporters. Note how the second squint from the upper chamber beyond cuts through the cresting of the monument.

The elaboration of the chancel included the lovely arcade on the s. side. The mouldings are encrusted with little wings for the Wingfields, leopards' heads for the De La Poles, and

Wingfield, St Andrew: the hudd

the knots of the Staffords. The **capitals** are carved with demi-angels and on both sides the two eastern bays are linked by a cresting above. Below stands the tomb of the man in whose memory the work was done, Michael De La Pole, 2nd Earl of Suffolk. He was with Henry V on his French expedition and died of dysentery before Harfleur. The Countess Katherine was one of his executors and probably erected the monument for them both soon after his death in 1415. The beautifully sculpted effigies are not of stone but wood, a very late and unusual example of the medium. They are in remarkable condition and her figure, in kirtle and a long mantle with a deep collar, is particularly attractive; the head-dress is patterned with flowers set in squares

and her veil is secured by a narrow band. Unfortunately, the gilded and coloured gesso decoration was painted over in the late C18. The range of niches on the s. and w. sides of the chest once contained the figures of the Duke's children, and a most unusual feature is the **sedilia** seats that are ranged along the n. side. The chancel e. window has some medieval armorial glass and a mass of fragments in the tracery, while the high altar frontal is a fine early design by **Sir Ninian Comper** – stylised grapes against a fleur de lys pattern. The altar in the Lady chapel to the s. of the chancel is a small **Stuart** table, and behind it hangs a panel of cloth that was used in Westminster abbey at the coronation of Queen Elizabeth II. There are large mutilated niches r. and l. which show traces of original colour, and they now contain figures of **Gabriel** and the **Blessed Virgin** which date from the 1930s. The piscina in the windowsill is the simplest type and it is odd that such a lavish chapel should not have had something more elaborate. The massive unstained dug-out chest in the chapel may well be C12 and also to be found there is a rare example of a 'hudd', the shelter used by late C18 and early C19 parsons at the graveside in wet weather. The only other known example is at Walpole St Peter in Norfolk, but that is like a sentry box whereas this one has merely a boarded top fixed to curiously bandy uprights. The simple chamfer decoration is just like that used on farm wagons of the period and it would have been made by the village carpenter.

Winston, St Andrew (D4): At a sharp bend on the Debenham to Helmingham road a lane is signposted to Hall and church. It is a pleasant spot and the little church has a plain C14 tower with **quoins** of thin red bricks all the way up. The simple w. doorway has been bricked up, there is a **lancet** belfry window, bell openings with 'Y' **tracery**, and brick battlements. On walking round, 'Y' tracery is seen again in the tall windows on the n. side of the C14 **nave**, and a **vestry** was added against the n. door in the late C18 or C19. Farther along, the old **rood stair** projects from the wall, and the **chancel** windows were probably copied from the originals when a restoration was carried out by **Phipson** in 1857. All of the outside walls were encased in flint at that time and the e. end was partially rebuilt, with a new window. There were problems of settlement, however, and in 1897 the architect W.D. Caröe had it rebuilt with a modest neo-**Perpendicular** window, probably because Phipson's window was overlarge. The s. nave wall is now plastered and one window has **Decorated** tracery. The diminutive **porch** is in **Tudor** red brick but makes the most of itself – a crow-stepped gable between octagonal buttresses that continue as stumpy pinnacles, and three niches above an outer arch that has deeply recessed mouldings.

Within, there is more Tudor red brick in the w. arch, and the thickness of the tower wall forms an interior porch to the little C18 door. There is a plain octagonal **font** with an C18 Creed board standing by, and a dark set of George III **Royal Arms** painted on board is framed over the n. door. The dinky vestry beyond is complete with fireplace. The nave ceiling is plastered but below it are C14 heavy **arch-braced tie-beams**, and the doorways of the rood stair can be seen in the n. wall by the C18 pulpit. This is a rather strange affair. It has a conventional body with plain bevelled panels, but it stands on three clusters of turned legs. Small monochrome panels of stained glass hang in the nave windows and are likely to be foreign C19 work. On the s. side: **St Peter**, and **St Matthias**, with **St Andrew** and **St John** to the e.; n. side: **St James the Less** and **St Jude**. A small and plain **piscina** on the s. side marks the site of a nave **altar**. There is now no **screen**, and in the chancel the outline of a door in the n. wall may have led to an earlier vestry. Although the wagon

roof is part of Phipson's work, he retained the medieval tie-beams, and did not disturb the nice early C13 piscina in the **sanctuary**. It is large, with detached shafts and remnants of stiff-leaf **capitals** below a **cusped** arch which has little **trefoils** on the cusps.

Wissington, St Mary (C10): The sign on the Bures/Nayland road points to 'Wiston church', using the local pronunciation, and the church is to be found surrounded by comfortable farm buildings in the lush valley of the Stour – a most beguiling setting. This is a **Norman** building and the restorers of 1853 decided to emphasise this by rebuilding the **apse** on the original foundations, enlarging the e. window, adding a neo-Norman **priest's door** and finishing it all off with a rib vault within. There is a glazed **porch**, two new windows on the s. side, a C19 w. window and n. **vestry**, but the tiny original **lancets** remain in **nave** and **chancel** and there are two ancient **corbels** projecting from the chancel walls. A large weatherboarded bell turret carries a vane pierced with the date 1722. Within the porch stands a fractured bell cast by John Thornton of Sudbury in 1719 and there is a large and lavish Norman s. doorway. It is very tall and the shaft to the l. is carved with alternating spirals up to a section of leaf carving below the **capital**. Its opposite number is cut as an octagon and decorated with **chevrons**. The deeply recessed arch has chevron, roll, and interlace mouldings and the **tympanum** is filled with chip-carved lozenges. To the l. of the doorway are two **scratch dials** and a faint but very delicate inscription is cut above the upper one. To the r. is a C15 **stoup**.

A heavy C19 **gallery** in two parts flanks the organ at the w. end and a **consecration cross** shows clearly below it on the n. wall. Overhead are the **Royal Arms** of George III in poor condition; it is interesting that 'Fear God and Honour the King' was lettered on the back, presumably for the benefit of the children who had to sit up there. Also suspended are two **hatchments**, the one on the s. side for Elizabeth Gibbons who died in 1798 and the other for a member of the Whitmore family. By going through to the vestry one can examine the n. doorway which is also Norman and has a massive rounded lintel below a plain tympanum and zigzag arch moulding. Both doorways have deep recesses in the **jambs** for security bars and the arrangement is probably as old as the church itself. While in the vestry, have a look at the pair of stalls with plain **misericords** and a nice **Jacobean** chest with some marquetry work on the front. Another stands opposite, but two of its panels have been badly damaged. Also of interest are two engravings from drawings by the antiquarian Henry Davy of the interior as it was in 1827 (i.e. before the restoration) and of the s. door. The early C15 **font** is a fascinating and unusual example; the double-panelled stem has three very worn lions lying at its foot instead of sitting up as usual and, on the s.w. corner, a sheep lies with its lamb – a possible reference to Isaiah's prophecy of peaceful cohabitation. The rim of the bowl is **castellated** and in four of the panels angels hold shields: e., the arms of England (with the lions facing the wrong way!); s., the star of the De Veres; n.w., a **Trinity emblem**; the n.e angel holds a crown, that to the s.e. plays a psaltery, and the last one holds a rebec, one of the earliest bowed instruments.

One of the most tantalising things about Wissington is that it obviously had a complete range of wall paintings in the second half of the C13 and although enough remains to show their extent, very little can be easily distinguished now. Professor Tristram uncovered and treated them in the 1930s but they are now very faint for the most part. There was on the w. wall a **Doom** of which hardly anything is recognisable, and on the s. wall of the nave an upper range of scenes from the life of Christ. **St Michael** stands dimly above the pulpit, a Nativity scene is farther w., with the archangel appearing to the shepherds alongside, and the adoration of the Magi is discernible over the s. door. In the lower section there were scenes from the lives of **St Margaret** and **St Nicholas**, and his figure and his ship's sail are still clear.There is a huge and flamboyant red dragon over the n. door and originally the n. wall displayed incidents from the life of **St John the Baptist**, but perhaps the most interesting survival is the shadowy figure of **St Francis** high on the n. wall at the e. end. He is shown preaching to the birds which perch on a scrolly tree. This is the earliest known example of the most popular of his legends and must have been painted within a few years of his death. The nave **roof** is an example of **king-post** and **tie-beam** construction. Below, the 1850s restorers indulged in pews with Norman-style blind arches carved in the ends and doors, plus a positively gross pulpit and matching reading desk. There are round-headed wall recesses at the end of the nave which no doubt housed **altars** and the e. arch is a grand Norman piece, wide and high with two widely separated zigzag mouldings. The supporting shafts vary, with spirals to the n. and mixed lozenge patterns to the s. It is highly likely that the original church had a tower beyond this arch like the one at Ousden [Vol.1]. There is a large lancet above the farther arch and a beast corbel which was probably re-set when the apse was rebuilt. In the floor is a **brass** with two shields and an inscription for John le Gris, who died in 1630, having been minister here for thirty-nine years. It was placed there by Elizabeth 'uxor amoris' (his loving wife). Beyond neo-Norman **communion rails**, the rebuilt apse has bright uncomplicated glass in C13 style by Wilmhurst & Oliphant – Crucifixion and Descent from the Cross in the e. window, the angel at the empty tomb in the n. lancet, and Christ bearing the cross to the s. The other stained glass in the church consists of very conventional and flaccid designs by Thomas

Baillie dating from the 1870s. The churchyard is a pleasant place in which to wander and there are some interesting headstones, including a fine modern example for Joyce Pike e. of the chancel, with excellent lettering and the **Chi Rho** symbol.

Witnesham, St Mary (E6): The main road dips steeply between the two halves of this straggling village and a lane leads from there to the church. The building dates largely from the late C13/early C14, and some two hundred years later a **clerestory** under a new **roof** was added to the **nave**. Although the s. **aisle** was built in the early C14, it has no counterpart to the n., and a group of conifers overshadows the wall on that side. The late C18 was often a time of neglect and this may be why the **chancel** was shortened and partially rebuilt. You will see that the e. wall is a mixture of brick and salvaged stone, and the e. gable of the nave was renewed in brick. Nevertheless, the C13 **priest's door** with original ironwork is still there on the s. side. There was a major restoration in 1845 and the n.e. **vestry** was added in 1868. In common with a number of other churches in the area, St Mary's has a tower on the s. side which is also the main entrance. Built at roughly the same time as the aisle, it has angle buttresses up to the bell stage, **Decorated** bell openings, and **flushwork** battlements. The s. face neatly illustrates the early history of time-keeping, with a **scratch dial** which has traces of numerals by the entrance, a sundial of 1729 in the buttress angle above, and a single-hand clock with a diamond face which was installed in 1737. The inner face of the archway has a whole series of chamfer mouldings which fade into the **jambs**, and the C14 inner door of lapped boards still has its strap hinges and centre closing ring.

The interior has a pleasant, spacious feel about it, and the **hammerbeam, arch-braced** roof of the nave has a plaster ceiling that masks everything above the collar beams. This is not uncommon but here the flat centre section is decorated with large raised roundels and diamond shapes. The placing of the tower shortens the aisle to no more than a two-bay chapel, and the contemporary **arcade** has wide **capitals** above the slender octagonal pillar and **responds**. The three-**light** e. window leans casually to one side, flanked by formless image niches, and the **piscina** with its renewed **credence shelf** shows that the aisle had its own **altar**. The floor has been newly relaid with nice bricks and there are benches ranged along the walls. These match the main suite in the nave and were made by **Henry Ringham** in the 1840s, a restrained design with good **poppyheads** and moulded top rails and ends. His skill lay in matching the remains of an original C15 set, and a careful look at those w. of the **font** will show how good he was. There is a medieval shield of the Weyland family arms set in the clear glass of the w. window, and although the font is a familiar East Anglian pattern it has been entirely re-cut. Witnesham has the best example in the county of the C18 wall texts that were the successors to the Elizabethan 'profitable sentences'. High on the walls, their small painted panels have been well preserved, and some of them are placed to make specific points of doctrine. Opposite the font over the blocked n. door you will see: 'Except a man be born of water …'; over the main entrance: '. . . this is the gate of heaven'; and near the pulpit the preacher is reminded: '. . . woe is unto me, if I preach not the gospel'. There are remains of a similar set at Hemingstone dated 1773 and it is likely that the same man painted both. In addition, there are slightly later Lord's Prayer and Creed boards in frames on either side of the chancel arch, and a matching **decalogue board** in the aisle. The attractive little animal in the C14 glass at the top of the s.w. nave window came, it seems, from the nearby chapel of St Thomas which was in ruins by the

C18. It has been tentatively identified as a beaver but I think that even at that time the characteristic tail was well known, and this one's is bushy. To the l. of the s. door is a memorial by **Thomas Thurlow** for Robert Carew King who died in 1842. The medallion portrait has him in profile, plump of chin and sporting sideburns. A plain tablet on the n. wall is rather odd in that it reverses the normal convention of a man boasting of his ancestry. Here we have 'Thomas Woolner (father of Thomas Woolner, R.A., sculptor and poet and of Sarah Ann Meadows) was buried in this churchyard.' Presumably Thomas junior couldn't resist the advertisement when he memorialised his father. On the other side by the chancel entrance there is an extreme example of the more usual human failing. In 1824 Philip Meadows was described among other things as 'the great, great, great, grandson of William Meadows who was first seated here in 1630'. The pulpit is **Jacobean** with excellent panel work, standing on a modern base, and the shapeless chancel arch was part of the late C18 rebuilding. Above it is a dark set of Charles II **Royal Arms**. There is another of the wall texts just beyond which relates to the Eucharist, and the Ringham choir stalls incorporate transverse C17 panels. The 'Gothick' arches along the fronts match the set of **communion rails** provided at the same time. John King's memorial of 1815 on the n. wall is by **John Bacon the Younger**, a plain tablet on a black surround, with drapes falling on both sides from an urn at the top; there is a neat little **achievement** below. Opposite, two early C19 brothers who died far apart in India and Canada are remembered on a graceful oval set on a black square. The dull and heavy stone **reredos** was designed by Robert Ireland in 1868, and the e. window is filled with 1840s glass by Edward Baillie. It is interesting historically because it precedes the flood of mass-produced glass that came later, but the colours are harsh blues, reds, and greens and Christ's figure in the Resurrection and Ascension panels seems to have strayed from a ballet.

Worlingworth, St Mary (E3): The church has a bold but fairly plain C15 tower, with four **set-offs** to its angle buttresses which are decorated with **flushwork**; there is more flushwork to be seen in the battlements. The shields in the **spandrels** of the w. doorway carry the emblems of the **Passion** and the **Trinity**, and the w. window has stepped **embattled transoms**. The mouldings of the n. doorway are decorated with **fleurons** and masks, the buttresses of the **nave** between large **Perpendicular** windows have flushwork designs, and there is a flushwork **base course**. The n.e buttress incorporates a **rood stair turret** with a tiny window, and there is a **priest's door** on the s. side of the early C14 **chancel**. Its e. window **tracery** is very attractive – a pair of **trefoils** in circles and a centre sexfoil above the four main **lights**. S. of the tower you will see the base of a **preaching cross** and the tall C15 s. **porch** has a handsome flushwork facade displaying **sacred monograms** and 'Ms' for the dedication. The outer archway spandrels are carved with **St George** and the dragon, there is a canopied niche above it, and over that, a sundial plate on the battlements dated 1663. The remains of two C15 benches (one with a dragon on the elbow) were relegated to the porch, and the inner doorway has a profusion of delicate mouldings and pairs of thin shafts.

The spacious, lofty nave has a lovely double **hammerbeam roof** which has not been stained. It has tracery each side of the **king-posts** that stand on the collars and above the hammerbeams, and the well-restored angels at their ends bear painted shields (a key to the heraldry is helpfully provided on the w. wall). Within the tower stands a fine example of a village manual fire engine. Restored in 1953, it was built by Newsham & Ragg in 1760 and was the

Worlingworth, St. Mary: C17 benches

first type to make use of compressed air, which enabled it to provide a continuous jet up to 150ft. Given by Lord of the Manor John Major, it served the village until 1930 and was last used on Guy Fawkes Night 1927. The massive pole that rests in the n.w. corner of the nave was the spit on which an ox was roasted whole in celebration of the Jubilee of George III in 1810 (it was carried in procession for Queen Victoria's Diamond Jubilee in 1897 – there was no ox that time). The village feast is shown in a delightful painting by the s. door, full of homely detail. Above the tower arch is a curiously offset door. It doesn't seem quite right for an entrance to the old w. **gallery** but I can think of no other possibility. Below in the floor is a 1622 **ledger-stone** with two **brass** shields and an inscription: 'James Barker to his dearest wyfe Susanna doth this last office of love for she was religious, chaste, discreet, loveing'. The **font** is a

common East Anglian design, with deeply carved bowl panels in which the **Evangelistic symbols** alternate with angels bearing shields – n.e., Passion emblems, s.e. **St Edmund**, s.w. Trinity, n.w. St George. There are very upright lions round the stem and a clear donor's inscription round the base: 'Orate pro anima Nicholai Moni qui isti fonte fieri fecit' (Pray for the soul of Nicholas Moni who had this font made). The tall cover was originally a telescopic model like Ufford's but it was altered at some stage, and there is an unusually complete record of its fortunes over the years painted on panels at the top: 'Repaired and restored 1706', 'Removed from the gallery by the Parish Nov. 1800', 'Repaired and beautified by the Honble John Henniker Major May 1801', 'Restaur By Public Subscription 1893', 'Conserved and regilded May 1963'. It is now very jolly in red, green, white and gilt, and the two other inscriptions are easy to read. One is a Greek palindrome (the characters read the same backwards and forwards) like the one at Hadleigh which translates: 'Wash my sin and not my face only'; the other is a quotation from St Paul's Letter to the Romans (2: 29): 'Circusisio cordis in spiritu non litera' (Circumcision is that of the heart, in the spirit and not in the letter). The cover is supposed to have come from the abbey at Bury although one wonders what a Benedictine foundation was doing with a font. By the door is a nice little poorbox which is dated by the worn brass plate on the top: 'W. Godbold gave me 1622'. Another plate on the front has: 'Proverbs XIX vearse XVII He that hath piti upon the poor, lendeth unto the Lord, & that which he hath given, he will pay him again 99'. The **Stuart** table with its turned and carved legs by the n. door was used in the C17 as the **altar**, and is interesting because the drawer in the front shows that it was designed for domestic rather than religious use. Nearby, the **Royal Arms** of George III are crudely painted on board and farther along there are vestiges of a wall painting with fishes at the bottom which could have been a **St Christopher**.

There are a number of good C15 sets of benches to be found in the county but C17 work of quality is rarer and Worlingham's suite is perhaps the best. The bench ends and the low doors are carved with blind-arched panels and there are squat **finials** supported by scrolls. At the w. end the ranges on both sides of the nave narrow to afford ample space around the font, and the front rail of the n. side is nicely carved with beast heads and strapwork together with the legend 'WGM 1630'. The excellent pulpit is contemporary – two ranks of matching panels and a six-sided **tester** suspended by a chain from the roof. Elizabeth Cordy died aged 11 in 1824 and her chaste tablet on the n. wall is by Smyth of Woodbridge. The one above it is by Clutten of Framlingham, who provided another on the s. wall for John Croydon who died in 1828, with a verse more C18 in style than C19. Two minor brasses lie

under the nave matting; halfway along there is an inscription and verse for Jaspar Hussie who 'came to this towne after a long sickness to take ye benefit of this aire' but died nevertheless in 1624, and at the e. end plates showing four sons and seven daughters are all that are left of an unidentified family group of about 1530. The rood stair lies in the n. wall and the small **piscina** by the pulpit shows that there was a pre-**Reformation** altar there. Only the base of the **rood screen** remains and fragments of its decoration show through a covering of dark brown paint.

The wide chancel has a C19 roof and on the n. wall is one of the better works of **John Bacon the Younger**. It is the large memorial in white marble for the Duchess of Chandos, who died in 1817. The figure of Faith with book and cross kneels by a sarcophagus, while on the other side Hope with her anchor and with her foot on a skull points upwards to the cross and crown. Farther to the e. is a memorial for Sir John and Dame Elizabeth Major provided in 1781 by a little-known sculptor, Cooper of Stratford le Bow. There is a grey obelisk at the top and the well-lettered tablet has a decorative backing in multi-coloured marbles with a coloured shield of arms inset below. On the opposite wall is a very good example of the use of Coade stone, an artificial substitute for marble popularised by that remarkable C18 businesswoman Mrs Eleanor Coade. Here we have a memorial for Dame Ann Henniker of 1792 – an epitaph panel with cherub's head below, small sarcophagus above topped by coat of arms and an urn, all crisp and attractive. By the priest's door is a **consecration cross** and in the **sanctuary** the early C14 angle piscina has a slim shaft and a stone **credence shelf**. In the head of the e. window the arms of John Henniker Major, 4th Baron, are beautifully painted in enamels on white glass and dated 1838, and the **reredos** in stone and mottled marble with a pair of white marble angels is unashamedly Victorian. John Wilson died in 1782 at the age of 116 and I searched in vain for his grave for no better reason than to ponder on the fact that his suppers for forty years were plates of roasted turnips. You may be luckier and hear the faint echo of an antique burp.

Yaxley, St Mary (B3): Now that the village has been by-passed the church enjoys a tranquil setting by a sharp bend in the street. As you enter the churchyard, note the hitching ring in the wall to the r. of the gate, and look for an interesting stone on the r. of the path for Robert 'Waterloo' Bond who died on Christmas Day 1878 and was given a military funeral on New Year's Day. The C14 tower has **flushwork** and chequer on the buttresses, a deep **ogee**-headed niche in the w. wall, and tall, narrow **lancets** at ground and first-floor level. There is a s. **porch** of 1854 and in 1868 the **chancel** was largely rebuilt with new side windows, although the e. wall and window are mainly original. It is interesting that the restorers took the trouble to add a flying buttress over the **priest's door** in emulation of the one at Eye. The main entrance is the C15 n. porch and this is a splendid affair with a beautifully proportioned and detailed facade. A pair of large windows above the outer arch light the upper room and they are flanked by elaborately canopied niches. Below, a line of crowned 'Ms' for the dedication is set in flushwork and more tall niches occupy the corner buttresses and the spaces each side of the archway. A line of shields runs below the crested parapet whose pinnacles carry seated beasts. The **spandrels** of the arch are carved with a giant and a **woodwose** and the vault within has mutilated **bosses** of the **Evangelistic symbols**, with a possible **Annunciation** in the centre.

The **font** is a plain octagonal bowl resting on an 1860s base and columns, and nearby is a very compact iron-banded C15 chest. The tower screen has a number of medieval glass fragments inserted but they are difficult to

appreciate without access to the tower. The s. porch now serves as a **vestry** and over the doorway hangs Yaxley's famous sexton's wheel. In the C14 and C15 when veneration of the **Blessed Virgin** was at its height, penitents would sometimes be directed (or would choose) to observe the Lady fast – either one day a week for seven years, or 365 days continuously on bread and water. If they chose the latter, they would come to the sexton to determine the day on which to begin. There are six days in the church's calendar set aside for the honour of the Virgin, and six long threads were tied to the wheel, each one identified for a particular feast. The sexton would spin the wheel and the devotee would grasp a thread at random to decide when the fast should start. There must have been hundreds of these wheels, particularly in churches dedicated to **St Mary**, but only two have survived – one here and one at Long Stratton, just up the A140 in Norfolk. There is a **hatchment** close by for the Revd Seymour Leeke who died in 1786 and another over the n. door for Francis Gilbert Yaxley Leeke; he was Seymour's illegitimate half-brother and heir, and died in 1836. In the s. **aisle** are three **brasses** – an inscription for Joan Yaxley, 1517; another for Alice Pulvertoft, 1511 at the e. end; and the 18in. figure of Andrew Feldgate, who died in 1598, in ruff and gown. On the s. wall there are wooden heraldic carvings which were once part of the tomb of William Yaxley, a Catholic Suffolk M.P. who married one of the Oxborough Bedingfields and died in 1588. It stood in the s. **aisle** until the great upheaval of 1868. In a n. aisle window the vicar who masterminded that restoration, William Henry Sewell, is commemorated by a Jones & Willis version of Holman Hunt's *The Light of the World.*

The s. aisle is separated from the **nave** by a three-bay **arcade** on octagonal **piers** and there is a **clerestory** on that side only. This was inserted when the new **roof** was built and the line of the old one still shows on the tower wall. The **arch-braces** are adorned with large flower bosses, the **wall plates** retain traces of colour, and the easternmost bay of the roof was originally decorated as a **celure** for the **rood** below. There are large patches of what was a painted **Doom** remaining on either side of the chancel arch but little detail can now be seen. The window overhead originally silhouetted the rood when the chancel roof was lower, and note that a support for the cross was slotted into the centre of the window frame. The entrance to a commodious **rood stair** is now largely masked by a superb pulpit of 1635. It has strapwork on top of the **tester** and displays the initials of churchwardens Thomas Dade and Thomas Fulcher. The back panels remind the preacher: 'Necessite is laid upon me, yea woe is me if I preach not the Gospel', and there are fine dragon scrolls on each side. The carving on the body of the pulpit is conventional for the period but unusually rich and vigorous. The nave pews date from the Victorian restoration and were supplied by Frosts of Watton in Norfolk. One of the ends on the s. side carries an interesting 1870s brass:

A stove has been placed near this bench in remembrance of a ... widow of about four score and nine years which departed not from the temple but served God and was buried in the s.e. part of the churchyard having desired that her name should not appear on her gravestone. May it be found written in the Lamb's Book of Life.

It seems like sneaking somehow to reveal that her name was Elizabeth Pretty, and judging by her engraved portrait she was a fine-looking woman.

The C15 **rood screen** is a late version of the type to be found in many East Anglian churches but is surprisingly large and elaborate for a church of this size. Although cruelly mutilated, enough remains to prove that it was once very beautiful. The **crockets** and **hoods** have been broken from the main **lights** but the centre arch still has fine triple ranks of **cusping**. The small lower panels have paintings of saints in the Flemish style and, despite defacement, the sword and wheel of **St Catherine** can be identified just to the l. of the entrance, and a recognisable **St Mary Magdalene** on the s. side. Next to her is **St Barbara**, followed by **St Dorothy** and **St Cecilia**. The figures are backed by an interesting variety of **gesso** patterns still in good condition. Overhead, the stumps of the **rood beam** can be seen just below the **wall posts** of the nave roof. The 1860s chancel roof rests on ebullient musical angel **corbels** and the organ blower's stool has a most engaging refinement – its oval top has a massive block to match which can be lifted off its securing pegs to accommodate a smaller size of boy. A very worn C14 effigy of a priest lies within a recess in the n. wall and there is a brass inscription for Alice Yaxle, 1474, in the centre of the floor. It is worth studying the medley of medieval glass arranged in the e. window by William Sewell in the 1880s. His own minuscule profile portrait is sweetly enclosed within the letter 'P' in the inscription in the r. hand light. There is a figure of **St John** above it, a beautiful head of Christ in the centre, a late head of St Mary in yellow stain farther down, and **St Andrew** with **St Peter** in the top **tracery**.

GLOSSARY OF TERMS

Abacus (plural, abaci): A flat stone slab set on top of a pillar or **pier** to take the thrust of an arch springing from it. Most often seen in **Norman** and **Early English** architecture. (Compare with **impost** and **capital**.)

Acanthus: A stylised form of leaf decoration based on a family of plants which include Bears' Breech. Used originally by the Greeks, it became very popular in the C17 and C18, particularly for use on mouldings and scrolls.

Achievement of arms: Heraldic arms in their full form with all or most of the following: shield of arms, crest, helm and mantling (its ornamental drapery), supporters (animals or humans), motto – as opposed to a plain shield of arms.

Agnus Dei (The Lamb of God): When **St John the Baptist** saw Jesus coming he said, 'Behold the Lamb of God who takes away the sin of the world'. The words were used in the mass as early as the C5 and by the C9 wax medallions were being made on Holy Saturday from remnants of the previous year's paschal candle. In the Middle Ages, the lamb bearing a cross or flag was widely used in painting and sculpture as a symbol of Our Lord.

Aisles: The parts of the church to the n. and s. of the **nave**, and sometimes of the **chancel**, under sloping **roofs** which give the impression of extensions to the main building. Which, indeed, they often were, being added to accommodate side **altars**, (see **chantry chapels** and **guild altars**), as well as larger congregations, and to provide processional ways – an important requirement before the **Reformation**. These are not to be confused with the 'aisle' down which the bride steps, which is the centre gangway of the nave.

Altar: The table used for the celebration of the Eucharist (Holy communion or mass), to be found within the **sanctuary** at the e. end of the **chancel**. Originally of wood, but stone altars (see **mensa**) became common in the early Church. When the practice of celebrating private masses became common in the Middle Ages, altars were set up elsewhere in the church (see **guilds** and **chantry chapels**) and the original altar became known as the high altar. At the **Reformation** there was controversy over the use of stone altars; more followed in Elizabeth's reign and in the C17 over the positioning of what was then called 'the Holy table' (see also **Laudian**). In recent years the practice has grown of siting an altar at the e. end of the **nave** to emphasise corporate worship.

Altar rails: See **communion rails**.

Anchorite/anchoress (female)/**anchorite's cell:** An anchorite – the word being derived from the Greek 'anakhoreo', retire – was a religious recluse who chose to be walled up for life in a cell attached to a church, in order to devote his or her mortal existence to prayer, meditation, and piety. A small outer window gave light and a way for food to be passed in – and for people to receive wise advice from the recluse. Another small window, or **squint**, gave a direct view of the **altar** so that the anchorite could watch the celebration of mass. See Cotton and Nettlestead.

Angle piscina: See **piscina**.

Anglo-Saxon: The Anglo-Saxons were the Teutonic invaders who overran Britain in the Dark Ages. Between the C5 and C7 Norfolk and Suffolk were overrun and were settled by the Angles, who gave their name to East Anglia. **Saxon** architecture, distinctive in its simplicity, existed until it was superseded by **Norman** building following the Conquest of 1066 (see **Styles of Architecture**).

Annunciation: Annunciation representations are a regular subject for stained glass scenes, as well as wood and stone carvings – the Archangel Gabriel bringing news to Mary of the Incarnation, that she would conceive a child of the Holy Ghost (Luke 1: 26 – 38). The Feast of the Annunciation is 25 March, otherwise known as Lady Day, an important date too in the rural calendar, when tenant farmers' rents were due and new tenancies were granted. Examples may be found in many churches.

Apostles: see under **Saints**.

Apse/apsidal: Rounded end of a building, usually the **chancel** at the e. end in churches. Derived from Romanesque architecture, semi-circular in shape, or consisting of five sides of an octagon, and often dome-roofed or vaulted; generally associated in Britain with **Norman** churches. It is said that the apse represents the raised platform of the secular 'basilica' or public hall which in Roman times was used as law court and treasury as well as meeting hall; another theory is that it is borrowed from the platform of the meeting rooms of early Christian **guilds**.

Arcades: A series of arches, i.e., those down each side of the **nave** of an aisled church – supported by pillars. Sometimes arcades are 'closed', 'blind', or 'blank' – a decorative outline on a wall or tomb or furnishing or, as may often be found, the result of an aisle having been demolished and the arcade bricked up, leaving its pillars and arches outlined.

Arch-braced roof: A roof carried on a simple, braced arch. (See **roofs**, fig. 4 for full description.)

Art Nouveau: An ornamental style that flourished throughout Europe during 1890 to 1910, characterised by long sinuous lines mainly derived from naturalistic forms, particularly the lily, rose, and peacock. Sometimes occurring in church furniture and fittings of wood and metal (there is a tablet at Bredfield), but more often seen as an influence in the stained glass of the period.

Arts and Crafts Movement: A movement active in the late C19 and early C20 which opposed the shoddy results of mass production and emphasised the value of hand crafts. One of the guiding principles was that the artist should be involved in every process, from initial design to finished work. Selwyn Image, W.R. Lethaby, **Christopher Whall**, Walter Crane, and Charles Rennie Mackintosh were among the leading figures. The movement's influence in church art is mainly to be seen in stained glass like Hugh Arnold's at East Bergholt and Robert Anning Bell's at Nayland, but there is a font cover and war memorial by Charles Sidney Spooner at Hadleigh and a **lych-gate** by E.S. Prior at Brantham.

Ashlar: Square hewn stone, often used as facing for brick or rubble walls.

Assumption of the Virgin: The translation of the Virgin Mary, body and soul, into heaven – a theme often represented by medieval artists in painting and sculpture. The Feast of the Assumption is 15 August, a festival first initiated in the year 582 by the Roman Emperor Maurice. The Eastern Orthodox Church, with a poetic touch, celebrates the Assumption as 'The Feast of the Falling Asleep of Our Lady'.

Aumbry: A small cupboard or recess in which were stored the Holy oils used in baptism, confirmation, and Extreme Unction (anointing of the dying person by the priest); also the sacred vessels/plate used for mass or communion. Sometimes the aumbry held the Reserved Sacrament – the consecrated bread, 'reserved' from a mass (see also **Easter sepulchre**). The aumbry is generally found on the n. side of the **chancel** (opinions vary about medieval usage), but sometimes near the **piscina** – which is almost always on the s. side – and in a few cases it may be near the **font**. Originally, very few parish churches had **sacristies** for storing the plate and valuables. The priest robed at the **altar**, his vestments meantime being kept in a parish chest, the vessels for altar and font being placed in the aumbry. Thus chest plus aumbry equals the later **vestries**. Occasionally the aumbry was used in the C15 as a safe for documents, not only those belonging to the church but also ones belonging to parishioners, as it would be secured by door and lock. Very few of these wooden doors remain today, though the hinge and latch marks in the stone can often be made out. Aumbries can be found at Bures (St Stephen), Great Wenham, Henley, Holton St Mary, and Needham Market.

Bacon, John the Younger (1777 – 1859): Something of a child prodigy, he was sculpting figures at the age of 11. Extraordinarily prolific and successful, monuments by him are legion. A good example of his work may be seen at Worlingworth with others at Assington, Edwardstone, Stoke by Nayland, and Witnesham.

Ball flower: An early C14 decorative ornament in sculpture. See **Decorated** under **Styles of Architecture**.

Baluster: A short, decorative column, often slightly pear shaped, i.e., bulging at the middle and tapering at top and bottom.

Banner-stave lockers: In the late medieval period, parish **guilds** proliferated and all had their banners to be carried in the processions which in medieval times were an important part of services on Sundays and Feast Days (see also **Galilee porches**). Between times, the banners would be placed in the guild chapels and the staves in their lockers, which explains the long, narrow upright niches in the walls of some churches which can seem so puzzling.

Bar tracery: Tracery in the heads of windows, constructed in separate pieces, as distinct from **plate tracery**, where the pattern is cut directly through the masonry. See **Early**

English under **Styles of Architecture**.

Base course: A horizontal layer of masonry, decorative in character, usually at the base of towers. See **courses**.

Basilisk: See **Cockatrice**.

Bestiary: A medieval collection of stories, each based on a description of certain qualities of an animal or plant. The stories all derive from the 'Physiologus', a C2 Greek text in which each creature is linked to a biblical text. Extremely popular in the Middle Ages, the bestiaries presented Christian allegories for moral and religious instruction, and many are illustrated, thus providing prototypes for many imaginative carvings.

Biers: Some churches – particularly, for obvious reasons, those with a long path between **lych-gate** and church – have a platform to carry the coffin to and from the funeral service. These curious conveyances can often be seen, discreetly tucked away at the back of the **nave** or in a side **aisle**. Most of them are Victorian but there are interesting C18 examples at Washbrook and Mendlesham (where there is a matching child's bier like the one at Brundish).

Billet: Billet moulding or decoration was particularly used in **Norman** work. It was formed by cutting notches in two parallel and continuous rounded mouldings in a regular, alternating pattern.

Black Death: Some time in the 1340s a horrific epidemic of bubonic plague ('The Black Death' is a modern expression coined in the C19) began, possibly in China, and by 1348 it had reached the south of France where it devastated the papal city of Avignon. By the end of the year it had crossed the Channel and begun the ravages which, in twelve months, would leave between a third and a half of the nation's population dead. It cut off in its prime the greatest flowering of English architectural beauty (see **Decorated** under **Styles of Architecture**). On 1 January 1349 the king, Edward III, issued a proclamation postponing Parliament because 'a sudden visitation of deadly pestilence' had broken out in and around Westminster, and by June the full fury of the plague had reached East Anglia. In the dreadful year ending 1350, it has been estimated that at least half, and probably more, of the population of Norfolk and Suffolk were swept away. Plague broke out again at intervals over the next three centuries until the last major outbreak, culminating in the Great Plague of London in 1665, when a quarter of the inhabitants died. What is remarkable, in considering the Black Death in relation to our churches, is that it was followed by one of the greatest ages of church building. It was first recorded in East Anglia at Little Cornard, and there seems to be clear evidence of its effect on church building at Kersey.

Blank/blind arcading: See **arcades**.

Blessed Virgin: See **Mary the Blessed Virgin** under **Saints**.

Blomfield, Sir Arthur William (1829 – 99): Son of a bishop of London and one of the successful architects of the Victorian era. He established his own practice in 1856 and was president of the Architectural Association in 1861. He carried out important cathedral restorations at Canterbury, Salisbury, Lincoln, and Chichester, and designed many churches in England and abroad. Apart from a number of restorations in the county, he designed Ipswich (St John the Baptist).

Bodley, George Frederick (1827 – 1907): Church architect and decorative designer, Bodley was **Sir George Gilbert Scott's** first pupil in the 1840s and established his own practice in 1860. From 1869 to 1897 he was in partnership with Thomas Garner and much of their work is indistinguishable. Bodley excelled in the use of late Gothic forms, and in furnishings his preference for rich colour enhanced by gilding shows in the many designs he provided for Watts & Co. He was also the first to commission stained glass from **Morris & Co.** Edwardstone is a tribute to the quality of his restoration work.

Bosses: A boss is the carved ornamentation seen at the intersections of **roof** beams or of the ribs in vaulted (see **groining**) ceilings. Usually they represent foliage or grotesque animals or figures, but often they are intricately worked with biblical scenes, portraits, heraldic arms, and symbols.

Box pew: Large pews panelled to waist height or higher, often with seats on three sides, and entered by a door from the **aisle**. Nicknamed 'box pews' from their similarity to horse-boxes or stalls. They came into favour in the late C17 and early C18 and were often embellished with curtains, cushions, and carpets. Most disappeared in the wave of C19 restorations. There are examples at Lindsey, Gipping, Brundish, Cretingham, Easton, Letheringham, and Gislingham, and a **Jacobean** set at Badley. See also **Prayer book churches**.

Brasses: Brasses are incised memorial portraits and inscriptions, usually found set into the floor or on top of tombs, although some may be seen fixed to walls and furnishings. Brasses

are made in an alloy called latten, a mixture of copper and zinc. This was chiefly manufactured at Cologne, where it was beaten into rectangular plates for export to Britain, the Low Countries, and elsewhere. Such memorials were for a long time favoured by a wide range of classes, from the nobility, through the priesthood, scholars, and monks, to merchants and families of local standing. The earliest brass to be seen in England is said to be that of Sir John d'Abernon at Stoke d'Abernon in Surrey, dated 1277, in the reign of Edward I. It was not until the first half of the C17 that the fashion petered out. In the 1830s, interest stirred again, and in the 1840s **Pugin** combined with **Hardman** to design and produce brasses in the medieval manner. Good examples of Victorian brasses are to be found at Yaxley and Ipswich (St Bartholomew). Effigies and inscriptions became popular, and although Hardmans were by far the major suppliers, many firms were at work. Very few were produced after the spate of war memorials in the 1920s. Suffolk is rich in medieval brasses, with particularly fine examples at Burgate, Brundish, Easton, Letheringham, and Little Wenham. But brasses are more than memorials: they are remarkable, pictorial commentaries on four centuries of our history, martial armour, manners, customs, dress, and fashion. See also **chalice brass** and **shroud brass**.

Broach spire: A spire which rises from a square base and then becomes octagonal by the insertion of triangular faces.

Burlison & Grylls: A firm of stained glass manufacturers founded by John Burlison and Thomas Grylls in 1868. They had trained with **Clayton & Bell** and had close links with **Sir George Gilbert Scott** and **G. F. Bodley**, for whom much of their earliest and best glass was done. Its accomplished drawing followed C15 and C16 precedents and the work was of a high technical standard. The firm closed in 1953. An excellent example may be found at Edwardstone and there is another window at Earl Soham.

Butterfield, William (1814 – 1900): The architect and decorative designer who will always be remembered for two London churches at least – All Saints, Margaret Street, and St Matthias, Stoke Newington. His was a highly individual interpretation of the Gothic style, often characterised by structural polychromy – bands and patterns of bricks in contrasting colours, and his strong sense of craftsmanship may have stemmed from his apprenticeship in the building trade. He was a staunch Tractarian and for many years directed the **Ecclesiological Society's** scheme for the design of church furnishings. He rebuilt Great Waldingfield chancel in 1866 and added a new nave and chancel to Ipswich (St Mary at Stoke) in 1870.

Butterfly head-dress: 'Butterfly' is a name given in the C16, and used ever since, for a style fashionable in the previous century, from about 1450 to 1485. Its high-fashion status is indicated by its appearance on effigies of the period in brass and stone. The head-dress consisted of a wire frame, fixed to a close-fitting ornamented cap, supporting a gauze veil spreading out above the head on each side like a pair of diaphanous butterfly wings.

Cambridge Camden Society: See **Ecclesiological Society**.

Canopy of honour: See **celure**.

Capital: The usually decorated and ornamented top of a column/pillar, from which springs the arch which the

pillar supports. (Compare with **impost** and **abacus**.)

Cartouche: Latin 'carta', paper. Sculptural representation of a curling sheet of paper.

Caryatid: Female figure used as a pillar or **pilaster**.

Castellated: Decorated with miniature battlements like a castle.

Cautley, Henry Munro (1875 – 1959): Diocesan surveyor from 1914 to 1947 and authority on church architecture and fittings. His only complete churches in the county are Ipswich (St Augustine), St Andrews and All Hallows, but many others bear witness to his work, and furniture of his design may be found at Flowton, Stowmarket, Westerfield and Stowupland. His *Suffolk Churches and their Treasures* was first published in 1937 and is still essential reading for those interested in the county's medieval heritage. The fourth edition was supplemented in 1982 by Anne Riches's *Victorian Church Building and Restoration in Suffolk*, a subject that Cautley resolutely refused to contemplate. His *Royal Arms and Commandments in our Churches* was one of the first monographs on the subject. A man of parts, he farmed at Butley, specialising in Red Poll cattle, and he enjoyed the gift of water divining. His father was rector of Westerfield and Cautley himself read the lessons there for over sixty years. The superb pews at Mildenhall are an enduring memorial to his love for ancient churches and to his generosity.

Celure: Otherwise known as a 'canopy of honour'. A panelled and painted section of the **roof** of a church, either over the **altar**, or at the eastern end of the **nave** over the position occupied by the **rood**. There are examples at Barking, Bredfield, Cotton, Dallinghoo, Eye, Kersey, and Yaxley.

Censer/Censing: See **thurible**.

Chancel: The e. end section of a church, containing the **altar**. Before the **Reformation** the chancel was restricted to the clergy and the celebration of mass, the people occupying the **nave**. Separating the two was a screen (thus the derivation of the word from the Latin 'cancellus', lattice). Traditionally, the parson was responsible for the repair and upkeep of the chancel while the parishioners cared for the rest, and this sometimes resulted in separate building programmes. In some cases it explains the difference in age and style between the two parts of the church. See **rood loft** and also note **weeping chancel**.

Chantry chapels: The most distinctive development in C14 and C15 church affairs was the growth of chantries. Instead of leaving money to monasteries or similar foundations, rich men began to favour their parish church and to endow priests to say daily masses for them and their families after their death. By the C15 all large, and many small, churches contained a number of such chantries – often with their own chapel or **altar** and furnished with vestments, ornaments, and sacred vessels. They provided light, profitable work for a priest, although the less well-endowed chantries had to make do with a part-time stipendiary chaplain. These priests were not under the jurisdiction of the incumbent and endless disputes and not a few abuses followed. For those who could not afford the luxury of a private chantry, membership of a local **guild** often offered a substitute. Chantries were abolished by Edward VI in 1547, ostensibly on religious grounds but really to meet an acute shortage in the Exchequer.

Chevron moulding: The chevron or zigzag is a characteristic decorative moulding of **Norman** architecture, its bold 'V' shapes being used from the early C12 around open arches and arches of windows and doors. See **Styles of Architecture**.

Chi Rho: See **sacred monogram**.

Christian, Ewan: (1814 – 95): As architect to the Ecclesiastical Commissioners and the Church Building Society, he designed a large number of rather dull churches. None of them are in Suffolk but he also directed over 300 restorations, including Bramford, Bures, Hoxne, Lowestoft (St Margaret) [Vol.3], and Mendlesham.

Christmas, Gerard: Carver to the Royal Navy, and pageant master to the City of London in the reign of James I, Christmas was an outstanding sculptor whose masterpiece is, perhaps, the Tanfield monument in Burford church in Oxfordshire. It is strange that, although he was an East Anglian by birth, there are only two of his works in Suffolk – the Drury monument at Hawstead [Vol.1], and the Crane monument at Chilton.

Chrysom child: When a child was baptised, it was swaddled for the Christening service in the 'chrysom' cloth or sheet, which often belonged to the parish. If the child died before its mother had been churched (i.e., had been to church after the birth to receive the priest's blessing and purification) it was then buried in the chrysom cloth, thus becoming a 'chrysom child'. In this form it was represented on tombs and **brasses**, as, for example, on a **ledger-stone** at Stoke by Nayland.

Churchyard cross: See **preaching cross**.

Cinquefoils: See **foils**.

Clayton & Bell: A firm of stained glass manufacturers founded by John Richard Clayton and Alfred Bell in 1855, and still continuing under Michael Bell. Their studio was one of the largest of the Victorian period and they were notable for the brilliance of their High Victorian designs and consistency in their use of colour. Their work of the early 1860s was of a particularly high standard. There are good examples at Assington, Stowmarket, and Wilby, with others at Baylham, Ipswich (St Mary le Tower and St Mary at Stoke), Ringshall, and Stradbroke.

Clerestory: An upper storey, standing clear of its adjacent roofs, and pierced with windows which usually correspond in number with the number of arches, or bays, in the **arcade** below. Its pronunciation – 'clearstorey' – explains the clerestory's function, namely, letting in light through clear glass windows onto the large covered area below.

Clerk: See **parish clerk**.

Cockatrice (also known as a basilisk): A fabulous reptile hatched by a serpent from a cock's egg. Both its breath and its look were supposed to be fatal. In medieval imagery it takes the form of a cock with a barbed serpent's tail. There is an example on a bench end at Stonham Aspal.

Collar beam: See **roofs**.

Collar of SS or Esses: A decorative collar of gold or silver composed of Ss linked together. There are many theories concerning the origin of this mark of honour and what the 'S' stood for (sovereign, seneschal, etc.). The earliest effigy shown wearing it in this country dates from 1371 and so it cannot, as some have maintained, have been introduced by Henry IV. He did, however, issue a regulation in 1401 limiting its use to sons of the king, dukes, earls, and barons, and to other knights and esquires when in his presence. During the reigns of Henry IV, his son, and his grandson, it was a royal badge of the Lancastrian house, with a white swan as pendant rather than the more usual portcullis. It was later restricted to the lord chief justice, the lord mayor of London, the heralds and kings of arms and the serjeants at arms. See Chilton.

Colonnette: A small column.

Commandment boards: See **decalogue boards**.

Communion rails: The rails against which the congregation kneel to receive communion (no doubt taking it for granted that this is and always was their purpose) were originally installed for quite other reasons. They were to protect the **altar** from irreverent people and even less reverent dogs – and the **balusters** were to be set close enough to ensure this. Before the **Reformation** the **chancel** was always closed off by a screen (see **rood loft/screen**), usually fitted with doors, and the people normally never entered it-they watched through the screen as the priest celebrated mass. At great festivals parishioners received the sacrament, sometimes going through the screen to do so. When general participation in services and the administration of the sacrament to the people became the norm, different arrangements were needed.

Archbishop **Laud** ordered that the altar should be railed and not moved from its n.s. position, and the rails often enclosed the altar on three sides. Whether there should be rails or no, Richard Montague, bishop of Norwich, made his position clear in a Visitation question in 1638: 'Is your communion table enclosed, and ranged about with a rail of joiners and turners work, close enough to keep dogs from going in and profaning that holy place, from pissing against it or worse?' The bishop further ordered that:

> the communicants being entered into the chancel shall be disposed of orderly in their several ranks, leaving sufficient room for the priest or minister to go between them, by whom they were to be communicated one rank after another, until they had all of them received.

This was to come into conflict with the Puritan habit of demanding that communion should be received by the congregation seated in their pews. In 1643 communion rails went the way of other 'monuments of superstition and idolatry', but at the **Restoration** in 1660 old habits were resumed and the taking of communion at the **sanctuary** rail became accepted practice. At that time three-sided rails were popular and examples can be found at Cretingham, Elmsett, Hoo, Letheringham, Lindsey, and Polstead. There are rails by William Cleere at Great Waldingfield and an Italian set of 1700 at Barham. See also **Prayer book churches** and **housel bench**.

Comper, Sir Ninian (1864 – 1960): Distinguished and highly individual architect of the Gothic Revival, who in the course of seventy years built fifteen churches, restored and decorated scores, and designed vestments, windows, and banners for use literally all around the globe, from America to the Far East, for both the Roman and Anglican communions. He designed the restored screen and much else at Eye, a window at Ipswich (St Mary at the Elms), and an altar frontal at Wingfield.

Consecration crosses: Painted or carved, they indicate the points at which the walls of the church, and the **altar** slab (the **mensa**) were touched with Holy oil by the bishop at the consecration of the building. On the altar were incised five crosses – one at each corner and one in the middle – signifying the **five wounds of Christ**. Medieval practice varied, but normally three crosses were marked on each of the four walls, both inside and out, and spikes bearing candles were inserted below them. The bishop's procession would circle the church before he knocked to be admitted by the single deacon within. The floor was marked from corner to corner with a cross of ashes in which the bishop would inscribe the Latin and Greek alphabets before anointing the rest of the crosses and the altar. In many cases a sacred relic would be sealed within or near the altar at the same time. Examples are not uncommon and include Bures (St Stephen), Creeting St Peter, Hoxne, and Nayland. There are seven at Kenton and an incised cross at Horham.

Corbel: A highly practical item which often doubles as a very decorative one. This is the support, set firmly into the wall, to carry a weight from above (see **roofs**) and it will usually be carved, either decoratively or with heads which may be reverent or formalised, delightfully (and irreverently) portrait-like or entirely fanciful.

Corbel table: A continuous row of **corbels** set into a wall to support the eaves of a roof.

Corinthian: A column of one of the classical (Grecian) orders, comprising a cushioned base, the shaft or pillar itself (usually fluted), and a **capital** (i.e., the head of the pillar) enriched with **acanthus** leaves.

Courses: A course is, in general terms, a horizontal layer of masonry. A **base course** will usually be at the base of the tower – a purely decorative course, a little above the ground, designed to set off the tower visually. In Suffolk, local flint is often used to great effect here, knapped and set flush into stone panelling (thus, **flushwork**) to create a most attractive contrast, as well as a visual impression of upward, vertical thrust. A string course is a continuous line of moulding projecting from a wall which, when used on a tower, divides it into stages. Finally, a drip course is, as its name indicates, a raised course doing the practical job of carrying off rain from the wall surface. See also **dripstone**.

Credence/credence shelf: This is a shelf on which the elements of the mass or communion (bread, wine, and water) are placed before consecration by the priest; usually found within the niche of the **piscina** beside the **altar**, or the site of a former altar. It can sometimes occupy a niche of its own.

Crockets/crocketting: This is an exuberant ornamentation of the **Decorated** period, in the first half of the C14, though it was to be carried through with enthusiasm into the later **Perpendicular** style (see **Styles of Architecture**). It is a little projecting sculpture in the form of leaves, flowers, etc., used in profusion on pinnacles, spires, canopies, and so on, both inside and outside the building.

Crossing/crossing tower: The crossing is the part of the church at the intersection of the cross shape of a church, where **chancel** and **nave** and n. and s. **transepts** meet. The crossing tower is

the central tower built over this point.

Cusps/cusping: From the Latin 'cuspis', a point (of a spear). These are the little projecting points on the curves of window and screen **tracery**, arches, etc., which give a foliated, leaf-like appearance.

Decalogue board: The decalogue (a word derived from the Greek) is the Ten Commandments collectively. The decalogue board, it follows, is a large board upon which the Commandments are written. These became a regular part of church furnishings in the reign of Elizabeth I, when it was state policy to clear churches of the decorations and adornments which were regarded as 'popish'. In 1560, Elizabeth ordered Archbishop Parker to see 'that the tables of the Commandments be comely set or hung up in the east end of the **chancel**'. The following year more explicit instructions were given: the boards were to be fixed to the e. wall over the communion table. The Creed and Lord's Prayer were not so ordered but were felt to be 'very fit companions' for the Commandments. Decalogues were also set up on the **tympanum** – panelling which filled the curve of the chancel arch to replace the discarded **rood loft** (see also **Royal Arms**). In most cases today, the decalogue boards have long since been moved from their position behind the **altar** and are usually displayed on a convenient wall of **nave** or **aisles**. There are good C17 examples at Kettleburgh and Saxtead, and an C18 set at Badley with an extra sentence.

Decorated: This was the high point of ornamented Gothic architecture in the first half of the C14. See **Styles of Architecture**.

Dogtooth decoration: An ornamental carving of the **Early English** period (see

Styles of Architecture) in the C12 to C13; it looks like a four-leafed flower. One suggestion is that it is based on the dog's tooth violet.

Doom: A picture of the Last Judgement, normally found painted over the **chancel** arch (which symbolically separated earthly from heavenly things). Christ is often represented seated on a rainbow, with souls being weighed below before being despatched to join the blessed on His right hand or the damned on His left. There are examples at Earl Stonham, Hoxne, Wissington, and Yaxley.

Dowsing, William (1596? – 1679?): In August 1643 Parliament ordered a general destruction of **altars**, pictures, and images in all churches, and the Earl of Manchester, as general of the eastern counties, appointed William Dowsing as his visitor in Suffolk to carry out the work. Dowsing had been born at Laxfield and later lived at Coddenham and Eye. He toured the county between January and October 1644 and is the best known of the despoilers, simply because he kept a diary. The original manuscript has vanished but a transcript was made in the early C18 and it was first published in 1786 (C.H.E. White edited the best edition in 1885). Dowsing employed deputies but took a personal delight in wreaking vengeance on all that he considered 'popish', often exceeding his brief in digging up floors and disturbing tombs. An eyewitness of his work in Cambridgeshire said:

> he goes about the Country like a Bedlam breaking glasse windowes, having battered and beaten downe all our painted glasse ... and compelled us by armed soldiers to pay ... for not mending what he had spoyled and defaced, or forthwith to go to prison.

It should not be assumed that all congregations and ministers in this strongly Puritan area were averse to the purge, but some churches saved their particular treasures by guile or obstinacy. Nevertheless, Dowsing exacted a terrible reckoning. At Clare [Vol.1]:

> we broke down 1000 Pictures superstitious; I broke down 200; 3 of God the Father and 3 of Christ and the Holy Lamb, and 3 of the Holy Ghost like a Dove with wings; and the 12 Apostles were carved in Wood, on the top of the Roof, which we gave order to take down; and 20 cherubims to be taken down; and the Sun and Moon in the East window, by the King's Arms, to be taken down.

His work done, he seems to have returned to obscurity and one of his name was buried at Laxfield in 1679. His was a very personal interpretation of the psalmist's: 'Let the righteous put their hand unto wickedness.'

Drip course: See **courses**.

Dripstone: A projecting ledge or moulding over the heads of doorways, windows, etc., serving the practical purpose of carrying off the rain. When the same architectural addition is used inside a building, as a decorative feature, it is called a **hood mould**.

Dropped-sill sedilia/window: See **sedilia**.

Early English: This is the style development of the mid-C12 which heralded the arrival of Gothic, or pointed, architecture in Britain – as well as the birth of a truly native style. See under **Styles of Architecture**.

Easter sepulchre: Immediately to the n. of the high **altar** a recess in the wall, ranging from the plain to the richly canopied, housed the Easter sepulchre. In some cases the top of a table tomb in the same area was used, and occasionally it was designed for this purpose. The sepulchre itself was normally a temporary structure of wood and a fragment of such a frame exists at Barningham [Vol.1]. On Maundy Thursday, a Host was consecrated (Latin 'hostia', victim – the bread which is the Body of Christ) and placed in the Easter sepulchre, to be consumed at the following day's Good Friday mass. This practice still continues in the Roman Catholic Church and in some Anglican churches today, the Host being 'borne in solemn procession ... to the altar of repose', to be processed back to the high altar the following day. Until the **Reformation**, the sepulchre would be watched over from Good Friday to Easter Day, partly from a belief that the final appearance of Christ would be early one Easter morning. Sometimes the watchers were paid. The sepulchre was often the setting for a dramatisation of the Resurrection. There are fine examples at Washbrook and East Bergholt, with others at Little Wenham (?), Mellis, Stradbroke, and Wingfield.

Ecclesiological Society: The Cambridge Camden Society, later to become the Ecclesiological Society, was founded by J.M. Neale, B. Webb, and others in 1839, and lasted until 1868. During that time it exerted an extraordinarily powerful influence on churchmen, architects, and laymen in laying down what it believed to be correct principles for church design, building, and ornamentation. Its activities coincided with the great wave of church building and restoration during the mid-C19 and much of what we see now is a direct result of its activities. The preferred style was **Decorated**; anything earlier was tolerated, but **Perpendicular** was stigmatised as 'debased' and classical architecture was anathema. Its critics have claimed that it destroyed more than all the Puritan iconoclasts put together, but the enthusiasm it engendered probably saved many medieval buildings that would otherwise have been lost.

Elevation squint: Central to the Eucharist (Mass) is the consecration of the bread and wine. During the Middle Ages, the standard practice was for the priest to raise the wafer of bread and the cup to symbolise the offering and for adoration by the people. Those kneeling close to the **chancel** screen could not gain a clear view, and the more determined sometimes bored a hole in the panel in front of their accustomed place so that they need not rise from their knees. These apertures have become known as elevation squints and there is an example at Badley. See also **squint.**

Embattled: Decorated with miniature battlements.

Emblems of the Trinity: Used extensively in wood, stone, and glass to represent the idea of the three persons of the Godhead: Father, Son, and Holy Spirit. The forms vary and include the equilateral triangle, the **trefoil**, three interlocking circles, and a widely used 'Trinity shield' which bears three inscribed and linked circles. Sometimes the image is pictorial, with God the Father holding a miniature Christ between His knees, and a dove superimposed to represent the Holy Spirit. There is a mutilated alabaster carving of this at Kersey, and other examples of the emblems may be seen on Hitcham porch and the **fonts** at Bildeston, Brome, Creeting St Mary, and Earl Stonham.

Encaustic tiles: The Victorians invented the process of burning-in different coloured clays onto tile and brick, to produce a stencil-like effect. In churches built during the C19, and in others 'restored and improved', these tiles were freely used on floors and walls.

Evangelistic symbols: On **fonts** and screens, in stained glass, etc., the symbols of the Evangelists are represented as man, eagle, lion, and ox, all winged. The biblical source is the four all-seeing, never-sleeping creatures around the throne of God, in the vision of **St John the Divine**: 'The first living creature was like a lion, the second was like an ox, the third had a face like a man, the fourth was like a flying eagle …' (Revelation 4:7). The Evangelists associated with the symbols are **St John**, eagle; **St Luke**, ox; **St Matthew**, man; **St Mark**, lion. There is an unusually good example in C14 glass at Great Bricett.

Evangelists: See **Evangelistic symbols**

Fan vault: A C15 architectural development in which the ribs of a vaulted **roof** were arranged in a fan pattern, rising in a trumpet shape from the walls and meeting at a **boss** or pendant; the spaces between the ribs were panelled and the effect is opulent. Seldom seen in parish churches, but there is an example at Eye. See also **groining**.

Finial: A carved or moulded ornament, often in foliage or floral form, or as a particularly decorative **crocket**, completing the points of arches, pinnacles, or gables. Any finishing in this sense, no matter how plain or simple, is still technically a finial.

Five wounds of Christ: On fonts and elsewhere, the five wounds of Christ are often represented. They are, of course, the wounds of the Crucifixion – to hands, feet, and side, recalling doubting Thomas's words: 'Except I shall…put my finger into the print of the nails, and thrust my hand into his side, I will not believe' (John, 20: 25). The **Easter sepulchre** at Mellis has five niches which may have been linked with the five wounds. See also the **instruments of the Passion**, which often accompany representations of the wounds.

Fleuron: A flower-shaped ornament used to decorate mouldings both in wood and stone.

Flint-knapping: Splitting flint across the middle, with craftsmanly skill, to achieve a shell-like fracture, and a lustrous, flat surface. See also **flushwork**.

Flushwork: This is the use of knapped flints, set flush into panelled patterns in brick or stone, a combination which adds visual beauty and striking impact to so many Suffolk and Norfolk churches.

Foils: From the C12, foils were a much used adornment in Gothic architecture. The **Early English** style produced the graceful **trefoil**, or three-leafed shape: it is said that this was intended to represent the **Trinity** – three in one and one in three – and that **St Patrick**, in C5 Ireland, so the story goes, put together three leaves of shamrock to illustrate to his converts in a visual way that profound mystery. Be that as it may, the trefoil was followed architecturally by the quatrefoil (four leaf), cinquefoil (five leaf), sexfoil (six leaf), and multi-foil.

Font: Receptacle for baptismal water, normally made of stone, but sometimes of wood or metal. The traditional place for the font is at the w. end of the church near to the main entrance, symbolising that baptism is the first stage in the Christian life. Medieval fonts were provided with a lockable cover to ensure the purity of the baptismal water and to guard against misuse or profanation. See also **seven**

sacraments.

Four Evangelists: See **Evangelistic symbols**.

Four Latin Doctors: 'Doctor' here indicates one who is learned, a theologian. The Four Latin Doctors were the leading theologians of the early Christian Church in the west – **Ambrose, Augustine of Hippo, Jerome**, and **Gregory**. See also **Saints**.

Gabriel: See **Saints**.

Galilee porches: Where a church has a western porch it was often called the 'Galilee porch' because it was the final 'station' in processions round the building. The priest at the head of the procession symbolised Christ going before his disciples into Galilee after the Resurrection. In medieval times these processions were an important part of certain services, particularly on Feast Days. There is a Galilee porch at Debenham. (See also **banner-stave lockers**.)

Galleries: These have a fascinating pedigree in churches. Before the **Reformation**, when every church had its **rood loft** in the **chancel** arch, singers might use the loft as a gallery, the singing being accompanied by a simple organ. In the couple of centuries that followed the Reformation and the destruction of the old rood lofts, galleries – usually at the w. end of the **nave** – became a common feature. There a simple orchestra would sometimes assemble to accompany the singing, and of their instruments a serpent survives at Barking and a bassoon at Stratford St Mary. Village choirs were common, although the robed and surpliced variety was a mid-Victorian innovation. When organs again became popular they were sometimes placed in a western gallery, and there they can still occasionally be found. Many more galleries were inserted in the C19 to accommodate the larger congregations of the period. There are galleries at Eye (C15), Boxford (C16), Little Stonham, Nayland (C18), Whatfield, Wissington (C18), Stowupland, Thornham Parva (C18), Wickham Skeith, Flowton, Hintlesham, Henley, Copdock, and Ipswich (Holy Trinity), and the C19 example at Old Newton has school seating.

Gargoyles: These are spouts jutting outwards from a wall so as to throw rainwater well away from the building. But there is much more to them than that. Almost always in ancient churches they are grotesquely carved in all manner of fanciful forms of weird beasts and dragons and devils and representations of human vices like the **Seven Deadly Sins**. This choice of subjects has a very positive aspect to it: if there is good in this world, there is assuredly evil; so also in the world of the spirit. To appreciate goodness and beauty, it is necessary to recognise the face of evil and ugliness – and this medieval man knew and practised. As his mixture of reverence and superstition also inclined to the view that dragons and demons were always prowling evilly round his church, what better way of keeping them at bay than putting their own kind on guard, on the basis, presumably, of 'it takes a devil to catch a devil'?

Gesso: This is a system of coating a base, usually wood, with a thick layer of plaster of Paris, or with gypsum (one of the powdered minerals used to make up plaster of Paris). When it is hard, the artist/sculptor carves into it his chosen design, to produce an incised effect which is then painted and, in church art, almost always gilded. The best example is the **retable** at Thornham Parva.

Green man: The green man is a foliate mask, often of demoniacal appearance, probably representing the spirit of fertility and often having living vines issuing from its mouth, and as such, an occasional device in wood and stone carving – a touch of persistent paganism in Christian art. Interesting examples can be found at Capel St Mary, Cotton, Great Waldingfield, Grundisburgh, Hintlesham, Little Waldingfield, and Nayland.

Griffin: Traditionally the guardian of treasure – but also used in church sculpture, carvings, and paintings. The griffin, or gryphon, is a mythical monster with an eagle's head, wings, and fore-legs; and the body, tail, and hind-legs of a lion. Heraldry uses this fabulous creature too (there is a griffin on the arms of the City of London, for example). In oriental folklore, a couple of griffins pulled Alexander the Great in a magic chariot up to heaven, while he was still alive, that is, just to have a look around. See an excellent medieval example at Shelley, others at Belstead and Eye, and a good modern version at Combs.

Grisaille: Geometric or leaf patterns painted onto white glass.

Groining: This is the creation of a vaulted ceiling, divided into segments by raised, intersecting lines – these lines, between the angled surfaces, being the actual 'groins'. Found in carved canopies, as well as in **roofs**.

Guilds/guild altars: In corners of churches, in the e. ends of **aisles**, etc., you will often see **piscinas**, and occasionally **squints** which, as is frequently repeated in the body of this book, indicate the presence of a guild or **chantry altar** in pre-**Reformation** times. Indeed, English guilds, according to one authority, 'are older

than any kings of England'. They were small local associations whose members banded together for a common charitable or practical purpose. Their religious commitment would often be shown by having their own altar in their parish church, served by a priest whom they maintained. There were two main divisions: craft or trade guilds, whose purpose was the protection of particular work, trade, or handicraft; and religious societies or, as they are sometimes called, 'social guilds'. The split was often one of convenience rather than a real distinction. All had the same general characteristic, the principle of brotherly love and social charity, and none was divorced from the ordinary religious observances daily practised in pre-Reformation England. Broadly speaking, they were the benefit societies and provident associations of the Middle Ages – a helping hand as ready to help the sick or look after poor children as to lodge pilgrims cheaply. Dr Jessop, a Norfolk local historian around the turn of this century, wrote descriptively of:

> ... small associations called guilds, the members of which were bound to devote a certain portion of their time and money and their energies to keep up the special commemoration and the special worship of some Saint's chapel or shrine which was sometimes kept up in a corner of the church, and provided with an altar of its own, and served by a chaplain who was actually paid by the subscriptions or free-will offerings of the members of the guild whose servant he was.

Nearly everyone was a member of one fraternity or another. One distinct help to the parish was the provision of additional priests for the services of the church. Beccles's guild of the Holy Ghost, for example, had a priest 'to celebrate in the church'. Beccles being 'a great and populous town of 800 **houseling** people ... the said priest is aiding unto the curate there, who without help is not able to discharge the said cure'. See also **chantry chapels**.

Hakewill, Edward Charles (1812 – 72): A church architect who was one of Philip Hardwick's pupils in the 1830s and district surveyor for St Clement Danes and St Mary-le-Strand. In 1851 he published *The Temple: an Essay on the Ark, the Tabernacle and the Temples of Jerusalem*. He carried out restorations and rebuilding at Ashbocking, Brantham, Crowfield, Grundisburgh, Kenton, Needham Market, Rushmere St Andrew, and Stonham Aspal.

Hakewill, John Henry (1811 – 80): An architect who enjoyed an extensive practice mainly in Wiltshire, Suffolk, and Essex, building many churches, schools, and parsonages. He was one of the consulting architects for the Incorporated Church Building Society and carried out the extensive 1870s restoration at Great Waldingfield.

Hammerbeam roofs: A brilliant conception, architecturally and artistically, of the late Gothic period, late C15 – C16, in which the thrust of the roof's weight is taken on 'hammer' brackets. See **roofs**, figs. 6, 7, and 8.

Hanoverian: The period during which the sovereigns were of the House of Hanover, from George I to Victoria.

Hardman, John & Co.: The family were originally button makers in Birmingham but John Hardman (1811 – 67) met **Pugin** in 1837 and they became friends. The following year they were partners in a new metal-working business which set out to provide church fittings and accessories of all kinds, for which Pugin provided all the designs in medieval style. Starting with small projects, mainly in precious metals, the venture blossomed. As Hardman and Iliffe, the firm took part in the Great Exhibition in 1851 and the medieval court displayed an extraordinary range of Pugin's designs and Hardman's craftsmanship. The revival of memorial **brasses** was largely due to them and Hardmans became by far the largest suppliers, producing some notable designs. In the early days, Pugin's influence was pervasive and stained glass was added to the repertoire in 1845. He was the chief designer in this medium until his death in 1852, after which the role passed to Hardman's nephew, John Hardman Powell, who continued until 1895. The firm's early work set standards for the Gothic revival in stained glass, and despite the changes in taste that have until recently dismissed it as unworthy of serious attention, it is of high quality and beauty. There are examples at Ipswich (St Helen) (?),Offton, Whitton, and Wilby, and the firm provided the lectern at Hadleigh.

Hatchments: Many churches display on their walls large, diamond-shaped boards, bearing a coat of arms and either the motto of the family whose coat it is, or the simple word: 'Resurgam' (I shall rise again). Dating from the second half of the C17 through to the end of the C18, these boards were carried in procession at the burial of the holder of the arms. Afterwards for some months they adorned the dead man's house, and finally they were transferred to the church. Samuel Pepys had a handsome one made for a relative in 1663 which cost him £4. The composition of the boards followed a formalised pattern – the background is black on the l. hand side if the dead person was a husband, black on the r. if a wife; for a bachelor, widow or widower, the whole background would be black. There is an early example at Debenham, and a good range at Easton and Coddenham.

Headstops: The decorative stops at the ends of **dripstones** and **hood moulds** over arches, doors, and windows.

Heaton, Butler & Bayne: A firm of stained glass manufacturers founded by Clement Heaton and James Butler in 1855, joined by Robert Turnill Bayne in 1862. They took over the role of the most original Gothicists from **Clayton & Bell** and produced an impressively varied series of high-quality windows in the 1860s which were fine examples of the High Victorian style at its most accomplished. There was significant collaboration with Henry Holiday and other artists of the aesthetic movement in the 1870s and the firm continued to produce glass until 1953. There are good examples at Brome, Ipswich (St Mary at Stoke) and Stuston, and others at Burstall, Eye, Gosbeck, Holton St Mary, Little Cornard, Oakley, and Willisham(?).

Herringbone work: A technique of positioning stones, bricks, or tiles in 'arrow formation', like the bones of a fish, with alternate courses in different directions, giving a zigzag effect. Not a decorative device, but a strengthening and supporting measure. The technique goes back to Roman times, but continued through the **Saxon** period and well into the **Norman** era.

High altar: See **altar**.

Holy table: See **altar**.

Holy Trinity: See **emblems of the Trinity**.

Hood mould: See **dripstone**.

Hour-glasses/stands: There was a time when long sermons were the rule rather than the exception, particularly after the **Reformation**, in Cromwell's Puritan period in the mid-C17, and in the C18 when preachers were renowned for their long-windedness. For their own guidance preachers often had an hour-glass on or near the pulpit, to indicate the passing time (though when the hour was up it was not unknown for sermonisers to turn the glass over and start again). Before the Reformation hour-glasses were used, though less commonly, to time private meditations, etc. There is a unique set of three at Earl Stonham and stands at Gislingham and Washbrook.

Housel bench/houseling people: In Old English 'housel' means 'sacrifice', and it was used in the English Church from **St Augustine** to the **Reformation** to mean the Eucharist. Houseling people were those in the parish who had received communion, and houseling benches were special seats placed in or near the **chancel** for them when they came up to the **altar**. The practice lingered on and the benches at Polstead may be a late example.

Howson, Joan: See **Townshend, Caroline and Joan Howson**.

IHS: See **sacred monogram**.

Impost: A simple bracket or moulding set as a 'lip' in a wall to carry a springing arch. A typical attribute of plain and massive **Saxon** architecture, in which field it is almost exclusively used in this book. (Compare with **capital** and **abacus**.)

Instruments of the Passion: Often used symbolically in carving and painting. They are: Christ's cross; the crown of thorns; the spear that was thrust into His side; the cup of vinegar; and the reed and sponge by which that vinegar was offered as Christ hung on the cross (John 19: 28 – 9). The dice which were used to cast lots for His clothing, scourges, pillar of scourging, seamless robe, pincers, hammer, nails and a ladder are additional symbols. Hitcham screen, Great Blakenham **font**, and Westerfield **roof** have good examples, with others at Baylham, Bramford, Brome, Earl Stonham, Gipping, and Kersey.

Jacobean: Style of architecture dating from early in the C17 with the reign, 1603 – 1625, of James I. See **Styles of Architecture**.

Jamb/jamb shaft: The upright of a doorway, or the side of a window opening: the 'shaft' is a decorative shaft or slim column at the angle of the window splay with the wall, and can often be used to remarkably beautiful and delicate effect.

Jesse tree: Isaiah prophesied: 'And there shall come forth a rod out of the stem of Jesse, and a Branch shall grow out of his roots.' This gave medieval artists a wonderful opportunity to illustrate the human genealogy of Christ as a tree (often a vine) springing up from the body of Jesse with each generation pictured as the fruits, with the **Blessed Virgin** and Christ child at the top. Occasionally, pagan figures, like Virgil and the sybils, slipped in. See the C15 doors at Stoke by Nayland and the C19 w. window at Ipswich (St Mary le Tower).

Kempe & Co. (Kempe & Tower): A firm of stained glass manufacturers founded in 1869 by Charles Eamer Kempe, a designer who had worked for **Clayton & Bell**. His nephew, Walter Ernest Tower, took over in 1907 and continued until 1934. Their work is generally in C15 mode, intricate and often sentimental, with a distinctive colour range

Kempe was one of the most successful late Victorian designers and there was little change in the style he adopted, even in the C20. His windows are sometimes signed with a wheatsheaf emblem, while those of Tower often have a castle superimposed on the sheaf of corn. There is a good range at Burgh, another of both Kempe and Kempe & Tower at Creeting St Mary, with other examples at Bildeston, Bramford, and Nayland.

Kennel head-dress: A style of head-dress fashionable from about 1500 to 1540, but not in fact given the name by which we know it until the C19. It appears distinctively on figures on **brasses** and tombs of the period, and on carved heads of **corbels**, etc. The head-dress consisted of a hood wired up to form a pointed arch over the forehead, with borders framing the face to each side. The early kind hung in folds to the shoulders behind; but after 1525 the back drapery was replaced by two long pendent flaps which hung down in front on each side of the neck. Both kinds will be seen represented. Examples are at Brome and Nayland.

King-post: An upright roof beam set between horizontal cross beams, or between cross beam and roof ridge, to prevent sag and give greater stability. See **roofs**, fig. 3.

Knapped/knapping: See   **flint-knapping**.

Label: A **dripstone** carried over a rectangular door or window, enclosing the top.

Lancet: The slim, pointed window which characterises the beginnings of **Early English** architecture from about 1200. See **Styles of Architecture**.

Laud: See **Laudian.**

Laudian: This refers to Archbishop William Laud, 1573 - 1644. His seven years as archbishop of Canterbury, during which he tried to impose certain disciplines of worship on the English and Scottish Churches, had far reaching effects, and resulted in his execution. Laud wanted to reform the English Church in a way compatible with Protestantism, yet without imposing the sweeping changes and austerities called for by the increasingly powerful Puritans. Brought down to its simplicities, he wanted a disciplined order and form of worship which centred on the **altar**, placed against the e. wall of the **chancel**, with an enclosing rail around it; and with the communicants kneeling within the chancel to receive the sacrament. But these were matters of bitter and violent debate (and disturbance – see the Monk Soham entry). From Elizabeth I's reign, the altar often had been placed 'table-wise', i.e., e. to w. at the **nave** end of the chancel, or a temporary table was set up in the nave – the intention being in each case for the communicants to be within sight and hearing of the priest at the altar. But there were those who refused to kneel, or even to enter the chancel, and who certainly would not tolerate, in the e. end altar, what smacked to them of a popish high altar, divorced from the people. The impression which comes down to us of the archbishop is of a man of honest intent whose every action seemed to turn people against him. He was accused of 'popery' and of warmth towards Rome; blamed for the disastrous and ineffective moves against Scotland, both judicial and military, intended to make its churches conform with his ideas; then he issued 'canons' (i.e., instructions) which appeared to many to enshrine the absolute rule and 'divine right' of King Charles I – whose position by now was seriously threatened. In December 1640 Parliament impeached Laud for treason, and he was imprisoned in the Tower. But it was not until March 1644 that he was put on trial and then it was a complete mockery of justice, for the House of Lords had decided in advance that he was guilty of trying to alter the foundations of Church and state. Nonetheless, they hesitated to sentence him until the House of Commons threatened to set the mob on them if they didn't. On 10 January 1644, staunchly declaring his innocence and good intent, William Laud, at the venerable age of 72, died under the axe, Parliament having graciously agreed that he should be excused the usual traitor's punishment of being hung, drawn, and quartered. The irony is that, by the end of the century, the forms of service which developed in the Anglican Church were much in sympathy with the things for which Laud fought and died. See also **Prayer book churches, communion rails,** and **mensa slabs.**

Lavers & Barraud (Lavers & Westlake): Stained glass manufacturers. The firm was founded by Nathaniel Wood Lavers in 1855; he was joined by Francis Philip Barraud in 1858, both men having been with **Powell & Sons** in the 1840s. Lavers was the craftsman and business head, relying on competent artists to design his windows; Barraud was a prolific designer for the first decade of the partnership, specialising in small figure medallions. In the 1860s the firm was much favoured by the leaders of the **Ecclesiological Society.** From then on, major commissions were designed by Nathaniel H.J. Westlake and he became a partner in 1868, doing the majority of the figure work. At that time their colouring was light and sweet, with a wide range of tints, and the leading was meticulous. Towards the end of the century there was a steady deterioration in aesthetic standards, with mass production methods being used to meet the heavy demand. Westlake was head of the firm in 1880 and continued to his death in 1921. There is a wide range of their work at East Bergholt, and windows at Brantham(?), Burgate(?), Great Bealings, Great Waldingfield, Hasketon, Kenton, Offton(?), Rushmere St Andrew, and Stonham Aspal.

Ledger-stone: When the art and use of monumental **brasses** declined in the first half of the C17, sculpture in stone began to come into its own in churches. But while those splendid, opulent examples which adorn wall or table tomb may be the first to catch the eye, it often pays to drop one's gaze to those dark, massive slabs in pavements of **chancel, nave**, and **aisles**, incised with arms, crests, and epitaphs. These are ledger-stones, a study in themselves, and many carry quite marvellous inscriptions which can easily be overlooked.

Lenten veil: It was the custom in medieval times to 'curtain off' the **altar** and also the **rood** during Lent with a veil. This was suspended from **corbels**, or hooks, of which a few examples remain set in the walls and roofs of Suffolk churches, as at Monk Soham. Some churches follow the custom to-day by veiling the **reredos**.

Lights: A word frequently used in these volumes. Very simply, it is the space between the vertical divisions of a window or screen. So if a window has just one centre **mullion**, it is a two-light window. (The term is not to be confused with an occasional usage of 'light' in the sense of candles or lamps kept burning before images, the **rood**, and tabernacles.)

Linen-fold panelling: This was an innovation in wood carving of the C16 in the **Tudor** period – an elegant and beautifully restrained representation

in wood of linen laid in crisp vertical folds. Seen on a range of church furnishings, with a good example at Shelley.

Long and short work: Distinctive of **Saxon** craftsmanship, upright stones alternating with flat slabs in the **quoins** at the corners of buildings. See also **Styles of Architecture**. There is a good example at Hemingstone and others at Claydon, Debenham and Gosbeck.

Low side windows: Almost as much nonsense has been written about low side windows as about **weeping chancels**. These small square or oblong windows were usually low down in the s. wall of the **chancel**, just e. of the chancel arch, and fitted with shutters so that the window could be opened. It has been suggested that they were 'leper windows' for these afflicted people to look in and thus share in the mass – a ridiculous assertion, since not even in medieval times would lepers have been allowed to roam at leisure. The actual use of these windows, most authorities agree, was so that, at the point in the mass at which the priest raises the cup and the consecrated bread for the people to see, a bell could be rung through the open window so that: 'people who have not leisure daily to be present at Mass may, wherever they are in houses or fields, bow their knees' (Archbishop Peckham, 1281). A hand bell may have been used but sometimes a bell was housed in a turret on the roof (see **sanctus-bell**). Sometimes the low side window was incorporated in a larger window, but many of the separate ones have been blocked up. Interesting examples can be seen at Combs and Raydon, with others at Burstall, Chattisham, Great Wenham, Little Cornard, Little Wenham, and Swilland.

Lych-gate: The word 'lych' is derived from the **Anglo-Saxon** 'lic' or 'lich', and from the German 'leiche', all meaning corpse. The purpose of the lych-gate is to provide a shelter and resting place for coffin bearers on the way to the church. In former times, the lych-gate would have had seats and a coffin table, on which the coffin would be set. Poor people who could not afford a coffin might be placed, temporarily, in the parish coffin; but otherwise they would be wrapped in a sheet and placed straight onto the coffin table, where they would be received by the priest, who speaks the first sentences of the burial service here. Ancient lych-gates are rare, but there are good C19 examples at Aspall and Framsden, and an excellent **Arts and Crafts** design at Brantham.

Marys: See **three Marys**.

Mason's marks: It was the practice of medieval masons to identify their work by cutting an individual symbol on selected blocks of stone.

Mass dials: See **scratch dials**.

Mensa slabs: In pre-**Reformation** times, all **altars** were of stone, topped with a slab or 'mensa' (Latin for table). Each had five crosses carved upon it, one at each corner and one in the centre, representing the **five wounds of Christ**. **Chantries** were dissolved in 1547, and with them went their altars. But stone high altars remained, until a movement was led by two bishops to have them removed and replaced by wooden tables. This was realised in 1550 when the king in Council commanded every bishop to order this change in all the churches in his diocese. There is a restored mensa at Mendlesham and another at Wilby. See also **consecration crosses**.

Misericords: In the **chancels** of many

churches remain ancient stalls with hinged seats. Underneath, the tip-up seats are carved, generally with very free expression and often with exuberant irreverence and humour: anything from the wildest caricatures to cartoonish domestic scenes and upsets. All are worth examining closely, wherever they are found. On the leading edge of these seats is usually a smooth, hollowed surface on which, during long services, the elderly, or just the plain sleepy, could lean and rest – thus the name, from the Latin 'misericordia', pity, compassion. There are examples at Bildeston, Denham, Framsden, Occold, Stoke by Nayland, Whitton, and Wissington.

Morris, William & Co.: Stained glass manufacturers. William Morris (1834 – 96) was a designer, poet, and prolific writer on artistic and other matters. In 1861, he drew together a group of artists which included Burne-Jones, Ford Madox Brown, Rossetti, and Philip Webb, to found Morris, Marshall, Faulkner & Co. The firm revolutionised British taste in furnishing and interior decoration and, from the outset, stained glass was an important part of their activities. Morris assumed responsibility for colour, and all cartoons were by the partners themselves. Rossetti dropped out in 1865 and from 1869 Burne-Jones was much more active, becoming sole designer in 1875, after which Morris gave only occasional attention to the work. Burne-Jones died two years after Morris in 1898 and thereafter John Henry Dearle was chief designer. He had worked with Morris for many years and echoed his style and that of Burne-Jones. Good design and technical excellence, combined with Morris's genius for colour, put their windows in a class apart, particularly between 1865 and 1875. Although Dearle followed them faithfully, re-using and adapting many of their designs, his work in the 1920s was an empty continuation of an outdated style. The firm closed in 1940.

In Suffolk there are windows by Morris & Co. at Bacton, Bedingfield, Freston, Great Barton, Hopton-on-Sea, Thornham Magna, Westerfield, and Whitton.

Mouchette: A **tracery** shape or motif, used principally during the **Decorated** period early in the C14. It is a curved dagger or spearhead shape, **cusped** and arched inside.

Mullion: Vertical bar dividing **lights** in a window.

Nave: The main 'body' of a church – from the Latin 'navis', a ship. Traditionally the nave was for the congregation, the **chancel** being for the clergy. Indeed, so much was it a preserve of the people that once services were over, it was used for parish meetings, as a courtroom, and perhaps for the performance of mystery plays. Its upkeep was normally the responsibility of the people, just as the chancel was maintained by the priest.

Nollekens, Joseph (1737 – 1823): Nollekens was to portrait sculpture what Sir Joshua Reynolds was to portrait painting – the choice of fashionable London. Having spent a decade in Italy in pursuit of his art, he had a ready-made reputation on his return. Adept in every form, from chimney pieces to memorial tablets, his busts were outstanding and they made his fortune. He had a complementary genius for meanness which he shared with his wife (see J.T. Smith's *Nollekens & His Times*, the most candid, pitiless, and uncomplimentary biography in our language). There are memorials by him at Helmingham.

Norman: The Romanesque form of architecture, with its distinctive rounded arches and massive round pillars, introduced to England following the Norman Conquest of 1066. See under **Styles of Architecture** for full description.

O'Connor, Arthur and William: Stained glass artists whose ' father Michael began in Dublin as an heraldic painter before moving to London in 1823. He had studied with Thomas Willement and worked with **Pugin** and **Butterfield**. He took his sons into partnership in the 1850s and when Arthur died in 1873, William George Taylor joined the firm and managed it from 1877 onwards. Much of the O'Connors' work is distinguished by fine colour and an effective deployment of lead lines – as in the Stoke by Nayland w. window. Other examples may be seen at Groton, Holton St Mary(?), Ipswich (St Mary le Tower), and Stradbroke.

Ogee: This is a lovely, flowing 'S'-shaped arch or moulding – a convex curve flowing into a concave one. Usually ogee curves are not very large because, by their very nature, they cannot carry heavy loads; but their grace lends them to the heads of canopies, to **piscinas, sedilia**, and the like; and sometimes also to doorways, giving them an engaging and curiously oriental look; as well as to the **tracery** of windows, screens, etc. Adorned with **crocketting**, ogee arches are still more attractive. They came into general use in the C14, playing an important role in the development of the sumptuous windows of the late **Decorated** period with their flowing tracery, of which the ogee curve forms an integral part. See **Styles of Architecture**.

Pamment: An unglazed flooring tile used widely in East Anglia; the average size is 9in. square, 2in. thick.

Parclose screen: The screens which separate **chantry** or side chapels, and/or **aisles**, from the main body of the church. See also **rood loft/screen**.

There are examples at Barking (matching C15 pair), Burstall (early C14), Combs, Grundisburgh, Hadleigh (C15 pair), and Wingfield.

Parish clerk: Not the clerk to the parish council of late Victorian, local government invention, but the holder of a paid office which was for centuries of central importance in church services. It was the job of the clerk to lead the singing and the responses to the prayers, and to voice a healthy 'Amen' both at the end of prayers and of the sermon. Sometimes he filled the role of choirmaster; certainly he would 'give the notes' on a pitch pipe, just as the conductor gives them today to unaccompanied choirs. After the **Reformation** in the C16, the clerk continued to exercise his role; indeed, the replanning of church interiors to meet the new Protestant requirements gave him a special seat in the **three-decker pulpits** which appeared at this time (see **Prayer book churches**). In the C17, under James I and later Charles II, the parish clerks, who had the dignity of being a London company, were given new charters which stipulated that: 'every person that is chosen Clerk of the Parish should first give sufficient proof of his abilities to sing at least the tunes which are used in the parish churches.' He sang on until soon after Victoria ascended the throne, when most of his duties were given to curates. Then came the local government acts of the late C19, which finally consigned him to history and left only his seat at the foot of the three-deckers to remind us of a 700-year-old tradition.

Parish guilds: See **guilds/guild altars**.

Passion emblems: See **instruments of the Passion**.

Paterae: Ornaments in bas relief, often used to enrich mouldings.

Pediment: The low triangular gable used in classical building but often employed in classically styled monuments in churches.

Pelican: The pelican has long had a special place in religious symbolism and may often be seen as a device used in medieval carving and embellishment. There is a legend that the bird tore its own breast to feed its young upon its own blood – the source of the idea, it is suggested, being that the tip of the pelican's bill, which usually rests on this ungainly bird's chest, is touched with red. In medieval art the ungainliness is replaced by a dove-like representation and the legend transmuted into a symbolism of man's fall and redemption through the Passion of Christ. Here we find that the parent bird was said to kill its young in a moment of irritation – then, 'on the third day', to restore them to life by tearing its breast and letting its own blood pour over them. The complete carving of the bird and its young is often referred to as 'the pelican in her piety'. In the C18 and early C19 a female figure with the pelican signified benevolence. There are examples at Aspall (C19 version), Baylham, Burgh (C20 version), Combs, Earl Stonham, Great Waldingfield, Pettistree, and Stoke by Nayland.

Perpendicular: The great age of church building, in the second half of the C14 and through the C15, in the style characterised by soaring upward lines in great windows and majestic towers. See full description under **Styles of Architecture**.

Pevsner, Sir Nikolaus: Author of the monumental and remarkable undertaking, *The Buildings of England* series – forty-six volumes, written between 1951 and 1974, meticulously recording the principal buildings, domestic, public, and church (including the detail and furnishings of the latter), of every county in England. It was masterminded throughout by Pevsner himself. His volume on Suffolk appeared in 1961 and a second edition, revised by Enid Radcliffe, was published in 1974.

Phipson, Richard Makilwaine (1827 – 84): As an architect he was not outstanding and sometimes verged on the incompetent, but he was very active in Norfolk and Suffolk from 1850 onwards. As joint diocesan surveyor from 1871 until his death, he had a hand in most of the restorations during that important period and by then had become well known, particularly for his work at St Mary le Tower, Ipswich, and St Peter Mancroft, Norwich. See also Bentley, Brandeston, Bredfield, Burgate, Ipswich (St Mary at Stoke, St Mary at the Elms, and St Matthew), Playford, Ringshall, Stoke Ash, Stowmarket, Stradbroke, Thorndon, Whitton, and Winston.

Pier: The architectural term for a column or pillar.

Pilaster: A miniature pillar, rectangular in section, usually based in style on one of the classical orders of architecture, and normally applied to a wall.

Pillar piscina: See **piscina**.

Piscina/angle piscina/double piscina/pillar piscina: A stone basin near an **altar** (its presence today indicates that there was formerly an altar there). In its simplest form it is merely a depression in a windowsill but usually it is set into a niche in the wall below an arch or canopy, sometimes projecting outwards on a bowl, which in turn may be supported by a small pillar. Occasionally too a piscina may be found let into a pillar. The piscina was used for cleansing the communion

vessels after mass; thus it has a drain hole in its basin, which allows the water used in the cleansing to run down into consecrated ground. It is obligatory that where water has been blessed, or has come into contact with anything consecrated, it must be returned to earth. Sometimes there is a small shelf in the piscina niche called a **credence shelf**. The angle piscina is one built into the angle of a window or **sedilia**, and opened out on two sides, often affording the opportunity for beautiful carving and design. Double piscinas (two side by side) may occasionally be found. These had but a short span of fashion in the late C13 to early C14: one was used by the priest for the cleaning of the vessels, the other for washing his own hands. A pillar piscina is not, as the name might imply, a piscina set into a pillar; but a piscina which protrudes from a wall, its bowl and drain standing on a miniature pillar, either attached to or standing clear of the wall. A **corbel** piscina has, instead of a pillar, its bowl supported by a corbel or pendant.

Plate tracery: This is **tracery** in the heads of windows where the pattern is cut directly through the masonry; as distinct from bar tracery, which is constructed in separate pieces. There are examples at Ashbocking, Debenham, and Little Wenham. See **Early English** under **Styles of Architecture**.

Poppyheads: The boldly carved floral ornament which graces the ends of bench pews, said to be derived from the French 'poupée', puppet, doll, or figurehead. It was during the great age of C15 church building and wood carving that poppyheads came into being and achieved their highest artistic expression. The carvers often seem to have been given a free hand, with diverse and interesting results including animals, grotesques, faces, and so on. Some Victorian craftsmen, such as

Henry Ringham, were capable of producing poppyheads that are well up to the medieval standard.

Porches: It was not until the C14 that porches came to be regarded as an essential part of the church plan, so few are earlier than that. This explains why **scratch dials** will often be found beside the inner door, inside the porch, where the sun could not possibly reach them. Quite simply, the porch was a later addition. Having become established, the porch assumed a practical importance in medieval times which we tend to forget today. Services of baptism began here; sentences were spoken from the burial service, after the first pause in the **lych-gate**; women were churched (i.e., purified and blessed) after the birth of a child; part of the wedding service was conducted here; in the porch the kneeling penitent received absolution; and the porch was one of the 'stations' in the regular Sunday and Feast Day processions. Sometimes, as at Eye, the porch contained a dole table where bread and other charities were distributed, and it was the place where debts, tithes, and church dues were traditionally paid, along with much other civil and legal business. Some porches also have a second storey originally intended as a priest's room, but later sometimes used as the first and only school in the parish. Examples of wooden porches are to be found at Bures, Boxford (Suffolk's finest C14 one), Great Blakenham, and Somersham (earliest?); there are particularly lavish porches at Kersey and Yaxley, and Nayland's is unusually placed.

Powell, James & Sons: Stained glass manufacturers. Founded in 1844, the business had one of the longest histories in the trade and did not close until 1973. It was among the most important and progressive firms, making a significant contribution both in technology and in the art form. Many of its designs came from artists of the calibre of Burne-Jones, Henry Holiday, and **Christopher Whall**. Good examples may be found at Aspall (1850s), Higham, and Stratford St Mary.

Prayer book churches: A phrase used to describe those churches where the furnishings and layout still embody the great shift of emphasis in church worship that came, first with the **Reformation** and then with the Puritans. The old, and strict, division of priest in **chancel** from people in **nave** was put away, and the English prayer book of 1549 required the laity to take part in all of the service; Matins and Evensong were to be conducted from the chancel and everybody had to hear the Lessons. The **altar** became 'the table' for the first time in the 1552 revision. After the Civil War, Sunday services (except on infrequent Sacrament Sundays) were conducted entirely from the reading desk, and soon the convenient reading-desk-cum pulpit became the rule (see **three-decker pulpits**). In the C18 virtually every church in the land had its pews (often enclosed for each family – see **box pews**) arranged to focus on the reading desk. Then, in the 1830s, a 'new wave' of churchmen were inspired by **Pugin** and John Newman's Oxford Movement to sweep away these things. Their vision was to have truly Gothic churches again, and C18 domestic church interiors were anathema. Today, very few of the sensible and seemly furnishings of the Age of Reason are to be found.

Preaching/churchyard crosses: The medieval churchyard was also a gathering place, and sometimes a market-place and fairground. Most of them had a preaching cross of stone, raised on steps so that the people could gather round it to hear their priest or an itinerant friar. Sometimes the stump or just the base survives, as at Athelington, Earl Soham, and Worlingworth.

Pre-Raphaelites: The pre-Raphaelite Brotherhood was a group of Victorian artists, much reviled in its day, who sought to go back to principles before the Italian master, Raphael (d. 1520), imposed his mark (one of the major figures in the world history of art, he was the painter of many celebrated works, including decorative work in the Vatican). The brotherhood had only three members, Rossetti, Millais, and Holman Hunt, and lasted only five years from its establishment in 1848. But its pre-occupation with biblical and literary subjects and the artists' urge for 'social realism' gave it great influence on several other artists of note, among them Burne-Jones. It was he who later, with **William Morris,** briefly tried to revive the brotherhood. Inevitably the pre-Raphaelite movement left its impression on the church art of the period, as evidenced in Burne-Jones's work.

Priest's door: Most **chancels** have a small door, usually on the s. side, which was the priest's 'private entrance'. It fits into context when it is remembered that, in pre-**Reformation** times, the **chancel** was the priest's particular responsibility (only occasionally entered by the laity) while the parishioners looked after the **nave**.

Pugin, Augustus Welby Northmore, (1812 – 52): English architect and designer. After intense study of medieval buildings, he established himself as an expert and designed much of the detail used on the Houses of Parliament. He had become a Catholic by this time and much of his work was for that Church. It was largely by his influence and through his writings that Gothic was revived as a full-blooded style. He worked with Sir Charles Barry at Westminster but illness dogged his later years and he died young.

Purbeck marble: References to Purbeck marble are frequent in relation to effigies and **fonts**. The first wave of fonts in this material came during the **Norman** period, and it was used for long afterwards. The grey stone is not in fact marble at all, but a hard limestone full of shells. Although much of it is now eroded, it originally took a high polish. It comes from strata stretching from the Isle of Purbeck, the peninsula in s.e. Dorset (famous for its quarries for a thousand years), and northwards through to Aylesbury.

Purlin: The purlin is the main horizontal supporting beam of a roof. See **roofs,** fig. 4.

Put-log holes: The holes where the horizontal members of the (timber) scaffolding slotted into the walls during construction.

Putti (singular, putto): Little naked cherub boys first seen in that form in the work of **Renaissance** artists in Italy; and regularly in the work of C18 and C19 sculptors in England in the adornment of monuments and tombs. It is possible that these cherubs have their origin in the naked Eros and Mercury representations of ancient classical, pagan belief, one of the many examples of 'Christianising' ancient deities, places, and practices.

Quarry: A diamond-shaped pane of glass.

Quatrefoils: See **foils**.

Queen-posts: Upright roof beams set in pairs on horizontal cross or **tie-beams** and thrusting up on each side to the main horizontal supporting beams, or **purlins,** of the roof. Designed, like the **king-post,** to prevent sag and give greater stability. See **roofs**.

Quoins: The outside corner stones at the angles of buildings. See also **long and short work**.

Rebus: A punning representation of a name or word by the use of symbols, normally in churches referring to the name of the place or the name of a donor.

Redundant Churches Fund: It having been recognised that Church and state should share responsibility for churches no longer required for regular worship and for which no suitable alternative use could be found, the fund was set up by law in 1969. Its declared aim is to preserve churches which are of architectural, historical, or archaeological importance, and it is financed jointly by the Department of the Environment (70%) and the Church Commissioners (30%), plus contributions from the general public, local authorities, and other organisations. The fund was caring for 250 churches in 1989, of which 17 are in Suffolk, and many of them are used for occasional services.

Reformation: In particular terms, the great religious movement in western Europe during the C16, founded on a return to biblical sources and their fresh interpretation, which led to the rejection of Roman and papal authority and the establishment of Protestant churches. In England the original motivations were more basic, being political and economic rather than theological. Firstly, there was a ruthless, single-minded, vastly vain and wholly autocratic monarch in Henry VIII, intent on putting away one wife and taking another by whom he could beget an heir. Secondly, there was his calculating eye on the wealth of the monasteries, backed by his aristocracy and gentry, who could not wait to get their hands on the spoils. Even when he had broken with Rome, however, Henry did his best to minimise the impression of any break with the tradition begun in England by **St Augustine** a thousand years earlier. The true religious, reforming Reformation came with his son, the boy-king Edward VI, who, though young, was a fanatical Protestant (see **Prayer book churches**).

Reliquary/reliquary chamber: A container for relics. The bodies of saints and martyrs were venerated by the early Church and wherever possible an **altar** would contain, or have housed nearby, a portion of bone or an object associated with a saint. Some became famous objects of pilgrimage and a source of revenue for the church. There is a reliquary chamber at Gedding [Vol.1] and a possible example at Ipswich (St Margaret).

Renaissance: A movement which began in Italy during the C14 in which there was a startling rebirth of culture, particularly in the arts and literature, which drew its inspiration from the classical models of Greece and Rome. It spread to the rest of Europe during the C16 and the style of architecture and decoration which originated in Florence in the early C15 gradually replaced the Gothic tradition. See also **Styles of Architecture, Jacobean /Caroline.**

Reredos: A screening at the back of an **altar**, usually richly embellished in painting or carving. Few old examples remain, many having disappeared at the **Reformation** and in the century following. See also **decalogue boards**.

Respond: This is the half-pillar, attached to a wall, which supports an arch, most often seen at the ends of **arcades**.

Restoration: The period from 1660, following the restoration of the monarchy after the Civil War and Cromwell's government, and the accession of Charles II.

Retable: A shelf or ledge at the back of an **altar** on which statues, lights, or crosses could stand (see Nayland). The term can also apply to a painted or carved panel in the same position, as at Thornham Parva. See also **reredos**.

Reticulated: (Latin 'rete', a net; 'reticulum', a bag of network – the link being that the **tracery** forms a net-like pattern.) A form of 'flowing' tracery in windows which was developed at the height of **Decorated** achievement during the first half of the C14 (see **Styles of Architecture**, fig. 17).

Ringham, Henry (1806 – 66): Master joiner and carver. During the C19, when many churches were restored, the standard of craftsmanship was high and, because methods and tools had not changed significantly, many joiners and woodcarvers were able to match the work of their C15 predecessors. In this, no one excelled Henry Ringham. He came to Ipswich from Lincolnshire as an unlettered teenager, and by a mixture of perseverance and native genius made himself the master of Gothic woodwork. He devoted his life to the restoration of churches, and in 1843 was entrusted with his first big commission at Woolpit. Roofs and benches were his speciality and before he died he had worked on eighty-three churches in the county including Bentley, Combs (?), Great Bealings, Ipswich (St Margaret, St Mary at the Elms, St Mary le Tower, St Mary at Stoke), Sproughton, Swilland(?), Tuddenham (St Martin), and Witnesham.

Rood screen/loft/beam/stair: The rood (Old English for wood) is the cross with the figure of the crucified Christ, the dominant symbol of atonement. Before the **Reformation** all churches were divided in two: the **chancel** for the clergy, the **nave** for the people. Between them was a wooden screen (often with a door) which stretched from pillar to pillar under the chancel arch, and in some cases right across the church. This screen is known as the rood screen because above it stood (or hung) the great crucifix, the rood itself. This sometimes stood on a separate beam (the rood beam) and was normally flanked by figures of the **Blessed Virgin** and **St John**. In many cases there was a loft built above the screen so that the images could be maintained (they sometimes had special clothes) and to carry lights. On occasion, the loft housed singers and during the mass the Gospel was read from there. Access to the loft was by stairs in one or both of the side walls. At the **Reformation** the rood and its images were almost universally torn down and destroyed in violent reaction against Rome and 'popery'. The fact that so many screens survive is due to Queen Elizabeth who, in a royal order of 1561, directed that while the great rood and its figures should go, the screens themselves should remain, and be topped with a suitable crest or with the **Royal Arms**. Where screen as well as rood had already been destroyed, a new screen – or 'partition', as the wording had it – was to be constructed: for the Elizabethan view was quite clearly that the church should be partitioned into two distinct sections. The issue of screens and their role was to rumble on for another century. In 1638 Richard Montague, bishop of Norwich, was pointedly asking his clergy:

> Is your chancel divided from the nave or body of your church, with a partition of stone, boards, wainscot, grates or otherwise? Wherein is there a decent strong door to open and shut, (as occasion

serveth) with lock and key, to keep out boys, girls, or irreverent men and women? And are dogs kept from coming to besoil or profane the Lord's table?

While rood stairs and screens are common, rood lofts are very rare. There is a splendid reconstruction at Eye by **Comper**. There is a rare example of a C13 to C14 stone screen at Bramford, and a high-level **piscina** to serve a loft **altar** survives at Bures. Rood beams are still in place at Athelington, Bentley, Debenham, Hemingstone, Horham (?), Kesgrave, Monk Soham, Somersham (?), Swilland (?), and Westerfield.

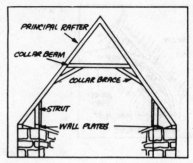

Fig 1.

Roofs: The development, structural variety and embellishment of church roofs is a fascinating field. Here is a potted guide to a richly complex subject. Coupled rafter roofs are a simple variety, which also serve to indicate the roof components (fig. 1). The principal rafters, the feet of which are secured to a **wall plate**, have a collar beam to support them and to prevent sagging. More support is given by the collar braces, with struts lower down giving more strength. Another framing system is the scissor beam (fig. 2), which can exist with the cross beams only, or with a supporting collar. As a precaution against spreading of the roof, a tie-beam was often added between the wall plates (fig. 3); but as tie-beams have a tendency to sag in the middle a central **king-post** served to prevent this. The **arch-braced** construction is where the roof is carried on a braced arch which incorporates 'in one' the strut, collar brace, and collar beam (fig. 4). The function of the tie-beam has already been seen in fig. 3. With a low-pitched roof, it is often used simply with struts upward to the principal rafters, and downward on brace and **wall post** to a **corbel** set into the wall (fig. 5) well below the wall plates. With the advent of the **hammerbeam** development (fig. 6), a new splendour was added to the roof builder's art.

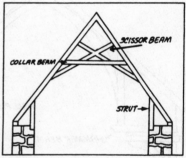

Fig 2.

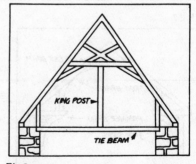

Fig 3.

Fig 4.

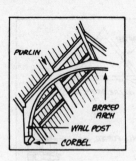

PURLIN

BRACED ARCH

WALL POST

CORBEL

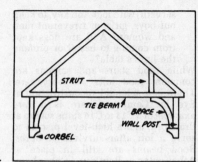

Fig 5.

STRUT

TIE BEAM

BRACE

WALL POST

CORBEL

Fig 6.

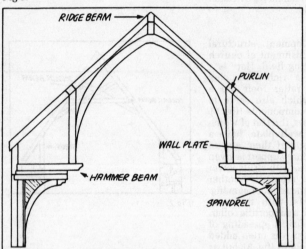

RIDGE BEAM

PURLIN

WALL PLATE

HAMMER BEAM

SPANDREL

Fig 7.

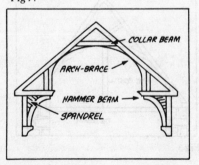

COLLAR BEAM

ARCH-BRACE

HAMMER BEAM

SPANDREL

Fig 8.

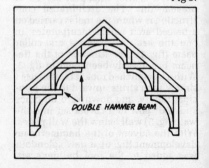

DOUBLE HAMMER BEAM

Instead of a tie-beam spanning wall to wall, there are hammerbeam brackets, from which spring a vertical strut, upward to the principal rafter at its intersection with the **purlin** (refer again to fig. 4), the main horizontal supporting beam. Continuing upward, curved arch-like braces meet either at the ridge beam, or at a collar beam, set very high (fig. 7). From there it was a natural development to the double hammerbeam. Fig. 8 is self explanatory. The ends of the hammerbeams are often embellished with angels or decorative carvings. Roofs of exceptional quality may be seen at Cotton, Earl Stonham, Grundisburgh and Needham Market.

Rope, Margaret E. Aldrich: Arts and Crafts stained glass worker. Born of an artistic family at Leiston, she spent her childhood at Blaxhall and studied stained glass under Alfred Drury at the Central School of Arts and Crafts. She assisted her cousin Margaret Rope at 'The Glass House' in making the Rope memorial window at Blaxhall in 1911, and after the war she returned to Fulham and began securing independent commissions. She continued to produce work of high quality until her retirement in the 1960s. Windows by her may be found at Earl Soham and Kesgrave Roman Catholic church, with others at Barnby, Little Glemham and Leiston [Vol.3].

Royal Arms: Many churches display Royal coats of arms, usually square and framed, painted on wood or canvas; though they may also be found in carved wood or stone, cast in plaster, or set in stained glass. Occasionally the arms are set up and painted in a lozenge shape, like a **hatchment**, but this is unusual. It was only during the reign of Henry VIII, when he assumed complete control of the English Church, that Royal Arms began to come into regular use. Catholic Queen Mary was later to order their removal, and the replacement of the old **rood lofts**. But with Elizabeth's accession,

they began to reappear; indeed Elizabeth directed their use and indicated that the **tympanum** (the top part of the **chancel** arch, panelled in) was the place to display them. Inevitably many disappeared during Cromwell's Commonwealth, for in 1650 his Parliamentarians ordered 'the removal of the obnoxious Royal Arms from the churches'. The **Restoration** Parliament in 1660 made Royal Arms compulsory in all English churches, a practice continued generally until Victoria's accession, ordering that 'the Armes of the Commonwealth wherever they are standing be forthwith taken down, and the Kings Majesties armes be set up instead thereof'. Hosts of Royal Arms will be found throughout the county but the following are notable: Dallinghoo (Tudor, not in situ), Denham and Mellis (Charles I), Cretingham, Earl Soham and Ipswich (St Margaret) (Charles II), Little Blakenham (James II), Kettleburgh and Swilland (Queen Anne), Easton (Hanoverian).

Sacred monogram: The two names of Christ and Jesus, originally written in Greek, were often reduced to the first two letters; or the first, second, and final; or the first and last. When written in Latin they became: IH-XP, IHC-XPC, or IC-XC. For centuries the symbol XP (known as the Chi Rho) was used in various forms. The name came to be written IHESUS in English and IHC became IHS. This was later taken to mean (conveniently but erroneously) 'Jesus Hominum Salvator' (Jesus, Saviour of mankind).

Sacring bell: A small bell rung at that point in the mass when the priest holds up the Host above the **altar** (the action known as the Elevation). See Somersham.

Sacristy: A room, often with specially strengthened doors and windows, where the vestments, church plate, and other valuables were stored. There are examples at Barking, Hitcham and Occold.

Saints: 'For all the saints . . .' On **rood screens**, on **fonts**, in woodwork and stained glass, a panoply of saints is represented in Suffolk churches. Almost all of them have some identifying emblem – which adds yet another element of interest for the church visitor. The following is a list of those to be found in that part of the county covered by this volume, with emblems, brief story background, and some representative locations.

Agnes: Her symbols are a sword, often thrust into her neck or bosom, and a lamb – Latin 'agna', a pun on her name. Ancient Rome, about A.D. 300, and 13-year-old Agnes refuses to marry the prefect's son. She was publicly stripped, but her hair miraculously grew long to cover her nakedness. They tried to burn her, but the flames declined to help. So at last she was stabbed. She is represented at Athelington, Bildeston, Creeting St Mary, and Eye.

Alban: Often represented with a tall cross or a sword, he is credited with being Britain's earliest martyr. He was a Roman knight who had been converted to Christianity in Britain in the C3. Ordered by his superiors to sacrifice to pagan gods, he refused to do so, and was condemned to be executed at Verulamium, the city which became St Albans. He converted the first executioner who tried to despatch him. The second was more successful and beheaded the saint, whereupon the man's eyes dropped out! Alban is the only saint to have enjoyed a continuous cult in England from Roman times. He is seen in modern glass at Creeting St Mary.

Alphege: Having been successively abbot of Bath and bishop of Winchester, he became archbishop of Canterbury in 1006. Five years later the marauding Danes seized Canterbury and took Alphege prisoner. Held captive for some months on their ships at Greenwich, he refused to tax the poor as the price of his release and was stoned before being beheaded. Buried first in St Paul's, his remains were transferred to Canterbury in 1023. His emblems are stones or a battle-axe, and there is a modern panel painting of him in the **sanctuary** at Ipswich (St Mary le Tower).

Ambrose: One of the **Four Latin Doctors.** Usually represented with a beehive – an allusion to the intriguing story of a swarm of bees which settled on the baby Ambrose's cradle. Also seen wearing his bishop's robes and holding a whip or scourge, recalling the penance he imposed on the Roman Emperor Theodosius. Ambrose became bishop of Milan in 374 and was a central figure in the early Church with powerful influence on the Roman emperors.

Andrew: The saltire (X-shaped cross, Scotland's part of the Union Flag) and fishing net are his symbols. One of the twelve disciples, he was a fisherman before he became a disciple. Legends of his later life are legion, including one that he visited Scotland, thus becoming its patron saint. He was martyred by crucifixion, it is said, upon an X-shaped cross. There is a C19 mosaic of his martyrdom at Layham and a bench end of the same period at Athelington.

Anne: According to the apocryphal Gospel of **St James**, Anne was the mother of the **Blessed Virgin** who, after years of childlessness, was told by an angel that she would bear a daughter who would become world famous. She vowed that the child would be devoted to the Lord and presented Mary to the Temple at the age of 3. Another tradition identifies her with the widowed prophetess Anna who was in the Temple when Jesus was received (Luke 2: 36 – 8). She is usually shown teaching the Virgin to read, and is represented at Edwardstone, Great Waldingfield, Kersey, and Oakley.

Apostles: The twelve chief disciples of Christ (the lists of names vary slightly, probably because the same person was known by more than one name). They were: **Peter, Andrew, James the Great, John, Philip, Thomas, Bartholomew, Matthew, James the Less, Simon, Jude** (Thaddaeus/Judas, son of James), and **Judas**. After the suicide of Judas Iscariot, his place was taken by **Matthias**. Both **Paul** and **Barnabas** are referred to as apostles in the Acts of the Apostles.

Appollonia: This poor saint is most often seen having her teeth forcibly removed with huge pincers or herself holding aloft a tooth, representing the torture which preceded the martyrdom by fire of this aged and pious deaconess in Egypt in 249. Not surprisingly, she is invoked against jaw- and tooth-ache. She is represented at Chilton.

Audry: An alternative name for **Etheldreda**.

Augustine of Canterbury: In the C6 Pope **Gregory** sent Augustine, an Italian by birth, with a band of monks to convert England. King Ethelbert of Kent received him civilly and was soon won over. Augustine made Canterbury his base and built the first cathedral there, but he travelled widely as a missionary. Guided by Gregory's wisdom he laid down those precepts which enabled the new religion to assimilate the pagans and their sacred places – 'Don't destroy their temples,

but just their idols, and then convert the place to Christian use' advised the pope. His figure is one of the modern series in the **sanctuary** of Ipswich (St Mary le Tower).

Augustine of Hippo: One of the **Four Latin Doctors** of the early Church; a profound and sustaining influence through the centuries on the Church's thought and teaching. Often represented holding a flaming heart in his hand or wearing his bishop's robes (he was bishop of Hippo in North Africa for thirty-five years to his death in 430) and carrying a pastoral staff. His saintly adulthood followed a dissolute youth, from which he was rescued by **St Ambrose**. Augustine, a man of flesh as well as spirit, is credited with the memorable prayer, 'O Lord, make me chaste ... but not yet.' There is a headless figure of him in medieval glass at Burgate and one of Ipswich's modern churches is dedicated to him because of his regard for his mother **St Monica**.

Barbara: A tower, and a chalice with the Host (the consecrated bread) above it are her emblems. This lady, goes the story, was an early Christian convert in godless Italy, to the fury of her father, who shut her up in a high tower. When she tried to escape he beat her before handing her over to a judge who condemned her to death. She was tortured and decapitated, whereupon, very properly, both father and judge were consumed by bolts of lightning. Barbara is thus patroness of architects and firearms, and also protectress from thunderbolts and lightning or any form of explosion. She is represented at Athelington, Bildeston, Eye, Wilby, and Yaxley.

Barnabas: The saint is described in the Acts of the apostles as a Cypriot who sold a field and gave the proceeds to the apostles. He was a 'prophet and teacher' in Antioch and was chosen to go with **St Paul** on his first missionary journey. They later fell out when Barnabas wished to take his cousin John Mark with them on another trip. He parted with Paul and went to Cyprus, where tradition has it that he was stoned or burned to death by the Jews. Seldom seen in medieval art, there is a modern glass figure of him at Wilby.

Bartholomew: One of the twelve, his emblem is the butcher's flaying knife, for thus, it is said, he was martyred somewhere along the Caspian Sea, being first flayed alive and then beheaded. More gruesomely, he is sometimes seen in medieval art carrying the skin of a man, with the face still attached to it. It follows that he is the patron saint of tanners. His figure is carved on one of the C19 bench ends at Athelington.

Blaise: During the horrific persecution of Christians around the year 300 by the Roman Emperor Diocletian, innumerable martyrs died various and nasty deaths. Blaise, bishop of Sebaste, in Armenia, was first torn with iron combs, and then beheaded. A large comb is thus his symbol in medieval art and it also conveniently made him patron saint of wool combers! It is interesting to note that Parson Woodforde, in his celebrated diary, describes a solemn procession in the saint's honour in Norwich in March, 1783. A figure at Eye has been identified as him but that is questionable.

Botolph: A shadowy C7 figure, possibly of Irish birth, he became the abbot of 'Ikanhoe'. One tradition has it that this was in Lincolnshire and that he 'dwelt in a dismal hut amidst the swamps of the fenland rivers', but his monastery may have been at Iken on the River Alde. The church at Burgh has been

claimed as his burial place, but if so his body was transferred to Bury abbey where there was a chapel dedicated to him. He has no definite symbol although he is properly represented as an abbot, occasionally holding a church in his hand. There are five churches dedicated to him in Suffolk, including Burgh where he figures in a **Kempe** window. One of the figures on Charsfield font probably represents him.

Catherine of Alexandria: The emblem of this saint is a wheel of the devilish variety, set with spikes and knives, on which she is said to have been martyred in C4 Egypt, and which in turn inspired the spinning firework that bears her name. The wheel, however, flew to pieces as she was spun on it, the knives etc. skewering her persecutors. Her head was then cut off and from the wound flowed milk, not blood, which could explain why she is patroness of nurses. There are many images of her, but the following are notable: Thornham Parva **retable**, Little Wenham wall painting, Wilby C15 glass.

Cecilia: Daughter of a C3 noble Roman family, she refused to worship idols and was beheaded. Her many converts to Christianity included her husband Valerian (with whom she lived in virginal wedlock) and one of her symbols is a garland of roses or lilies because an angel is said to have brought them one each from Paradise. When she heard the organ playing at her wedding she 'sang in her heart' to God and dedicated herself to His service. Thus she is the patron saint of music and her common emblem is a harp or an organ, although this was never used in English pre-**Reformation** pictures. She is represented at Creeting St Mary, Eye, and Yaxley.

Christopher: Patron saint of travellers, pictured on many a dashboard medallion, he was probably a C3 martyr in Asia Minor. Legend describes him as a giant who wished to serve the greatest king in the world. A hermit preached the Gospel to him and suggested that he live by a dangerous river nearby and help wayfarers across. As he carried a child over one day, the waters rose and he seemed to bear the weight of the whole world on his shoulders. When they reached the other side, the child was revealed as Christ Himself. The saint is invariably represented as a giant holding a huge staff as he fords the river with the Christ child on his shoulder. He was so popular that nearly every church had a statue or painting of him. It was normally placed opposite the main door so that passersby could see it easily, for it was believed that:

If thou the face of Christopher on any morn shalt see,

Throughout the day from sudden death thou shalt preserved be.

Examples are common but note those at Creeting St Peter (with a variation of the text), Grundisburgh, Little Wenham, Oakley, Sproughton (**Arts and Crafts** glass), and Wilby.

Columba: No special symbols. He was a prince of C6 Ireland with a talent for founding monasteries. He left Ireland in 563 when he was 41 and with a few companions headed for Scotland and the island of Iona, where he established his own monastery and lived until his death in 597. A potent evangelist in Scotland and Northumbria, he was also a scholar and poet and work survives which is believed to be his. There is a modern glass figure of him at Debenham.

Cuthbert: Born about 636, he was a Tweedale shepherd lad who, having had a vision of angels bearing the soul of St Aidan up to heaven, entered Melrose monastery. He made many missionary journeys into Scotland and in 664 was chosen to be prior of Lindisfarne. Retreating to even sterner self-denial on the Farne islands, he relented to become bishop of Lindisfarne for two years before returning to his cell on Farne to die in 687. He had great influence over the Northumbrian kings and his work with the sick and the poor became a legend in the north-east. His body now rests in Durham cathedral. There is a painting of him on the C15 screen at Nayland, where he is shown with the head of **St Oswald.** This is because the king's head was buried at Lindisfarne and placed in St Cuthbert's coffin when the island was threatened by the Danes in 875.

Denys, or Dionysius: His symbol is a severed head. Patron saint of France and first bishop of Paris – where his missionary zeal so roused the fury of the pagans that they put him to terrible tortures, from which he emerged miraculously unharmed. So they took him to Montmartre and beheaded him – only to have him rise and bear his severed head to his chosen resting place at St Denis. And that is why the kings of France were traditionally buried there. There is a modern glass picture of him at Oakley.

Dominic: Born of a noble Spanish family in 1170, he pursued a conventional clerical career until he became convinced of the need to reform the Church in southern France. In 1218 the pope gave him authority to establish his order of friars preachers and his zealous missioners became known as the Black Friars by the colour of their robes. They reached England in 1221. Illustrations of the saint are rare but one may be found on the **retable** at Thornham Parva.

Dorothy: Usually shown holding a spray of flowers and/or a basket of fruit. During the persecution of the Emperor Diocletian in the early C4, she was threatened with terrible tortures unless she rejected her Christianity and married the prefect. Her reply, it is said, was:

> Do to me what torment thou wilt, for I am ready to suffer it for the love of my spouse, Jesu Christ, in whose garden full of delights I have gathered roses, spices and apples.

On her way to execution, she was mocked by a young lawyer who scornfully asked her to send him some of those roses and apples. After she had been beheaded, an angel appeared to the lawyer, bringing from Dorothy in Paradise the requested gift, whereupon he was converted and followed the saint to martyrdom. She is represented at Eye and Yaxley.

Edith: There have been two saints of this name and it is not always possible to say which is intended. St Edith of Polesworth was a sister of King Athelstan and abbess of Polesworth during the C10. St Edith of Wilton was a daughter of King Edgar and the nun Wolfrida (whom he had abducted). She took her daughter back to Wilton abbey where she was educated. She founded the church at Wilton and died there in 984 at the age of 23. The saint (take your pick) shares a C20 window at Edwardstone with Melchizedek and Abbot Samson.

Edmund, King and Martyr: Crowned at Bures (St Stephen) and king of East Anglia from 855 until 870, when the Danes defeated him in battle and took him prisoner. He refused to renounce his faith and they tied him to a tree, shot him with arrows, and finally beheaded him. His murderers left his head in a wood to rot, but those that sought it were guided by its ability to cry 'Here! Here!'. They found it guarded by a great grey wolf; the wolf followed the cortège to Bury and then returned to the wood. The great abbey church was dedicated to St Edmund and his shrine became a principal place of pilgrimage. Hoxne is the traditional site of the martyrdom although one school of thought prefers Hellesdon near Norwich, and another Bradfield St Clare. The saint's usual emblem is an arrow or arrows but the wolf's head is sometimes seen (as at Hoxne and Stonham Aspal). Representations are naturally plentiful, but note in particular the figure on the **porch** at Bramford, the wall paintings at Boxford and Thornham Parva, and the screen panels at Belstead, Eye, Nayland, and Kersey.

Edward the Confessor: Usually seen in kingly crown, and holding aloft a ring. This deeply pious king of England, immediately before the Norman Conquest of 1066, built Westminster abbey – the price for not having kept his vow to make a pilgrimage to the Holy Land. Confronted once by a beggar asking for alms, the king, having no money, slipped a ring from his finger and gave it to him. The beggar, it seems, was really **St John the Evangelist**, who returned the ring to English pilgrims in Palestine and foretold the king's imminent death. This is alluded to in the painting at Nayland and there are other representations at Bures (St Stephen), Eye, and Ipswich (St Mary le Tower).

Eligius, or Eloy: Patron saint of farriers, his symbol is a blacksmith's hammer and tongs and occasionally a severed horse's leg. Eligius was a charitable and devoted bishop in C6 France and Flanders. His most famous exploit was to lop the leg off a difficult horse which was refusing to be shod, fix the shoe to the severed limb, and then put the leg back on again; a sign of the cross, and the beast trotted thankfully away. He is represented at Freckenham [Vol.1] and possibly at Ipswich (St Matthew).

Elizabeth: No distinguishing symbol, but usually represented at the moment of the **Visitation**, when the **Blessed Virgin** came to tell her of the visit of the angel to announce Christ's birth, Elizabeth already being near her time with the child who would be **John the Baptist**. She is represented at Great Waldingfield, Newton, and Thornham Parva.

Erasmus: His symbol is a windlass. He fled from Roman persecution, about A.D. 300, to a cave where he was cared for by a raven. Later, when he resumed his inspirational preaching, his death was ordered by Emperor Maximian and he is said to have been martyred by having his entrails uncoiled and wound upon a windlass – which explains why he was invoked against colic and stomach troubles. A figure on the screen at Ipswich (St Matthew) may represent him.

Erkenwald: A member of the royal family of East Anglia and brother of **St Ethelburga**, he was abbot of the monastery he founded at Chertsey. In 676 he became bishop of London and founded St Paul's cathedral. Little is known of his life but its sanctity is vouched for by the Venerable Bede. He figures among the selection of English saints in the **sanctuary** panels at Ipswich (St Mary le Tower).

Ethelbert: He was king of East Anglia in the late C8 and was executed by King Offa of Mercia. The story goes that he sought the hand of Offa's daughter but aroused a jealous passion in her mother Queen Cynethritha, who persuaded her husband to behead him. In contrition the king built Hereford cathedral, dedicated it to Ethelbert, and made a shrine for the saint which became known for miraculous healings. There are four churches under his patronage in Suffolk and a modern painting of him can be found in the **sanctuary** at Ipswich (St Mary le Tower).

Ethelburga: A daughter of the East Anglian royal house, she became the first abbess of the convent founded by her brother **St Erkenwald** at Barking in Essex. She lived a life of exemplary piety, experienced prophetic visions, and died in 676. There is a modern painting of her in the **sanctuary** at Ipswich (St Mary le Tower).

Etheldreda: No special emblem, but generally represented as a royally crowned abbess. Daughter of a C7 king of East Anglia and born at Exning, she was twice married before becoming a nun. She founded a nunnery at Ely, became its first abbess and was known for her deep devotion and piety. After death her body remained incorrupt and its miracle-working powers made Ely a great centre of pilgrimage. She is represented at Bramford and Ipswich (St Mary le Tower).

Eustachius, or Eustace: A saint whose name is coupled with **St Andrew's** in the unique dedication at Hoo. Eustachius was a Christian who suffered martyrdom with his wife and two sons under Emperor Hadrian about the year 120. Legend adds that he was Trajan's master of horse and was converted by seeing a luminous crucifix between the horns of a stag he was hunting. A similar tale is told of St Hubert and they share the same emblem of a stag with crucifix.

Faith: Her symbols are a palm branch and the grid-iron upon which she was roasted in France about the year 287. Legend says that a thick fall of snow came to veil her body during her suffering. She figures in 1930s glass at Boulge.

Felix: Usually seen as a bishop, he came to England in the C7 from France to preach the Gospel, and in 630 became the first bishop of Dunwich. For the seventeen years of life that remained to him, he worked steadfastly to establish the Church on the eastern seaboard, founded schools, and preached extensively, with the friendly support of the king of the East Angles. A favourite subject for C19 and C20 artists in Suffolk churches, he is pictured at Boulge, Capel St Mary, Earl Soham, Ipswich (St Mary le Tower), Swilland, and Tuddenham (St Martin).

Francis of Assisi: Usually seen as a friar holding a cross, often accompanied by the animals and birds with whom he is always associated; sometimes also with the 'stigmata', the wounds of Christ in hands and feet and side. Oddly, this much loved saint is only occasionally represented in medieval art, though his story is so well known – his birth in wealthy circumstances in C12 Italy; his decision as a young man to devote himself to poverty, prayer, and charity; his establishment of the Franciscan Order; his healing powers; and, not least, his rapport with wild animals. He died, aged only 45, in 1226, and was canonised two years later. We are fortunate in having at Wissington the earliest known example in this country of a painting which shows him preaching to the birds. Dating from the second half of the C13, it was completed not many years after his death.

Gabriel: One of the seven archangels mentioned in the Book of Daniel and in **St Luke's** Gospel. He is the archangel of the **Annunciation** and appears in many carvings and paintings with the **Blessed Virgin**, and alone at Boulge, Brantham, and Capel St Mary.

George: The martial knight, armoured and mounted, and England's patron

saint, famed for his exploits in rescuing the beautiful maiden from the terrible dragon, and then killing the fire-breathing beast. All this took place in Palestine, where subsequently George was horribly put to death for refusing to sacrifice to idols. It was during the Crusades to Palestine that he was adopted as England's patron. King Richard Coeur-de-Lion is said to have had a vision of him, assuring him of safety and victory in a forthcoming battle against the Saracens. Commonly seen, but note the wall painting at Earl Stonham and the **spandrels** at Athelington.

Giles: His emblems are a doe or hind at his side, sometimes with an arrow piercing his hand or leg, he being dressed as a monk or as an abbot with crozier (crook). He lived as a hermit in C8 France, with his doe for company. One day a king and his companions hunted the doe, which fled to the saint for protection. However, an arrow loosed off by the king by chance struck Giles. In penance the king built a monastery on that very site and Giles became the first abbot. About 150 churches are dedicated to him. He is represented at Bramford.

Gregory (the Great): Represented as a pope, with a dove, and a roll of music in one hand. One of the **Four Latin Doctors**, he was born of noble Roman stock in 540. He became a monk and founded several monasteries, into one of which he retired. It was he who, seeing fair-haired British slaves in the Rome slave market, commented: 'Not Angles, but angels.' It is said he came briefly to Britain as a missionary but was recalled to be elected, much against his will, as pope. He sent **St Augustine** to these islands and gave his name to Gregorian chants (thus the symbolic roll of music). One of the best-known incidents in his life came to be called the mass of St Gregory. It is said that, in order to sustain the faith of a sceptic, the sacred elements of bread and wine were transformed on the

altar into a vision of the risen Christ as the pope celebrated mass. It is illustrated on a screen panel at Wyverstone [Vol.1].

Helen: Represented wearing a crown and holding a cross, sometimes an Egyptian cross, like a letter 'T'. Mother of Emperor Constantine the Great, but her own parentage is mysterious. One story says she was an inn-keeper's daughter. Another (much more colourfully) says she was the daughter of King Coel of Colchester, Old King Cole of the nursery rhyme. What is certain is that she married an emperor and bore another; and that as an old lady she set off on pilgrimage for the Holy Land, where she found fragments of the True Cross and brought them to Europe. She can be seen in C15 glass at Wilby and there is a possible representation at Easton.

James the Great: Usually seen with a sword, or with the pilgrimage necessities of staff, wallet, and scallop shell. One of the **apostles** closest to Christ and subsequently one of the leaders of the Church, he was executed by Herod Agrippa in A.D. 44 (Acts 12: 2). Many traditions surround him; enough churches claim relics to make up half a dozen bodies. Strongest, however, is the belief that his body was put into a boat, without sails or rudder, which travelled unaided out of the Mediterranean, around Spain, and fetched up at Compostella, on the northern coast, where James's shrine became throughout the medieval age one of the greatest places of pilgrimage. One of the Athelington bench end carvings may represent him.

James the Less: His emblem is a fuller's club, a curved implement like a hockey stick, used by a fuller (a cloth cleanser) to beat cloth, with which he was killed by a blow on the head after he had survived either being stoned (one

version) or being hurled from the pinnacle of the Temple in Jerusalem by the Scribes and Pharisees. This occurred after James, one of the twelve, presided over the great synod in Jerusalem which reached agreement on how far Gentile converts to Christianity should be made to observe Jewish rites and customs. His figure appears in C19 foreign glass at Winston and possibly on one of the Athelington bench ends.

Jerome: Usually seen with a cardinal's hat; sometimes with an inkhorn, and with a lion at his feet. One of the **Four Latin Doctors**, he became secretary of the Roman see about 381, after much travel and study. (From medieval times, this office was held by a cardinal; thus Jerome's hat.) Later he travelled again, coming at last to Bethlehem, where he founded a monastery and fulfilled his ambition of translating the Bible from its original languages, Hebrew and Greek, into Latin: the Vulgate of the Roman church (thus the inkhorn). There is a charming story that a lion came to his monastery with an injured paw. The saint healed it, and the animal stayed on as his faithful companion.

John the Baptist: His story needs no telling in detail; he was the man who baptised Christ and 'led the way', and who died at a whim of Herod's daughter Salome. He figures in modern glass at Brantham.

John: As one of the four Evangelists (see **Evangelistic symbols**), his emblem is an eagle, but he is often shown with a cup or chalice from which a snake or devil is emerging. This is a reference to the story that he was offered poisoned drink but made it harmless by making the sign of the cross over it. John, 'the disciple whom Jesus loved', and whose figure normally stood on Christ's l. hand on the **rood**, was hurled into boiling oil in Rome but emerged unharmed. He was banished to Patmos and is said to have spent the closing years of his long life at Ephesus. He is represented in many churches.

Joseph: Little is said in the Gospels about St Joseph but stories abound in the literature of the early Church. It is said that he was a widower chosen under divine guidance by the high priest as a husband for the **Blessed Virgin**. He continued as a carpenter until Christ saved his body from corruption at the age of 111 and entrusted his soul to the hosts of heaven. Joseph normally figures in Nativity scenes and in the Flight into Egypt.

Jude, or Thaddaeus: Most often seen holding a boat, though sometimes with a club or carpenter's square. One of the twelve, he is said to have preached in Mesopotamia, Russia, and finally in Persia, where he was attacked and killed by pagan priests, says one tradition; another says that he was hung on a cross at Arat and pierced with javelins. He is seen in C15 glass at Stratford St Mary, in C19 foreign glass at Winston, and on a bench end at Athelington.

Lambert: Seen as a bishop holding a sword. He was bishop of his native city of Maastricht in the Netherlands from 670. There, according to the *Golden Legend*, he 'shone by word and by example in all virtue'. But around 709 he was the victim of a revenge killing. Unknown to him, his servants had killed two brothers who looted his church, and their relations took revenge on the bishop. There is a picture of him at Stonham Aspal.

Laurence: He shares with **St Faith** the emblem of a grid-iron (both were martyred by being roasted on one). He is usually shown in the vestments of a

deacon, an office he held under the martyred Pope Sixtus II. During the diabolical persecutions of Emperor Valerian in the C3, Laurence was ordered to reveal the treasures of the Church, whereupon he disappeared into the noisome alleys of Rome to return with a retinue of cripples and beggars. 'These are the Church's treasures', he declared. It was an answer which earned him an agonising death. There are nine churches dedicated to him in Suffolk, including Great Bricett and the Waldingfields; he appears on the screen at Belstead, and in C19 glass at Bures (St Stephen), Bramford, and Creeting St Mary.

Leger: Bishop of Autun in C7 France. His political partialities and involvements earned him the hatred of a royal chamberlain, one Ebroin. When Ebroin rebelled and sent an army against Autun, Leger offered himself so that the inhabitants might be spared. Ebroin promptly had the poor man's eyes put out, tortured him further, and finally beheaded him. His emblem is an auger (a 'T'-shaped tool like a large corkscrew), with which he was blinded. A fragment of medieval glass at Polstead may be a rare picture of him.

Longinus: Rather confusingly, legends assign the name both to the soldier who pierced Christ's side and to the centurion who was converted at the Crucifixion when he exclaimed: 'Truly this man was the son of God.' It is said that he was beheaded later for his faith. Oakley has a picture of him in C19 glass.

Lucy: She is shown holding a sword; or with a sword driven through her neck; or with light issuing from her gashed throat; or holding aloft a plate or a book on which are two eyes. Martyred in Syracuse about the year 303, legend says that when she was sentenced to death nothing could move her, not even yoked oxen. So faggots were piled around her and lit, but she would not burn. At length she was killed by a sword thrust to the throat. The rays of light, and the eyes, probably refer to the similarity between her name and the Latin word for light – 'lux'. There is a picture of her on the screen at Eye where she is shown carrying her bloody eyes on a book.

Luke: One of the four Evangelists, his special symbol is an ox (see **Evangelistic symbols**), probably a reference to the sacrifice in the Temple at the beginning of his Gospel, while tying in neatly with Revelation 4: 7. **St Paul's** 'fellow worker', he was with him on his later journeys and was referred to as 'the beloved physician', hence the tradition that he was a doctor. There is another story dating from the C6 that he was a painter who gained many converts by showing them portraits of Christ and the **Blessed Virgin** – the first ikons. Thus he is also the patron saint of artists.

Margaret of Antioch: Her emblem is a writhing dragon, which she transfixes with a cross. Thrown into prison in Antioch for her Christian beliefs, this legendary lady was tempted by the devil in the guise of a terrible dragon. Some have it that the dragon was miraculously decapitated; others that he swallowed her but burst when her cross stuck in his throat; others still that she simply made the sign of the cross and he faded away. That she is guardian of women in childbirth presumably has something to do with her 'caesarian' irruption from the dragon. There are fine C15 glass panels illustrating her life at Combs, a painting of her on the **retable** at Thornham Parva, C13 paintings at Little Wenham and Wissington, and other examples at Athelington, Belstead, Chattisham, Edwardstone, Grundisburgh, and Wilby.

Mark: One of the four Evangelists, his symbol being the winged lion (see **Evangelistic symbols**). The significance of the lion is intriguing – in ancient lore it typified the Resurrection, based on the curious idea that the lion's young were dead for three days after birth, and were then brought to life by the roaring of their parents. An interesting parallel is the symbolism of the **pelican**. Mark's story as Evangelist, and his missionary travels, thread through the New Testament. There is a tradition that later he went to Rome, then to Alexandria, where he became the city's first bishop, and was subsequently martyred during Nero's reign. What is certain is that in the C9 his relics were taken to Venice, whose patron saint he became and has remained, and where his lion symbol is much in evidence.

Mary the Blessed Virgin: The mother of Christ, pre-eminent among the patron saints of the medieval Church. Out of the 500 in Suffolk, over 150 churches are dedicated to the Virgin, and no other individual saint reaches a third of that. Originally, a number of them will have been associated with one of her specific Feast Days such as the **Assumption**, but it is now rare to find instances that can be substantiated. Aspall, however, uses the variation 'St Mary of Grace'. Acclaimed as 'the only bridge between God and man', she became the primal intercessor, 'Queen of Pity', and few churches will have been without at least an **altar** of Our Lady. The Assumption and **Annunciation** scenes were popular subjects for paintings and carvings, and hers was the attendant figure on Christ's r. hand as part of the **rood** group. She figures also in some **Doom** paintings and is sometimes shown as a child being taught to read by her mother **St Anne**. The Blessed Virgin's usual emblem is a lily and her badge a crowned 'M' or 'MR' for 'Maria Regina', (Queen of heaven).

Mary Magdalene (Mary of Magdala):
She was one of a number of women
'healed of evil spirits' mentioned in **St
Luke's** Gospel, and was among those
who stood watching the Crucifixion.
Both **St Matthew** and **St John** tell how
she came to the sepulchre on the first
Easter day, heard from the angel that
Christ was risen, and hastened to tell
the disciples. The first appearance of
the resurrected Christ was to her as she
wept by the tomb. From the earliest
times, some commentators have
identified her with Mary of Bethany,
sister of Lazarus, and also as the un-
named woman who, as a sinner,
washed Jesus's feet with her tears,
dried them with her hair, and anointed
them with ointment. Thus she has
become the archetype of the Christian
penitent and her emblem is the pot of
ointment. According to an early tradition she was martyred at Ephesus, but a
livelier story was current by the C9. In
it, her enemies cast her adrift with
Lazarus and Martha in a rudderless
ship that fetched up at Marseilles
where Lazarus became a bishop and
Magdalene preached the Gospel.
According to this version she spent the
last thirty years of her life as a
contemplative near Aix-en-Provence.
There is a C13 painting of her at Little
Wenham and later examples at Badley,
Belstead, and Ipswich (St Mary le
Tower).

Matthew: According to his own Gospel,
Matthew was a customs officer in the
service of Herod Antipas when he was
called by Jesus to become one of the
twelve **apostles**. He was the Levi at
whose feast Jesus and his disciples
scandalised the Pharisees and an early
tradition tells of him preaching to the
Hebrews. His commonest symbol is the
creature that 'had a face as of a man',
one of the four mentioned in
Revelation (see **Evangelistic symbols**).
He is said to have met his death by the
sword for opposing a king's marriage to
a consecrated virgin and so a sword is
sometimes substituted. To confuse

things further, he may carry an axe like
St Matthias, or a carpenter's square.
The commonest alternative is a money
bag in reference to his early profession.
He can be found in many churches.

Matthias: Though not in the least
martial, Matthias is usually shown
with a weapon – axe, spear, or sword,
because he was beheaded in Jerusalem
by the Jews. He was the disciple chosen
by lot to take the place of Judas Iscariot,
after the betrayer's death. He figures in
C19 foreign glass at Winston.

Michael: A very popular choice for
medieval dedications. In the Old Testament, Michael was 'the great prince
which standeth for the children of the
people', the guardian angel of the Jews,
and the Revelation of **St John** portrays
him leading the angelic host against the
devil and all his works. And so he
appears as a winged angel in shining
armour striking down the dragon, but
his role as the weigher of souls was a
popular notion and he is often seen in
Doom paintings with the scales of
justice. There is a C13 painting of him
at Wissington and later examples at
Boulge and Capel St Mary.

Monica: She is the saint who illustrates
the ideal of a devout wife and mother.
A native of North Africa, she converted
her husband to Christianity, having
endured rough treatment. She grieved
over her son **St Augustine's** early
waywardness but went with him to
Milan and rejoiced in his conversion
under **St Ambrose** in the year 387. She
is pictured in a window at Ipswich (St
Augustine).

Nicholas: Very few facts are known
about this C4 bishop of Myra in Asia
Minor, but the legends are spectacular,
and he was a popular choice for
dedications. There was once a famine
in the land and an inn-keeper, with

nothing to set before his guests, cut up three boys and put them in a pickling tub. Along came the bishop and smartly restored them to life, providing a subject popular with medieval congregations and, incidentally, assuming the role of the patron saint of children. The sign of the three golden balls is seldom seen now in city streets but they were another of St Nicholas's symbols and he was the patron saint of pawnbrokers too. The balls stand for the bags of gold that he left secretly at the house of an impoverished nobleman in order that his three daughters should not lack dowries. The Russian Church called him 'Sant Niklaus', which came in time to be our own 'Santa Claus', that answer to an adman's prayer but still part of the children's magic. There is a C13 version of him at Wissington and a modern window at Boulge.

Olave: Patron saint of Norway. After some years fighting the Danes in England, he became a Christian and returned to his native country to defeat Earl Sweyn and become king in 1016. His agressive stance against paganism was summed up in the challenge: 'Be baptised or fight', and he was forced by a rebellion to take refuge in Russia. Returning at the head of a large army, he was killed at the battle of Stiklestad in 1030 and his shrine at Trondhjem became a focus for pilgrims in the Middle Ages. He occurs in a **Kempe** window at Creeting St Mary.

Oswald: The son of Ethelfrid, king of Northumbria, he fled to Scotland in 613 after his father's death and was converted to Christianity by the monks of Iona. He recovered his realm from Caedwalla and helped in St Aidan's missionary work. He died while fighting Penda, king of Mercia, at the battle of Maserfield and his body at length came to rest in Gloucester in 909. His hands migrated to Bamburgh and his head to Lindisfarne, but the latter

journeyed on with the body of **St Cuthbert** to Durham cathedral eventually. That is why it is shown with the figure of St Cuthbert on the C15 screen at Nayland.

Osyth, or Sitha: She was a granddaughter of King Penda of Mercia and apparently fled from her bridal feast to take refuge at Dunwich, where she took the veil. Having founded a nunnery at Chick in Essex in 673, she was beheaded in an attack by Danish pirates. She then, so the story goes, walked to the nearest church, carrying her head. She appears on the Belstead screen, in C15 glass at Wilby, and on a modern panel at Ipswich (St Mary le Tower).

Paul: A sword is this **apostle's** symbol, usually pointing down. With this weapon his head was struck off at the order of the Emperor Nero, about the year 66 in Rome, when his success in converting eminent people to Christianity became too much to tolerate. Upon his beheading, it is said, milk flowed from the wound. Paul's life story is too well related in the Acts of the Apostles, and in his own Epistles, to need retelling here. Representations of him are common.

Peter:

> Thou art Peter, and upon this rock I will build my church.... I will give unto thee the keys of the kingdom of heaven.

So Christ spoke to his beloved apostle. And so, always, Peter's symbol is the keys. The Gospels tell his story during Christ's ministry on earth, but not his ending. He was crucified – upside down, at his request, as he did not consider himself worthy to die in the same way as his master – in Rome by the Emperor Nero, at about the same time that **St Paul** was beheaded there. Examples of Peter and his crossed keys are legion.

Peter Martyr: A Dominican friar who was born at Verona in the early C13. His eloquence and reputation as a worker of miracles led to his appointment as inquisitor to rid northern Italy of heresy. He met his death at the hands of hired assassins who cleft his head with an axe and drove a knife into his heart, and so he is normally shown with a blade in his head. There is a painting of him on the **retable** at Thornham Parva.

Philip: One of the twelve, Philip is seen either with a cross – for like his Lord he was to suffer crucifixion, at the hands of pagans in Asia Minor – or with a basket of loaves and fishes, recording his connection with the story of Christ's feeding of the 5,000. He occurs on a bench end at Athelington.

Polycarp: In his youth, Polycarp was instructed in the faith by **St John**, who consecrated him bishop of Smyrna where, for forty years, he was one of the resolute leaders of the Church in Asia. In the year 167 he was arrested on a charge of atheism and the Roman authorities tried in vain to persuade him to renounce his faith. Under the pressure of mob opinion he was condemned to be burnt at the stake and an eyewitness account describes how the flames seemd only to form a canopy around him so that a sword thrust was necessary to kill him. He is seldom seen in English churches and has no characteristic emblem, but he figures in a modern window at Eye.

Raphael: One of the seven archangels. He is described in the Book of Tobit as the angel who hears the prayers of holy men and brings them before God; in the Book of Enoch, he is said to have healed the earth defiled by the sins of the fallen angels. He is represented at Capel St Mary.

Richard: Having been a brilliant student at the universities of Paris, Bologna, and Oxford, Richard de Wyche was appointed chancellor of Oxford and Canterbury. After his archbishop had quarrelled with Henry III, he left for France with him and became a Dominican friar at Orleans, adding asceticism to his learning. Returning in 1244, he was elected bishop of Chichester and combined generosity to the poor with strict discipline over his clergy. He died in 1253 and his shrine at Chichester became a place of pilgrimage. He figures in C19 glass at Swilland.

Sebastian: Recognisable at once, the saint riddled with arrows – or at least holding an arrow in his hand. This fate befell him in early Rome, where the saint preached and converted, and comforted Christian prisoners – until the vengeance of the Emperor Diocletian fell on him in 287. He was popular in the Middle Ages as a patron against the plague, which struck as swiftly as an arrow. There is a picture of him on the screen at Belstead.

Simon (the Zealot): He is named as one of the twelve **apostles** in the Bible but no other details are given. All stories about him come from the *Golden Legend* and he is supposed to have preached in Egypt and gone with **St Jerome** to Persia. Once there, his miracles so discredited the pagan idols that he was hacked to pieces. Later, he was identified with Simon the 'brother of the Lord' (i.e. son of Cleopas and Christ's cousin). His usual emblem is a fish to show that he was a fisherman, but confusing alternatives crop up: an oar, an axe, or a saw. He is represented at Athelington.

Stephen: Shown always with a heap of stones in his hands, or on a platter or book. The first Christian martyr, he was stoned to death by the Jews of

Jerusalem, when he fearlessly answered their charges of blasphemy (Acts 6 and 7). The Church tests the faithful by celebrating his martyrdom on 26 December. He can be seen on the screen at Belstead and in a **Kempe** window at Burgh.

Thomas: The **apostle** who is chiefly remembered for refusing to believe that the other disciples had seen the risen Lord, the original 'doubting Thomas' for whom Jesus reappeared that he might be 'not faithless but believing'. The C3 Acts of Thomas record that he was taken to India to be a carpenter for King Gundaphorus, but he spent his time preaching and working miracles, which led to his being arrested and run through with spears. His emblem is normally a spear but it can also be a carpenter's square, and he is the patron saint of builders and masons. He is represented at Athelington, Badley, and East Bergholt.

Thomas of Canterbury (Thomas Becket): Represented always as an archbishop. Occasionally he may have a sword or an axe, a reference to his famous martyrdom at the hands of four of Henry II's knights in Canterbury cathedral at Christmas 1170. Thomas's shrine became a place of veneration and miracles. Four centuries later, Henry VIII branded him traitor, rather than saint, which is why representations of him are often defaced with particular savagery and thoroughness. He is represented at Belstead(?), Eye, Gipping(?), Ipswich (All Saints and St Matthew(?)) and Nayland(?).

Uriel: In Jewish apocryphal texts he is one of the four chief archangels who stand in the presence of God. He is represented at Capel St Mary.

Ursula: Very seldom seen, but normally portrayed crowned, with a sheaf of arrows in one hand, and young women in some profusion at her feet and under her cloak. The story has it that she was a king's daughter in early Britain who, to escape the attentions of an unwelcome suitor, set off for Rome ... accompanied by 11,000 handmaidens. It has been suggested that this startling entourage stems from an early translation error because Ursula's maid was called Undecimilla – probably misread as a number. Be that as it may, Ursula and companions arrived in Rome where the pope received her – and perceived in a dream that she was to suffer martyrdom, at which intelligence he took off his tiara and set off with it to Cologne. There they were beseiged by the Huns, who took the city and slew the lot – except for Ursula, whom the Hun prince wanted to marry. When she refused he shot her with an arrow. She can be seen on the screens at Belstead and Eye, and (possibly) Bildeston.

William of Norwich: In 1144 the Jews in Norwich were accused of crucifying this 11-year-old boy and burying his body on Mousehold Heath, just outside the city. His body was found and reburied in the cathedral where it became the focus of miraculous cures and subsequent pilgrimages. The full story can be found in *A Saint at Stake* by M.D. Anderson. Seldom seen outside Norfolk. There is a painting of the saint on the screen at Eye.

Sanctuary: That part of the church containing the **altar** (or, if there is more than one altar, the high altar. It is normally bounded by the **communion rails**.

Sanctus-bell/turret/window: At the point in the mass at which the priest raises the consecrated bread and the chalice of wine for the people to see, a bell was rung (and sometimes still is) so that 'people who have not leisure daily to be present at Mass may, wherever they are in houses or fields, bow their knees' – the words of Archbishop Peckham in 1281. Some churches have a small turret on the e. gable of the **nave** to house the bell used for this purpose – there is an example at Coddenham. In other cases, a sanctus-bell window is to be found in the interior wall between tower and nave, placed so that it has a clear view of the **altar**. Such an arrangement allows a ringer to use one of the tower bells for the same purpose. See also **low side windows**.

Saxon: The period, with its distinctive architecture, preceding the Norman Conquest of 1066, a vital era in the general establishment of Christianity in the British islands. See also **Anglo-Saxon**, and **Saxon** under **Styles of Architecture**.

Scissors-braced roofs: A roof in which the beams are crossed and interlocked diagonally in the shape of an opened pair of scissors. See **roofs**, figs. 2 and 3.

Scott, Sir George Gilbert (1811 – 78): One of the leading architects of the Gothic Revival in England and one of the great names of the Victorian era. Stimulated by **Pugin's** enthusiasm, he designed the Martyr's Memorial in Oxford, one of the early key works of the new movement. Prolific and successful, he worked on hundreds of churches, either as designer or restorer, and subsequently much of his work attracted bitter criticism. Westminster Abbey and Ely, Salisbury and Lichfield cathedrals all bear his mark – not to mention the Albert Memorial and St Pancras station. His one complete church in Suffolk is at Higham [Vol.1], and his most extensive restoration and rebuilding was Bury (St James) [Vol.1] before it was promoted to a cathedral. The n. **aisle** of Ipswich (St Matthew) is his.

Scratch dials: On or near the s. doorway of many old churches may be seen circles incised in the stone, usually about 6in. across, with lines radiating down from a centre hole. A wooden or metal peg was put in the hole and its shadow marked the time of day, forming a primitive sundial with a specific purpose. The marks related to the times for morning mass, noon and vespers (evensong) and were used to assist priest and people to be punctual in the days before clocks and watches. Sometimes the dials were divided into four 'tides' of three hours and, occasionally, the line for mass is thicker or identified with a short crossbar. There are cases where lines have been added to the top half of the circle, no doubt by mischievous young hands. Interesting examples can be found at Great Bricett (earliest?), Horham and Witnesham (numerals), Swilland (significant placement).

Screen: See **rood screen**.

Sedilia: These are seats (usually made into decorative and architectural features, with miniature columns, arches, and canopies, and detailed carvings) on the s. side of the **chancel**. Generally there are three seats. These can be all on the same level; or 'stepped', i.e., on descending levels; and/or 'graduated', i.e., under separate arches but contained within a composite pattern, frieze, or frame. In many cases, a simple seat is created by building a low window sill; the result is called dropped-sill sedilia. The three seats were specifically for the priest, the deacon (who read the Gospel), and the sub-deacon (who read the Epistle). Though three seats are the norm, numbers can vary between one and eight, and they may be found beside subsidiary **altars** as well as by the high altar. In places where the seats seem impractically low, it may well be that the floor levels have been raised as part of reconstruction or restoration (the

Gothic revivalists were particularly keen on the ritual significance of steps leading up to the **sanctuary** and altar, and these were often not there originally).

Septaria: Nodules of limestone or ironstone which contain other minerals, frequently used as a building material in the s.w. of the county.

Set-offs: The sloped, angled surfaces on buttresses at the points where the buttress 'sets-off' another stage further out from the wall it is supporting.

Seven Deadly Sins: Pride, covetousness, lust, envy, gluttony, anger, sloth. Pride was always pre-eminent and the others encompassed other human failings; drinking went with gluttony, suicide was linked with anger, and spiritual idleness was seen as a form of sloth. Pictures of them were often placed close to the **Seven Works of Mercy** to give them greater emphasis, and they were occasionally used to decorate bench ends (as at Tannington and Wilby)

Seven Sacraments: The sacraments of the Church are: baptism, confirmation, mass (Holy communion), penance, ordination to the priesthood, marriage, Extreme Unction (anointing of the dying). The theme was used to decorate a fine series of seven sacrament **fonts** of which there are thirteen in Suffolk, twenty-three in Norfolk, and one each in Kent and Somerset. All are octagonal and the carving in the eighth bowl panel varies, with the Crucifixion being used on the example at Monk Soham. The sacraments were also illustrated on sets of bench ends at Tannington and Wilby.

Seven Works of Mercy: Sometimes called the Corporal Works of Mercy,

they are: to feed the hungry, to give drink to the thirsty, to welcome strangers, to clothe the naked, to visit the sick, and to visit prisoners. Derived from **St Matthew's** Gospel (25: 34 – 9), the six works are normally augmented by a seventh, the burial of the dead. Part of a set on bench ends survives at Wilby; there is an incomplete version in glass at Combs, another at Hoxne, **Ward and Hughes** windows at Ipswich (St Margaret), and Great Bealings, and another by **Lavers and Barraud** at East Bergholt.

Shroud brass: A brass on which the corpse is shown wrapped in a shroud ready for burial. There is an example at Stowmarket. See also **Brasses**.

Sound holes: Instead of windows at the first-floor level, some towers have square, oblong, or shaped openings, often treated very decoratively. These are very common in Norfolk and their purpose is not, as might be supposed from the name, to let the sound of the bells out (the bell openings higher up do that) but to light the ringing chamber and allow the ringers to hear the bells.

Spandrels: The triangular space between the curve of an arch or the supporting braces of a roof, the wall or upright brace, and the horizontal line above. Often filled in with rich and delicate **tracery** (see **roofs**).

Squint (or hagioscope): An opening cut obliquely through a wall or pillar to give a view of the high **altar** from side chapels and **aisles**. During the mass, the squint made it possible for the act of consecration by a priest at a side altar to be coordinated with the celebration at the high altar. This was necessary because **chantry** and **guild** masses were not allowed to take precedence over the parish mass.

Where there is a squint in the outer wall of a church it may point to the existence of a former chapel or, much more rarely, an **anchorite's** cell. The idea still persists that squints were provided so that lepers could watch the mass, but there is no basis for this at all. It is sometimes possible to determine the original site of the high altar by taking a line through a squint, useful in those cases where the **chancel** has been shortened or lengthened. Squints are not uncommon and there are examples at Copdock, Hadleigh, Hintlesham, Layham, Little Waldingfield, Nayland and Nettlestead. See also **low side windows** and **elevation squints**.

Stone, Nicholas (1586 – 1647): Greatest sculptor of his century, he was born the son of a quarryman in Devon, but soon moved to London, and then to Holland, to gain greater experience. In Holland he apprenticed himself to Hendrik de Keyser, a famous Dutch master mason. The story has it that one piece of work he carried out so delighted his master that Stone was given the hand of de Keyser's daughter in marriage. By 1614, Stone was back in London as mason and statuary; and quickly gained such a reputation that he was employed by the king on the royal palaces and on great buildings in London. Only five years after his return from Holland, he was made master mason to James I, and in 1626 Charles I confirmed him in that appointment. The Mannock tomb and Lady Dorothea's **brass** at Stoke by Nayland are probably by him.

Stops: See **headstops**.

Stoup: In the **porches** of many churches, or just inside the main door, there are basins, usually recessed into the wall. More often than not they are very plain, and where there was once ornament or decoration it has usually been defaced because these were one of the targets of the Puritans. This was because the stoups held holy water which was mixed once a week before mass. On entering the church, worshippers dipped their fingers into the water and crossed themselves as a reminder of their baptismal vows. To prepare the water, salt was first exorcised and then blessed, the water itself was then exorcised and blessed, the salt was sprinkled over it in the form of a cross, and then a final blessing was given to the mixture.

String course: See **courses**.

Stuart: The Royal House of Stuart, which inherited the Scottish throne in 1371 and the English throne, on the accession of James I, in 1603. The Stuart period is taken to be their years of English kingship: those of James I, Charles I, Charles II, James II, William and Mary, and finally Anne, who reigned 1702-14. After the death of Anne, George I, the non-English-speaking German from Hanover, succeeded to the English crown and the Stuart day was over, its last fling being the '45 Rebellion of Bonnie Prince Charlie, 'The Young Pretender'.

Styles of Architecture: From the days of the Saxons, before the Norman Conquest of 1066, through to the Georgians in the C18, architecture both sacred and secular has passed through many developments and details, fads and fancies, inspirations and inventions. The names we use so easily to describe those phases – **Early English, Decorated**, etc. – interestingly were coined only in the last century, being given convenient, even precise, dates. But such dating can be more than misleading. Just as fashions in costume took time to filter through from city or court to provincial outposts, so changes in architectural ideas were only gradually assimilated. For example, there are instances of the lush shapes of the Decorated style still appearing after the **Black Death**, well into the 1360s and 1370s where, presumably, masons with the old skills had survived the pestilence. Window shapes and **tracery** offer the clearest guide to individual styles and are normally the most helpful features for the layman.

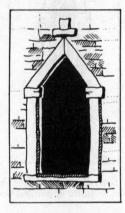

Fig. 9. Saxon triangular-headed form.

Saxon: From the C7 to the Conquest. Characterised by roughness of construction, crudely rounded arches, and triangular-headed window openings (see figs. 9 and 10). Equally distinctive of the period is their **long and short work** at corner angles of buildings. This is where upright stones are alternated with flat slabs, often re-using Roman tiles and other materials salvaged from local remains. Saxon work can be seen at Stuston(?), Thornham Parva, Aldham(?), Framsden, Gosbeck, Hemingstone, Hasketon, Debenham, and Syleham.

Norman: From the Conquest to about 1200, including the **Transitional** phase, spanning the reigns of William I and II, Henry I, Stephen, Henry II, and Richard I. Massive walls and pillars are typical features, mighty rounded arches and, still, small round-headed windows, though they might be used in groups, with heavy pillar-like **mullions** between them. But after the **Saxon** crudity, here is growing craftsmanship and artistry, with rich, bold ornamentation. The small windows of the period are usually deeply splayed (see figs. 11 and 12). These would

Fig. 10. Typical Saxon round-headed window with crude arch.

Fig. 11. Norman slit window – interior view of typical deep 'arrow slit' embrasure.

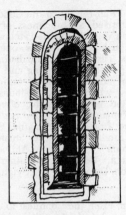

Fig. 12. Norman slit window – exterior view.

originally have been filled with parchment or oiled linen – glass came later. Examples of Norman work are found at Horham, Bedfield, Tuddenham (St Martin), Hasketon, Swilland, Letheringham, and Wissington.

Transitional: This is the phase of the changeover from the rounded, Romanesque architecture of the Normans to the Gothic movement in England – the triumph of the pointed arch and, as it seemed then, a new age of learning and faith. It took three or four decades, to about 1200, for the changeover to take full effect. Massive pillars during this time became slimmer and lighter, and might sometimes bear a pointed arch, carved in **Norman** character. These attractive, slimmed-down columns would also be used in clusters, and would continue to be so used during the full flowering of **Early English**. Examples at Henley, Kenton and Tannington.

Early English: Gothic has now fully arrived, and with it the first really native English architectural style. It spans roughly the 100-year period from

the end of the reign of Richard, through John and Henry II, and into the time of Edward II, to about 1300. The simple, elegant **lancet** made its appearance, first used singly (see fig. 13), then in groups.

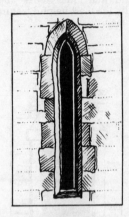

Fig. 13. Early English lancet – the first arrival in England of pointed Gothic.

As ideas developed, the space between the heads of two lancets placed together was pierced with an open pattern, cut directly through the masonry: this is known as **plate tracery** (see fig. 16). From there it was but a step to fining down the tracery by constructing it in separated pieces, that is, **bar tracery**. In the **Decorated** style which followed, this technique reached a wonderful zenith. Intermediate, however, about the year 1300 (and a most useful dating device), came a most distinctive phase, the 'Y' traceried window. (Fig. 14 is self-explanatory.) A development of this was the extension of the Ys through three or four **lights** producing the simplest interlocking tracery with slim and graceful pointed heads. Everything at this time became finer in conception: bold buttresses, effortlessly thrusting arches, beautiful foliage carving, and, most distinctive of this period, the trefoil, or three-leaf decoration. (See **emblems of the Trinity** and **foils**.) This was much used in window tracery and in decorative carving. Also popular was the **dogtooth** moulding, which looks like a square, four-leafed flower, said to be based on the dog's tooth violet.

Fig. 16. Simple geometric plate tracery.

Fig. 14. The typical 'Y' traceried window of around 1300.

Fig. 15. Early English lancets composed in a group.

Decorated: This supreme time of architectural achievement and marvellous confidence in the use of shape and decoration had but a half-century of full life – during the reigns of the first three Edwards – before the catastrophe of the **Black Death** struck Europe in 1349 – 50. In East Anglia, it has been estimated that half the population died. This was, then, the high point of ornamented Gothic. Windows grew larger, **tracery** became progressively more flowing and adventurous: from the 'geometrical', with circles, trefoils, quatrefoils, lozenges, etc. (see **foils**) dominating the tracery, it burgeoned ultimately to the virtuosity of **reticulated** or net-like tracery (see fig. 17) and the creative beauty of form as seen in fig. 18. Rich ornamentation and carving abounded, including the distinctive **ball flower**, a little globule whose carved petals enclose a tiny ball; and also a sculptural explosion of pinnacles and **crocketting**, both inside and outside the church, from gable ends to tombs. There are many Suffolk examples but Raydon and Washbrook chancels are notable.

Fig. 17. The flowing beauty of the Decorated style's reticulated form.

Fig. 18. Decorated artistry in imaginative flow – the butterfly or four-petalled flower motif.

implies, is one of soaring upward lines, drawn in great windows by vertical **mullions** (see fig. 19); by majestic, clean-lined towers; and by meticulously panelled buttresses and parapets and the ornamented bases of walls (see also **flushwork**). Rich decoration is typical, though it usually has more of the grandly formal than of a purely aesthetic beauty. The majority of churches embody something of the style, even if it is only a window or two. Boxford, Eye and Gipping are prime examples.

Fig. 19. The classic Perpendicular window, its mullions thrusting to the head of the arch.

Perpendicular: This style takes us from the aftermath of the **Black Death**, through Richard II's reign, and successively those of Henry IV, V, and VI, Edward IV, and Richard III to the time of Henry VII, until around 1500, when the **Tudor** adaptation took place. The Perpendicular style, as its name

Tudor: Here we are talking of roughly the century to 1600 spanned by Henry VIII, the boy-king Edward VI, Mary, and Elizabeth. It is not so much a style as an adaptation, in that the Tudor mode, as far as churches are concerned, is basically the flattening of the **Perpendicular** arch, while otherwise retaining the same features (see fig. 20). Decoration had become stereotyped, with interminable repetitions of the royal badges, the rose and the portcullis; and family heraldry followed the trend so that badges and shields of national magnates and coun-

Fig. 20. The Tudor contribution – a flattening of the arch over a Perpendicular window.

ty gentry are to be found carved in wood and stone. Red brick had become a fashionable alternative to stone, and in some cases it displaced the local flint as a basic material which could be laid quickly and produced locally. Examples of the period are Little Waldingfield and Great Bealings **porches**, Charsfield and Ashbocking towers, and the s. **aisle** at Akenham.

Jacobean/Caroline: From the early C17 with the reign – 1603 – 25 – of James I (Latin 'Jacobus'), and continuing with the reigns of Charles I and II (Latin 'Carolus'). It was during James's reign that a stirring towards a **Renaissance** expression of architecture truly began in England. It was a style, and a movement, which employed the principles of the ancient Greek classical building concepts, much classical detail and ornamentation, and, as in the Elizabethan period, a copious use of bricks. This stylised approach found expression in furniture too, as will be found in many examples in churches. During James's reign, the Renaissance movement found its resident genius in Inigo Jones (d. 1652), whom James

appointed surveyor general of the works. After Jones came another genius, Sir Christopher Wren. And if his masterpiece, St Paul's cathedral, remains one of our greatest Renaissance buildings, it was nonetheless in country houses and grand mansions that the Renaissance spirit was most evidenced. In our churches, the Jacobean title applies as often as not to wood carving, pulpits, typically high bench backs, etc., and to aristocratic monuments.

Symbols of the Evangelists: See **Evangelistic symbols**.

Tabernacle work: Representations of canopied stalls, niches, and pinnacles, particularly in stained glass and wall paintings.

Talbot: An heraldic hound or hunting dog, seen in the arms of a number of families, but particularly associated with the Talbots, earls of Shrewsbury.

Tester: Flat canopy above a pulpit, acting as a sounding board.

Three-decker pulpits: After the Civil War, the normal Sunday service was conducted entirely from the reading desk, and only on the infrequent Sacrament Sundays would minister and people move to the **altar**. Convenience demanded that pews be grouped round a focal point, and the C17 to C18 solution was a three-decker pulpit. The service was read from the second tier, and the minister climbed to the pulpit above to deliver his sermon (if the curate took the service, the rector would sit in the pulpit until sermon time). The **parish clerk** led the responses, and conducted the singing from his special pew below, and the three compartments were combined in a number of ways, often ingeniously.

Some churches made do with two-deckers wherein the reading desk and pulpit were planned as a unit, and separate accommodation was found for the clerk, but such arrangements are occasionally the result of later alterations to suit changing needs or parsons' predilections. For decades the three-decker was the focus of congregational worship (with spasmodic acknowledgement of the altar's pre-eminence), and it gathered to itself cushions for the ledges, candlesticks, **hour-glass**, wig-stand, and the odd hat peg. There are examples at Gislingham and Cretingham. See also **Prayer book churches**.

Three Marys: In **St Mark's** Gospel **Mary Magdalene**, Mary the mother of James, and Salome visit the sepulchre to anoint Christ's body, but in some medieval accounts they were called Mary Magdalene, Mary Jacobee, and Mary Salome, and in one Bible text of the Middle Ages the last one becomes Maria Joseph. From this has come the convention of calling them the 'three Marys'. **St Anne** is credited with three husbands by which she had three daughters, all Marys – the **Blessed Virgin**; Mary the mother of **James the Less, St Simon** and **St Jude**; and Mary the mother of **St James the Great** and **St John**. These too are sometimes referred to as the 'three Marys'. The women at the tomb feature in modern glass at Earl Stonham, Bentley, East Bergholt, Great Bealings, and Wilby.

Thurible: Known also as a censer, it is a pierced metal container used for the ceremonial burning of incense. The incense is burned on charcoal and the thurible is usually suspended on chains so that it can be swung in the hand of the thurifer as he censes the **altar**, the priest, or the congregation, thus fanning the charcoal and directing the smoke at will. The thurifer is sometimes attended by a boy bearing a boat-shaped vessel containing incense for replenishing the thurible.

Thurlow, Thomas: A native sculptor born at Saxmundham in 1813 who spent his whole life in the county and did most of his work there. He exhibited at the Royal Academy between 1846 and 1872 and died in 1899. The majority of his pieces are in East Suffolk but there is a medallion portrait by him of Robert Carew King at Witnesham.

Tie-beam: The wall-to-wall cross beam or truss supporting a roof. (See **roofs**.)

Touchstone: A smooth, fine-grained black stone (jasper, black marble, or similar) widely used in the C16 to C18 for funeral monuments.

Townshend, Caroline (1878 – 1944) and Joan Howson (1885 – 1964): Arts and Crafts stained glass workers. Caroline Townshend studied at the Slade and then became a pupil of **Christopher Whall** in 1900. Her first commission was in 1903. Joan Howson had studied stained glass at Liverpool and became her apprentice before World War I. They became partners in 1920, with Townshend designing and Howson collaborating in the making and specialising in the repair of medieval glass. Miss Townshend died in 1944 but Joan Howson continued to work, mainly on restorations. An example of their work can be seen at Pettaugh.

Tracery: Ornamental open-work in wood or stone, especially in the upper parts of windows and screens; the term also applies to similar patterns on solid panels.

Transepts: Projecting 'arms' of a church, built out to n. and s. from the point where **nave** and **chancel** meet, to form a cross-shaped or cruciform ground plan.

Transitional: Though 'transitional' can refer loosely to any change from one phase of architecture to another, it is particularly applied to the transition from the 'rounded' Norman to the 'pointed' Gothic, in the second half of the C12. (See under **Styles of Architecture**.)

Transoms: The horizontal crosspieces in window **tracery**, most noticeable in **Perpendicular** windows.

Trefoil: See **foils**.

Trinity: See **emblems of the Trinity**.

Tudor: The dynasty founded by Henry Tudor, victor of Bosworth Field against Richard III ('My kingdom for a horse . . .'). He was crowned Henry VII in 1485; Henry VIII followed, then Edward VI, Mary I (Bloody Mary), and finally Elizabeth I, who died on 24 March 1603, 'the last of the Tudors and the greatest of Queens'. For the Church, it was a cataclysmic time. Various aspects of this are dealt with under the headings: **communion rails; Laud; mensa slabs; Prayer book churches; rood screen;** and **Royal Arms**. The interiors of churches were changed beyond recognition during this era, but the Tudor influence upon church architecture as such was negligible. (See under **Styles of Architecture**.)

Tudor roses: A typical flower decoration of the period. (See **Tudor** under **Styles of Architecture**.)

Tympanum: Space over head of door, or in head of filled-in arch, plain or carved. See also **Royal Arms** for special connection.

Unicorn: A swift and fierce little animal from the **bestiary**, with the well-known single horn on its forehead. The only way to catch it was to lay a trap with a virgin. The beast was so attracted by her purity that it would run up, lay its head in her lap, and fall asleep. Thus it became the symbol of purity and feminine chastity, and for the **Blessed Virgin** in particular.

Uriel: See under **Saints**.

Vestry: That part of the church in which the vestments are kept and where the clergy robe for services. It sometimes doubles as a **sacristy** and occasionally as a choir robing area.

Virgin Mary: See **Mary the Blessed Virgin** under **Saints**.

Visitation: Having been told by the Archangel Gabriel that she would bear a son, whose name would be Jesus and whose kingdom would have no end (Luke 1), the Virgin Mary hurried to tell the news to her cousin **St Elizabeth**, already near her time with the child who would be **St John the Baptist**. This meeting is commemorated on 2 July as the Visitation. See Bildeston, Newton, and Thornham Parva.

Wall plate: See **roofs**.

Wall post: See **roofs**.

Ward & Hughes: Firm of stained glass manufacturers founded by Thomas Ward and James Henry Nixon in 1836. They traded as Ward & Nixon until 1850, when Henry Hughes became chief designer. After Hughes's death in 1883, the firm continued under Thomas Curtis until the 1920s and some later windows are signed by him. They were the largest suppliers to Norfolk and Suffolk in the C19, and their 1850s – 60s High Victorian work was well drawn and often pleasing in design and colour. In 1870, their massive production was rationalised and it was often dull, repetitive, and poorly designed thereafter. There is some of their early work at Horham and good windows at Clopton and Ipswich (St Mary at Stoke).

Warrington, William (1833 – 66): He described himself as 'artist in stained glass, heraldic and decorative painter, plumber, glazier and paperhanger'. He designed in medieval styles and some of his detailing was distinctly fanciful. The firm continued under his son James until 1875. An example of his work can be found at Shelley.

Weathering: The sloping surface of a buttress **set-off**, or section of a wall designed to throw off rain-water.

Weeping chancels: Much nonsense has been written (and is still being perpetuated in some church guide books today) about chancels which incline away from the centre line of the **nave**. The popular fallacy is that this is intended to indicate the drooping of Christ's head on the cross onto His right shoulder, as He is always shown in medieval representations of the Crucifixion. As **Cautley** put it with splendid acidity, the idea is 'too absurd to be credited by any thinking person'. In any event, it should be noted that there are as many chancels which 'weep' left as right. The explanation is simply that mathematical accuracy was not the forte of medieval masons, and the chancel being 'out of true' with the nave was a result of ground-plan inaccuracy or expediency. It was often the result of a rebuilding which affected only the chancel or the nave. There is an extreme example at Thrandeston, with others at Akenham and Saxtead.

Whall, Christopher (1849 – 1924): Arts and Crafts stained glass worker. For ten years he designed for the firms of Saunders, **Hardman**, and the **Powells**, but became disenchanted with their mass-production approach and the lack of opportunity to control the whole process, from cartoon to installing the window. He was fortunate in his contacts with leading architects and was able to influence others through teaching, while his high standards of craftsmanship and insistence on continous involvement made him a leader in the movement. His book *Stained Glass Work* is still one of the best handbooks on the subject. His finest work is in Gloucester cathedral but there are lovely windows at Herringswell and Sproughton in the county.

William and Mary: The 'joint' reign of William III (1688 – 1702) and Mary II (1688 – 94), he a Dutch Protestant, she the daughter of the deposed Catholic James II. Architecturally, a period of gracious houses and fine furniture.

Woodwose: A wild man of the woods, bearded and hairy, and usually carrying a club, as he can be seen in some churches in carvings on **fonts** and on woodwork. In **bestiaries** he is frequently found fighting with lions, and they alternate round the bases of many East Anglian fonts. One medieval text describes the woodwoses as wild men of India who fought the Sagittarii – they were naked until they had slain a lion, after which they wore its skin. The Sagittarius represented man's body and the woodwose his soul; as the lion was slain, so the soul overcame the vanities of the world, and this was used as an appropriate theme for a baptismal homily, with the figures round the font or in the **roof** overhead as illustrations. Examples can be found at Barking, Mendlesham, Old Newton, Stradbroke, Wickham Skeith, and Yaxley.

Wyvern: A mythical winged dragon with two eagle's feet and a snake-like barbed tail. There is an example at Mendlesham.

Zachariah: A Jewish priest who was **St Elizabeth's** husband and **St John the Baptist's** father. Having been struck dumb for his refusal to accept the archangel's message, he praised God in the canticle known as the Benedictus when the child was named (Luke 1: 64). There is a tradition that he was martyred in the Temple for refusing to tell Herod where his son was. His figure forms part of the lavish **Kempe** window in the s. **aisle** at Bildeston, and can also be found in a **Lavers & Westlake** window at Great Waldingfield.

NOTES

NOTES

NOTES

NOTES

NOTES

NOTES

NOTES

The Popular Guide to Suffolk Churches
by D. P. Mortlock

No 1. West Suffolk
ISBN 0 906554 01 1

No 3. East Suffolk
(in preparation)

Together, Norfolk and Suffolk form the real East Anglia,
and the churches of the two counties have so much in common
that they deserve to be studied as a whole.
There is a companion series
that makes this possible:

The Popular Guide to Norfolk Churches
by D. P. Mortlock & C. V. Roberts

No. 1 North East Norfolk
ISBN 0 906554 04 7

No. 2 Norwich, Central and South Norfolk
ISBN 0 906554 07 1

No. 3 West and South-West Norfolk
ISBN 0 90655 09 8

Order from your bookseller
or direct from the publisher:

Acorn Editions
P. O. Box 60
Cambridge CB1 2NT